JUMPING INTO JEOPARDY

CHRIS HASLAM

JUMPING INTO JEOPARDY

*The physical and psychological challenges
facing the 21st century National Hunt jockey.*

First published in Great Britain 2024

ISBN: 978 1 3999 8095 1

Copyright © Chris Haslam 2024

Typeset by Karen Langridge.
Graphics by Jason Conway.
Formatting and Internal Text Design by Kimberlee Kessler, Sydney, Australia.
Printed and bound by Short Run Press, Exeter, Devon.

25% of all proceeds from this book will go to Racing Welfare charity.

Cover photo: by David Dew. Nick Oliver takes the final fence at Chaddesley Corbett on Mr. Cee, trained by Caroline Walker.

"If you are going to try, go all the way. Otherwise, don't even start. This could mean losing girlfriends, wives, relatives and maybe even your mind. It could mean not eating for 3 or 4 days. It could mean freezing on a park bench, it could mean derision, it could mean mockery — isolation. Isolation is the gift. All the others are a test of your endurance, of how much you really want to do it. And, you will do it, despite rejection and the worst odds. And it will be better than anything else you can imagine. If you are going to try, go all the way. There is no other feeling like that. You will be alone with the gods. And the nights will flame with fire. You will ride life straight to perfect laughter. It's the only good fight there is."

- Charles Bukowski, *Factotum* -

"Anyone immune to the delicious lunacy of horse racing is suffering a deprivation for which mere solvency cannot compensate."

- Hugh McIlvanney -

"Winning's just the easy bit."

- Ruby Walsh -

FOREWORD

If jump racing has a future - as I earnestly hope and believe it does - it will be because of the support of people like Chris Haslam. You only have to spend a short time with him, chewing over the latest news about the great game, to see evidence of his deep knowledge, longstanding enthusiasm and continuing curiosity.

The sport is not as fashionable as it was back in the 1980s, when Desert Orchid's durable charisma made it an easy sell, when there was no internet and only four TV channels in Britain, and racing would be on two of them simultaneously most Saturday afternoons. These days, every part of the entertainment industry has to fight for its audience and there are obvious challenges for jump racing, which embraces risk, in an age when the general instinct is to insulate against danger.

More than ever, we need to communicate to a sceptical wider world why this game matters so much to us, why it's important that it should continue to thrive. With his eloquence, insights and avuncular manner, I fully believe Chris is the type to kindle new enthusiasms in previously doubtful hearts.

I met him while working on a book about the incredible Scudamore family of jockeys: Michael, the Grand National winner; Peter, the dominant champion, and Tom, the rider of Thistlecrack, who had the longest career of them all. Chris had known them for decades and done much of the spadework for the book, including many hours of interviews with Michael, then in the final months of his life, who trusted Chris enough to share all his old stories.

Without that effort on Chris's part, those great yarns would have lived only as long as the man himself. Whenever we lose another of those high-achieving horsemen from distant days, it bothers me that we're also losing a chunk of the sport, the chance to learn what it was really like for them when the mud was flying.

And so to this book, which seems to me an attempt to take us into the collective mind of all jump jockeys, so far as that can be done. With his careful probing and guidance, as agile in its way as anything Ruby Walsh ever did in the saddle, Chris has elicited any number of illuminating comments from those he has spoken to.

His aim is to help us share in the concerns and the pressures which jump jockeys shoulder each day, so that we can get our fix of action. There are highs as well - without which no one would climb in the saddle - but they are set in their proper context, something to be aimed at and dreamed of, but far from a regular reality for most participants.

While Chris wants you to understand the jockey's perspective, this is also a deeply personal work, amounting to one man's meditation on his favourite pastime. He is capable of taking a romantic view, as we all are, but his gaze is at other times unflinching and he tackles the most difficult of subjects in these pages.

Don't expect any of the PR man's gloss, then. This is a sincere work, full of grit and grime, and it can take you closer to the game.

Chris Cook
Senior Reporter of the *Racing Post*

A JOCKEY'S DAY

04:30 -   Alarm shatters silence and sleep... he fights the strong urge to doze... limps onto the scales in his boxers: too dark to see the numbers...

04:40 -   Eats half an orange, looks over at a pile of grapes, takes two, can't have more: "Ridiculous"... puts kettle on, filling cup to the brim... scalds his lips...

04:47 -   Walks to his car... raining, a cold November morning; long winter ahead... embers of broken collarbone jar as he climbs into the driver's seat... can't make fuss about that... mustn't let on it's still painful... just keep grafting...

04:49 -   He is away... ahead of him, 40-mile drive to the trainer's yard... no other cars on the road... rain increases, but he is looking forward to riding out... one horse at this trainer's yard has potential: only young, last time out he rode it to a gallant second...

05:19 -   Puncture! Curses loudly... morning is truly cold... changes wheel, not easy with his collarbone... rain lessens a little... he is under pressure for time now...

06:27 -   Arrives at yard... greeted by sarky comments on his time-keeping... rides three, though not the good one... wonders why...

08:31 -   Back in the car, wraps himself up in plastic bags and two more jumpers, turns heater on full... "If only they still had saunas in the weighing room."... riding at Catterick today, a 200-mile drive... his agent rings... tells him best mount for the day has gone lame... only two rides now... more curses...

13:47 -   Arrives Catterick racecourse... windy... climbs out of his plastic bags, takes kit to weighing room... sets off for run around the track...

14:35 - Raining again now... heavy going on the track... first horse pulls up before half-way... disappointing...

16:18 - Falls at second last hurdle when in with a shout... collarbone banged... whip lost... realises how hungry he is as doctor checks him over... wolfs down a tuna and sweetcorn sandwich: tasteless... does his hunger no help at all...

17:17 - Back to car... falls into plastic bags and dons the two jumpers... sets off on long road home... "Why the hell am I doing this?"

18:46 - Stops at service station... people stare at his plastic bags... feels like Michelin Man... he is Michelin Man... buys a packet of nuts...

19:23 - Agent rings with plans for next day... Taunton... just two rides... quells more questions in his mind... turns up radio, avoiding racing results...

20:19 - Car phone rings: trainer with usual preamble, then a pause... hears the name of that good horse... "Nothing to do with me, mate... owner's not happy... wants to put up Neil Shilston... says the horse needs a real jockey... you know how this game works..."

This book is dedicated to:

David Bass
Nick Oliver
Tom Scudamore
Sam Thomas
Four Horsemen of our Apocalypse

with mighty thanks for their wisdom, laughter, and the finest examples they set...

...and to Lorraine,
outrageous encouragement, always...

CONTENTS

1.	The Horse	1
2.	What Is Winning?	13
3.	Back In The Day	21
4.	Becoming A Jockey	31
5.	Keeping Your 'Bottle'	41
6.	The Weighing Room	55
7.	Past Masters	65
8.	Injuries	77
9.	The Injured Jockeys Fund	87
10.	Jockeys 1 – The Complete Package	99
11.	Female Jockeys	109
12.	Coming Second – And Not Giving Up	119
13.	Trainers	127
14.	Jockeys 2 – Wear And Tear	139
15.	Sam Thomas: Early Days	149
16.	Sam As A Top Jockey	159
17.	Duel In The Cotswolds	167
18.	Sam Post-Denman	175
19.	Sam Thomas Trainer	187
20.	Taking The Ultimate Step	201
21.	Mental Health	209
22.	Mental Health 2	219
23.	Jockeys 3 - Vicissitudes	229
24.	Deaths	241
25.	The Emerald Isle	253
26.	Retirement	273
27.	Emperors Of Their Craft	287
28.	Tom Scu	299
29.	The Jockey Who Thinks Out Of The Box	309
30.	Where To From Here?	321

CHAPTER 1: THE HORSE

"A great horse will change your life:
a truly special one can define it."
- Declan Murphy - 'Centaur' -

" There is symphony in the movement of a horse. The gallop is a four-beat rhythm: hind leg, hind leg, fore leg, fore leg. It is musical, beautifully poetic when you listen to it. This is the gait of the racehorse; it strikes off with its non-leading hind leg, then the inside hind foot hits the ground before the outside fore, just by a split second. The movement concludes with the striking off of the leading leg, followed by a moment of suspension when all four hooves are off the ground. Even at 35 or 40 mph, when the animal appears to be flying, it follows this classic, controlled cadence. In truth, it is not flying at all; it is dancing.

"It is amazing what a horse can do for our soul. Horses empower humans: because the horse is a prey animal and survival instinct defines its existence, its response mechanism is immediate. So, even at the quietest of moments, it is intensely aware of its surroundings, acutely able to understand human behaviour, and reflect it. This endows the horse with a gift, which enables the animal to be a perfect mirror for our feelings. Horses accept us for who we are, not who we are supposed to be.

"Horses are wonderful with people who have physical or mental disabilities, because they are able to bring out the human element that often lies dormant within us. They are intelligent and honest; their innate ability to read human emotion is perhaps what lies at the core of the man-horse relationship.

Patient and gentle, they offer their insight and empathy, responding naturally to emotional issues, offering their companionship, their silent support. And in doing so, they enable us to win back trust in ourselves." Declan Murphy

For many of us there are few things better than watching horses canter uphill on a dark, grizzly, grey morning: when they walk back down, dragon-smoke puffs out from their flared nostrils. They give us hope. The horse, with beauty unsurpassed, strength immeasurable and grace unlike any other, still remains humble enough to carry a human being on his back. Shakespeare's Henry V acknowledges this:

"When I bestride him, I soar, I am a hawk.
He trots the air. The earth sings when he touches it."

When riding a horse, we borrow freedom.

Our 21st century racehorse has evolved over the past 45-55 million years, from a small multi-toed creature, Eohippus, into the large, single-toed animal of today. All our thoroughbreds can be traced back to three horses imported into England between 1680 – 1730 the Byerley Turk, Darley Arabian and Godolphin Arabian. There are currently around 14,000 race horses being trained in Britain and just over 9,000 in Ireland. Until relatively recently, jump racing was considered by some a lesser sport than flat racing, which is more regulated, watched by society's finest, more concerned with bloodstock, breeding sheds, world-wide recognition – and money. But things are changing here.

In either code, the racehorse is badly designed for the pressure we put it through to race. For the amount of sheer power than runs through it at speeds of up to 40 mph, the frame of its legs is desperately thin. Man would never design a racehorse like that, but it works: it shouldn't, but it does, and we are in awe to watch/witness the beauty of a racehorse in full flight, even when we've asked it to carry a weight of up to 12 stone on its back.

Standing in its stable, a horse has a heart-rate of between 36- 42; this can go up to 225 at the climax of a race. "A racehorse in full flight is a thing of beauty: an artist, an enigma, an elite athlete that bursts into life in a bid to perform. Every minute at full gallop, a thoroughbred pumps 1,800 cubic litres of air in and out of its lungs. Its heart beats 250 times – nearly 5 beats a second – to pump 60 litres of blood around its body, all to achieve that singular goal: speed. When they are reaching speeds in excess of 35 mph, racehorses have the highest requirements for air flow, and are therefore likely to have their performance limited by even modest airway obstructions. Thermal imaging cameras can detect when a horse is over-heating post-race; MRI scanners, x-rays and endoscopes can pick up health conditions before they deteriorate, all instrumental in improving today's ever-evolving equine welfare.

An appreciation of why the horse craves admiration came in a book on Seabiscuit, one of the USA's greatest racehorses. "The horse swoops over as much as 28 feet of earth in a single stride, and corners on a sixpence. His body is a paradox of mass and lightness, crafted to slip through the air with the ease of an arrow. His mind is impressed with a single command: RUN. He pursues speed with superlative courage, pushing beyond defeat, exhaustion, sometimes beyond the structural limits of bone and sinew. In flight he is nature's ultimate welding of form and purpose. To pilot a racehorse is to ride a half-ton catapult: it is without question one of the most formidable feats in sport."

Horses are built to run. In the past, their speed enabled them to escape predators; they possess a superb sense of balance, they can sleep standing up, and have the largest eyes of any land mammal. As Melanie Reed, a fine horsewoman, has observed, "They are supremely good listeners, they soak up human pain" – as she knows only too well – they "pass no judgement, are a leaning-post, a sounding board, and solace for the soul. They give us a kind of magic, a depth, a fascination, which lies beneath the thrill of riding." But, when things go wrong, as they did for her in 2010, "They can be the harbingers of a cruel harvest."

Many people have a sense in which their horse is an extension of themselves. In Mongolia, horses' skulls are sacred and made into musical instruments, whose sounds comfort mourning souls. In Peru, the Incas thought the arriving bellicose Spanish were gods, because they were on horseback, which had never been seen before: they surrendered forthwith. An ancient Bedouin text rejoices in this beast: "In creating the horse, God has moulded it from the wind, and tied good fortune to its mane. It will fly without wings. It will be the noblest of animals."

John Steinbeck, some of whose novels reflect the steadfastness of horses, as in *The Red Pony*, concurred: "A man on a horse is spiritually, as well as physically, so much bigger than a man on foot," and Winston Churchill, rider and owner of racehorses, wrote: "There is something about the outside of a horse that's good for the inside of a man."

Horses, and the depth of companionship they offer, have inspired many great words. In *Rough Magic*, the account of Lara Prior-Palmer's adventures in the Mongolian Derby, the author expresses her admiration for 'equus' throughout the book: "For all the empires horses helped build, and all the land they captured for us, what they really invoke is an opposing set of forces: fleeing, giving away, leaving behind…" Partnering horses is different each time, so riders are addicted to surprise. And there is something complete in a horse: "I am enough as I am, the horse says to himself. Himself in all his blatant being." The horses of yesteryear have left their mark. Down the centuries across Britain, 16 massive carvings of horses have been etched into her chalk hills, as at Uffington, where The White Horse, allegedly a 374-foot legacy from the Bronze Age, leaps across an escarpment on the Berkshire Downs, an uplifting landmark.

They have been used in warfare from time immemorial: their current participation in sport has even been seen as war in disguise. In The Crusades; for Genghis Khan; at Bosworth Field, where Richard III uttered the immortal:

"A horse! A horse! My kingdom for a horse!"

and on the battlefields of Agincourt, they have played a vital role. During the Middle Ages, there were three types of war horse: the destrier, courser and rouncey. But in the First World War they were no longer huge cavalry chargers, they were rather working beasts carrying and pulling supplies, ammo, artillery and the wounded. Almost a million horses were used on the Western Front, where gas, artillery, machine guns, mortars and tanks made it a terrifying place for them. Nose plugs were at first improvised; later horse gas masks were developed, often to no avail, as barbed wire caused vast injuries to horses, not least by transmitting infection. When the war ended in 1918, over 484,000 horses had been lost – one horse for every two men. Most surviving horses were destroyed or sold for meat, while only the healthiest and youngest animals, a mere 60,000, were brought back to the UK.

Horses are empathetic, which is why they are perfect for many children and people with mental health challenges: this is seen in the number involved with Riding for the Disabled. Genuine horses share their empathy: if spooked, they will try to put themselves right for the rider, and it is widely believed that horses in a stable get to know us by our footfall. It has been said that horses are God's way of apologising for men.

The explosion of mental illness in our age has been caused by many elements, not least the dramatic speed with which life and communication have evolved within a single generation. In this context horses have not changed; their heartbeat and affiliation with people have become a steadying, rooting influence on all involved with them. Especially jockeys. For them, there always has to be hope amongst the hoofbeats; racing offers the chance of improvement and renewal. Horses have to go out and run: they demand the belief that winners – and good days – can return.

It is the great horse, more than any other feature of the sport, that brings in the crowds. National Hunt horses bring with them few of the commercial opportunities of the Flat: mostly they provide joy. But their longevity holds huge appeal; they are not dashed off to the breeding sheds, but come back year after year to entertain, endear and earn our admiration.

Over the years, followers of The Sport of Kings have all doubtless had their favourites and those long in the tooth (an expression of equine descent?) can still recall the glory days, albeit in black and white, almost as far back as Phar Lap, Indonesian for 'lightning', the 1930 Melbourne Cup winner and hope-lifter in the Depression. Such luminaries as Nickel Coin, Merryman II, Wily Oriental, Blessington Esquire, Pas Seul, Scottish Memories, Saffron Tartan, Kirriemuir, Dagmar Gittell, Green Drill, Tea Fiend, Out and About, Red Alligator, Different Class, Badanloch, Spanish Steps, Salmon Spray, The Fellow, Pappageno's Cottage, Lanzarote, Ekbalco, Royal Athlete, Kapeno, Rondetto, O'Malley Point, Buona Notte, Nicolaus Silver, Durham Edition, Greasepaint, Cab on Target, Noddy's Ryde and Twin Oaks – were all magical names that brightened the racing's cosmos. As a kid growing up to the alluring new world of racing, I thought the Queen Mother – or her racing manager - named her horses eye-catchingly: Makaldar, Escalus, Double Star, Laffy, Silver Dome, Special Cargo, Game Spirit and, especially, The Rip.

Horses shone more than ever in that chiaroscuro world: Golden Miller ground down his opponents with his relentless pace; Arkle, champion of Ireland, the freak of nature known as 'Himself', who consumed a pint of Guinness every day, won three Gold Cups (1964-66), an Irish National (1964) and countless other chases under jockey Pat Taaffe, of whom Hugh McIlvanney wrote, "Nobody sweated more for his brutal trade;" only injury to the horse put paid to further glory. Uniquely in racing history, his dominance led to handicappers having two weighting systems: when he ran, and when he didn't. Letters addressed simply to Arkle, Ireland, always found their way to his box. Flyingbolt is still reckoned by some shrewd judges the equal of any other: Champion Hurdlers Night Nurse and Sea Pigeon are in every true racing man's pantheon, as is Red Rum, the horse that 'saved' the Grand National through his exploits and popularity: 'Rummy' won three Grand Nationals (1973, 1974, 1977) and finished second twice. Peter O'Sullevan's commentaries on his triumphs remain legendary; the horse even appeared in the studio on BBC's *Sports Personality of the Year* programme. Desert Orchid was the powerful front-running grey who liked to take hair-raising leaps from outside the wings of a fence; he won the Gold Cup in atrocious conditions in 1989, together with four King Georges. More recently we have followed and revelled in the exploits of Dawn Run – still the only horse to have won the Champion Hurdle and the Cheltenham Gold Cup; Irish wonder horse Istabraq; Best Mate, victor in three successive Gold Cups; Kauto Star, the only horse to regain the Gold Cup, and Tiger Roll, winner of two Grand Nationals.

A horse never permitted by the fates to realise his full potential, and rated by Richard Pitman as his mount of greatest promise, was Killiney, the novice chaser, trained by Fred Winter, who considered him the best horse he ever looked after. The horse won six hurdle races, as well as all nine of his steeplechases, jumping expertly and pulverising his opposition by halfway. He stormed home in the Champion Novice Chase at Cheltenham, but in his next race, at Ascot, he 'put down' into the open ditch, catapulting his pilot into the turf. Richard was concussed and dislocated a shoulder; the horse broke his own shoulder and had to be destroyed.

The grey, One Man, captured hearts with his never-say-die attitude, bold fencing and huge spirit. When he died, Steve Dennis wrote his obituary: "His death leached the last lees of joy out of racing's little world. When he went, he took the fun with him. He was grey: that always helps. He was a joyful animal, full of ebullience and flamboyance. Those qualities rebounded on us: that "little rubber ball" put a spring in our step. He jumped with the deft certainty of a professional knife-thrower; it's a stirring sight, a dashing grey in full flight."

More recently Synchronised, Douvan, Annie Power, Quevega, Native River, Cue Card, Sprinter Sacre, Moscow Flyer, Altior, Paisley Park, Kemboy, Shishkin, Bénie des Dieux, Vautour, Faugheen, Energumene, Honeysuckle and Chacun Pour Soi have earned a special place in the hearts of race-goers; everyone has their favourites. Native River wove himself further into the fabric of jump racing every season. With endless stamina reserves, he embodied the spirit of the sport with every leap; in an era where greatness is conferred on guarded campaigning and unbeaten records, he proved that the best equine careers - and perhaps human careers - are characterised as much by failure as by success. Un de Sceaux was a loveable tearaway under blue and orange silks: an intelligent animal, his win in the Ryanair Chase in 2020 was breath-taking for all, not least his owners, the O'Connell family: "He slipped into the hands of nobodies like us." He became the people's horse, tough, hard on himself, physically and mentally. Horses gain a following. The more obscure horses' lack of celebrity doesn't prevent them brightening our lives, and when these horses win, with ears pricked, eyes sparkling, they are a vivid advert for the theory that they relish their five-star lives.

Racing history teems with the bravest of tales, most colourful of facts, most admirable of horses, right down to Cornishman V, dual Olympic Gold Medal winner in the Three-Day-Event, who, in the hands of John Oaksey, leaped a level-crossing for the film of Dick Francis' first novel, *Dead Cert*.

Many horses, like Faugheen, Denman and Energumene, graduate from the point-to-point world, as do young jockeys. Will Biddick, with over 450 winners, terms point-to-points, "The grass roots of the sport: that's what makes them so important; they're a leg up, a stepping stone for horses, jockeys and trainers too. At the other end of the spectrum point-to-points offer horses in the twilight of their careers the chance to bow out at a lower level, but well."

Just occasionally, the horse is forgotten in post-race interviews and fall-out. But, as former jockey Jerry McGrath has said, "We jockeys couldn't do our job without them." Their bravery knows no bounds: it shows a spiritual independence complete in itself. They are so much more than "bearers of little profits and little losses." (Peter Shaffer: *Equus*.)

Racehorses in full flight over a fence are at the pinnacle of what they can do, but their athletic ability is always on a knife-edge: legs can break so easily, and, unlike dogs, they cannot manage on three. If a racehorse breaks a leg, the jockey hears a loud crack and knows instantly. They then will often stand with the animal until the vets arrive, a tranquiliser is applied, and the green screens go up, for privacy. When the jockey has a particular attachment to the horse, sometimes they will stay with it until the end.

At the Punchestown Festival 2021 a horse broke its leg just before a fence: he would have been entitled to turn over and fall to the ground. But in this case, adrenalin kept him going, even though the jockey tried to pull him up; he still jumped the fence. The jockey was unseated, the horse crumpled on landing, but stood up, patiently waiting to be euthanised. Racehorses who are badly injured on a course are put to sleep by humane lethal injection; this must only be carried out by a vet. Having been sedated, the horse will collapse gradually, experiencing a rapid loss of consciousness, followed by cardiovascular arrest. The vet will remain with the horse until it has died and all natural reflex reactions have ceased. The animal will not be aware of any discomfort or pain as life leaves its body.

Alan Lee wrote about horse deaths on course, explaining how grief and glory go side by side in the fervour of jump racing: "When a horse dies, or has to be euthanised, people want someone to be accountable, they want racing to suffer even more than is obvious from the naked grief of all those involved with the stricken animal, and the silent shock that stuns the racecourse. But there are some things we cannot prevent, things not easy to understand, never mind explain." Alastair Down feels such a day takes away far more than it gives; sometimes the most innocent-looking fall can cause the most damage. As Peter Scudamore has said, "Accidents happen, that's what accidents do. Death is a fact of racing: there is no point hiding it or being embarrassed, but every reason for the never-ending work to minimise it."

"Horses are incredibly tough animals: brave, hardy and durable. At the same time, in the wrong combination of circumstances, they may as well be made of glass," wrote Chris Cook in *The Guardian*. When a horse breaks a leg, it is not possible to repair the bone, because it is then in lots of little pieces that won't heal together. 'Plate deformation' means that the bone bends before it breaks, and it is the bent piece that is preserved in the pieces. Then, if it were possible to put the pieces back together, they would end up with a badly bent bone. There is very little soft tissue covering the bone, so often the bone penetrates the skin, turning it into an open fracture. Even if there were a remote possibility the bone might heal, the horse could then contract laminitis (inflammation of the structures attaching the pedal bone of the foot to the hoof wall, which is extremely painful, and incurable), so to euthanise the horse is the only option. But by far the majority of racehorses do not lose their lives on the track, or on the gallops.

So, what happens when racehorses retire? Some 5,000 horses a year leave racing: many, especially those who have incurred an injury, are content out in a field. But a huge number are not: they still have fire in their belly: they need a second career. Founded in 2000, Retraining of Racehorses is British Horseracing's official charity for the welfare of retired horses; it is well-known, and well supported, with former equine stars appearing at racecourses to advertise their well-being in a new role. Dressage, polo, show jumping, eventing, hunting, horseball and showing are among the most prominent of these roles, offering the animals a new lease of life, and horses thrive in their new discipline, while some are happy to act as hacks. Greatwood Charity fulfils a future for former racehorses, closely linked in to the education of children and young people with special needs, aiming to equip these youngsters with emotional well-being, even mindfulness: inclusion in every possible aspect is at its heart. The Racehorse Sanctuary provides a lifeline for ex-racehorses in need of homes, helping them to avoid the slippery slope of being sold off from one owner to the next. Some of its residents arrive at the Sanctuary mentally scarred. Even though it is full, with a long waiting list, it aims to expand, which inevitably needs funds. Horses are herd animals: they need companionship. More and more provision is being provided for erstwhile stars of the turf by organisations such as these.

But British racing has faced significant public scrutiny of late, with particular focus on the welfare of our horses throughout their lives. After-care of these animals is not just the responsibility of the sport's regulators, but of everyone, which requires a fundamental shift in the way we go about this. A highly controversial *Panorama* in summer 2021 showed racehorses having their lives ended in an abattoir near Swindon that was not fit for purpose; the programme claimed 4,000 plus had been slaughtered in Britain and Ireland since the start of 2019. Its soulless portrayal of slaughter made grim viewing and caused a furore. In response, the Horse Welfare Board (HWB) stated, "When used appropriately and ethically, euthanasia is an essential component of equine welfare." "Appropriately" and "ethically" are key.

The Royal College of Veterinary Surgeons defines euthanasia as "painless killing to relieve suffering." So, when their lives do not come to an end naturally, human intervention is necessary. Newmarket trainer John Berry said, "…as humans we have to play God and decide when the time is right. When a horse reaches a certain level of physical deterioration, it can no longer enjoy life: the time has come. Almost the worst thing is to realise you should have taken the decision six months earlier." James Given, Director of Equine Health and Welfare at the British Horseracing Authority (BHA), concurs: "Euthanasia, often in consultation with a vet, may be considered the most humane outcome for a horse to prevent it falling into neglect or living an unsuitable lifestyle."

But where death occurs in an abattoir it is more commonly referred to as slaughter, with the carcass then used for food. To have a horse put down at home, in familiar surroundings, done expertly under veterinary care, costs a few hundred pounds; by contrast an abattoir will pay the horse owner for the carcass. Most racehorse trainers, including Nick Alexander, are convinced that abattoirs are just not acceptable. Berry, who sees the situation as "losing a horse," does it at 2 p.m., when there is no-one in the yard, ensuring other horses' boxes are shut so they do not see one of their number being winched on to a wagon. Owners have to pay, but see it as an obligation, thus avoiding what he calls "that combination of parsimony and callousness," whereby the last eight hours of a horse's life can be infinitely stressful. James Given is certain euthanasia is "about showing respect for the service that horse has given, and affording it dignity."

Research into the area of equine slaughter is currently thin: "We do not know nearly enough about horses who leave racing," admitted Lee Mottershead in *Racing Post* August 2021. So, traceability is now a top priority. The HWB is implementing *A Life Well Lived* strategy to ensure the highest standards of racehorse welfare throughout the animals' lives, preventing the horse entering a spiral of decline before ending up in the slaughter house's carnival of death. The primary responsibility of all equine owners is to ensure their animals enjoy a good life, and, at its end, have a good death.

But the loss of any horse is a sadness. Horses have always inspired admiration, as novelist Jane Smiley pinpoints: "The eyes of a horse always tell you something a little bit beyond your comprehension, always ask more of you than you are able to give, are a metaphor for life's beauty and generosity, a worthy object of repeated, ever-changing contemplation." Horses represent not our freedom from the storm, but peace within us: to have control of them is to give up that control. When we ask questions of them, they shouldn't answer, but they do.

The naming of a racehorse is a joy – and a challenge: there are rules here: no more than 18 letters, no figures, nothing vulgar, obscene, or offensive, and not named after any living person. Whilst the names of sire and dam are often melded, some of these monikers are dire: "a woeful smash-up, ill befitting such a graceful animal." And the likes of Big Buck's (aggravating apostrophe) and Definitly Red (spelling) raise the eyebrow. With that extra thought, a strong name can be invoked: rarely is a great racehorse saddled with a poor name, and some are inspired, not least the animal by Desert Prince out of Spartan Girl christened My Tent Or Yours.

Horses' names illuminate our lives. And many horses in history had memorable names: Bucephalus (Alexander the Great); Marengo (Napoleon); Sir Briggs (knighted for his role in The Charge of the Light Brigade at the Battle of Balaclava in 1854, when wounded); Sefton (who in 1982 survived the IRA attack in Hyde Park) and Copenhagen (the Duke of Wellington's horse at Waterloo). In mythology, as if spilling out of the Trojan Horse, came Hercules' Pegasus, Sir Gawain's Gringolet and cowboy Pecos Bill's mount Widow-Maker, while literature has given us Rocinante (*Don Quixote*); Gandalf's Shadowfax (the Lord of All Horses in Middle Earth); Gabilan

(John Steinbeck's *Red Pony*); Conan Doyle's Silver Breeze; C. S. Lewis' Narnian horse Bree, and, more recently, Topthorn in Michael Morpurgo's *War Horse*. The Grim Reaper's horse is called Mr Jeepers!

Winners are universally fêted, but there have been several famous losers, not least at the Cheltenham Festival, whose coming to grief at the final obstacle prevented an almost certain win. Annie Power was still in second gear in the Mares' Hurdle of 2015 as she breezed into a huge lead, with just the last hurdle to jump – but she hit the floor, taking with her millions of pounds in multiple wagers. Goshen, for the popular Moore family, was miles clear in 2020 Triumph Hurdle until, after jumping the final flight, his two left legs somehow became stuck for a second, unbalancing the horse and sending Jamie Moore crashing to the turf. In 2022, Paul Townend on Galopin des Champs was imperiously clear when they crumpled dramatically on landing after the final fence.

Perhaps the unluckiest loser of all was the Queen Mother's Devon Loch in the 1956 Grand National, who collapsed – still inexplicably – sprawling to the ground, slithering to a halt on his belly, his forelegs splayed out in front of him and hind legs dragging over the Aintree turf. He was just 50 yards from the winning post, with the race at his royal mercy, thereby igniting a battalion of 'what ifs'. The jockey quickly dismounted, fearing his horse might be injured, but the vets reported no lameness in Devon Loch. Francis, who went on to become the internationally acclaimed crime novelist, always maintained the noise of the crowd, "a tremendous crescendo" had been the cause; other stories, like the horse suffering a sudden muscular cramp, still abound…

How different would things have been if Devon Loch had won?

CHAPTER 2: WHAT IS WINNING?

"For nothing can seem foul to those that win."
- Shakespeare: Henry IV Part 1 -

Racing is defined by winning. The word has a strong ring to it: triumphant, victorious, vanquishing, conquering, first, successful, top: all are positive in the extreme. We take it for granted that everyone wants to win. And so many axioms are part of our everyday language: "Winner takes all," "He is on a winning streak," "Everyone loves a winner," "Winning is everything," but is it? The macho language makes it hard to question.

We know what winning means for a jockey: succeeding, often having overcome difficulties; being acknowledged for the manner of their winning after hours of toil; reward for dedication and disappointment; aiming for and reaching the extraordinary. The urge to win builds physical and mental resilience; every day a jockey trains, and every night they dream. It has been said by one of their number, "Winning is the most important thing in life after breathing."

Horse racing is a dangerous, exhilarating, ennobling, cruel, demanding sport; for many, winning is everything, no matter the cost. On the flat, money is absolutely key, but 'over the sticks' still has the vital ingredient, whereby small-time owners, farmers, horsemen and even the odd schoolmaster can enjoy all aspects of 'The Sport of Kings' by banding together to form a syndicate. But there is huge risk involved, of course; to train, ride, even back a winner is the ultimate aim in every race; there can, however, be only one winner; winning cannot be shared.

Natural sportspeople have an intrinsic love of their sport: the challenge for them is how best to nurture – and sustain – that love. Pressure is good, but they have to understand that pressure. They have to get a balance to play hard and play well, and also to enjoy themselves. All too easily enjoyment can be disregarded, even cut out; there needs to be a sense of fun. What is fun to the young jockey? How do they make it fun? How can they get the most out of their sport so they are able to sleep at night, not spending hours looking at the ceiling?

Winning in sport has its own language. Nick Oliver, amateur jockey, who won his first race in Declan Murphy's boots, is son of Henry, the trainer, and older brother of young Henry, now also a trainer. Nick learned from Richard Davis, Vince Slattery and Warren Marston. He has strong views on winning: "Winning is an esoteric thing. Many judge it, mistakenly, on race results or numbers at the end of the season. Perhaps they don't truly understand. Or they have given in to fear/doubt. But despite this, winning is within us all. It is a heart thing, the quality of pursuing an ideal, or dream, or love, without compromise, or apology. In life, it can be indomitability of spirit in the bullied, the sick or the broken-hearted. In sport, I believe it is the mixed pain, joy and emotion we all carry with us from our journey, a journey that started the day we decided to pursue our dream, irrespective of the odds against reaching it… it is the trials and criticism, as well as the little wins of which we don't speak. We do it for love, willingly accepting the risk of injuries, or worse still, being forced to stop. For me, conquering my fears to pursue the thing I love is winning. It is not the race itself, but the road from the beginning (of our journey) to the start (of a race). What happens after that is… racing."

For Nick, that first win was one Saturday at Worcester in October 1995: the lad was still at school, Cheltenham College, and had Saturday morning lessons, so was thrilled to avoid them, be picked up by Dad, Henry, in his humble Daihatsu and whisked off to the course. Nick was riding Fairy Park in a 20-runner field: though momentarily left at the start, the pair gradually made up ground: "It felt unreal," says Nick, "like being in a western" – and came through to win, beating Jim Culloty, Robert 'Choc' Thornton and Richard Johnson. Nick was 16.

He still believes the bond between animal and human is never to be taken for granted. "Horses trust their riders: forming that bond is the opposite of ego – it's humbling, a privilege, bound up in mutual awe." He is grateful for all that horses have given him down the years and his riding remains a spiritual thing, "My peace, my freedom, my church."

Winning in jump racing is about the pain jockeys go through after making the decision to be a professional rider: doing the little things well every day; defiance of obstacles; maintaining that unbreakable spirit under sometimes extreme pressure; having the mental attributes every sportsperson must have.

But nobody goes undefeated the whole time. Perhaps winning can mean not always coming first, but doing better than ever before? Perhaps winning craves a wider perspective, about the achievement of whole lives, not just short-term results? Crossing the line first, feeling that surge of adrenalin, holding that trophy are all split-second moments; do they need translating into meaning beyond that split-second if winning is to be a long-lasting positive experience? And what about not winning? A long period of falls, unplaced rides – or injuries – can cause jockeys to suffer let-down, depression, or worse. Tiger Woods has said: "Winning solves everything." I wonder if it is quite that simple...

The vast majority of us will have enjoyed our own victories down the years, but I suspect riding a horse over jumps to win any race, let alone a prestigious one at Cheltenham, Aintree, Punchestown or Fairyhouse, must give that jockey a feeling that is hard to put into words. Jockeys have always tried to explain that feeling, not least in their immediate post-race interviews, when they have hardly had time to let victory sink in – their words come up short. It is impossible to describe the feeling, which psychologists term being 'in flow': when you are so completely immersed in endeavour, something takes you over, as initiative, instinct and some extraordinary innate atoms fuse for those moments in time. It is more than exhilaration, and though we less courageous mortals may experience a nuance of this feeling, in love, work or recreation, in the last analysis it defies definition – as it has to. To define the feeling would be to profane it.

But that must make the winning feeling all the more precious: to be on a horse jumping like a stag and then to cross the line first, buzzing because you have made that horse win; that feeling is, all jockeys say, impossible to replace. Champion Irish jockey, Paul Townend, gave his thoughts on winning in an interview: "You have to dedicate your life to being a jockey: it's a bug, a drug to us. There's no comparison between winning and losing, but you learn to live with both. We are all professional, we want to win every day we go out; even riding an outsider, we'll convince ourselves this horse has a chance. If we don't do that, there's no point in going out to try. You pick the positives in everything, especially regarding your own mount, the negatives in all the other horses, and you go out with that mindset. And you put as much effort into the losers as the winners, sometimes more."

When Paul won his first Cheltenham Gold Cup on Al Boum Photo in 2019, a first victory in the blue riband for Willie Mullins, after six times training the runner-up, it took winning to a whole new level and "felt like nothing else." Paul enjoyed a pure adrenalin rush for days, yet remembers the race more than what happened afterwards. "After that, I lost the run of myself a little. To win was brilliant, to lose heartbreak. If you are 5th or 6th you can hear everything: if you have a winning chance, your focus is so sharp, so concentrated, you can't hear a thing – adrenalin and focus drown everything out."

It's not about money: something deeper drives jump jockeys. Distilling all the hype, betting, unpredictability, dreams of winning huge prize money (unlikely in Britain at the moment) and the Dick Francis-like romance, jockeys are left with two things: the decision to keep doing something hard against the odds, and the horses' trust and willingness. In times of hopelessness, when they think their journey will end in failure – in the unforgiving eye of the racing public – it is the heart that drives them forward; they have to keep their heart in it. Everyone may slate them, abuse – even death threats – pile up on Twitter, and, even as they realise theirs is a physical, precarious, duplicitous sport, they have to keep going forward, always readjusting their perspectives. Winning is about keeping going.

Yachtsman Warren Richards sees winning as a collective thing, even in an individual sport like jump racing: "Jockeys cannot succeed without the support of their team – and the benefit of those unsung heroes of the past who shape them. It's about trying to make the right decisions, to keep pushing on, go and go again, never deviating, easing the bruising (physical and mental) and relentlessly chasing the chosen goal."

All the time jockeys need to be nimble in mind and body: to change and adapt, not just in every race they ride in, but in their whole approach. Keeping their eye on the prize, they may need to try different methods, different routes. They need to be given freedom, space, scope to talk about objectives, what's working and what isn't, their fears, blazing hopes, set-backs, injuries, and private lives away from the racecourse. With such a fierce will to win, they can become blinkered and miss the obvious. But it all comes down to trust, for every member of their team. The importance of mutual trust cannot be exaggerated.

The team, and knowing where and how they fit in, is everything in racing: Warren compares the jockeys' operation to flying with the Red Arrows: "Jockeys must know their ability, their full role, their objective, and fit into the formation of that team so it can work at its zenith, like the Red Arrows. And we, the racing public, must play our part to acknowledge and encourage that fine team spirit, not least by appreciating jump jockeys in everything for which they strive, day in, day out."

Multi-talented sportsman Nick Sketchley, 37, was aiming high – with no mean success – when a freak accident as a teenager took away his opportunities for winning. He can appreciate, fiercely, what he missed: the joy of participating, and the thrill of coming out on top. Before his injuries, he took his sporting success for granted: it gave him his identity, his way to shine; now he knows sport, and aiming to win at any level, is a privilege, not a right. He advocates the need always to be aware of what is happening, both internally and externally; addressing little things that go wrong to stop them snowballing into bigger things; being open about mistakes made; maintaining self-confidence, especially during hard times; being around positive people; having, and keeping steadfast friends; not being afraid to show emotion; being – and remaining – yourself (never easy for a jockey), no matter what befalls. In practice that constitutes a great, and on-going, challenge. Those who rise to that challenge will usually succeed – whatever that means for them – to some extent. The question is: to what extent? And who is judging? Whose definition of winning is guiding and motivating the jump jockey?

Do these definitions change with time and/or circumstance, and why is winning so essential?

For a jump jockey, winning will always be at a price, often the price of pain. Clare Balding has said that pain "is all about mind-set, and there's a part of every top sportsperson that actually enjoys pain; they learn to like it because they know that by pushing their body they are working towards the ultimate reward."

But the winning feeling is clearly like no other. Sport shows winners with a clear lens, but a probing one. Ex-jockey Declan Murphy has written: "I think after all the falls and scrapes, defeats and near wins, blood and bruises – to my body and my ego both – I have finally learnt this: there is a definite attitude to winning. And this comes only from experience, from confidence, from the taste of having won before. This is what propels you to win again. It inspires you, drives you, pushes you – almost to madness. And you don't rest until you quench those fires of desire. Until you reach perfection. Until you ride the best race of your life. Then, you breathe. There is a stillness then. A state of nirvana."

Rugby player Will Nelson acknowledges that many sportspeople who are winners inevitably have setbacks, but acquire that vital resilience to come back: those who wallow in the lack of winning never achieve. And the question must be asked, "Will a life obsessed by driving onwards and upwards have been worth it?" Jonny Wilkinson's podcasts go a long way to answering this question. True champions only get going when they're losing; they only count their press-ups when they're tired. And many sportspeople remain counting. But many of those who do not win at first end up victorious later, thus coming to experience the full meaning of winning, because they have thirsted for it for so long.

In jump racing the obsession with winning can be hard to master, though one jockey said: "Winning isn't everything, but wanting to win is." Perspective is essential here, and that is hard to maintain in such a fiercely competitive sport: everything in racing depends on the result. And every jockey has their own definition of winning: for a few, even competing/taking part in the experience is a win: there are so many ups and downs in a jockey's journey, and no-one can win all the time (though AP McCoy did more than his best to disprove this!). Knowing you've done your best can be – sometimes has to be – enough. That experience of learning often goes deeper than a medal round the neck.

But in order to learn, grow, take feedback and criticism, they need time, something jockeys do not have. Acceptance only comes with time, and this can shed a different light on jockeys' achievements, give them different insights. They may not have won in the way they expected, planned or hoped, but they can still be winners.

The fact winning can never be guaranteed in any sport is a huge part of its appeal. But, when it happens, we understand why jockeys, having experienced its depth of emotion, crave more of it. This has been compared to the dilemma of a pilgrim who reaches his destination after much toil, endeavour and probably discomfort, but cannot bear to stop there, so carries on walking… jockeys are always searching for the next win, always chasing the horizon.

Is winning the same as refusing to lose? Can there be any joy without winning? If so, where does that joy come from? Can jockeys celebrate their journey, not just the destination? Can they celebrate their sport? Are they only any good if riding winners? Does winning need a wider viewpoint? What's on the other side of winning? Is there a more creative aspect to winning? Might jockeys one day lose the meaning of winning? We are always inventing new goals, bewitched by the promise of progress, forever aiming onwards and upwards; there is never enough. Perhaps the fact that the winning feeling can never be fully defined is because it is in itself a mystery, and will remain a mystery, forever sought after, forever hungered for, but ultimately fleeting, as Richard Burridge said following Desert Orchid's Gold Cup victory: "Winning is a funny thing; it sort of dissolves in front of you…"

CHAPTER 3: BACK IN THE DAY

"Things ain't what they used to be."

- 1942 Jazz Standard -

There has been an increasing awareness that, while they can never be completely avoided, dangers can be reduced, and that the men and women – of whom there is an increasing number who put themselves in harm's way riding over obstacles – need proper looking after. Dr Michael Turner, chief medical advisor for the Jockey Club and the BHA 1992 to 2013, has led the way in many fields, not least the need to improve protocols, to no small extent triggered by Richard Davis' tragic death in 1996. National Hunt racecourses now have three ambulances in attendance at every meeting: trauma-trained doctors must be on hand, and, when a jockey takes a fall, a doctor or paramedic must attend them within one minute. All injuries are recorded and reported, and, obviously, a jockey must be examined before they can think of riding again. It was not ever so...

In his book *Warriors on Horseback*, John Carter has charted the evolution of those brave riders who enthral us with their skills. The name 'jockey' originally meant horse dealer or owner, because, at the start of the 18th century, owners were usually well-heeled establishment figures who rode their own horses in match races (contested by just two horses.) As the 18th century attracted more and higher gambling stakes, owners delegated riding responsibilities to minions, or 'jockeys' as they came to be called. These jockeys were dressed like servants or grooms and treated accordingly. Not surprisingly, they behaved as such: there were no codes of conduct, so jostling for position and roughhouse tactics were encouraged, often leading to fights. Jockeys could be savage with whips and spurs on their equine mounts, and on each other. Northern jockeys were particularly aggressive, riding in "dirty jackets, dark greasy corduroys and gaiters of similar complexion." As stakes increased at a vertiginous rate, it was win-at-all-costs.

The first jockey to capture public imagination was Samuel Chifney senior, born 1753, who raced in ruffles, frills, ribbons and lovelocks, and was dubbed "a luminary of the first brilliancy" riding for the aristocrats of his day. But he was not just an egocentric dandy: he knew how to win on a horse, and was the first jockey known to employ tactics in race-riding. In the Georgian era, most jockeys went at breakneck gallop from flag-fall to the winning post: Chifney held up his mounts for a late, often decisive swoop as the front-runners tired. But he was not an honest jockey, even when riding for the then Prince of Wales: it was said that Tattenham Corner at Epsom, with its notoriously sharp bend, was "straighter than Chifney."

As the 19th century progressed, horses were no longer the preserve of the aristocracy, and louche characters took the sport into disrepute. Racing became shady, and corrupt, and jockeys were not exempt here. In 1835 the owner of the 1,000 Guineas winner, Preserve, said in the press, "The sport of horse racing has a peculiar and irresistible charm for persons of unblemished probity. What a pity that it makes just as strong appeal to the riff-raff of every town." Gradually, in Victorian England, skulduggery and underhand dealings gave way to more honesty and efficiency, and the start of the 20th century continued this trend, though excessive gambling, the nobbling of horses, doping and substituting one horse for another are not unknown, even today.

The first known steeplechase had, not surprisingly, taken place in Ireland, the country renowned for its love of breeding and racing horses, and the cradle of many greats, equine and human. In 1752, just outside Limerick, County Cork, Edmund O'Brien and Cornelius O'Callaghan raced over 4½ miles for a cask of wine. They started at Buttevant village church, and rode over fields, bushes, hedges, walls, brooks and ditches dug in farmland to the church at Doneraile: steeple-to-steeple or point-to-point.

The first such race in England over fences (eight of them, 4'6" high), the Great St Albans Steeplechase, took place at Bedford in 1830, organised by a pub landlord, and racehorse trainer, Thomas Coleman. Captain Martin William Becher, a soldier in the Napoleonic Wars, was one of sixteen starters, racing four miles from Harlington Church, Bedfordshire, to the obelisk in Wrest Park, near Silsoe; this race drew huge attention, and was such a success it was run again the following year.

After that, racing's popularity grew fast. The first race at Cheltenham was run near Andoversford in 1834, while the Vale of Aylesbury saw racing in 1835, also the year of the initial meeting at Aintree, which staged its first Grand National in 1839, won by the aptly-named Lottery. People converged on Liverpool by railway, steamer, coach, gig, wagon, on horseback and on foot. Hotels slept four to a bed. Becher, a roisterous mimic, raconteur and ladies' man, then 40, rode a 20-1 shot, Conrad, and he led the charge to the steep fence with a brook on the landing side. Conrad hit the paling at speed, catapulting his jockey into the brook's cold waters. Becher bravely remounted, unaware he would be forever immortalised by the fence being named Becher's Brook, but was again decanted into the water at what is now Valentine's Brook.

From 1900 onwards a formal jockeys' championship title was awarded to the rider notching up the most winners each season. Frank Mason won that title, and the next five. Fred Rees won five titles, as did Billy Stott. Gerry Wilson won seven championships, but is best known for his partnership with the mighty Golden Miller, who won the Cheltenham Gold Cup five times. Racing then culminated in two celebrated spring festivities, at Cheltenham and Aintree. In 1934 Golden Miller became the only horse to win the Gold Cup and Grand National in the same year.

In the days of Gerry Wilson jockeys wore little protection: they remained exposed to the inevitability of injury: Fulke Walwyn won the Grand National 1936 on Reynoldstown, but fractured his skull two years later and lay unconscious for a month, while Fred Rimell – four times jump-racing's Champion Jockey – broke his neck in a career-ending fall in the 1947 Gold Cup. There were no back-protectors, or goggles; crash-helmets were made of cork, with no chin-strap, so invariably came off, or split on impact. And medical supervision was primitive: if a jockey felt he could ride, even after a bad fall, he could; there was no Injured Jockeys Fund, and insurance companies ignored what they saw as a 'foolhardy pursuit'.

After the Second World War the sport attracted a band of strapping, gutsy, fearless men contesting the major races and titles, a lion-hearted group who had survived the wartime years and now took up the challenge of riding professionally. Theirs was a cavalier attitude, not giving safety a second thought – nor did those in charge of the sport. Stewards enjoyed lunches at the course, served by a butler, with fine wine and vintage ports. Jockeys went out to ride after a warming tot of whisky.

Tim Molony from County Limerick came to England after the war, and was Britain's Champion Jockey five times. He won the Champion Hurdle three consecutive years on Sir Ken and four times on Hatton's Grace. His brother, Martin, won the Gold Cup in 1951 on Silver Fame. Aubrey Brabazon won three successive Gold Cups on Cottage Rake, but was allegedly nervous before the first one in 1948: having weighed out, he had a large port and brandy before mounting. Bryan Marshall was regarded as the most polished rider of his time, and won two Grand Nationals on Early Mist in 1953 and Royal Tan in 1954. In September 1948, he had won the first five races at Folkstone, all for eccentric Dorothy Paget: when he was beaten into second on her sixth runner, in the last race: she was incensed (she backed her horses heavily). Bryan had better luck with another owner, the Queen Mother, on Manicou and Devon Loch. Johnnie Gilbert concentrated only on hurdles; in 1959, he rode ten consecutive winners, a feat equalled in 1986 by Phil Tuck.

Fred Winter, it is reckoned, jumped 120,000 fences, galloped more than 10,000 miles in 4,000+ races, winning nearly a quarter and being placed in half; he nurtured a sense of pace, balance, tactical nous – and the winning edge. And was as strong as an ox. Astute judge John Oaksey labelled Winter, "the best jumping jockey I ever saw." His 121 winners in 1952-53 was a record that stood for fourteen years; he won the 1957 Grand National on Sundew, and famously, in 1962, steered his mount, Mandarin, already winner of that year's Gold Cup, around the challenging fences of the Grand Steeplechase de Paris at Auteuil, in the Bois de Boulogne, without a snaffle, hauling the horse, unsteered since the fourth fence, over the line to win by a head.

Of that feat, John Oaksey wrote: "They have surely earned a place of honour that will be secure as long as men talk, read, or think of horses." Eventually Winter lost his edge, telling jockey Tommy Smith, "Courage is like a bank account: if you draw too many cheques, sooner or later one bounces." He became a celebrated trainer, and remains the only person to have won the Cheltenham Gold Cup, Champion Hurdle and Grand National as both jockey and trainer.

Terry and Tony Biddlecombe, Michael Scudamore, Dave Dick, Bill Rees and Peter Jones were all tough, courageous, talented and determined: they rode hard and played hard, embodiments of the brave Corinthian spirit. After drinking late into the night, they sweated it out next morning in Turkish baths, before catching the train to that day's races in far-flung places like Bogside (erstwhile home of the Scottish Grand National), Buckfastleigh, Hurst Park, Rothbury, Stockton and, almost always on a Monday, Wye, where Michael Scudamore rode his only winner for the Queen Mother, Gay Record in October 1966, the 500th victory of his career. This was to prove his last win over fences. Brough Scott has said, "My outstanding memory of Wye is that it was such a hairy place: the course was notorious for its tight bends." "Riding round Wye was like racing around Wimbledon dog track," recalled former jump jockey Joe Stevens, and another ex-jockey, Pat Mitchell, said, "Wye was a lovely place in terms of atmosphere, but terrible by way of facilities. It was on a field that grazed sheep, which were herded into the middle of the course on race days. Occasionally the sheep got out during a race; an electric fence was installed, but that proved even more hazardous, with falling jockeys landing on it, or loose horses running into it." Wye was the only course where a bell was rung to warn the jockeys they were going out into the final circuit; the course was closed in 1975. There are around ninety courses that now exist only in the imagination – or the depths of memory for horsemen granted longevity, though one or two have been resurrected as point-to-point venues.

Michael Scudamore was a true Corinthian. Despite family connections with racing, getting started was no sinecure: Michael went 56 rides before his first success, on Wild Honey at Chepstow in February 1950. There were no agents fixing up rides back then: jockeys would go racing without any booked rides and reasonably expect to pick up a mount or two. Those making the rules and running the sport had very likely fought in the First World War trenches; the people jockeys rode for had often been shot at in the Second World War; health and safety were unheard of, which meant in those post-war days there was a different level of fearlessness. But the bond between Michael, Terry and Tony Biddlecombe, Stan Mellor, Dave Dick and Johnny Lehane was truly tight. Michael laughingly recalled sitting in saunas with Terry Biddlecombe, drinking champagne cocktails to make the heart beat faster and thus lose weight. There was no concept of a jockey's long-term future but, "We had no end of fun together."

They drove almost everywhere, at 30 mph across a land of no motorways. When Michael took a fall at Kempton riding for Fulke Walwyn, and was kicked in the face and chin, a doctor stitched him up there and then, before bidding him a hearty "Off you go!" If the meeting was south of London, the young bucks would stay in the capital at the Savoy Baths on Jermyn Street "for thirty bob a night," nipping out to Wheeler's Fish Bar, and then soaking the night away, with great bonhomie. Taking a train next morning to southern courses, they would be joined on the journey by Lambourn lads and play rummy "for a penny a spot," often including strangers in their games. The hardest part of racing was getting home at night: there were certain "stopping-places" where they were well-received: they'd been wasting all day so much looked forward to their 'pint'. Michael's 'local' had long been The Black Swan at Much Dewchurch (always known as The Dirty Duck); the pub never closed, and Michael once walked in at 6.40 a.m.

The kit they sported then sounds ludicrous nowadays: ladies' stockings under their breeches; a woollen jersey, often polo neck; neckscarf fixed with a safety pin; cork helmet and stirrups of aluminium. To ride out, or school, they wore a cloth cap, turned the wrong way round to cope with the wind. Asked in 2012 whether he would want to be a jockey in the 21st century, Michael's eyes twinkled more than ever, "Well, the money's better. No, I'm not complaining. The way things were in those days suited my style – the fences were bigger and stiffer, and you had to be a horseman as well as a jockey. Leicester, Manchester, Haydock, they all took a lot of jumping." He clearly revelled in being a jockey: "I met some lovely people, and some wonderful losers." (How many of today's sportsmen and women would say that?) "How lucky we were."

He crossed paths with some great characters, none more colourful than the aforementioned rich and fiercely eccentric Dorothy Paget, on whose Legal Joy he finished second in Teal's Grand National of 1957. Michael recalls how she would rush into the paddock at the very last minute, always wearing the same coat and hat, having driven there in her own Jaguar. A huge gambler, she liked to sleep all day, and the bookies happily took her bets after the race, knowing she'd been asleep. But when jockeys got hurt she could be generosity itself, sending them crates of champagne. Dave Dick had several cases under his bed.

The doctor for whom Michael Scudamore had most respect was Bill Tucker, who had played rugby for England in the 1920s, and whose London clinic stayed open seven days a week, so was ideal for sportsmen who needed to get back into action as quickly as possible. "When you hit the ground, and before you finished rolling, you had Tucker's phone number in your head. He was a genius; he gave us so much confidence. One time he said, "I think you need a drop of brandy: it'll do you good," said Michael, who always smiled roguishly when recounting his colourful escapades.

Michael's last year in the saddle was "the most enjoyable ever." He'd won the Gold Cup on Linwell in 1957, the Grand National on Oxo in 1959, and the King George VI on Rose Park in 1956, beating the Queen Mother's Devon Loch nine months after that horse's exaggerated belly-flop at Aintree. By supreme irony, Michael's career-ending fall happened between obstacles at Wolverhampton on November 1st 1966. Terry Biddlecombe had been due to take the ride, but couldn't do the weight, so Michael rode Snakestone in a handicap hurdle. Either the horse clipped heels or slipped up while rounding a bend, but he fell and brought down three others: the thrashing legs of four horses caused Michael broken ribs, a collapsed lung, six or seven fractures of the jaw, two cracked cheekbones, a broken nose, split palate and several nasty cuts to his head. Worst of all, he lost 90% of vision in his left eye. All the jockey could think was that he wouldn't be able to jump Becher's again. A surgeon put his face together like a jigsaw, but at 34, his career as a jockey was over. He did not complain once; his was the generation that just got on with things. He'd won the big races, had struck up a particularly rewarding partnership with prolific chaser Crudwell, had enjoyed ten Cheltenham Festival successes, and ridden in the Grand National sixteen consecutive times – a record until beaten by Richard Johnson in 2012. Grandson Tom was to ride in nineteen Nationals. He thinks his grandfather's favourite horse was the big, handsome Greektown, on whom Michael won the Arkle Chase in 1964 (the Cotswold Chase as it was then) on his first run over fences – an extraordinary achievement. He thought nothing of riding in a 40-runner novice chase round Hereford: when he fell, his helmet would hit the floor before he did, as there were no straps in those days. He was amused to recall that when he was racing, the only time he'd ever see himself on a horse was in a shop window photograph, or on Pathé news.

Many folk revered Michael Scudamore, but he was utterly self-effacing: "You just throw your heart over a fence, and go after it," he said. And because he loved racing so much it was hard having to stop suddenly. But he kept his friends – always, "as long as you don't go dropping them in it in books." He didn't make much money, but that mattered not: "I'd do it all for nothing, because I loved it." A jockey's financial rewards were by no means generous in his day: often he'd be given cash on the day from owners, if they were present: "a dab in the hand was expected and two wins might get you a tank of petrol." The jockey he revered was Bryan Marshall, who was very strong and didn't move over a fence: he was good to watch. Bryan improved jockeys' style, which was further honed by David Mould, one of the Queen Mother's jockeys.

After being forced to stopped riding, Michael missed the weighing room, not to mention the "blow-out meal once a week on Saturday night: steak and greens, no spuds and a small glass of wine." And he missed the quirks of jump racing folk, like the trainer who would give him "a drop of port in the morning." Grandson Tom, who had a strong bond with Michael, described him as "tough, physically strong, and fearless, utterly fearless, but, perhaps most of all" – he chooses an adjective not often used these days, but in no way old-fashioned – "he was very, very fair."

Michael won over 500 races in Britain, not to mention four or five in Norway, and remained refreshingly modest to the end. One day he mentioned

Owen Glendower; it had been suggested the Scudamores were directly related to the Welsh warrior. Michael gave his trademark smile, and said: "…connected, not related."

I had the great pleasure of interviewing Michael over several weeks for Chris Cook's book – *The Scudamores: Three of a Kind*. We usually talked in the dining-room of his Herefordshire cottage, a simple room, self-effacing of course (if a room can be self-effacing). I recall two pictures from fellow jockeys: *The Worst View in Europe* (coming up to Becher's), and *The Best View in Europe* (a day out hunting). There was a photo of son, Peter, with Lester Piggott; one of Michael junior with his Welsh rugby cap; one of two of Tom's three girls, Margot and Myrtle; a small cigarette case from Norsk Jockey Club; the trophy he'd won for Oxo's Grand National, and, to me most gently striking, a portrait of Michael riding King's Nephew, a stalwart, but perhaps not one of his glory horses.

They don't make them like Michael Scudamore any more.

For many years there was an informal ritual in the jump jockeys weighing room at the end of each season when riders would congratulate each other on their survival with the simple words, "One piece." This does not happen so much now, but that does not mean jockeys take their survival for granted – quite the reverse.

From the sports' first days, every jockey has been well aware that their fortunes – and their future – could change in an instant. One moment they could be in the heart of the action, gripped up by the contest, fuelled by adrenalin, their body taut and at one with their mount as they covered the ground at 25-35 mph: the next they could be unceremoniously ejected from the saddle, hurtling towards an uncertain future. The rider might be shot down into the turf at speed, be kicked, and stamped, not only by their own horse but by the rest of the field, even though horses do their best to avoid stricken riders. But a horse might still land on them; half a ton of racehorse is many times the weight of a jockey, and can cause irreparable damage. The jockey is left alone and deserted out on the course.

Ron Atkins began his career in the 1960s: "When I first started we didn't wear any protection at all. I'd school a horse over fences in just jodhpurs and a t-shirt." Back then a jockey could be knocked out in the first race, but still ride in the third or fourth. Michael Scudamore, Peter Pickford and Dave Dick became punch-drunk, at times slurring their words in normal conversation… a lot of damage was done that wasn't picked up on.

As safety standards gradually improved, jockeys had a back-pad made of foam rubber, shaped like their back, strapped round their waist. Ron had a humorous view of this: "Every jockey in the 1960s was going out like the hunchback of Notre Dame." John Francome then developed his own version – today's modern body protectors are based on his self-designed model. When a horse and jockey fall – they hate having that 'F' beside their name almost as much as the 'U' for unseated rider – it is often the horses landing behind them that do the damage. So jockeys try to roll themselves into a ball, and keep still. But they can still be kicked, or landed on top of, by that half ton of horse. And until relatively recently racecourses had wooden running rails with concrete uprights. Joe Mercer's brother, Manny, was killed cantering to the start at Ascot when his mount unshipped him – he hit a concrete post head-on. Racecourses now have splinter-proof plastic wings and railings. Medical support was provided by the St John's Ambulance Brigade, and Red Cross, but they were volunteers, "who looked ancient," said Ron. There was always a doctor, but it felt to the jockeys he was there purely to have a 'g and t' and, if a jockey had a fall, it was 'a bloody nuisance'.

Ex-jockey Peter Jones still lives near Cheltenham, and made a "tidy living," but it was not possible to have all the top bookings a jockey's agent arranges today. "In those days jockeys were jockeys, and trainers were trainers, there was none of this hugging and kissing they do today," and the Cheltenham Festival, now the apotheosis of every National Hunt season was just the 'March Meeting'. But Peter Jones has a particular claim to fame: in one of the many evenings spent with fellow jockeys Michael Scudamore, Stan Mellor and Terry Biddlecombe at The Tump Inn, Wormelow, outside Hereford, they together set up what was in time to become The Professional Jockeys Association – so they were the founding fathers of a group to represent the jockeys' best interests… Things were starting to progress…

CHAPTER 4: BECOMING A JOCKEY

"A jockey grew up wanting to be a fighter pilot,
but decided to live dangerously, and became a jump jockey instead."

- Alan Lee -

Potential jump jockeys now are given far better training than they were in the past. The British Racing School in Newmarket and Northern Horseracing College in Doncaster are the two main providers of training in the industry. The first step is the foundation course, Level 1 Diploma in Racehorse Care, which allows potential riders to work full-time in a trainer's yard as a racing groom. Then, if they think them competent enough to progress, the trainer will apply for the groom to attend a Jockey Licence Course. Both Newmarket and Doncaster offer an ever-widening range of courses at all levels for people looking at horse racing as a future career, and those already working in the industry wishing to develop qualifications and skills. Many of these courses are available online, at least for the theory.

Most come to the Racing Schools eager to learn and already committed. Much of this is thanks to the strong positive role models who are succeeding in this toughest of sports. Tom Scudamore, Aidan Coleman, Paddy Brennan, Daryl Jacob, Brian Hughes, David Bass, Sam Twiston-Davies et al all execute their art with minimum fuss and maximum resolve, setting the best possible examples to younger jockeys. An increasing number of young jockeys have come up through pony racing, like Sean Bowen, which teaches them much. This learning is communicated to younger, less experienced, but up and coming aspirants, who can only benefit from their elders in the weighing room.

Aspiring jockeys need to go to the right stable to start out; they may not stay there forever, but they will have a grounding that will last them a lifetime. Of the jockeys who begin their training course, only 10% complete their apprenticeship by riding out their claim, i.e. riding enough winners to lose their probationary allowance of 7 lbs, 5 lbs or 3 lbs - depending on their number of winners - when competing against those more experienced. Half of those who do ride out their claim drop out in two to three years and only 5% of would-be jockeys make it to 10-15 wins a year.

Those who stick at it now work closely with a jockey coach. This comparatively recent innovation sees all conditional jockeys (apprentices) allocated to a fully qualified jockey coach to support them from a technical and pastoral perspective, improve their riding skills and develop them as all-round sportspeople. They benefit from a holistic approach to all aspects of their future careers, not least in motivation, confidence, fitness and communication skills. Jockey coaches had been missing until 2011, which is surprising: in almost all sports the player has a coach. Current jockey coaches have all ridden at the highest level: they know not just what they are talking about, but how they themselves have been taught, and how best to pass on knowledge and experience. Every race is different, so to be offered friendship and this depth of support is essential. Today's jockeys need someone to talk to, especially after a bad day, someone who has been through it. Good coaches make young jockeys realise they will always make mistakes – multiple champion AP McCoy attests to that, and what young jockeys think they are doing may not be what they are actually doing.

There can be nothing better for potential jockeys than riding under the keen eyes of a jockey coach. Recently-retired jockey Wayne Hutchinson, having ridden out (exercised a trainer's horses on the gallops), like so many before him, when still at school, went on to complete his jockey qualifications, and achieved no mean success in the saddle. He still sees his time learning the trade as being of excellent value: "You become totally involved in a sport with the animal you love, and you get to meet so many different people. You need to work hard, have a strong work ethic, to listen, and learn." Now, his son is following in Wayne's hoof-prints.

Much time is spent on the equicizer, designed by the Injured Jockeys Fund (IJF), a riding simulation machine used to improve a jockey's style.

Riders are encouraged to work at every aspect, not just at their technique, but their whole approach to, and understanding of the sport. The coach puts their "determination into gear," as one jockey said. Often, the coach will walk the course before racing with his mentee, or just take them out onto the track to talk with them in private. Most recipients of this experience progress quickly thanks to such individual attention. They are taught not just what to say, for example to an owner after their race, but how to say it. If successful, the coach will help them cope with suddenly earning good money, preparing them for the fact that good money/success means people will treat them differently. One jockey summed up his time with his coach as a chance not to dwell on "one-dimensional things." When things go badly, as inevitably they will, the coach will talk to his charge – at length – and get them back on track. So the coach has to work hard too. It's a tough profession, one of the toughest; there will be lots of hurt along the way, but there is no denying that they are all better prepared, and thus better jockeys because of their coaches.

When potential jockeys first seek to enter the profession and start to learn of its demands, they are offered a PDP (Personal Development Plan), which is designed to run alongside their career, setting short, medium and long term goals. This challenges them in terms of what to aim for, and how they might achieve this. They are taught that being a jockey is what they do, not the person they are: learning that is a huge step on the way to the mental resilience they will need – in spades: to identify as a human being, not just as a jockey. As well as receiving advice on important matters, like finance, they are encouraged to have another interest totally unrelated to racing, for example playing squash; that will help put things into perspective, something that can so easily be lost, without them realising it. On the racecourse they will probably experience more bad days than good, and could well be taken over by what one jockey terms 'race brain'. Having another focus, albeit a minor one, aids the recovery of that perspective, and also increases forward thinking.

Three months after the initial course and discussion of their individual plan, Phil Kinsella, Personal Development Manager at the Jockeys Education and Training Scheme (JETS) and a retired jockey himself (having ridden for Keith Reveley and Malcolm Jefferson before two injuries in 2011 forced him out of the saddle), will post a copy of their plan to them, reminding them of the goals set. Many jockeys admit to having forgotten all about the plan – Phil realises that no-one can control having winners, but wants young jockeys to be in control of as much as they can. An essential feature to work on is communication. Talking to owners, trainers, other jockeys, agents, the press and TV is all about making connections: if they give themselves the best opportunity to express their opinions, ideas, fears and hesitations they will be on track, and hopefully stay there.

Jockey Matters is a series of podcasts made by JETS in tandem with the Professional Jockeys Association (PJA), opening riders' eyes to the opportunities open to them and dealing with a plethora of issues confronting every jump jockey in the 21st century: fitness; resilience; nutrition and wellbeing; injury and rehabilitation; substance abuse; loss of earnings; safer driving; performance psychology; loneliness; personal development; dealing with defeat on a regular basis; concussion management; preparation for retirement and, increasingly, mental health are among the most prominent. Wayne Hutchinson acknowledges, "I really needed JETS to lean on and provide the support I needed."

Besides being among the most dangerous of sports (as one jockey has termed it, "We are all only one ride away from paralysis"), racing is a fickle mistress: loss of form can leave even the most committed of those who don the coloured silks to doubt themselves; in the worst cases, this doubt rolls on and on. Hunger, tiredness and disappointment can snowball, and everyone has dark days. The question is, what to do with that day? Mood swings can soon cause irritation, then unusual behaviour, which puts pressure on the jockey's family and those surrounding them, as he or she comes to hate, at least for a while, the thing they love most of all – racing. Michael Caulfield, for 15 years CEO of the PJA, and now a top sports psychotherapist consultant, has seen this multiple times, and always urges those who are suffering to seek help, help which is increasingly available and which comes in many forms, before things lurch out of control. As he succinctly puts it: "We don't wait for our car to break down before we take it for a service."

Perspective is easy for the outsider to apply from the comfort of an armchair in front of the TV; it is not so easy for those whose self-worth is determined by what happens on the racecourse, even if it is in essence "just horses running round a field." Self-worth is vital, perhaps being determined by what sort of person we are, but try telling that to a jockey pencil-thin, existing on one meal a day, sometimes not even that, who gets up at 4.30 a.m. every day, Sundays included, is fighting to ride out any horse while recovering from injury, and whose mind is full only with negatives.

Not surprisingly, alcohol is prevalent in the diet of many jockeys; all too soon it can take over and lead the addict (though many deny the use of that word) on a merry-go-round: they drink to stop feeling, hold on to the negatives because they experience far more lows than highs, and end up in a vicious circle that then becomes a perilous vortex. Often lonely, and sometimes ashamed, they may then seek crack cocaine and heroin as not just the pain killer but the panacea for what often amounts to raw fear: that fear is exhausting. The phrases 'Just one more', 'I'll sort things out tomorrow', 'I can still make a better job of things' and 'What will people say?' cavort around in the heads of the sufferers, without them realising it, as they wait to hit rock bottom…

But waiting to hit rock bottom inevitably makes everything harder. Paul Struthers, ex-Chairman of the PJA, was among those leading the way to support jockeys with ways of recovery. He saw racing as a very forgiving sport, urging jockeys not to wait for a positive dope test, if using drugs, but to reach out their hand for help. As Prince William is advocating with other sportspeople, that first step is so often the hardest: many young riders do not know how to make it; whom to trust; what will happen to them if they open up; whether admitting they are struggling will cost them their job; what the worry will add to a family that perhaps has other deep-set worries; what the racing fraternity will think of them etc. As Struthers always said: "It's not about judging, certainly not about condemning; it's about understanding why…" The behaviour may not be exemplary, but the individual is salvageable… and several high-profile jockeys like Ray Dawson and Kieran Shoemaker are testimony to Struthers' words – they, too, are urging sufferers to grab the hand reached out to them; to tell their stories, and come to realise that second chances are always possible; they still have so much ahead of them.

Many of us still think all counselling is the same, sitting in a falsely cheerful room, with a cup of tea and a box of tissues on the table, facing a cosy middle-aged lady in her twin-set and pearls. Not so: counselling today comes in many forms. Some ex-jockeys are counsellors now. We are all human beings, and human beings make mistakes. Despite all the pressures, problems, bad days, lost races, untimely weight gains and falls at 30 mph, perhaps this generation of young jockeys will prove the best so far to realise that help is out there, that they can - and will – make a better fist of things tomorrow.

For all their ever-growing experience of race-riding; all the hours of grind at their craft, often in wild winter conditions; for all their hardness and ability to banish thoughts of injury from their mindsets, jockeys are always determined to improve. As John Carter puts it: "Tactical acumen comes with time." So patience is hugely important, not easy in an age that demands everything be done yesterday. But, if a young jockey is determined enough, he realises the whole package takes time. Graham Lee, until recently a flat jockey, but previously a jump jockey, who won the Grand National on Amberleigh House, was mentored by Michael Caulfield, who instilled into Graham his professional, well-prepared, well-rounded approach. Many of the lessons learned by a young rider over the sticks are by definition hard ones, often costly, but they are essential if that young rider is to keep improving.

Three areas in which jockeys are now given more guidance and support are preparation, physical conditioning and the management of personal relationships. Jockeys must do their homework, study both the *Racing Post* website and race replays, and thus get to know their opposition in every race. They must watch their weight with the eye of an eagle, adjust their eating accordingly, and many walk the course before racing to assess ground conditions.

Riding a horse in a race is an intense physical activity: a study in conjunction with Exeter University has proved jockeys' bodies work as hard as Olympic athletes during every race. Some riders have a personal trainer; all agree that fitness is paramount. Jockey coach and ex-rider Steve Smith-Eccles, that one-time jester of the weighing room, is wise here: "The technical stuff you can teach, but holding the normal body position on the bridle expends energy, and a tired body affects the mind, which in a race situation is dangerous."

A pillar of professionalism for jockeys, John Carter states, "is the management of a network of connections; the whole racing industry is built upon an ever-shifting foundation of alliances." Jockeys are one third of the triangle with owners and trainers, with whom they have to build relationships using skills quite alien to those they need on a horse. And then, of course, there is the media, not least when leaping jackal-like onto a rider who has just ridden a winner, for the first interview, which some jockeys do not enjoy. Increasingly, jockeys who did not bring home the spoils are also encouraged to express their feelings on camera: there is no hiding place.

Loyalty is not a universal feature in the racing world. It is by no means uncommon for riders to be 'jocked off' in favour of another pilot. Here again, pressing media persons are not always the best to have around. At the big meetings, this is particularly challenging. But the weighing room helps here, there is always banter and real camaraderie, even when stakes are highest, as in the intense cauldron of emotion at the Cheltenham Festival. Michael Caulfield believes, "That week is all about performing well, yet under the pressure the jockeys remain courteous, there is no cheating or conning. It is just raw competition. The jockeys' manners are impeccable under pressure, it's competitive, it's feisty but it is based on manners and standards that have been handed down over the years." A code of conduct under which jockeys must operate is now in place after the controversial case in 2021 when female jockey Bryony Frost complained she had been bullied by fellow rider, Robbie Dunne.

Each jockey builds a team around them: valet, agent, accountant, friends and family; every person in that team is invaluable. But such harmony is not always practical… the wheels can, and do often fall off, and therein lies the potential not just for time out with injury, but loss of earnings, the forfeit of regular rides, slow draining away of self-esteem, loss of confidence, mental health anxieties… and even worse.

Jockeys need 'horse sense', fundamental and intangible. They can ride racehorses competently in the "text book shape of a cocktail glass, with their head, elbows and heels in a vertical line," but that is not enough. American journalist Jim Murray has written: "You have to be half-man, half-animal to be a jockey, you have to think like a horse, sense his mood, gauge his courage, and cajole him into giving his best." It has been said that AP McCoy had a sixth sense, knowing what he wanted his horse to do in a race, the horse realising this and responding. It was a natural gift. That gift is hard to define. Two-time British flat racing champion jockey in the 1920s Charlie Elliott acknowledged: "There's a lot of mystery. There's something strange and marvellous that happens between the horse and certain men and women who get on his back; you can't explain it, you can only demonstrate it by getting up on the animal." Some jockeys, like musicians, are born with natural talent, natural flair; others have to work inordinately hard. But the consensus remains they have to be good horsemen in order to be good jockeys; the two are different. They have to get inside the heads of horses, as Dale Gibson, the PJA's Executive Director, has avowed: "Every horse is different, and you have got to work them out pretty damn quick. You can study their form, hear their trainer's views and watch riders in previous races, but sometimes it is split-second stuff." As with all arts, the best practitioners make it look easy, but, however gifted they may be, they have always had to graft. No jockey would contest this fact. They work on their style, continually seeking to hone it for better results; they learn from riding different horses on cold, dark mornings; they study a horse's past performance, and their experience grows all the time.

Acquired through nature, nurture and practice is the art of balance. American legend Bill Shoemaker recognised "the uncanny ability to achieve and maintain perfect balance so the weight appears to be taken off the horse's back: the jockey thus transmits confidence down the reins and through the bit, so the horse's mouth will not be abused; revelling in freedom the horse can use his speed to the full, responding to every request from the saddle so horse and man are as one." Centaurs.

Judgement of pace is another vital skill learned by experience, trial and error. This becomes an innate weapon in the jockeys' armoury. As their tactical acumen grows, so they can react instinctively, able to compute the mass of data being received through the senses as they race: how rival horses and jockeys are faring; where and when a gap will appear; how much each horse has left in the tank; being aware of the jockey preparing to make a move, in a word, seeing what is about to happen before it happens. Steve Smith-Eccles thinks: "Riding a horse in a race is like building a jigsaw. You build up your jigsaw as the race progresses; the final piece is when you jump the last, but that jigsaw is formed by the horse you ride."

Race-riding experience can only be gained slowly, brick by brick: no-one can become a master craftsman overnight. Becoming the whole package takes time… and the best young jockeys will be constantly looking, listening, learning, never ceasing in their fierce endeavour to improve…

CHAPTER 5:
KEEPING YOUR 'BOTTLE'

*"Those who seek the path to enlightenment must dictate terms
to their mind; then they proceed with strong determination."*

- James Willoughby -

Jockeys' lives are defined by winning. Mick Fitzgerald remembers, "Before a big race you feel you could walk through a brick wall," and now, in retirement, wishes he could have bottled that feeling. Jockeys need enormous reserves of stamina to spend their professional life controlling an animal ten times their bodyweight, an animal that could bolt with them onboard at any minute. Not every jockey can keep up this inordinately punishing schedule. We have wondrous admiration for those men and women who find themselves propelled into a whirl of tumbling horse flesh and flailing hooves, then swear, get up and start the long trek back to the weighing room to change into their colours for their next ride. They need to be supremely fit to ride; every race requires huge physical effort, and they have to be 110% fit to fall. Jump jockeys are taller and heavier than flat jockeys as they need more strength and stamina for their longer races.

As Edward Stroud, Head of Rehabilitation for the IJF affirms, "It is too late to catch a fallen jockey and repair them: the sport needs to prepare them for the inevitable falls that will come their way, and the impact that will have on them in both senses of the word." Brian Hughes, thrice Champion National Hunt Jockey, is a strong advocate of this essential preparation: "Obviously some falls are worse than others, but the fitter and stronger you are, the more chance you have of a quick recovery" – not rocket science, but he backs this up with his own experience. He used to spend a lot of time running and power-walking – now he believes circuit-training with short sharp exercises in resistance, together with boxing, keep the heart rate up and are thus beneficial: he says it is similar to interval training with horses. Whereas rugby players train themselves to take the impact of other bodies and sometimes the ground, jockeys have to train themselves to hit that ground at 35 mph, with half a ton of horse: they need to psych themselves up for this eventuality, for it will surely happen.

The three Injured Jockey Fund centres at Newmarket, Malton and Lambourn play a vital role. Many people assume jockeys only go to these rehab centres after an injury: not so. The superbly equipped centres have everything a rider needs, not just the machines but the highest possible degree of expertise, and the IJF encourages riders to take advantage of all this while they are fully fit. To keep weight off, they are encouraged to do a lot of impact training, loading their bones: this strengthens those bones, which will then suck up the nutrients they are taking in with their high protein/low carb diet. As Gavin Sheehan admitted, "Jockeys may well not do this on their own, they need direct encouragement, which is now provided." The result of this attention to their physical strength and fitness will lead to a mind primed, focused and keen. Jockeys will be hydrated enough, will not tire as the race unfolds (many falls not surprisingly take place at the latter end of races, when the tempo has increased) and that state of fitness will carry them through. Brian Hughes has asserted, "With three centres offering the best possible facilities, with every jockey's best interest at heart – for free – if a rider is not taking advantage of these centres, he has only one person to blame."

Jockeys are daring and brave. Many enjoy the risk factor in their everyday job, believing that sharpens their senses and heightens their love of what they do. To us, they seem fearless in a way we cannot understand, but jockeys do not boast of this essential chromosome in their make-up: they are well aware injuries will happen, but they blank out this fact in their minds, they have to, in order to be able to keep riding.

In his autobiography, AP McCoy wrote: "If you get on a horse and are afraid of falling, afraid of pain, then it's time to stop. As long as you are happy to ride the horse that has fallen in its last three races, knowing that if you get round it has at least a chance of winning, then kick on," (a phrase used tellingly by Sam Thomas' father, Geoff). To have that mindset – to keep it – even after 20 years in the saddle, is remarkable. Not surprisingly for some, over time, a sense of fear, and awareness that the notion of falling is starting to creep into the subconscious, however unbidden, can gnaw away "in the recesses of their grey matter" (John Carter). It is the most unwelcome of visitors. Jockeys will not admit it is happening; on the contrary, they will try even harder to subdue this dark shadow of anxiety. But others, not least their fellow jockeys, will spot this trait: they know each other well and will sense courage is starting to ebb: "Maybe instead of giving the horse a kick, they hold back. Once or twice you might overlook this, but if it keeps happening you know their bottle has gone. If that happens, you can't help them; in truth you probably look to take advantage of it. Our sport is man to man, it is not a team game, the camaraderie is great, but when you are out there on the racetrack it's every man for himself."

With jump jockeys nowadays taller than they once were, it is hard to avoid putting on weight. Whereas before they ate one meal a day, now they are better fed, better educated and thus better equipped. Jerry Hill, Chief Medical Advisor to the BHA, in association with George Wilson of Liverpool John Moores University, now advocates a low calorie, high fibre, protein diet with low saturated fat, i.e. eat more and lose weight.

In the past, jockeys would not eat for two days, and were really hungry all the time; to think of losing pounds was draining, physically and mentally. Now jockeys can take on board a far better diet, complemented by a planned exercise regime; as a result, well-being and performance are enhanced. They can allow themselves five to six feeds a day, small amounts of protein and low carbs, followed by a power-walk to get the metabolism going. Scientists, like those at John Moores, can assess jockeys' individual fitness and put in place a personal diet plan to assist them, treating them as professional athletes with access to world class sports science and facilities. This is a huge step forward from the days when they were subjected to endless mental torture – and left to it.

Some jockeys still look "skeletal to the point of anorexia," writes John Carter, "their waxwork faces pale, gaunt and sallow... more akin to willowy pencil-thin supermodels." And they have no respite, weighing out

30 minutes prior to every race, and weighing in immediately after. They have little opportunity to refuel or rehydrate, unlike boxers, who weigh in just once 24 hours before a fight. With jockeys, the weight changes from race to race, so every time they step onto the scales, (which they could do up to 28 times a day), the pressure is on. Small wonder their race day demeanour in the paddock can be "more akin to that of an undertaker than that of a clown."

But there is no short cut to success: bone health has to be strong to minimise the effects of fractures (when a jockey is 'wasting', bone density decreases). Dehydration is detrimental to health: it can lead to kidney failure, slower reaction times and decreasing muscle strength. Jockeys need a shift in their mindset to increase their value of themselves, and it is best if they can get this when young. Finding time may be hard, with days off rare and relaxation hard to master, but in expert hands jockeys can easily find and establish their correct weight management regime and be informed of the latest developments in nutritional advice. Being a jockey is a pilgrimage of perseverance, so professional nutritionists see it as their duty to spread the light of their knowledge: from every healed wound life lessons are learned, which become healthy scars of experience. The days of hours sweating in the sauna are long gone; with all the advice/support now available, jockeys can not only find their fighting weight but – the most difficult thing of all – hold that weight and thus enter the arena in the best possible shape. Even so, as ex-PJA Jockeys President David Bass admits, "Every so often, you have to break out."

For all that a jump jockey's professional life is – or can be – ablaze with colour, dash, excitement and trophies, it can be cruelly demanding, and fortunes change dramatically in seconds. Jockeys cannot take their feet off the accelerator. Whether they are scraping a living, swimming in rough waters, or riding high, they have to work with and depend on other jockeys, all the time grasping any opportunity that arises, even if that is to the disadvantage of their fellows. If they do not climb the ladder, they could slip down a twisting snake: everything depends on the demon luck. Risking body and mind every time they go out for a race, they are forever in the grip of their personal tornados, driven by fear of failure. They need to soak up the view, take in the bad weather and the good, for they are not the storm.

It has been said that jockeys are scrutinised as much, if not more, than any other sport practitioners; with social media, they can have no secrets: they are open to criticism all the time. Many feel it is not the horse, the trainer, the course, the weather, or the going, but the jockey who is blamed the most when losing a race; riders also feel the dismay at getting beaten more than most. Abuse on Twitter happens all the time: jockeys are too available on social media sites, but have to be on it for their survival.

And temptations abound. In a sport built around gambling, as Robin Oakley wrote in *The Spectator*, September 2014, that is an obvious risk to integrity: "If a jockey whose career is in decline is offered £1,000 by unscrupulous manipulators to make minimum effort in a race he probably won't win anyway, you can see the temptation, compared with a return of just £221 for a day's work and a 300-mile drive."

The most noble of animals can attract the most duplicitous characters. And relationships can become abusive: young people go into the game with abandonment, and love for a job connected with horses: all of a sudden they find themselves in a ruthless industry.

An intriguing, but ultimately sad story of alleged skulduggery in jump racing came to some sort of light recently: Cornishman, Barrie Wright was a West Country jockey from late 1970s to early 1990s, riding such horses as Butler's Pet and Doc's Coat for trainer Trevor Hallett. Known as 'Bazza', with his initials B.W. emblazoned on his helmet, Barrie was a colourful character, with a glamorous lifestyle. But some of his connections were not necessarily savoury, leading the jockey to trial at Southampton Crown Court on charges of importing cocaine. He was acquitted, but, having given evidence- along with Graham Bradley- about selling information, he was banned from racecourses in Britain for 15 years. He moved to the continent, based in Belgium... On February 7th 2020, he left a meal with his family in the Brasschaat district of Antwerp and vanished. He was 64 at the time. Talk of a ransom fuelled belief he had been kidnapped... he has not been seen since. Belgian police closed his file in April 2023; thus preventing a satisfying Dick Francis-like dénouement...

Safety is paramount at racecourses now. Three vets follow the race in cars sporting an orange flag, so as to be able to act as quickly as possible if a horse is injured. In addition there is a vet at the finish and one in the treatment boxes: nothing is left to chance. With two ambulances always on stand-by, doctors' cars also follow the race, their flag red and white check. If a jockey or an animal is hurt, screens will be swiftly erected. That used to be only if it looked as if a horse had to be euthanised; now the screens are used to set up a private, quiet space, where beast or human can be treated. Even if all seems well with the animals, they are watched closely post-race, especially if they have overheated, bled or had a cut, say on the back of the fetlock joint. Any wounds are cleaned up before they are returned to the racecourse stables.

Stricken jockeys receive the best possible care. Those who suffer an injury at a racecourse on race day will be seen by the RMO (Racecourse Medical Officer) on duty, who will register details of the injury. With the ambulances on hand, they are promptly assessed. If the jockey needs to be hospitalised, the Jockey's Injury Notification Procedure will contact next of kin and provide further support. The IJF will then call or text as soon as possible, liaise with the BHA Chief Medical Advisor and, if the jockey is in hospital for more than one night, will offer a visit. The jockey will have access to a team of experts at the IJF, who will provide a specialist rehab programme to help them return to riding as quickly and safely as possible.

Declan Murphy, the Irish jockey, severely injured in 1994, who told his story in *Centaur*, subtitled *The Memoir of the Jockey who came back from the Dead*, knew the full gamut of life as a jump jockey: "The ability to ride a horse well is the ability to embrace a partnership that is unique. It is a partnership between the horse and the rider in which the understanding is implicit – the horse is the true athlete; the rider is simply the enabler. And to enable the horse to run its best race, to enable the horse to win, is to master the art of balancing authority with kinship. The key to success is the ability to empower the horse to understand your will, while still allowing it to follow its natural competitive instinct. There are a lot of things about race-riding that can't be learnt, they have to be felt. A jockey has to feel every movement of the horse underneath him and understand what each one means.

"Nobody sees the fight within you. They see what they see with their eyes; they don't see your spirit. From the moment I got on a horse,

I shut everything else out. This was my way – blocking out the world, distractions fading into the background, giving way to a laser-like focus. When I am in this state of 'flow', nothing else matters. And so, just like the blinkers on my horse, I had blinkers on my mind. My only objective was to win.

"Throughout my career as a jockey, my riding skill and my intelligence worked in unison. Using a combination of gut feeling and judgement, I developed a strategic, perfectly instinctive approach to race-riding. Before I even got on a horse, I had a game plan, measured and calculated. I would analyse everything, pre-race and post-race, strive to correct past mistakes, strive to surpass past expectations. And then, when I got on my horse, just while cantering to the start, I would consider my options, judge my pace, determine my tactics – I wasn't riding for show; I was riding to win. And so every stride was thought through with careful deliberation, split-second decisions were taken with split-second precision. I didn't just go out and ride. I used my brain."

Declan's brother, Pat, understands what jockeys put themselves through day after day: "As a jockey, you are actually placing your destiny on to a horse's back, you are offering it up. So you are 'master of your destiny' when you decide you want to do it, but you are still back into the lap of the gods, once the race begins…"

Nowadays, no jockey can truly shine without a good agent, whose job is to connect opportunities for jockeys and find them the right horse at the right time. Dave Roberts, 'The Kingmaker', who retired in April 2022, was the master in this sphere, at one point looking after 57 jump jockeys – "a nice round number." Initially the spotter of young talent, he helped build the career of Adrian Maguire, the first Irish jockey to make it big in the UK, and, in his considered opinion, "the best jump jockey never to be champion." From October to May, Roberts was rarely seen: he could be on the phone from 12 to 20 hours a day, speaking to at least 40 different people. His aim was not just to secure rides for jockeys, but to secure the best rides: he knew which horses his charges should be riding and which they shouldn't, so his was a fine-balancing act, with a huge amount of juggling involved. Spotting opportunities, making links, always planning ahead, he still maintained this was his hobby, "so it wasn't like work." That said, his hours were antisocial,

"I don't recommend marriage for a jockeys' agent," and he admitted he had become the architect of his own slavery.

The title Jockeys' Agent may sound glamorous; Roberts says he was simply a salesman of jockeys, he linked them with trainers, whom he rang to help them place horses in a race in which they had a winning chance; it was then up to them to make their choice of racecourse and of jockey – "Everyone has their preferences." His knowledge of racing, of horses, of the jockeys he managed, was gargantuan. If need be, he would take a jockey off mounts he considered too risky a proposition: "We don't need to take chances." But the top jockeys rode the vast majority of those he selected for them, and he knew his jockeys inside out; he was "a bit like an agony aunt to them as well." He understood jockeys' temperament and mindset – these warriors have to be in the public eye, the only way that can happen is by showing their talent in riding winners. He had no contracts with his jockeys, but was always planning ahead; he struck up a rapport with them, not least AP McCoy who gave him brilliant feedback, analysing everything, conscious the future was rarely about today. But for all his industry, for Roberts the bottom line was plain and simple: "That jockeys came home in one piece: that was the only thing that mattered."

Chris Broad was a jockey, and a trainer, before setting out as an agent in 1996. Agents were a new thing then, but he had become a tad disillusioned, and was encouraged to have a go by Carl Llewellyn and Warren Marston, who knew he sought something different. Despite the job proving a constant treadmill, in the office from 5.15 a.m. until 6 p.m.; aware his wife was bringing up the kids; having Christmas day off if he was lucky, Chris revelled in the constant roundabout of his role. Competing with other agents, directing jockeys' careers, he went for quality, not quantity, his main goal being to get his jockeys on the right horses, ideally with chances in the big races. He regarded his lads as part of the family, which meant many trips to hospital bedsides, and ICU, often on the other side of the country. Career–ending falls, head injuries and smashed eye- sockets never lay well, despite being part and parcel of the job; they were hard always hard to deal with, as when Jason Maguire was badly hurt one year at Stratford, on the very cusp of the Cheltenham Festival.

Despite the tough life, he is proud to have known and worked with such proficient riders, even if they sometimes had to be treated with asbestos gloves! Picking them up when they were 'down'; knowing one jockey's strength was another's weakness, 'feeding' things right to them; so they could find the positive in such an individual sport, he was determined they did not feel they were on their own. He looked after Tommy Murphy from a conditional, and Jim Culloty from an amateur, and found Sam Twiston- Davies and Daryl Jacob particularly good value. Following 25 years as an agent, rarely having time to speak to people properly, Chris is now a safety officer, but still goes and has a word with riders, counting himself a fortunate man, despite all the blood, tears and sweat his charges had to endure.

Aside from riding out and racing, jockeys have no real routine. They only know 48 hours before a race their book of rides, so have to plan on an ad hoc basis. Very few make big money; many outsiders feel they are mad to do the job they do. Wives and partners have to be strong when jockeys bring their disappointments home. If jockeys seem always to be in a hurry, this is because always people are always snapping at their heels; only when running laps of the racecourse can they find any peace at their workplace.

In 1995, just a year before Richard Davis' untimely death in a race at Southwell, at a time when many jockeys were leaving school at 15 with nothing to fall back on, JETS, the brainchild of Bob McCreery and others, had been registered as a charity in Newbury. Founded by contributions from jockeys' prize money and support from the Injured Jockeys Fund (IJF) the charity is a development scheme helping jockeys to plan, and then achieve, a secure future after race-riding, through the provision of career coaching, training, grants, scholarships and employment advice. Training days were instigated, with tutor support on a range of skills such as business management; IT; bloodstock; marketing; office/secretarial work; saddle-making; accounting; bookkeeping; sport psychology; web design; journalism; racing admin; stewarding; groundskeeping; yard management; starter training; broadcasting and farriery. Richard Davis had been one of the first to start planning for his future, aware that he would need advice to help develop new skills, not only after retiring from the saddle, but also whilst riding. The venture called for initiative, forethought, effort and determination, all of which the 26-year-old had in spades.

In 1997, in addition to having an annual race instigated in his memory at Worcester, the trophy designed by racing sculptor Philip Blacker, the Richard Davis Awards were introduced because of his connection with the charity. These are presented every year at Cheltenham's November meeting to recognise and honour the career development of current or former jockeys. Interested parties can apply for the Jockey Club Achievement Award and the IJF Progress Award, and these are then assessed by independent judges, JETS trustees and IJF almoners. These awards are important in raising awareness for the good work of JETS, and acknowledging those jockeys who have gone on to forge successful second careers thanks to the charity. In 2020, the top award was won by Kylie Manser, flat jockey turned firefighter.

JETS changed their moniker, from Jockeys Employment Training Scheme to Jockeys Education Training Scheme in order to reflect the charity's wider remit to develop "jockeys throughout their careers," rather than just focussing on career transition. There's now a new Richard Davis Award for current jockeys who have shown the most commitment to their continuing personal development, with two new sponsors, the Jockey Club and the British Racing School, joining the IJF.

More and more jockeys are appreciating the need to be able to communicate well and build up their media skills, to survive under today's media spotlight. In addition, the scheme runs regular media training days with fees heavily subsidised and there is a wealth of computer/IT training available, delivered in all sorts of formats and venues. *Racing to Learn* is the racing industry's online learning and development platform, to help promote ever-increasing opportunities in the sport.

JETS has also produced a series of films in association with PJA, under the title *Jockey Matters*, to help riders take in aspects of the profession of which they may not have been aware, and thus become better, happier jockeys.

Phil Kinsella (based in the north, working for much of his time at Jack Berry House) exemplifies the second career that JETS now offer jockeys, signposting them to all parts of the industry. With the emphasis now on education rather than employment, he encourages today's riders to aim for a second career early, taking a holistic approach to this preparation for what happens when they stop riding. "Being a jockey is all-encompassing, all-consuming, but there is more to them than the job, so implementing a dual career plan from as early as possible is essential. Retired jockeys who are good role models, like Andrew Tinkler, speak to their younger counterparts, and we run workshops for them to fit in with racing commitments and riding out, so fitness, nutrition, finance and mental health are discussed openly from the start." Jockeys are encouraged to start putting into place plans for their immediate future and also to set long-term goals themselves, goals that will give them a different identity. Follow-ups to those plans take place regularly, the key thing is starting the process early, as Richard Davis did in 1995-96, hence the Awards: for a current jockey planning their next stage, for an ex-jockey now into their second career, and for a jockey excelling in that second career.

JETS offers a personal relationship, not a paper exercise. Being a jockey is about what you are, not who you are, so the jockey may have developed an identity, but the person may not; they need to acknowledge themselves as that person. Often, this represents a sea-change for the professional rider, which can be prepared for by JETS running alongside a jockey's career, showing them opportunities unrelated to racing, which is vital if they are to avoid 'race brain'. Thinking beyond the track can thus start at any time and jockeys have to take their minds, or have them taken off, all-consuming thoughts on racing. Phil posts targets to jockeys he is looking after, small goals they may have forgotten about (e.g: "eat little and often, stay off the Red Bull"). Rounded people not only ride better and have a sharper sense of perspective, they will experience fewer anxieties about what they want to achieve and how to achieve it.

Jump jockeys put enormous pressure on themselves. If they are anxious, that anxiety transmits to their mounts. They have to be durable and never get stale, staying on the hamster-wheel for most of their professional life. They cannot live in the past, but have to move on to the next race, their lives are all about the future, all the while the fire is burning inside them. Being a jockey is eternally complex. Whereas footballers play once or twice a week; golfers' tournaments last four days maximum; boxers' fights can be over in seconds, and county cricketers play regularly in the summer but have a long lay-off season, jump jockeys' lives are relentless. They can ride six or seven days a week, and, at present, a bone of contention for many, there is no proper hiatus between one season and the next.

Resilience is key, both mental and physical. Sacrifices have to be made, again both mental and physical. With many weddings still happening on Saturdays, invitations have to be turned down, the same with weekend parties, especially with the breathalyser. Jockeys must be 100% professional on and off the course (it is reckoned only the top half a dozen jockeys can afford to have a driver). Eating "nothing but white fish and a bit of lettuce" (John Carter), inevitably takes its toll when aligned to endless hours of driving, wasting, physical and mental pain; enduring this relentless lifestyle with its many deprivations is testing, to say the least.

Michael Caulfield has acknowledged the fact that not only is racing the sport where you lose and get beaten most of all, it is the one where you know you will inevitably get beaten often: "This takes a different mindset, you need the sheer perseverance to go through hell. Jockeys have to get past the 'f… it' factor [i.e. when they want to say "F… it, I can't do this anymore, it's just too brutal and painful"]. Most of them get past this; some, of course, do not."

Barry Geraghty has proved, "Being a jockey is a high-wire act: things can turn in a heartbeat, for better or worse. It all happens in the blink of an eye, as you feel a horse change underneath you in the final strides before a fence: there has to be constant communication/conversation between jockey and horse; everything is about the hands. The best jockeys have a lightness of touch, the nuances of their message changing with the slightest variation in the tension of the reigns – it's a shared responsibility, animal and human. Jockeys have to read the subtleties of a race that is developing around them every second. There are dozens of ways to win a race, but the tactical ride, meticulously plotted, executed with precision, is the best. It's a good clean fight till the last half mile – then the gloves come off.

Jockeys need to block out bad moments, and disappointments, to focus on the next race. A chain of events can unfold: when all the links come together that's perfect, but take out any one link and that chain collapses. Jockeys go in and out of fashion; cockiness and confidence are often confused, and, always, jockeys are in the crosshairs of desperate punters, disconsolate owners and worse…"

Self-belief is crucial, but this is not a constant, it can vary from day to day, from race to race, even from minute to minute, so maintaining a precious balance here is essential. Again, Michael Caulfield knows the score: "Self-belief is important in any walk of life, you need it throughout your career, belief comes from loving what you do, because you know you will crack it in the end. The majority of those jump jockeys who survive for 20 years have a strong self-belief; they have got lots of evidence to back it up, but they wouldn't keep riding without that absolute cast iron belief in their own ability. The ones who don't have it, don't last."

Caulfield saw this self-belief manifested nowhere better than in Richard 'Dicky' Johnson, for him, "The man most respected in professional sport, because he had done it for 20+ years, day in, day out. It was his ability not to get too high, not to get too despondent; he was remarkably consistent, he didn't leave a single piece of effort behind him, so he knew he had given everything to his profession. There was nothing else he could have done. He was a perfect role model and did it for the sheer joy of it. Of course, he got rewarded for it, which he should do, but he had such a desire in doing what he did; he was always hungry to win, but that was underpinned by belief in his own ability and love of doing it: he didn't need to do it, he just loved it, chasing coveted wins with an ever-raging thirst." Dicky rode just shy of 21,000 mounts, in races totalling 50,000 miles, that's twice round the world, over $\frac{1}{4}$ of a million obstacles.

Top jockeys have an edge. John Carter believes: "They seize opportunities to win with the icy, killer instinct of an assassin. Their behaviour might be more obsessive, riven, blinkered and competitive than other, perhaps more rounded human beings: they are not like most of us. Fred Archer was not normal. Richard Dunwoody was not normal. AP McCoy was not normal. Lester Piggott was once described as "always greedy for winners as if he'd never had one before." Each is driven in his own way. Ruby Walsh, when asked whether his glittering tally of wins at the Cheltenham Festival wasn't a bit greedy, paused for a moment before his reply: "There's a bit of greed in most sportspeople who enjoy any bit of success. AP was as greedy as hell. Somewhere in there, there has to be a little bit of selfishness that makes you want more, makes you push yourself that little bit harder. Yeah, I'm a bit greedy."

Jump jockeys' overarching element is their courage; theirs is a bravery that knows no bounds: it shows a spiritual independence complete in itself.

CHAPTER 6: THE WEIGHING ROOM

"National Hunt jockeys have a hard and brutal life, but they also have free entry to the world's greatest brothel of the senses."
- Simon Barnes -

Racecourse weighing rooms are usually a network of areas, for stewards; valets; the press; jockeys' changing, male and female; a medical section, including physiotherapy access; CCTV monitors; a kitchen/canteen; declarations desk; and the ever-important scales: there is no hiding place for jockeys when it comes to weight. The weighing room is the nexus, the holy of holies, for jockeys on race days. Security is tight: no-one is allowed in without jurisdiction, so riders cannot be pestered within its sanctuary. Jockeys always have with them their medical book: it is their passport, with details of all their injuries.

Each horse in a race has to carry a certain weight. To make sure it does so, jockeys have to 'weigh out' before the race to show they and the kit together weigh the right amount. That weight includes compulsory body-protector, boots, saddle, crash helmet, whip, pairs of goggles, the horse's bridle, blinkers, hood, visor, eye-shield, and anything worn on the horse's legs. If the jockey is lighter than the weight allotted, thin strips of lead are put into the saddle-cloth to make up the difference. Once a jockey has weighed out, he hands the saddle to the trainer to go and saddle the horse. After a race, jockeys must 'weigh in', to confirm they carried the right weight. The size of the saddle is crucial, and on half a ton of thoroughbred racing at full throttle, riders need to be sure they can stay 'in the plate'. Before they go to face the clerk of the scales to be weighed out, jockeys use a practice scale in the weighing room and adjust accordingly.

Pivotal to its workings are the jockeys' valets (pronounced in English rather than French), licensed by the Jockey Club to look after the riders whenever and wherever they ride. Their job is to lay out on the jockey's peg their breeches, white polo shirt, the colours of the owner for whom they are riding, string gloves, and pairs of tights, for warmth, lightness and protection from chafing. They have to dress their jockeys, fit their saddles with the correct weights and girths, add breastplates or blinkers and pamper their charges. These vital cogs work inordinately hard, arriving early on race day, transporting much of the riders' gear from course to course, washing it, cleaning and mending it, driving thousands of miles a year, thus becoming essential to the jockeys they look after, to the extent that they never fail to arrive at the course in good time: getting stuck in traffic is not an option.

While jockeys bring their own saddles, often two or three of differing weights, (though Paul Moloney had five or six), and the trainer brings the colours, valets take care of everything else, and take great pride in so doing. Washing machines and tumble driers are continually whirring: the valet is a master of the quick turnaround. If a jump jockey falls in the first race on a wet day, sodden breeches can be clean, dry and ironed ready for the third race. Valets are party to all the conversations, jokes, worries and inner thoughts of their charges, often looking after up to thirty of them.

Valets know the meaning of hard work. All jockeys are individuals, with their own routines, fads and superstitions. Tensions run high at times; all in the weighing room are aware it is the danger that bonds. Valets have to get things right, not least when it comes to ensuring the jockey is carrying exactly the right weight. Saddles are crucial here. They vary in weight from seven pounds down to three pounds (known as a 'pancake'). During the racing day, jockeys will need their valet's full personal attention.

Valet Neil Painting, 'Bagsy', had been racing forever. He revelled in 'the big circus', where the lads got on well, seeing the job as great fun, not least with jockeys like Nico de Boinville and David Bass. The worst thing about being a valet, he reckoned, were 'wet days', with all the sodden jockey kit they inevitably caused, but for him the good days always outweighed the bad.

On arrival, jockeys may greet their rivals like long lost pals, even though they have battled each other the previous day. Laughter and action are the remedies for pressure, and the weighing room can become one continual comedy show. Sabotage is a common entertainment: e.g. shortening a rival's stirrup leathers so that the horse might try and throw its jockey in the parade ring, or applying the diuretic/dehydrating pill: placed into a mate's cup of tea it can produce remarkably quick results. These, and many other harmless juvenile tricks, coupled with the continuous flow of jokes, make the dangers of the job seem far away. And the room sees a lot of laughter. Steve Smith-Eccles for a long time played the role of Chief Jester, the role was then taken over by Mattie Batchelor, and one jockey has likened the weighing room to a school classroom, when the teacher nips out, just for a minute. Humour is essential in the weighing room because it alleviates the grim seriousness of jump racing.

At the end of the day, when the last jockey has left the weighing room, there remains a mountain of mud-caked boots, saddles and breeches. On a wet day, as much as four hours' work remains for valets before everything is washed, dried and saddles oiled. So the valet is the ultimate backroom boy, a fusion of nursemaid, washer-woman, confidant and PA.

But the culture of this racecourse hub works, because racing is the ultimate leveller. In no other sport would you eat together, change together, travel together, have nights out together and compete against each other – ferociously. A Premier League footballer once asked to sit in the weighing room at Huntingdon to watch the day's events unfold. Afterwards, he was noted to say that if he could take what he had witnessed back to his own dressing room, his team would win the Premier League: He had witnessed: "People from all backgrounds, all walks of life, jockeys who come back covered in blood, spitting teeth out, and all they were bothered about was how their brother jockeys were." Sam Twiston-Davies echoes this: "When you're injured, the weighing room is the place you look forward to getting back into. The camaraderie is great. It's a safe place, a tight-knit fraternity. It doesn't matter if you don't see eye to eye with whoever is changing next to you - that person might well be coming to your rescue next day." Jockeys are always busy between races, but will be aware if a colleague's clothes have been hanging on his peg for some time. If that jockey has been hurt, one of the riders will take their injured pal's clothes to the hospital, and, providing things are not too serious, drive him home.

Until recently, the atmosphere of the weighing room had been the traditional club-like ambience of its all-male members. Ginger McCain, trainer of Aintree hero Red Rum, described it as "a man's domain; you had that smell of men's bodies, sweaty and masculine." With the ever-increasing number of female jump jockeys, much has changed since then. But how much? The weighing room, having gradually evolved over centuries, had, for a long time, its own special culture. This, though ethically far from perfect, provided a reassuring sense of spirited togetherness. Richard Pitman, back in the day, wrote, "A lot goes on in the weighing room that may be frowned on by certain parts of the community, but it is a hive of activity, where your own personal problems are always overshadowed by your mate's disasters. The alliances formed there last long after the right to enter that room is lost." But Richard was writing some time ago, well before the recent escalation of numbers of women jockeys. This sudden opening-up of the profession inevitably brought tensions with it, which led to serious questioning of the 'culture' of the jockeys' sanctuary that had obtained for so long, culminating dramatically in 2021, when, in a high-profile challenge, a female jockey filed a complaint of harassment against a male counterpart. A new PJA code of conduct, stating that "Areas where riders mix should be free of fear, intimidation and discrimination," swiftly became central to an ongoing and extremely heated debate.

Tensions can run high in the fierce cauldron of high level competition that is the weighing room. Millie Wonnacott, an ex-jump jockey, now riding on the flat, who returned to the saddle after breaking her neck in a fall at the Cheltenham Festival in 2021, said, "We're all competitive, and things get said in the heat of the moment. Five minutes later, it's usually all over." But perhaps not always, if a jockey has committed the unpardonable sin of "going up the inner" (i.e. trying to squeeze into a gap that may or may not be there in order to save ground), theoretically thus giving their mount a better chance of winning. This is seen as highly provocative and can, on occasion, put a horse through the rails.

Yet the feeling persisted in several quarters that racing's internal disputes were best kept out of the public eye, for fear the nuances, motivations and daily realities in this odd little world would never be understood by outsiders. This line of argument suggested that inevitably tempers would fray, voices would be raised, altercations would occur, and anger would surface, as trainer remonstrates with jockey, jockey with jockey. But there is all the difference in the world between coercive behaviour to make a point, and corrective behaviour to do so. Peter Scudamore still sees the weighing room as a surprisingly non-violent place for the level of competition, but he stands up for the jockey's right to speak their mind plainly to rivals. Brian Hughes concurs: "There's a good mix of people, boys and girls, and plenty of older figures, more than welcoming to the younger generation. When a jockey gets injured, then you see people's true colours come out. You know someone is going to help you."

That said, it can still be a lonely place for some, as was the case during Covid, when jockeys saw less of each other, and there was no lingering after the last ride of the day. Jockeys felt more isolated than in normal times, so some tensions ran particularly high. Spats in this fulcrum of activity are bound to happen, and young jockeys are usually 'sorted out' if they get cocky. Until recently, what happened and was said in the weighing room stayed in the weighing room, and 'normal service' was resumed. But there is a narrow line between bullying and banter: it is only banter if both sides are laughing. The 2021 high-profile complaint of harassment had been provoked after a long saga that began in September 2020, when, during a two-mile chase at Southwell, Bryony Frost, Britain's most successful female jockey, moved across Robbie Dunne, causing his horse, Cillian's Well, to fall. The horse was killed, and Dunne blamed Frost's riding, allegedly threatening to hurt her, or "put her through the wing of a fence." Frost felt bullied and abused and complained at the treatment received at the hands of Dunne: the case went to the BHA, where it stayed for over twelve months. In that time Chris Watts, the BHA's Head of Integrity Assurance, quit his job and disappeared. The antipathy between Frost and Dunne festered and continued, until at last the tribunal took place: Dunne was charged with 'conduct prejudicial to the integrity and good reputation of racing'.

Battle lines were drawn: Bryony had always been popular, not least for her exploits on Frodon in big races, and Lee Mottershead in the *Racing Post* acknowledged: "her way of communicating, which makes you feel as though you experienced the race with her." She was seen as the victim, even before evidence had been heard. A press leak had added gall to the muddiness of the case, and the weighing room came under heavy fire. Tom Scudamore said that similar incidents took place every third day, and other experienced riders reiterated the need for understanding the difference between coercion and correction. After an inordinate and needless delay, the case was heard, although a fair trial was hardly possible after both parties had been subjected to 'trial by media'.

Several senior jockeys gave evidence, one of whom said, "It's a code of conduct in the weighing room to stay as neutral as possible, not to get involved." The trial polarised opinion, though many in racing sided with Bryony, who they thought had been bullied and preyed on, and saw as the scapegoat. What was the truth?

But, Frost vs Dunne was not the only case investigated around that time. In December 2021, an inquiry into the incident at Kempton in 2016 that led to Freddie Tylicki being paralysed, revealed that evidence had not been fully investigated at the time, because people did not speak up, which meant the grim situation could not be brought into the light and then dealt with. Clearly it did no good to stay neutral. Old-school thinking was outmoded and needed reform, with jockeys codified to desirable behaviours. The role of jockey coach, expanding all the time, has become vital here for representing support for all riders in the weighing room.

The final verdict banned Dunne for eighteen months – later reduced to ten - after he was found guilty of deliberately targeting a colleague whose vulnerability he intentionally exploited. But the enquiry also concluded there was a cultural issue in which threatening behaviour is condoned and not reported in the weighing room, which needed to be addressed: it described the weighing room culture as "rancid." David Bass, then Jump Jockeys President of the PJA, denied there was a cultural issue and said things had: "been blown out of proportion: the weighing room was not a negative environment. Senior jockeys went out of their way to resolve issues in a respectful way." In his official role, he was keen to improve jockeys' wellbeing and sort things out quickly, so there were fewer weighing room disputes. Ex-champion

Richard Johnson echoed David's thoughts, saying the weighing room was a "great place to be and very safe. Jockeys revel in the company of like-minded colleagues and rivals, where they feel supported and understood."

In line with the thinking of the Freddie Tylicki findings, one conclusion that came out of the Dunne versus Frost case was that: "There is a cultural issue in which threatening behaviour is condoned, not reported, in the weighing room." David Bass was backed up by former jockey Andrew Thornton: "The weighing room is an inviolate way of trying to make sure people ride as safely as they can. The last thing anyone wants is for horses or people to get injured out there and sometimes that means you need to be having words." But, he pointed out, stewards and valets were always in and out of the weighing room, which allowed for a wider group of people to see what was taking place between jockeys. He was not alone in feeling the BHA had made a real mess of things, which made it unfair on both parties. Carl Llewellyn, himself a jockey coach with the BHA, supported David and Andrew: "My first impression has always been that this can be a dangerous sport, and people from early on need to be told this – if what they're doing might cause others to get hurt."

On his return to the saddle after his ban, Robbie Dunne apologised for his reaction that day at Southwell; he said a long line needed to be drawn under it all, and it should now be left in the past.

Lewis Porteous' article on *The Pulse of Racing* made more cheering reading when he focussed on the weighing room early in 2022, soon after its culture had come under such vivid scrutiny and criticism with the Frost vs Dunne case: "When your day starts earlier than the milkman's, and there's always a chance it could end in A&E, it wouldn't be much use riding over jumps if you were a glass-half-empty person." Porteous found the weighing room upbeat: Nick Scholfield, en route for his best season in years, was typically positive, even with only one ride, a 50/1 shot in a maiden hurdle race: "I never look at it as one ride, as that horse might win three or four runs down the line. You've got to make decisions to suit you best. I never mind where I go or who I'm riding for – financially everyone is paid the same, which in other sports isn't the case. Prize money is increasing, albeit slowly, which it needed to do, and our career-ending insurance has just been rebooted. We have good backing, with the whole team at PJA doing their best for us. We're catching up on nutrition, and are getting treated more like athletes than we ever were. I look forward to going into the weighing room for the banter. We're all in the same sort of huddle every day, have a good time and always look out for each other. From the outside you probably don't appreciate that."

Supporting that view, Sean Bowen felt the collective voice of the weighing room was often ignored: "A lot of people say how great a place the weighing room is, yet for some reason nobody tends to believe us. The PJA try their best, but I think they get overlooked, like we do. Hopefully they'll get heard soon. Riding is hard work and always will be, but you get to see your best friends every day and it's a great place to work. Not many people get to enjoy their job as much as I do."

Sam Twiston-Davies agreed that he could understand the negativity, but praised the PJA: "There's a help-line which we can always ring. We confide in each other and help each other out. Going forward, there's a lot of things being put into place which could see the sport flourishing. To me the weighing room is still a healthy place, but there are always improvements that need to be made." Charlie Todd found the competition for rides fierce but relished the challenge: "There's a lot of positive energy in the weighing room – it's a very supportive environment."

Tom Scudamore, for a long time elder statesman of the weighing room, believed: "There's been great strides made with jockey coaches and support networks. It's a lot different from when I started riding. I was lucky because I had Dad [eight-times champion jockey Peter], but a lot of people were left to their own devices. Some things are better now, but much still needs to be sorted, not left to fester like the Dunne/Frost case. Everyone involved is part of the racing family."

Much of what is positive about the weighing room was being flagged up. But sports writer Paul Hayward brought us down to earth, seeing the times in which we live as a strong negative force. In media discussions, he warned us, the minority always get highlighted. He disliked wagons being circled. And he reminded us that, thanks to Bryony Frost as the whistleblower, we're in a different world now, sadly, a world not concerned with manners and respect. He asked where these are in the wider world, and called for a pool of mentors and neutral guides, rather like a tutor at school, aiming for better vigilance: the environment would be made more welcoming to female jockeys, and there would be a better mind-set all round. Up until now, he thought the weighing room might have been as it was in the fifties, and it needed to move on. It was a pity that everybody had been tarred with the same disturbing brush. As Ruby Walsh said, simply: "What divides should unite."

Paul Hayward was right to be challenging. Jockeys deserve a weighing room with top-quality facilities that will encourage a top-quality atmosphere. They have been putting up with inadequate facilities for too long. Much is being done now, but on some courses, men and women still do not even have separate areas (hardly rocket science). Showers are perennially cold. Saunas have been abolished, replaced with warm-up areas and cycles; food is on the way to being improved. "But the whole legacy of racing needs to be looked at, and adapted; with jockeys now receiving more educational well-being, and able to feed back their concerns, this is more likely to happen. Riders require that vibrant code of conduct to be put in force, that will support a top-quality culture. The best of the past must be respected, however, and positively embraced. The right facilities and the right balanced atmosphere are both crucial to the future of the jockeys' precious sanctuary. There can be no room for complacency... these warriors deserve to go into battle with every element of their armoury blazing."

Realising things needed to change, the PJA mounted a campaign for immediate improvements to the inadequate changing facilities available to jockeys at some tracks. Riders needed more space: they had been living through a legacy of racing putting up with things. Too many suggestions had been woefully short-term. With such a demanding fixture list for jockeys, a new mind-set was called for to enhance their well-being, including better planned menus (feedback here was noticeably good), so better conditions could complement their being given a better all-round education. Amid all the conflicting opinions and passionate writing, amid all the current and planned improvements to facilities being effected, one thing remains and will remain: a combustible atmosphere within the weighing room, engendered by the all-demanding nature of the winning post. For when jockeys stride out in their bright silks to embrace their next challenge, there is, for all of them, the same discernible gleam in the eye. Jockeys believe they're going to win that next race, even if the horse appears to have little chance. Indeed, they say that once you lose that belief, it's time to hang up your boots... and bid a permanent farewell to the weighing room.

CHAPTER 7: PAST MASTERS

"You look at all the elite sportspeople: they've all got a wonderful madness inside them, all got a psychopathic switch, which means you'd die for it, rather than fail."

- Peter Thomas on champions -

There have been many favourite jockeys down the years: Dick Francis, Jack Dowdeswell, Arthur Freeman, Dave Dick, Pat Taaffe, Johnny Haine, Willie Robinson, Ron Barry, Derek Ancil, Stan Hayhurst, Gerry Scott, David Mould, Bobby Beasley, Andy Turnell, Bob Davies, Tommy Carberry, Fred Winter, Bill Rees, Josh and Macer Gifford, Stan Mellor – the first jockey to ride 1,000 winners and the man aboard grey Stalbridge Colonist, who, in the 1966 Hennessy Gold Cup, beat the mighty Arkle, in receipt of 35 lbs – Terry and Tony Biddlecombe, Paddy Cowley, Graham Bradley, Dick Saunders, Jonjo O'Neill, Eddie Harty, Robert Earnshaw, Phil Tuck, Tom Morgan, Neale Doughty, Michael Scudamore et al. More recently, and due in no small part to the advent of jockeys' agents, who have changed the landscape of 'our beloved game' (Jeremy Richardson), a small number of titans have graced the jumping stage and left a mighty legacy.

Richard Pitman, "born a long time ago, but getting younger recently," was, in his own words, a slow burner as a jump jockey: winnerless for four years at 22, his next three years (making seven since he turned professional) averaged three victories a year, "but like the tortoise, I eventually arrived. Surely every jockey sets out with delusions of grandeur: was I a failure? Only hope keeps you going through long periods of bad luck." As a lad, he had often played truant from school when Cheltenham races were on;

he recalls one such day in his autobiography *Good Horses Make Good Jockeys*: "The seven runners topped the crest of the hill and surged towards my fence, the noise increasing with every stride. Packed tightly together, they rose as one: birch flew into the air; the grey horse, bellying the fence, grunted as the air was knocked out of him. A shout came from one jockey, and a curse from another. There was a thud as the horses landed, then a cracking of whips – the spoils were in sight – and then, the noise fading, the moving shapes on a wedge of green grass disappeared amongst the mass of colour made up of the paying public.

"To a boy, now standing alone half a mile away, the distant crowd might have been a garden party at Buckingham Palace. I had been a non-paying, unwanted witness to a steeplechase at Cheltenham. But I was drawn to this spectacle, which was already like a drug to me. I needed more. I waited half an hour before the next race. My parents would be angry, the headmaster would see through my forged sickness note, but no price was too high. I would stay there – little knowing that that very fence was to play a vital part in my undoing in the 1974 Gold Cup. Indeed if it had been suggested then that I would ever gallop down that slope I would have laughed."

He rode against Arkle, at a time when the weighing room was "full of genuine characters, who really enjoyed riding and living," and knew a jockey had to be many things: dietician, acrobat ("there's no such thing as a nice fall"), showman and long-distance rally-driver: "Riding is like driving: you are continually making split-second decisions." He saw a neurologist every summer "to check the condition of my skull – and its contents" – and was a pioneer in getting jockeys compensation when they had to retire after a fall. He rode 427 winners – "and 4,000 losers" – in his career.

He left school without any 'O' levels, being by his own admission, "bright but cocky." Being also small and light, he got a job as a stable hand for a local trainer in Cheltenham, earning "a couple of quid a week." Every day he'd ride three or four horses to the top of Cleeve Hill, 3,000 acres of common land that overlook the racecourse at Prestbury Park: "The only troubling part was when fog descended quickly, and you happened to be galloping – because there was a great big cliff edge.

"I rode in an era of cavaliers, with Terry Biddlecombe leading the charge.

We jumped everything. We didn't see it as a danger, just a part of life, though jockeys didn't really have a voice in those days. Nothing was frightening. God, though, we were mad. We just used to say, "If in doubt, give them a kick in the belly." So much has changed since then. When I was riding, the best liar got the race in the stewards' enquiries. Awaiting my first winner, I was waiting outside the stewards' room with Terry Biddlecombe… In there, he'd lied his head off. The stewards gently asked, "What do you think, Terry?" When my turn came, I was addressed as 'Pitman'. The stewards used to go hunting with Terry; I was shafted." (*Good Horses Make Good Jockeys.*)

After he stopped riding, a career that took in the Champion Hurdle on Lanzarote (1974), the King George VI Chase (twice) on Pendil, the Whitbread Gold Cup (Royal Toss) and the Hennessy (Charlie Potheen) and will forever be associated with those great horses, along with the gallant Crisp, he joined the BBC racing commentary team, and wrote, with co-author, Joe McNally, five racing novels, as well as his autobiography.

Bob Champion's legacy was an unusual one: the man is aptly named. Hero of the 1981 Grand National, on his partner, Aldaniti, the horse recovering from two serious tendon injuries and a fractured hock, Bob had been diagnosed with cancer eighteen months beforehand, and underwent gruelling chemotherapy, leaving him emaciated, but not giving up, primarily out of loyalty to the horse's connections, Josh Gifford, trainer, and owner, Nick Embiricos.

Despite all tribulations, the pair made it to Aintree, where Bob was, oddly, confident. That confidence, allied to his faith in the horse, put him in that rare mental state – often hoped for but seldom achieved – where mind and body work together: something else takes over, a part of us is outside of us, looking in and we somehow excel our usual selves. Needless to say, this state cannot be conjured up. Their courageous victory did a huge amount for racing – but also for cancer sufferers up and down the land, then and since. As he passed the winning-post, Bob's first thoughts were for his fellow patients, many of whom had sent him telegrams, wishing him luck. The Bob Champion Cancer Trust he set up is still going strong, 40 years later, having raised more than £16 million. Once he had retired, the jockey devoted himself to this cause; he still receives letters from people struck down with the disease, acknowledging the influence his courage has had on them, and the confidence he has given to many who are afflicted. Those letters, he has said, have meant the most to him.

AP McCoy saw Richard Dunwoody as the most complete rider: to his mind, the Irishman from County Down raised the standard of jockeyship single-handedly, and had a great pain threshold. But since his retirement Richard has spoken openly of the torment he carried through stages of his remarkable career in the saddle, torment that included sauna marathons, insomnia and self-loathing, as well as litanies of injuries. An ambassador for the Jockey Club, he was understated, determined and intensely talented. Three-times Champion Jockey, twice after protracted battles with Adrian Maguire, he won two Grand Nationals, a Cheltenham Gold Cup, Champion Hurdle and four King Georges, always breaking through ceilings: "Every race you ride in, you pick up something: you're getting better because you're more tuned in." Until AP overtook him, he'd won more jumps races than anyone else (1,874) achieving unheard-of things with his body because winning was the only thing that mattered. He rode many good horses, including Remittance Man, Waterloo Boy, Very Promising, Kribensis, West Tip, Charter Party, Desert Orchid and One Man. Ted Walsh thought him the most complete jump jockey, having brain, horsemanship and riding strength. But behind the goggles, all this was at the expense of his brain: as his autobiography Obsessed admits: "Ambition almost destroyed me." He was his own most savage critic, so single-minded about racing that other emotions were being shut down, unable to admit and then cope with his mistakes, the source of his turmoil; torturing himself mentally; incapable of moving on from defeats; being inexpressibly angry and permanently exhausted by wasting and a massive workload: there was no expression strong enough to describe his interminable nights and deep-set anxieties, before and after races, as, like AP McCoy, he waged unrelenting war on himself. In his own words he had become "a horrible bastard."

Fortunately for him, a friend convinced him he could have a life, as well as a career; he took the advice of Michael Caulfield, and consulted sports psychologist Peter Terry, who advised him to control the uncontrollable, go freelance, stop doing light weights and spend more time riding in Ireland.

Richard also relocated from Lambourn to London, an unusual move for a top jockey, but one that gave him a break from the racing world. When it emerged he was seeking help, *The Sun* ran a headline: *'Dunmaddy Off To Sports Psychiatrist'*. His long and hungry search for winners, and punishing schedule, had taken its toll; it was driving him crazy. Always craving that little extra bit of edge, he needed to focus on doing his own job, controlling the uncontrollable.

Gradually the fear of failure, of making mistakes, and the quest for the unattainable diminished: over his final seasons he did not punish himself the same, finding a balance between pressure and enjoyment. He particularly loved riding at the Irish festivals. But then injury forced his reluctant retirement: he had wanted to ride until he was 40, so having to stop was a massive challenge in itself; he trekked for 48 days to the South Pole in the steps of Ernest Shackleton ("the toughest thing ever") where, again, failure was not an option; eyeballed a polar bear; walked 2,000 miles, the length of Japan, for Sarcoma Cancer Charity, and ran marathons, including in North Korea. A second book was written: *Method in My Madness*. As he is the first to admit, his retirement took some coming to terms with, not least because it was enforced – and he was still obsessed with racing. The question 'What do you do?' suddenly became tricky, and he needed to ask himself, 'Who am I?'

Now he has found several niches, but he advocates the need, after hanging up the boots, to stand back for a while: "If that is possible, take a breath, and give yourself some time." He still loves travel, and now leads tours to remote kingdoms like Mongolia, where the horse is well respected (he has helped promote the Mongolian Derby), Kyrgyzstan and Afghanistan – and these are no cosy tours. He has become a fine photographer, but it has taken time. Finally, he is happy in his skin, having found a new perspective. He now lives in Spain, 40 miles north of Madrid, with partner and daughter, supports charities, and allows himself to enjoy being a photographer. He has little to do with racing: "It wasn't a normal life: to be at the top you couldn't be normal. What I had then was a totally different life. It was a totally different me, as well. Now I realise the big wins don't mean much when you're walking down a street in Madrid."

Peter Scudamore – 'Scu' - is a collateral cousin of Sir Peter Escudamor IV, of French descent, a knight and West Country landowner, who served in wars on the Continent, and made the first-known use of the stirrup in the Scudamore arms: this appears on a seal attached to his charter of 1323. Closer to home, Peter was bred to be a jockey: horses run in the Scudamore blood. His great-grandfather, John, though never involved in racing, was a "marvellous rider, a real horseman," recalled his grandfather, Geoffrey, himself a fine point-to-point jockey before riding under rules in the 1930s. Then he became an RAF pilot and was shot down over the Ruhr, which landed him two years in Stalag IVB: a bunk in a barrack-house sardine-packed with 700 prisoners of war. When he returned home, son Michael was already a capable horseman. Jump racing is full of characters – most of them marvellous, warm people with a rich sense of humour and a willingness to give their last penny if your need is greater than theirs. They did not come much better than Michael Scudamore.

Peter was only nine months old when his father won the Grand National, "But it has probably influenced me for the rest of my life. Although I remember nothing of the ballyhoo in our part of the county after his success, I know just how much Liverpool meant to him in the years that followed, and how much he missed riding in the race when he was forced to pack up." Peter did not have the good fortune to win the National, but he was Champion Jockey nine times, and in the season 1988-1989 he broke Jonjo O'Neill's then record of 149 wins in a season, booting home 221. His style, driving commitment to win, and single-minded concentration on the job, approached with a pale face and searching eyes, reflected his conviction "every day you must strive for perfection." This hard work had been his trademark at school at Belmont Abbey, where, whatever he set his mind to, he did, quietly and doggedly, as with his 'A' levels. Sons Tom and Michael junior have inherited this depth of resolve.

Peter rode some truly great horses: Corbière, Burrough Hill Lad, Celtic Shot, Broadsword, Bonanza Boy and Sabin du Loir (his favourite). "Great horses have a gait, a rhythm," he says, "you never feel you're going flat out, and you've got all the time in the world. Yet, in a funny sort of way, time seems to slow down: you have always got a choice." All heart, he didn't know when he was beaten. When that happened and he lost a race, his instinct was to wonder what he'd done wrong, and then to investigate till he found out.

John Francome, champion before him, admired Scu's "determination to dislodge me as champion: it gave me a new incentive in a way which endeared him to me and many others in the sport." Scu is unfailingly polite, always showing what has been termed a 'velvet courtesy', and disliking idle talk. Unique among jockeys in Britain, he prayed regularly throughout his career: "I was closer to God at the start of a race than at any other time in my life."

In sharp contrast to the Scudamore dynasty, John Francome was born in Swindon, the son of a fireman on the railways, later a self-taught builder, with no racing connections. At the age of six he rode a donkey at Barry Island: it was enough to captivate him. He had great success as a young show-jumper on his pony, Red Paul, winning team gold for GB in the European Championships, a fact dismissed with one line in his autobiography *Born Lucky*. He was also Young Riders Champion at Hickstead in 1970. On leaving school, he realised show-jumping offered little financial security; at 16 he joined Fred Winter, as an apprentice – and stayed with him for 15 years.

The lad who started out by driving a hot dog van to the course, and selling those hot dogs between races, ended up as an artist in the saddle, riding 1,138 winners and being Champion Jockey seven times, including in 1982 when he had been neck and neck with Peter Scudamore, who was narrowly ahead of John, but then got injured. With generosity of spirit, John drew level with his great rival, then stopped riding, and the two shared the title.

He loved life, loved laughing, and is still a great person to be with; confident and brave, he gave horses time, coaxing them through a race. Tactically brilliant, he was meticulous in his homework, always looking for 'that edge'. His first ride, on Multigrey, at Worcester in December 1970, was a winning one; on his next ride he broke his wrist. He attributed much of his winning career to Osbaldeston, who ran up a sequence of victories, which gave him the confidence he needed to take his riding to new levels. No stranger to controversy, he once referred to race stewards as "cabbage-patch dolls."

Being one of the lads, with his mate Steve Smith-Eccles, he loved the camaraderie of the weighing room, which revolved around him; with all its laughter, ribbing, sharp one-liners, pranks and practical jokes, he experienced endless fun. In his time jockeys were not breathalysed at racecourses every day, so they could have 'the odd night out'. He was always well aware the jockeys' lifestyle is dangerous, demanding discipline and sacrifice, but "the rewards make it all worthwhile, and they are what drive jockeys forward when times are tough."

He derived great pleasure from teaching horses to jump, and jump properly, and knew what to do if they didn't. Outstanding in the schooling sphere, he was a great judge of stride: Richard Pitman, who called John 'Rattletheladder', rated him the best presenter of a horse at a fence. He won the Champion Hurdle in 1981 on Sea Pigeon, the best hurdler he ever sat on, exhibiting a masterclass of coolness for the cheekiest of wins. In 1983, he won the Colonial Cup in America on Flatterer; the following year, he won the Hennessy and King George on Burrough Hill Lad, and thought Wayward Lad, gallant runner-up in Dawn Run's Gold Cup, the most athletic horse he ever rode. In 1978 he won the Gold Cup on Midnight Court, Fred Winter's only winner of that race. Admired for his quick wit, and momentous iron will, he believed jockeys hungry for winners create their own chances, though he was always aware things could go wrong in a race, no matter how careful the jockey.

He quit the saddle suddenly in April 1985 at Chepstow when his mount, The Reject, hung him up in a fall at the open ditch: "I looked up: the stirrup leather was wrapped round my shin, my foot was jammed in the iron, and I thought, if this horse takes off, I'm dead: he didn't, I wasn't, but after that I just didn't feel right, my head wasn't in the right place." He knew he had reached the point where he had more to lose than to gain: if he was not in racing to be the best – and John McCririck always termed him "greatest jockey" – he would rather not be in it at all. He had planned to retire at the end of that season, and remains, as *Born Lucky* attests, appreciative of what comes his way.

Having tried training for 18 months, he worked with Andrew Franklin for Channel 4 as a presenter for 27 years, and wrote 22 racing thrillers, only stopping when he "couldn't think of any more ways of killing people." He is a vice patron of IJF ("Racing's proudest achievement, which has so many strings to its bow"), and is still renowned for his quick, dry sense of humour. He built and owns Beechdown Farm, Lambourn, which holds 96 horses and is currently rented by Clive Cox. His is always a refreshing take on racing, advising today's jockeys to "Ride every horse as though you own it; know your worth; don't let people walk over you, and make sure you work for someone who gives you a chance. Your job is to make everything as easy as possible for your horse." He is a strong advocate for people taking responsibilities for their actions, and rates loyalty highly – he stayed with Fred Winter, even when offered the Martin Pipe juggernaut. He has always admired horses, even though as a jockey he saw them as business partners, to whom jockeys cannot afford to get attached. "You and they are out there to do a job. In 1900 there were 100,000 horses in London; people saw them every day: now they don't see them until they go racing, when they realise their beauty, power and courage." He believes horses attract good people, he has a strong work ethic, and is adamant, "Horses must enjoy jumping, even though, at the end of it all, you're out there to win."

He has said, "We don't breed characters anymore, we breed champions instead, jockeys not jokers. But when you meet them, when you know them, you are dealing with courage." Once described as 'poetic perfection' in his riding style, he has not missed race-riding since giving up, though he still rides out daily. But he may not have given up the pen: "Richard Phillips and I might write a sitcom; that'd be worth watching."

No jockey is indestructible – though AP McCoy tried hard. Now Sir Anthony, AP is the Don Bradman of jump racing – born in Moneyglass, Co. Antrim, Ireland, in May 1974, he rode a record 4,358 winners – and a record 15,000 losers – and was Champion Jockey in Britain 20 consecutive times. Champion Conditional in his first year meant he had never not ridden as the reigning title-holder. He rode his first winner in 1992, aged 17, and retired on the last day of the jumps season 2015, leaving a monumental legacy. At the end of the 2001-2002 season he had ridden 289 winners, thus beating Gordon Richard's long-standing record of 269 (on the flat) set in 1947.

AP raised the racing bar to a stratospheric height; his statistics are sans pareil. He made huge sacrifices, could endure pain and discomfort as no one before him, and was insatiable in his pursuit of winners on the racecourse. He knew the damage he'd done before a doctor examined him: "You only worry about your head or spinal column – everything else – some way or another – will repair in time."

His success is so remarkable that he has been termed, with affection and admiration, 'a freak of nature'. With his veracious appetite for winners, he drove himself relentlessly towards every new goal, nowhere better exemplified than when he once broke his back in a fall at Warwick: he fractured his T12 and shattered T9 and T10. He was operated on, and the prognosis was that he would be out of the saddle for months. But he had heard about cryotherapy, a Japanese practice from the 1970s, which uses extremely low temperatures to aid and accelerate healing. The body starts to turn red, goes numb, then pimply with little white spots: you think it's going to crack in places, as in cartoons. AP went to a health farm, undergoing one to three minute sessions of cryotherapy several times per day. He started off in a chamber at -65° C, and progressed to -100° C. But when he heard that a professional footballer held the unofficial record at -145° C, he withstood a session 5 degrees cooler than that. Seven weeks after that accident he was back in the saddle.

But he can always explain this extremity of thought. "The more injuries that happen, the easier it has become to cope. Your pain threshold gets higher: you learn that's part of your job and the job is getting back from injury as fast as you can." He demonstrated that admirably. Clearly he had an extraordinary pain threshold; his brain was not wired like 'normal' people. But he admits that much of the pressure he put on himself was based on fear: "The fear of not being champion was an overriding feeling, not excitement at the prospect of being champion." Although always aware that "we live in a little horse racing cocoon" he also confessed to a huge amount of greed in his quest for winners. Fear of failure, of not winning, would let his very high standards drop. "There was pressure on me every day to win, self-imposed of course. I just wanted another number to add to the total, another winner, another tick."

John Carter has written: "Jockeys mentally divorce themselves from the emotions that usually go with pain, injury and enforced absence from plying their courageous trade. They take time off (very little), heal, and get back on the horse soonest. Their diets consist of fresh air and not much else; for AP eating 12 grapes a day felt like an act of rebellion: his breakfast being tea with sugar, lunch two jelly babies and supper fish and steamed veg., a dollop of mayonnaise his 'guilty pleasure'. They know they'll be injured at some stage, so pain –and the inevitable expectation of it – becomes an accepted part of their lives. They have to develop a high pain threshold."

AP now recalls with humour one fall he suffered which was exceedingly painful, even for him. "My lower leg was pointing in a direction it shouldn't have been pointing as I lay on the ground. A trainer drove up, immediately greeting me with, "What makes you think your leg is broken?" Before I could reply the man spouted, "You know your trouble, McCoy? You're too soft," whereupon he got back in his jeep and drove off."

AP was restless, always desperate to learn from his mistakes. No matter how good a day he'd had, something had gone wrong: there was always something he could have done differently, something that might have made a difference. He was stubborn and single-minded, his aim being simply to get a horse from one side of a fence to the other as quickly as possible. He was happy wallowing in his own misery, and never trusted a horse to do the right thing: he always felt he needed to get the horse to do what he wanted. Dave Roberts, his agent, was obsessed with finding winners for him: "Every win was another notch. Everything got to AP: the wasting, the treadmill his life had become, the pressure, the fear of not being Champion Jockey; everything was governed by that fear. He never allowed himself to think he had it in the bag: that would cause him to ease up, take his foot off the accelerator. Statistics were everything – he was robotic. Having gone all-out to win the championship, he won it, and then it was back to zero at the start of the following season – a mere six days later."

From Martin Pipe AP learned detail and the need for information, finding out everything he could, going out to ride knowing he had everything covered, every horse covered, and by the time he came back into the winners' enclosure, he was thinking: "Where is this going to win next time? Martin Pipe turned me into a robot, but in the best possible way, because he made my mind need to do it." He never thought he had delivered, or was any good at his job until he won the Gold Cup on Synchronised in 2012: this was his first "really felt fulfilment. Being a winning jockey is selfish: the only way it works is if it's all about you. It's not a very attractive trait, but you've not got to care what anybody says about you, or what they want from you."

His Grand National win on Don't Push It in 2010 sealed his immortality in jump racing. He, Richard Dunwoody, Peter Scu and John Francome had all exhibited tunnel vision: they were winning machines; Richard Pitman had just been happy with a good ride.

CHAPTER 8: INJURIES

"When you are injured, life slows down to a glacial pace."
- A current jump jockey -

Jockeys have to be supremely fit, both mentally and physically, to get up early; drive to a yard; school three or four horses; drive to the course; go for a run; ride up to six or seven times, and then drive home. Often having been patched up so as to pass the doctor next day. Mick Fitzgerald, a Gold Cup and Grand National winner, understands the pressures their lifestyle entails: As a jump jockey, you go out to ride every day, knowing it could be your last. But you never think it could happen to you, it always happens to someone else… if you were thinking about getting injured, you wouldn't be able to do your job. Of course injuries occur – often."

Jump jockeys are well aware how prone they are, always, to injury. On average they fall every ten rides. Most of the time, after hitting the ground at thirty miles an hour, they sit up slowly, rise to their feet, and start the long trudge back to the weighing room. Most of the time…

Declan Murphy was not so lucky; he has catalogued everything that has happened to him in his memoir, *Centaur*. He was riding Arcot, favourite for the Swinton Hurdle at Haydock Park in May 1994, when his mount, very much in contention, reached too early for the final hurdle and snapped his pelvis in mid-flight. He dragged his lame rear end down to the ground, smashed into the timber of the hurdle's frame with a deafening crash and catapulted his pilot, now unconscious after colliding with the horse's desperate head, into the turf in the path of the galloping field behind him, one of whose hooves hit the jockey's head, shattering his skull in twelve places.

Declan described the event graphically: "The dull hollow thud of hoof hitting head - life hitting life – reverberated hideously through the air. Then followed a deathly hush. In a cloud of dust the other horses galloped past me to finish the race they had begun, the sound of their hooves drowning out the sound of silence. Spectators gasped, colleagues prayed, reporters clocked the seconds and everybody waited – frozen faces, bated breath – for me to awaken. But I lay in a deep, silent sleep while the blood gushed out of my mouth and on to the ground at Haydock Park, staining it a deep, vivid red."

Within minutes Sir Peter O'Sullevan announced gravely, in his distinctive measured tone, "We will bring you news of Declan Murphy when we have it." In the weighing room the air hung thick and heavy, like a jockey's lead cloth. Declan now acknowledges: "A typical fall off a horse is no more than eight foot to the ground. What can't be measured is how far the mind falls." Having been blue-lighted to Warrington General Hospital, and then to the Walton Centre for Neurology in Liverpool, he was on a life-support machine. A Roman Catholic priest was brought in to read him the Last Rites; in London the *Racing Post* prepared the headline: "DECLAN MURPHY DIES AFTER HORROR FALL." This obituary, having been penned, was stopped only in the nick of time. The jockey underwent extensive and intensive brain surgery at the hands of Professor John Miles, who told him the dire consequences should he survive… probable blindness in one eye, loss of memory, paralysis, loss of feeling in all major limbs. But, by a miracle, he did survive…

Coming out of his coma, and months of rehab, went hand in hand with despair and agonising frustration, but: "I had to heal, bit by bit, part by part, body, mind, soul." *Centaur* chronicles how hard this was, but how he managed it: "Obstacles didn't stop me. I cleared them – you have to. You have to leave them behind. My spirit was my lifeline. It fuelled me." But raw fear still ran amok inside his head: "The terror of a nightmare when you are asleep does not compare to the terror of a nightmare when you are awake. There were riots inside my head; there was nowhere to hide; it was complete entrapment." With raging hallucinations, he became desperate "to get away from myself." Gradually, with immense grit, he repaired the physical side, but not the mental: his mind remained in torment. For years afterwards he was afraid of being alone, but in his words he had been "spared his life so he had to save it" and take control of his destiny.

It was horses who ultimately saved him: "The warmth of their body against mine, each muscle independently alive, twitching, responding to my own tentative touch. The smell of them – the dusty, earthy, grainy richness of it. Their noise – exhaling, nickering softly, that low reverberating rumble from deep inside their throat. At your finest hour as a rider, it is trust that joins you to your horse. You put your life in that horse, giving it your complete trust."

Finally, in disregard of his doctor's orders, and the concern of his family and friends, he decided to ride in a race again, aware that he had escaped the jaws of death once, and had no right to tempt fate. It was not bravado that made this decision: "I was searching for my soul." Adhering to his long-held belief: "You've got to ride the race to suit your horse, not your horse to suit the race," he found himself 'in flow', thanks to the spirit of the animal beneath him, its swiftness, strength, majesty, gentleness and grace, he was at ease with his horse: "a liminal being - centaur." He won the race. Then he could stop riding. "Inspiring" is not enough of a comment on Declan. His autobiography goes beyond that, "piecing together slowly and painstakingly the scattered pieces of a giant jigsaw that make up the life of a man."

Mercifully, not all injuries are so serious, though they are bound to cause jockeys to look at the game in a different fashion, especially if they recur, as with Jack Kennedy. More than in any other sport, jockeys suffer from concussion, when a bump, jolt or blow to the head causes the brain to move or twist inside the skull, which can result in physical damage or chemical changes to brain tissue. Apart from the obvious headaches, nerve damage in the brain's messaging system can cause confusion after head trauma; often the person feels 'in a fog'; mood or behaviour changes can sometimes be observed in the hours or days following the injury; there can be problems with balance; sensitivity to noise and light; loss of memory; forgetfulness; nausea and/or vomiting; blurry or double vision; anxiety; sleeping problems and feelings of depression. Not only do jockeys face the dangers of being rocketed into the ground at over 30 miles an hour, they risk being kicked in the head by the horses' hooves, all of them shod with iron. Statistically, female jockeys suffer more from concussion than their male counterparts.

The majority of jockeys with concussion recover fully within seven days of the bang; those who need longer are told to rest body and mind, not easy when they have to earn a living that depends on them riding as much as possible. Once their symptoms have cleared, they must consult the BHA medical department to arrange a post-concussion review – (all jockeys have to complete a baseline test every two years). But concussion does not necessarily mean a knock on the head; it can come from any impact that goes through the body and gives the brain a shaking, thus affecting its rotation within the skull. Concussion is different for everyone and different each time it occurs. A not-so heavy fall does not mean no serious concussion.

Most concussions do not cause a lack of consciousness. Often they leave a short-lived impairment of neurological function, after which the brain reboots itself. After the Second World War, 'punch drunk' jockeys would often try to drive home after a blow to the head. We now know that riding on when concussed exposes sportspeople to further injury, or possibly even death. Nowadays this type of brain injury is taken very seriously, and a doctor has to confirm no bleeding has occurred before the individual takes any medication. Long gone are the days when established jockeys could evade the racecourse doctor, convince him there was no pain and 'carry on regardless.'

Racing is fortunate in one respect, because unlike rugby or football, there are thirty to thirty-five minutes between races, which gives time for jockeys to be tested for concussion. This protocol was introduced under Dr Michael Turner, who became Medical Director of the International Concussion and Head Injury Research Foundation, after his time as Chief Medical Officer to British Horse Racing with his *Don't be a Headcase* programme. Jockeys who suffer repeated brain trauma may come to experience a syndrome known as Chronic Traumatic Encephalopathy (CTE), which triggers progressive degeneration of the brain tissue, not helped by the build-up of an abnormal protein called tau. These changes in brain activity can start months, years, or even decades after the last concussion, and no small number of sports are putting this condition under the closest scrutiny; as yet, there are more questions than answers. But research is progressing all the time, as

Paul Struthers, then Head of the PJA, advocated. He expressed the view that if ex-jockeys donated their brains after death, much would be revealed.

But several falls in a few weeks can result in cumulative concussions. Jockeys keep battling on; they have got to be seen, head down and grafting, not taking time out. Concussion is unlike any other injury; sufferers think they're fine and don't realise they're suffering. They see another person creeping into their life they didn't know, and they don't realise what is going on. They go to rehab and are knocked for six when they realise the full extent of their concussion: it slows them down; their instincts and ability to keep out of trouble are dampened.

Delayed onset concussion is common. Jockeys can seem fine, but won't necessarily be so. They need a proper assessment, good advice and the right treatment. They need to be told they're going in the right direction, and there is light at the end of their tunnel. Jockeys feel it is up to them to control moods, but sometimes are reduced to being a recluse, not leaving the house. When concussions settle, there can be depression, but the chances of them seeking out a sports psychologist are – as yet – not high. And, always, there is 'something inside' that urges them to get back on a horse.

It is very difficult for jockeys to rest when they feel physically fine. But because concussion is a disease that rots the brain, there may be a price to pay. Every jockey wants to get back to the saddle, but cannot ignore the symptoms. Jockeys are becoming more open with trainers, and the relationships are better for it, but there is some way to go. And no jockey is indestructible, however well they have prepared for every eventuality. This injury is now receiving more attention from the authorities; in November 2023 a symposium on concussion took place at Cheltenham racecourse.

Andrew Thornton reminds us that, when out of action due to injury, it is vital to keep the mind active: "JETS is so accessible; it should be second nature for jockeys to make use of its schemes, programmes and teaching. When a jockey is laid low with injury, retaining the positive attitude that keeps them in the saddle is needed more than ever; they need reserves of patience to do what's right physically and mentally. The two go hand in hand. Overthinking their situation is almost inevitable, but recovery cannot be forced. A holistic approach is essential. At times it feels as if they need to start again from scratch."

AP McCoy acknowledged the pressures of injury. Typically, he saw that pressure, "a different type of pressure from race-riding, was in fact good." Injury was an opportunity to work on physical and mental qualities not yet developed, and thus to bring positive out of the negative: "The only thing holding you back is your head: don't panic. If the worst comes to the worst, you can do something else. But there is always the chance you can return to racing, physically, mentally, tactically and technically better." As the multiple champion proved many times over.

In football, former players are now acting as welfare officers with the Professional Footballers Association (PFA). Racing needs to do something similar. Change has to happen. Incidences of dementia in footballers after years of heading are on the increase, with players who have had serious concussion three and a half times more likely to die from dementia. Alan Shearer and Gareth Southgate are helping the London School of Hygiene and Tropical Medicines Heading Project, backed by the FA, to help protect future players and children at grass roots level. Much research is being done into the effect of players having long headed heavy footballs: of the England World Cup winning team of 1966, five of them ended up with dementia – perhaps no coincidence?

In rugby, retired players are registering concerns about neural damage caused by head impacts during their playing careers. *The Times* has launched a podcast series, *Stories of our Time*, to explore this situation, with a top scientist researching into the long term threat of contact sports: "Rugby is just another sport waiting to explode." It is believed more than 400 players from rugby league and rugby union have died early due to neurological defects from playing the game: there is a call for the sport to make "substantive, immediate changes to prevent players from suffering the same." Incidents in the 2022 Six Nations have brought Head Injury Assessment Protocols under fierce scrutiny. The RFU is trialling use of 'smart' mouthguards which will hopefully provide critical information on head impacts: a clip inside the mouthguard measures head movement, particularly acceleration and deceleration. James Haskell, aided by sixty brave and forward-thinking players, helps every year with Restart Charity, brainchild of the Rugby Players' Association, to talk through issues, while there is still time.

For jockeys, broken collarbones are par for the course, but the potential for damage to heads, necks and backs to turn lives upside down, not just for the jockey but for the jockey's family, is huge. They may learn there's a skill to falling, but in the end it comes down to luck whether and where a jockey is injured. They end up alone and deserted on the green turf, often some way from the weighing room.

In 2016 former Champion Jockey Richard Dunwoody, who had seven hundred falls, took part in a research project examining the long term effects of concussion on sportsmen. The study, *Concussion in Sport*, sought to establish whether retired sportsmen and women had increased incidence, or earlier onset of, neuro-degenerative disorders. Richard said jockeys gave little thought to the long term effect of repetitive head injuries. Having won the jockeys' title three times in seventeen years, his career was ended in 1999 by a neck injury. He was lucky, and wise, to stop when he did, like John Francome. Several ex-jockeys have suffered progressive memory loss, or CTE, which, sometimes, leads to early onset Alzheimer's and dementia.

Sam Thomas was at Bangor when JP (not JT) McNamara broke his neck in a fall: his horse slithered on landing after a fence and the jockey was thrown into the turf. Sam visited JP in hospital in Oswestry. Seeing his mate so badly injured didn't make Sam ride differently, but it slightly altered his perspective. Sam was present when doctors told JP he had a 1% chance of riding again.

The enemy jump jockeys face every day is paralysis. For a long time JP joined what paralysed writer Melanie Reid, in her autobiography *'The World I Fell Out Of'*, has termed "the fellowship of the damned." Lives have to be re-forged, loss and guilt somehow, and with extraordinary resolve, turned into a positive, while you remain a prisoner of circumstances, unable to challenge the surreal spinal injury scraping at your soul. There is an unrelenting urge to control your story – the desperate hope to live again, albeit in such a very different way. She pinpoints the full gravity of paralysis: "The future is already with you, just not very evenly distributed, as you lie helpless to conceal the reality of your plight in order to protect those you love from the depths of their own suffering." All too often severe spinal injuries lead to premature demise caused by pneumonia, sepsis, pulmonary emboli, heart disease and suicide, of which the two most frequent methods, according to research, are overdose and gunshot. The unending anxiety and patience of hospital staff, family and friends are tested to breaking point. Sam's friend JP fought and fought – he is now back on his feet. Many are not that lucky...

One of the many horses adored by the Irish was Dorans Pride who, along with Danoli, grew into charismatic Irish folklore. In 1995 Dorans Pride won the Stayers' Hurdle at the Cheltenham Festival, ridden by a young jockey, Shane Broderick, who was making his mark as a rider of potential. But on Easter Monday 1997, Shane took a fall from the ironically named Another Deadly at Fairyhouse, where he had just ridden the previous winner. He broke his neck, badly damaged his spinal cord, and was paralysed from the shoulders down – a quadriplegic. Francis Woods fell at the fence before Shane, whom he saw lying on the grass, not moving: "He was a grey colour. I'd never seen it before in anyone who'd had a bad fall. It was as if his whole system had locked up." Shane lived. Never in twenty-five years of racing in Ireland had a jockey received such serious injuries and survived. Christopher Reeve, himself the victim of a riding accident, heard of the jockey's plight and sent a message that nourished him. Reeve was convinced neither of them would be in a wheelchair for a lot longer. Alas for Reeve... Thanks to almost two million euros raised by Shane's mates, racing folk and the public, many of whom had never met him, he refused to be seen as a tragic figure, and now trains from his specially adapted residence in County Tipperary.

In 2016 Brian Toomey fell horrifically from his mount in a hurdle race at Perth. For six to seven seconds he was clinically dead. Top jockey Brian Hughes had to ring his folks in Ireland; at the same time the BHA prepared a statement announcing his death and sending condolences. In fact he clung to life, but he was given a 3% chance of survival: "Not sure how they worked that out," he reasoned in a recent interview with Nick *Luck on Sunday*. But his parents were making arrangements for a funeral and had already agreed to donate his organs: "I was quite upset about that." His recovery was slow, not least because, due to the swelling in his brain, doctors had to remove a part of his skull. He spent 157 nights in hospital.

His memory is slowly coming back now, but he was on lots of medication for seizures. Being a jockey, he didn't let on quite how hard his situation was.

He hit a big low during recovery, which was hardly surprising. Anxious as to how much more he would recover, he kept that to himself. Looking back, he wonders if it would have been better to speak out. He tried to play it down and to rush things, so keen was he to get back on a horse. When reporters and family endeavoured to slow him down, he saw that as a barrier: "I didn't feel sorry for myself and kept as busy as I could, but I think perhaps I was too independent for my own good." Even now he can hardly recall anything of his life before the fall, so has to gently put that puzzle together: "I was just so driven before." Eventually he put himself first, keen to prove everyone wrong in their advising caution, patience, acceptance - not part of a jockey's vocabulary. He had a wicked sense of humour and wanted to get that back, together with his personality: "I couldn't remember the old Brian."

He's back in the saddle now, riding out for trainer Clive Cox, who is "keeping me in the know," and in December 2023 trained his first winner, on the flat. The irony of his situation is not lost on him: the sport so nearly finished him, yet now it is reviving him. He succeeded in getting back his licence for race-riding, but was aware jockeys who raced with him might not feel safe, while owners and trainers were understandably concerned that they could be the indirect cause of further damage. In the end, after some eight hundred rides in all, his comeback did not work out. "I was – still am – disappointed." He had wanted to be successful, to be better than ever – it was not to be. In his last race he was brought down, his horse fatally injured, and that was it.

When jockeys are injured, they can understandably overthink the harm done, the move that caused that injury, and how long they'll be out of the saddle. But things are changing here. Injured jockeys spur them on. Injury can be seen as an opportunity, if they can flip time away from racing on its side, and Danny Hope, strength and conditioning coach for the IJF, encourages them in an aim to go back better athletes. First and foremost they need to understand and control their feelings, and help to do this is readily available now. "The bottom line of course, we will always remind them, they don't have to remain a jockey."

Liverpool's John Moores University has set up a programme for jockeys on the injured list, not least with diet – one of the jockeys' most difficult challenges is holding their weight. With practices like sitting in a sauna no longer obtaining, jogging, nutrition, circuits, interval training, boxing, warm up bikes, are now the way back to fitness, and then maintaining it. And the effects of these more modern practices will last. It is too late to catch a fallen jockey, but today's riders are more prepared for a fall than ever before. And times are changing. Medical care on racecourses is now second to none. If you have to have a medical emergency, the racecourse is not a bad place to have it.

Daloni Lucas has done much research on the human physiological demands of horseracing, investigating epidemiology and injury prevention aspects of the hazardous profession. Some jockeys do not have a healthy lifestyle when it comes to eating. Hardly surprising when the pressure on them is to keep their weight down. 92% of jockeys miss lunch. Grabbing a pasty at motorway services on the hoof, rather than something nutritious, does them no good. They have become conditioned to the feelings of dehydration, which reduces reaction times. Lucas particularly used jockeys' rehabilitation time after injury to help them adopt more positive self-management to make them healthier, fitter and able to continue riding for longer. Safety measures are being improved all the time, not least with regard to body protectors: three-day-eventers now sport inflatable protectors attached with a lanyard: when they are projected from the saddle, the protector bursts open with a bang. Paul Struthers realises: "The practicalities of jockeys wearing such kit are tricky. Apart from the noise, the protectors can be easily dislodged, and their weight is not insignificant. So it is still work in progress."

For jump jockeys, injuries are out of sight, out of mind: they don't want a sick note, they want to be sorted. By far the most significant and effective treatment for riders hurt in executing their vocation, has been the establishment of IJF, the Injured Jockeys Fund.

CHAPTER 9:
THE INJURED JOCKEYS FUND

"Our prime purpose is to provide help, financial and otherwise, to those jockeys past and present who are injured, unable to ride or generally in need."

- IJF Credo -

John Oaksey has been described by Marcus Armytage as the greatest racing writer of the post-war era. As John Lawrence, he combined two careers – jockey and racing columnist for the *Daily Telegraph*. In 1963, as an amateur, he was beaten in the dying strides of the Grand National on Carrickbeg, a fate he had ironically imagined in a film preview of the race that saw him ride the full course and have victory dramatically snatched from him. On the day, after this narrowest of defeats, he promptly changed out of his colours and proceeded to pen 800 words for the next day's paper with stunning honesty and aplomb.

Always hands-on, the warmth and strength of his personality was striking, if read, met or watched. He won the Whitbread and Hennessy Gold Cups, proof of his unquenchable love for the horse racing game. His father, Geoffrey, had been a presiding judge at the Nazi Nuremberg Trials, but John abandoned the Eton, Oxford, Yale law route to become a true Corinthian. Days before his final law exams, he told his father he was not going to complete his legal studies: he intended to be a jockey, to which his father said, "John, you will be the luckiest man in the world if you can find someone to pay you for what you want to do most." As a rider, he became accomplished; as a writer his words had edge and clarity. Friends paid tribute to his fairness, over-riding sense of duty, engaging personality and high principles.

In December 1963, ex-Champion Jockey, Tim Brookshaw, aged 34, was riding the inappropriately named Lucky Dora in a hurdle race at Aintree. At the fifth obstacle, the horse suddenly jinked left, sending her jockey crashing through the wing of the hurdle. Despite an operation on his spine, the dairy farmer was paralysed, though he regained enough movement to take part with distinction in Tokyo's 1964 Paralympic Games in discus and javelin.

In the following year's Grand National, Paddy Farrell, 33, married with four young children, and riding Border Flight, broke his back when his mount plunged through The Chair. He never walked again. Together, these two incidents proved a catalyst for change. A group of leading lights in the National Hunt world, including John Oaksey, resolved to open a fund "for the benefit and assistance of all professional jump jockeys." Originally the National Hunt Jockeys Fund, the IJF – Injured Jockeys Fund – began to receive generous donations – and has continued to do so ever since. For 60 years the fund has provided a safety net for countless jockeys, and their families, when times become truly tough.

The IJF provides support in matters financial, medical, emotional, and logistical. A national team of liaisons (almoners) works with the stricken jockey and their families. As well as riders injured in a race, or an accident on the gallops, the IJF also looks after those jockeys who might have fallen into gambling, drink and drug addiction. Since its inception, the Fund has helped more than 1,000 jockeys and their families, and paid out £19 million in charitable assistance, realising its vision as enablers to improve the lives of injured jockeys and the lives of those looking after them, growing all the time in its mission to provide appropriate support in a prompt, constructive and sympathetic manner for those in need.

To this end, in 2009, the IJF opened Oaksey House, in Lambourn, as its first rehabilitation and fitness centre. Named after the man who, together with his wife, Chicky, worked tirelessly to promote its ethos, Oaksey House provides treatment and support for physical and neurological injuries. As well as a state of the art gym and training facilities, physiotherapists and strength/conditioning coaches are on hand, ready to give education in nutrition, fitness and lifestyle, advice on how to help reduce the risks of further serious injury, and help with sports psychology, an increasingly vital aspect of life for any jockey. There are now two further centres: Jack Berry House, in Malton, opened in 2015, and Peter O'Sullevan House in Newmarket, opened in 2019. In March 2023 a new IJF hub for the South West was opened at Taunton Rugby Club. Jockey coaches who assist here are funded by the BHA. The charity recognises the increasing need for, and importance of mental well-being, and places huge emphasis on supporting those who find life difficult – at any stage. It works closely with the PJA, which runs a 24-hour Helpline for currently licensed jockeys, whilst former riders can access help from Changing Minds, as well as the mental health charity, MIND. The majority of these vital services are free of charge to professional licence-holders, including conditional, amateur and point-to-point riders. The Fund's only income is from its charity activities, of which the renowned Christmas cards and gifts provide a huge chunk every year.

John Oaksey was never a fan of shaking cans for charity; it was his bright idea to sell the world-famous cards at Christmas. In addition, supporters arrange – and promote – fundraising events, like participation in the London Marathon, but also including calls to action, like the 2020 '9 Lives Challenge', brainchild of Wayne Burton, who broke his back in a hurdle race in Exeter in 2008. For this event, nine beneficiaries covered the 560 miles from Oaksey House to Peter O'Sullevan House to Jack Berry House and back to Oaksey House: walking, pushing a wheelchair, cycling, running, even swimming part of the distance, each of them supported by an IJF partner. Sir Anthony McCoy is the current president of the IJF, whose vice patrons, with John Francome, include Clare Balding, Frankie Dettori, Peter Scudamore and Lady Oaksey. The liaisons work directly with beneficiaries, providing that first vital point of contact; among their other duties they organise supervised race days, as well as holidays, both in the UK and abroad, which are fiercely popular.

Affectionately referred to as 'My Noble Lord' John Oaksey worked tirelessly for IJF, and made it fun. But reading about Oaksey House is nothing to experiencing the centre for yourself; the warmest welcome awaits everyone: no hospital aromas, it's like a plush hotel, though not a swanky one. The feel-good factor can be sensed immediately: it is a safe environment and jockeys know straight away that they are with their own. Everything about the place is positive and down-to-earth, its primary aims being to treat the person, not the injury, and to get the jockey back riding as soon as possible. There is no doubt that, for those in need of acute care, this is the best place to be. Every piece of apparatus is highly adapted, with low-level beds; wet rooms; an anti-gravity treadmill; hydrotherapy pool with lift and hoist, and an astonishing variety of gadgets and gizmos.

Across the courtyard sit 12 specially-adapted apartments, all unique, some of them able to accommodate carers (it is rare for badly injured people to be able to live independently where they are having their treatment). Long-term needs can be housed here; there are five permanent residents. With liaisons their ears and eyes, anyone who has ever ridden under rules or held a licence, comes under the IJF wing. Those who can do so pay a small contribution to the running of the centre, but if a jockey has landed on particularly hard times, they can apply to the charity for assistance. Racing Welfare charity also offers support to stable staff with mental health challenges, which are rife. The government boasts that mental health on the NHS is good; this is far from the case. Cash has been stripped back to pay for largely unwanted projects, like HS2. In culinary terms, the NHS cake, while plain sponge for all, is nowhere near big enough to go round: if you want sprinkles on the cake, go elsewhere. The IJF gives you sprinkles, cherries, icing and jam; be it for a week or for a year, injured jockeys will get what they clinically need. Often modern-day riders are so single minded, so focused, they 'park' their problems, which then grow and grow, and end up all-consuming. The IJF constitutes an ever-present antidote to such stress.

Oaksey House, whose site was found by John Francome, president of the IJF after John Oaksey, has the more complex cases, including spinal injuries, for which neurological specialists are on hand. Crucially, the centre encourages jockeys to make the most of its facilities while they are fit and healthy, the mantra being, "Don't wait until it's broke…" When things are broken, help is immediately on hand. In conjunction with PJA, Sporting Chance, set up by ex-Arsenal and England footballer, Tony Adams, affords strugglers the opportunity – with residential rehab – to come to terms with the array of challenges with which they are faced: lack of rides, time off with injury, weight struggles, financial insecurity, expected wins not coming off, just life. In the case of mental health problems, jockeys are given their first consultation within 48 hours of initially asking for help, so approved specialists can begin building resilience with a person whose mind is either whirring too fast, or just not whirring at all. Underpinning all the attention, consolation, treatment and post-recovery care, both physical and mental, are the well-being checks that are permanently on offer.

The IJF also offers opportunities for jockeys at full fitness to work on physical qualities not yet developed. Then, if and when injuries occur, rather than sit back and feel sorry for themselves, jockeys are helped to make peace about, and with their injury; they can discern the wider picture, realising that often the only thing holding them back is their head.

No other equestrian discipline has this vast safety-net behind it. There is no golden bullet: recovery takes time, but jockeys are elite athletes, and IJF makes a huge impact on them by maintaining, then improving their quality of life, be it a spinal injury, MND, Parkinson's or more temporary damage. When the jockeys go back to racing riding, facilities at courses are improving, due in part to Edward Stroud's plan 'Fit to Fall': having had much experience in the army medical corps, he has been instrumental in seeking better equipment for jockeys at their place of work.

More and more social activities are being arranged by IJF for all in the industry: hog-roasts, walks, coffee mornings, Cheltenham preview nights, lunches for racing secretaries, carol services, Newmarket heath mornings, a monthly Beneficiary Bulletin and digital drop-in classes to improve technical skills: so much is on offer. Debbie Gray, Head of Operations, knows: "It's so important to get people into healthy mindsets, recognising how their physical and mental well-being are so closely aligned."

The IJF emphasis is proactive in the extreme: it doesn't just signpost help, it accesses it, and answers the question, "What can IJF do that you need right now?" It works closely with JETS. All three national centres relish the challenge of meeting every individual's needs. Every week there is a multi-disciplinary meeting of doctors, psychologists, physios, nutritionists, rehab-therapists, strength coaches, welfare, and liaisons to discuss each case and work towards Gold Standard outcomes. From the moment a jockey hits the turf to the point where they're ready to return to race-riding, for which they must undergo an assessment, the support offered is outstanding and sustained.

Among new initiatives is the Jockey Profiling Day, to gain insight into each jockey's individual situation. Data is gathered to benefit the jockey in question by highlighting specific strengths/limitations and creating a bespoke programme to work on these key areas. Such days incorporate mental health talks from clinical psychologists, nutrition advice, next career discussion from JETS and technical coaching sessions, ending with a social event – further evidence of how IJF not only supports, but sustains jockeys.

Whilst never blowing its own trumpet, IJF wants to make people aware of all that is on offer: "You can tell people, but they only hear it when they want to hear it." All sportsmen and women face trials and tribulations: thanks to IJF, racing is up there with the very best in terms of care, its wide-ranging facilities burgeoning all the time... and if, during recovery, a jockey has a setback, IJF picks up on it immediately; it is thus living out John Oaksey's vision: "Once a jockey, you're always part of the IJF family."

Not all jockeys are as fortunate as Jimmy Uttley, though he never rode over fences, only hurdles. He won the Champion Hurdle three times on Persian War, but in fourteen seasons riding he never broke a bone.

Jeremiah (Jerry) McGrath is a jump jockey who has Oaksey House to thank; he recalls a certain day only too well: "It was Monday January 16th 2021." With winter weather playing havoc with turf jumping fixtures, replacement 'bumper' (flat) races were arranged for that day on the All-Weather Track at Lingfield. "I had six rides booked; it should have been an 'easy money day'." But it turned out to be no such thing...

Jerry rode two favourites and three horses for his boss, then Champion Trainer, Nicky Henderson, with whom the jockey had been almost throughout his career. Having grown up in Cork, "the biggest county in Ireland," he says – no wonder so many jockeys are Cork men – the youngest of three, and named Jeremiah after a great uncle, he'd enjoyed a blessed childhood, but always wanted to be a jockey. He'd been to work for Brendan Powell in his long summer holidays, didn't think he'd make the grade, but got the bug. His mum wouldn't let him commit to racing until after the Irish equivalent of 'A levels', but he secured those and came to England at 18, with further education courses in his homeland a backup if he failed to make the grade. He re-made the Powell connection, then got the job with Nicky Henderson, where he learned his trade, alongside David Bass. He rode his first Cheltenham Festival winner for Henderson, Une Artiste, at the age of 21, thought the game "just brilliant," but then found things got quiet. It was seven years, during which he experienced a big lull, before his next Festival success, on evergreen stayer Beware the Bear. In 2020 he had nine rides at Cheltenham: only two got round. January 16th, with its promise of six rides at Lingfield, if not the quality of Cheltenham, would give him a good day...

He rode five losers, but in the sixth race was on his most fancied horse of the day. With no jumps to negotiate, the race was crowded, especially when the big-price horses came back to the peloton. Jerry's filly clipped heels with one of these - and that was it. The horse fell, the jockey came down, the horse behind tripped and landed on top of him. "When I was on the ground one of the horses was on top of my leg, and when they took him off I didn't feel anything. I'd hit the all-weather surface, and you don't bounce on that. I was conscious and remember being in the ambulance with the blue light flashing; it was fairly humbling; it brings you back to reality."

Jerry did not lose consciousness: "I wish I had... I've never felt pain like it. I knew my hip was 'wrong' because of the way it was twisted. Yet when the horse was lifted off me, the pain was worse..." For 90 seconds (a surprisingly accurate assessment of how much time had passed), he felt nothing, as paralysis cast its grim pall on his supine body. "I never want to feel that again... if I'd been knocked out, I'd never have known." Now, whenever he sees someone in a wheelchair, which, of necessity in rehab, was often, he feels how lucky he is. When the 90 seconds had slogged past, he was aware of "Something... anything else was a bonus."

But that spasm of relief was only the beginning of his long haul back to fitness. In Brighton Hospital, he underwent an operation to put the hip, and then the shoulder back, and was under anaesthetic again for eight hours as both were pinned, then plated. He lay in agony for days. But though the bones hurt, his mental fight was far worse. With Covid still flexing its greedy muscles, no visitors were allowed. "It was the worst ten days of my life." He got sick of talking on the phone – he didn't want to talk anyway. But, he appreciated his good fortune that both hip and shoulder surgeons had been present to operate on him at once – a stroke of luck in Covid days, and he was determined to return to the saddle, however long the road to recovery.

By chance he had the bed by the window: every day a lone seagull tapped on that window, becoming his talisman. Jerry needed that: the man in the bed next to him, whom Jerry never saw, tried to commit suicide: with Covid horrors, he had nothing to live for. The nurses gave the man tough love. Jerry, never seeing his face, found the man intrigued him: he gave the ailing jockey something to think about, other than his own suffering. The three other men in the ward received not a single phone call: they had given up on themselves. Jerry saw how some folk live, that he was lucky, even though in an unlucky situation; he didn't want pity, he wanted – needed – to get back to his world...

Two months later he went to the sales at Newmarket, his first real outing, to meet mates and contacts face to face: the day did not work out as planned. The young Irishman had long thought of going into the bloodstock business when he hung up his racing breeches, but his enthusiasm took a severe blow that day: "Four people asked me the same, painful question, "Will you come back?" Did they all think that was it? Did even racing folk think I was older than I am? I knew the question was not meant badly, but it went round and round in my head... horrible. Was I overthinking the whole thing? I certainly thought of Formula One racing with its cut-throat *Drive to Survive*."

There is much to weigh up with any injury: jockeys miss the buzz, the 'fix' of race-riding, whilst concentrating their considerable energies on the soonest possible recovery. Jerry was transferred from the Brighton hospital to Oaksey House after ten days: Oaksey is all on one level. After three or four days there, he contracted Covid: he couldn't move (though he was essentially crippled anyway), and had to endure two weeks in isolation. His immune system was at rock bottom; he felt utterly rough and raw. For six weeks he could not put his leg down on the floor, let alone place any weight on that leg. And his doctors erred on the side of pessimism: there was no chance of his returning to the saddle that season: a tough prognosis. The months February to May are busy for jump jockeys; not earning makes things harder; riders run their own business; they have to make things work financially. Jerry faced stalemate.

But he is not a tunnel-vision jockey, and here he is akin to his friend David Bass, in thinking out of the box. Both men are realists. If Jerry could not be back by the end of the 2020-2021 season, so be it: he was not going to rush back, he was going to heal.

He was mindful of a great mate who played loose-head prop for Munster: the two are chalk and cheese, but get on famously. The rugby man had a contract, whether he was match-fit or injured: Jerry had no such contract. For the first time in his career he was confronted by serious worries. In order to look forward – which jockeys always do – to next season, they all need security. "Only when you're not riding do you realise how good a sport racing is. Does one fall make it a bad day? No way – as long as you can drive out of the course in one piece, it has been a good day. I want to make sure I ride for as long as I can. When you're healthy you have to appreciate it." Jerry reckons he got "massive support" from most people; you need that to keep spirits up, to keep things fresh. Owners were good to him; he usually built up a rapport with them, though some surprised him: "You can feel let down."

The buzz of race-riding, "on a horse anything can happen," is similar, in Jerry's view, to bidding against someone for a horse at the sales. For a time unable to do either, he was aware of the inevitable withdrawal process that jockeys can sink into: "Not getting that regular 'fix' is hard." In many ways jockeys are scapegoats. Jerry was no exception: "You have to take the flak, however much you hate it. Social media is a strange one: I need information on horse breeding, but am content to use social media as a tool: others use it as a platform to promote themselves."

He has one great asset: "You can't show any weakness in the weighing room, but I love poker. I'm quite good at keeping cards close to my chest. You need that in racing." He also makes – and keeps – friends from outside the jump jockey circus. But when a fellow jockey loses his life it is desperately tough for his colleagues, as Jerry experienced with Liam Treadwell.

Jerry has a supporting family: "They've come on the journey with me, even though it's in another land, literally and metaphorically." His farming father was a teetotal pioneer. AP McCoy is teetotal; as a youngster Jerry wanted to be like AP – in every way possible, but he knew that was unrealistic, and enjoyed his first drink at the Galway Festival. He thought hard about winning: "Riding winners is brilliant, but you've got to be content doing it, and you need good mates." For him there had to be a happy medium between riding and family life – "The latter is the leveller, take Walter Swinburne (on the flat): would he have been happier if he'd only had half the success he ended up with? There'd have been less pressure, fewer demons." The young Irishman with no racing connections remained obsessed with it all, and was determined to return to the saddle just as soon as he could.

The weeks went by: the prognosis was not good: his complex injury needed more surgery: a nerve redirective graft. There are no rules to the way nerves heal, making the process different to, and more difficult than, bone healing. The jockey had been recovering for 14 weeks already; his next operation could not take place for another four, during which time he had to get his shoulder moving, as his arm would be in a sling after the op. The hardest thing was the fact there was no timeline for his recovery. When he heard this news he was downcast; a day later, his sang-froid had been summoned back into control. He'd been aiming to return to the saddle by September 2021: that could not happen now: "It was in the lap of the gods." But he was no fool, was aware that one day the phone would stop ringing and faithful owners start to look elsewhere, though he was generous about the retirement of Theinval, a horse he usually rode, who went out on a winning note at Ayr on Scottish Grand National Day, 2022. The owners had lunch with him as a thank you. As he planned his recovery, he realised he had the chance to do other things: not only would that make the time go quicker, it would broaden his experience and range of choices for later life. He began to delve deeper into the bloodstock world, whilst still working hard on his injuries, in the hydropool and on an electrical nerve stimulator. In Oaksey House everything was done straight away: "The staff are shrewd in knowing how we are feeling, which can differ from day to day."

But in January 2022, when he was 31, the extent of his injuries finally forced him to retire. He had known in his own head six weeks prior to Christmas that his twelve year career in the saddle was over, so had become determined to take the positives into his new life, despite conceding defeat in his year-long battle to return to race-riding. His hip had healed, but not the shoulder: "There's a lot of metal in there and there was a lot of nerve damage... my bicep ruptured... I've got what's called Popeye Syndrome, where my bicep is constantly tensed... strenuous exercise like riding makes it pop out. Dr Jerry Hill agreed there was not much we could do. I'll miss the adrenalin, but maybe it's easier I haven't had the buzz for 12 months. In a weird way, I've been weaned off racing. Oaksey House were brilliant, a massive help, and they still are. They always said getting back would be touch and go. Things progressed, but the body said no. I suppose I'm lucky I've had to retire, but the flip side could have been a lot worse. I could have been in a wheelchair for life. I remember everything about the accident, not feeling any pain, and then it being excruciating – but you can live off that moment forever, and end up ruining your life thinking about it. That day should have been money for jam, but something happened. I wouldn't say I'm totally at peace with retirement; I'd have loved another five to six years, but I knew my fate, and have accepted it better than I thought. I don't want this to be the end of the world or a sob story. I've had some brilliant days, got some great memories and my life isn't over."

Simonsig was his favourite horse. His second Cheltenham Festival win, on Beware the Bear, was vital: "I'd have been gutted without that second winner to know the difference in feeling from my first." Now he helps Nicky Henderson with race-planning and, under the guidance of David Minton, has become closely involved with the bloodstock industry, for which 'Hendo' thinks he is tailor-made. Despite his brave face, the reality of retirement was tough: "I thought I'd come to terms with it until I got bombarded with all the calls and texts. It really hit home when it was in print. But I have met great people and nobody can take that away from me. Now I'm looking forward to the next chapter, just waiting on the free bus pass to come through."

CHAPTER 10: JOCKEYS 1 –
THE COMPLETE PACKAGE

*"Every successful jockey
must have a screw loose somewhere."*

- Sam Waley-Cohen, ex-jockey -

Steve Dennis has written that jockeys are: "Just like us, and utterly removed from our experience." It is a crazy lifestyle. In their demanding profession they live only for the life, see only the next race, the run at Cheltenham, the good ride. They don't – they cannot – think of mortality; instead they ride a never-ceasing roller-coaster of emotions, "pawns to the silent assassins of chance, irony, and accident." Theirs is a "cocooned existence, almost incestuous." Trophies, cups, tankards, whisky decanters on the mantelpiece are memory-prompters, but the jockeys' memory banks contain more challenging images... They need resilience and fortitude, always, in the face of sustained endeavour and adversity. Many of today's jockeys possess these virtues in large measure; Peter Scudamore reckons our current generation of jump jockeys is "faster, fitter and better" than in his day.

Like many, if not most, top athletes, jockeys are wary of dropping their guard: theirs is often a private struggle, with themselves as much as their competitors. David Jennings has written: "Paradoxically, the more we know about them, the less we know them, which renders them likeable rather than loveable. So, when you meet them for more than a cursory evaluation of a horse's performance post-race (and jockeys are notorious for dashing off, not wasting words) it is a privilege."

If a soccer player breaks his leg, he is almost immediately on the operating slab, under the best surgeon around: when jockeys fall, they sometimes have to make their own arrangements, though the IJF is hugely involved and supportive here. The PJA helps with insurance, as well as with disciplinary matters, motoring offences (handy, considering the number of miles jockeys travel, and the huge potential for speeding points), medical expenses, and, should it be needed, help both practical and psychological with career-ending injuries. When they are injured, however badly, jockeys call upon a self-defence mechanism that demands they make out they are not seriously damaged, however hard the fall, and grim the pain. It is a sobering thought that, back in the day, jockeys like Steve Smith-Eccles counted the laughs first, the pounds and breakages later.

In addition to being martyrs to the scales, with all that involves, and being good judges of the pace of a race, knowing what sort of horse they have underneath them, when things happen in a race, as they invariably will, jockeys need to improvise: having the trainer's backing here is vital, for without that backing the jockey will feel on a knife-edge, so, more often than not, their mounts do not get the best ride. Some trainers will stand up for stable jockeys even when they know that jockey is 'in the wrong'. When this does not ensue, it can easily feed the jockeys' fear that they are not good enough. They need constant reassurance about their prowess, their ability.

Many jockeys spend their early mornings schooling prospective mounts at their stables; it is a way of securing rides. By schooling, often in cold blood, they get a feel for a horse and help the trainer make a plan: when to run, over what distance, on what ground, at which track, in which race. Together, they build the profile of a horse, and try to make the right decisions for it. This riding out is a part of the job; it's not always appreciated, and often jockeys do not get paid for doing it. Only between riding work, schooling and travelling to the races do jockeys have a slice of prime time to communicate with their agents, fellow jockeys, or another trainer for whom they might have picked up a 'spare' ride.

A healthy sense of humour is essential, and jockeys have a distinctive one. Battling danger, potential disaster and extreme pressures on their mental and physical resources, they share the thirst for light relief, quick – often sharp – banter and one-liners that shoot from their ever-teeming brains. The question as to who is the most intelligent jockey garners rich replies: "The lads who've retired," "Nico de Boinville and Aidan Coleman because they do the crossword"; "None of us, considering what we do for a day job," and "Tom Scu: he went to school." Humour releases tension – though it doesn't remove it – and ex-jockeys retain it long after hanging up their boots, Ruby Walsh with his penetrating, dry wit, being as fine an example as any.

Mattie Batchelor was renowned for being the joker, the man of pranks, guaranteeing much-needed jollity in – and out of – the weighing room. But he could also be deadly serious: "In this game there's no point being bitter. You've got to have a bit of balls to say, 'Right, I can get back from this'. He achieved recognition riding Carruthers for the Oaksey family, but kept a sense of proportion: "There's better jockeys than me, there's bigger jockeys than me (not just in stature) that have achieved much more, but no-one can take away recognition by a knowledgeable sporting public: Carruthers made me a somebody, well, a little somebody, anyway."

"Winning!" is the instant reply from Nick Schofield to the question as to why he is a professional jockey, "The buzz of winning," He instantly tempers that with, "But you can't escape the ups and downs. You lose so much more than you win, which makes you appreciate the wins even more." He is known and respected as a cheery rider, but that does not belie his steely determination, unwavering self-belief, and fierce will to succeed. "You'd sacrifice anything to do this job, with the chance of doing your best for the owners, the trainer and the horse. But it's not easy trying to please everyone: there's a lot of blood and tears."

Having turned freelance after years with Paul Nicholls, Nick now enjoys playing for a lot of different teams: "A win for a small trainer is massive," and while there are different winning feelings involved with bigger trainers, he is well aware there are always pressures: "You try and make as few mistakes as possible, to do your very best, but it's a huge responsibility: the trainer has done all the hard work for three or four months: a jockey has six minutes to bring that work to fruition, or undo it."

Born in Exeter, Nick was novice point-to-point champion, joined Nicholls from school and won the amateurs' title, watching Ruby Walsh, Noel Fehily,

Christian Williams and Sam Thomas, his idol: "Sam was so natural, so stylish. When I started out, he was at his pinnacle." Nick's first Festival win, on Hunt Ball, "was every bit as good as I'd imagined – and better… something you can't describe, but once you've had a bit, you want more." For a long time associated with the Jeremy Scott-trained Melodic Rendezvous, he won again at the Festival in 2021 on Sky Pirate.

Nick knows about the bad times, the injuries, how they happen out of the blue, like the freak accident sustained at Fontwell in November 2020, when, having just crossed the line fourth in a chase, he was broadsided by a loose horse and broke his leg in three places, the worst injury of his career. He endeavours to see the setbacks as character-building, though even when coming out with his mantra "positivity builds creativity" the fact that this is no trite aphorism for a man of his experience can be seen in his wide, but knowing smile. "Returning to the saddle as a freelance, after time out, is not easy. You're self-employed, with no guarantee of rides, so there is uncertainty: you have to work for it, but that gives you the drive."

Charlie Deutsch's father was a point-to-point rider, whose son was mad on horses, galloping through pony racing and then his own point-to-points, "always on the slippery slope." Having left Charlie Longsdon's, he moved to Venetia Williams' powerful stable in Herefordshire, already aware that "You never know what's around the corner." Despite a much-publicised time-out, during which the trainer stuck with him, Charlie learned a lot: "You shouldn't fear things quite as much. Everyone's got anxiety, and if you let fear get the better of you, you can end up in a worse situation. There's always a chance: you've just got to keep looking forward, and, as long as you keep your mentality right, have good people around you, and a bit of luck, you can overcome these things."

He has overcome much already, having become mentally tougher and more appreciative, not least with his trainer, whose care for her horses, and skill in training them he rates as highly as did Sam Thomas: "When you rely on animals, so much can go wrong. And horses don't have to do it for you, they can always surprise, or make a fool of you, but riding a winner [and he's ridden plenty of those] for the team is great: everyone has a slice of that success." One of his greatest successes to date came in the 2021 Ladbroke's Trophy, when he won on Cloudy Glen for his guv'nor. He is a thoughtful jockey: "I think people nowadays can be quite throwaway, quite caught up in the moment, and make snap decisions; I think it a mistake not to think things through and give people another chance." He has firm inner belief: "As long as you think you can do it, and can always improve, I think you will. It's not what you do, it's the way you do it."

On rare days off, Charlie tends a patch of land: his 'something else', to which every jockey needs to look forward, something that completely distracts them. "In winter, racing's on every day and you can't be consumed by it completely." For now, he relishes the fact "there's so much to the sport." He loves the mornings, going in to work at the yard, making the most of every opportunity, every race. And his recent partnership with L'Homme Pressé has given him a golden stab at the fates.

Army Captain Guy Disney was the first jockey to ride a winner with a prosthetic limb. On a tour of Afghanistan in July 2009, with his troop of Light Dragoons in Helmand Province, his vehicle was hit by a RPG (Rocket Propelled Grenade), which released a jet of molten metal. The eighteen year-old next to Guy was killed instantly; Guy himself knew at once he had lost his lower right leg.

He had grown up with Tom Scu on the pony club circuit; now his army career was over, he turned his thoughts to horses. Having ridden out for Kim Bailey, and taken part in a charity flat race ("a great test"), he applied for a licence, and was turned down. He promptly accompanied Prince Harry on his Antarctic expedition, *Walking With The Wounded*. But then Dr. David Carey took Guy's case to the BHA. In the meantime, Guy worked for months with the help of toe-stoppers, stirrup irons where the foot is prevented from slipping forward; he'd been coached by Yogi Breisner and had plenty of practice on the equishoot, which throws you off your horse. Expecting a hard battle with the BHA when he reapplied, he was surprised to be told he could obtain his amateur licence, and compete against regular jockeys, both amateur and professional.

Tom Scu told him about the David Pipe-trained Rathlin Rose, a big horse with a long neck that would suit Guy, and the pair combined at Sandown to win the Royal Artillery Gold Cup – twice. He also lined up for the Aintree Foxhunters over the Grand National fences. "They're still huge to jump." The former captain found everyone encouraging, not least Richard Johnson, then Champion Jockey. Guy is now a fierce advocate of appealing to new people to come into racing, so they can see how things are with new, and different eyes.

Harry Enright (18) from SE London was born without his left hand, but is still chasing his boyhood dream to be a jockey. Inspired by Guy Disney and his own parents, the lad attended the BRS – and completed the course there. Now a work-rider for Lawney Hill, he has been hugely helped by a custom-made prosthetic with magnet and wire release system, specially designed by Andrew Braithwaite at BRS. Harry is making strides; seen by his teachers as "hard-working, cheeky and dedicated," he regards his every challenge like a Grand National fence: "The wall of green firs comes at you like an Atlantic wave on a Donegal beach – you have just got to jump the fence!" He feels it quite natural to be on a horse and float away up the gallops, and is realistic about the magnitude of his ambition, one day to sport silks; meantime, he is training his brain to get used to the new limb. His Instagram account carries the motivational message: 'Breaking barriers single-handed.'

Guy Mitchell is the only jockey riding in Britain today with one eye: he lost his right eye to a tumour at the age of six. Despite being twice turned down in his bid for a jump jockey's racing licence, he persevered until, in 2019, his determination was rewarded with a mandate to ride on the flat, as an amateur. Having been to medical school, and taken part in triathlons, his determination has grown over the years; married with children, he is fully alert to the demands of race-riding: shatter-proof goggles have made a huge difference in helping to protect his other eye. He had his first ride in 2019.

At 46, Guy, the racecourse doctor at Goodwood, enjoyed his first – and landmark – victory on his fourth ride, when he partnered 50-1 shot The Game Is On to win an amateur jockeys' race at his home track, despite having nearly fallen off at the start. Confessing his win left him "in utter disbelief – and knackered," he said, "All of a sudden I found myself in front: it was very odd: it all went quiet, and the line couldn't come soon enough, because I was absolutely spent. To win a race is just brilliant; it always goes to prove if you have a crack, sometimes you can pull it off. I am always aware of other horses near me; I absolutely don't want to cause any issues for anyone, so I'd rather ride wide round a bend than squeeze someone for space. That probably isn't very good jockeyship, but we're all fair here." He was inspired by his namesake, Disney, and is delighted both that medical standards have advanced, and that racing has become more inclusive.

Between 1996 and 2019 there had only been two Champion Jockeys. AP McCoy, twenty times, and Richard Johnson, four. As a 7-stone teenager in Newtonhamilton, Co. Armagh, Northern Ireland, Brian Hughes had the burning ambition to make it as a jockey. Working when still young for trainer James Lambe, he schooled over racecourse fences on a 4-year-old, who'd never before left the yard. As Lambe says, "He was like Robocop: relentless."

Having come to England in 2005, he was Champion Conditional Jockey 2007-2008: he has always been dedicated to a fault. As a young rider he learned much and took inspiration from Graham Lee, with his composed riding style, conserving energy and gliding over the obstacles. Brian eats, sleeps and breathes racing, does his homework, and doesn't miss a trick. Being based in the North of England, once the powerhouse of steeple chasing greats Bobby Renton, Neville Crump, Ginger McCain, Willie Stevenson, Gordon Richards, Michael Dickinson and co., but now seen by some as the poor relation (which it is not), could put Brian at a disadvantage. He is first jockey to Donald McCain, and rides a lot for Nicky Richards, where relationships are built on trust. But for a time he had nothing like the fire-power available to Harry Skelton, Harry Cobden, Sam Twiston-Davies and co. down south, which made his being crowned Champion Jockey in the curtailed 2019-20 season even more momentous. He was leading defending champion Dicky Johnson by 19 winners on 141 before the season was brought to a premature end – ironically on St Patrick's Day 2020 – when racing was suspended, due to Covid. He was out on his tractor, rolling the fields at his father-in-law's farm, where he lives with wife, Luci, and two small children, when the news came through. With it, he became the first northern-based Champion Jockey for forty years, since Jonjo O'Neill, and he was generous in receipt of the honour: "I thought my being Champion Jockey was something everyone in the north could take a bit of credit for. They've waited a long time for it!"

Brian himself had to wait a while before he received his trophy. Mick Fitzgerald realised the situation and drove up north to present it to him. The new champion, while visibly delighted, remained endearingly humble on unwrapping the trophy, engraved on top of which are the four words: TALENT, BRAVERY, RESILIENCE, DEDICATION, to which he gently added... "and LUCK." But he had no chance to celebrate. He has become synonymous with the north of England's passion, dogged edge, and ability not just to survive, but to shine in the shadows of their counterparts in the south. "Winning at Hexham, Cartmel, Kelso or Sedgefield on the heavy, mist-drenched turf, muck on the face, fog in the air, doesn't hold the same allure as riding up in front of the rollicking stands of Cheltenham," has written one racing sage, but winners are winners. Brian has always been a winner: as an infant of eighteen months, diagnosed with meningitis, he was given the Last Rites: he pulled through. Now, his levels of courage and intelligence on horseback and off are introducing a more subtle edge to his arsenal. That intelligence can be seen in his comprehensive blog, nowhere more evident than in January 2019, when he paid tribute to Natasha Galpin, who worked for trainer Iain Jardine, but lost her life, aged just 22, after a gallops incident in which she took a terrible fall: "Her loss is a grave reminder of the importance of caring for people who are the backbone of racing. We absolutely must do our best to boost and encourage the likes of Racing Welfare, who do such excellent work supporting grooms and racing staff at all levels."

According to Donald McCain, the north's leading trainer, Brian is "always in the right place. He makes it look easy, very smooth and simple. Becoming champion in 2020 gave him more confidence; this game is all about that." Having lost that title to Harry Skelton in 2021, Brian picked up the pieces, and it was battle on to recapture the crown. As soon as the next season began, he came out all guns blazing, and set a ferocious pace, riding for a lot of the smaller stables: "I got a lot of support from good people," to whom he is grateful. "It was heart-warming that they thought enough of me to say ride what we have; they said that twenty times over, wanting me on their team, even for one ride. That's real sport." Proud of his working-class Irish family, where silver spoons were unheard of, he was kept grounded in normality – and still is. When not riding, he revels in being Dad at home.

He has been with agent Richard Hale for 16 years, ever since coming to England, and is a great believer in longevity: "The thing needs consistency." If things go wrong Hale says so: Brian values that opinion.

Teetotal, he likes to stay level at all times: "Then you're keeping your performance the same." He sets short-term goals and targets which he believes achievable. Losing his title to Skelton made him appreciate things more, taught him to know who's in his corner, and made him a more complete individual… it also made him more hungry to wrestle back the title, which he did in 2022, 99 winners clear of the runner-up, Sam Twiston-Davies. He was again Champion Jockey in 2023. That done, he would still like to be the one to beat for the next couple of seasons, "But you never know what's ahead in this game." As he is well aware, "One race can change your season, for good and bad." He has been mercifully free of serious injuries from his time in the saddle − so far.

He remains, as he has to be, "obsessed. Yesterday's gone, it's history." He's self-deprecating: "I don't like fanfare or headlines. I try to do my job." The man thrives on routine. Being based in the north is not easy, and in Cheltenham Festival week (where he needs big wins but realises, "You have to get on the right horses for that"), he often rides at Sedgefield, rather than Cheltenham: "I've no divine right to any of that." But his determination has been compared to that of AP, about which he demurs; the main thing on both their minds being where the next winner is coming from, the gimlet mindset of a champion.

He is a candid, steely, quiet member of the jump jockeys' fraternity, though he confesses he was not so quiet in his youth. About social media he is trenchant: "I don't need all that negativity and hype; it's insignificant to me." On the question: is his part in racing only about winning, he pauses; "That's hard to answer. Everyone is in racing to win, not to take part: that's the ultimate goal." All he thinks about is riding winners, "That's the way I have to be. A horse of any calibre can win a race or two." As long as the owner and trainer are happy, he is happy. He is essentially self-critical, keeping a low profile despite all his achievements. When he rode his 1000th winner he never told anyone: "The press picked it up 10 days later." If he does a good job, he knows it, but he is hard on himself, he has to be, and well aware if he messes up.

Regrets he has none, certainly not in big races. And in small ones he has too many to know: "You wish you could have done it again, but you learn from it." Years ago James Lambe saw in Brian "the complete package, utterly dedicated: the man even rode out on his wedding morning!" In regaining his title in 2021-22, he passed Tom Scu as the winningmost jockey still riding in Britain; he rode winners for 32 different trainers. He also joined an elite roll of honour: AP, Richard Johnson and Peter Scudamore, in riding 200 winners in a season. Despite his runaway lead in the championship, he never allowed himself to be complacent, riding every race with the mentality he was five winners behind; he achieved number 200 in April 2022, to the congratulations of his weighing room colleagues, who came out to acknowledge him: "I was a bit taken aback by their warmth, but I really appreciate people's good wishes."

He remains full of ambition and drive, as fit and competitive as ever, busier than anyone else, with huge commitment: "That's why he wins titles. Brian is a thinking jockey who would never blow his own trumpet." He still looks forward – always - to the next challenge: "Every jockey will throw their hat into the ring, but I'll still be committed as long as trainers want me. When I'm not riding as well as I could, I'll know. My racing career has been a slow-burner, not riding over jumps till I was 20. And I'm lucky I don't have a lot of weight problems." He would love to win at the Cheltenham Festival, but will not go there on a 100-1 shot: "That's like lining up in a Formula One race in a go-kart." Ayr and Aintree are more his bag, though his Grand National record is not sparkling: "I've had enough falls in that race to last me a lifetime."

CHAPTER 11: FEMALE JOCKEYS

"Jockeys are brave men and women, who accept crashing falls and desperate injuries as natural punctuation in their working lives, who sometimes need so many metal bolts and pins to hold shattered bones together, they joke about bequeathing their remains to a scrapyard."

- Hugh McIlvanney -

It is no coincidence that the majority of those now participating in the British Racing School apprentice course are female: more and more girls are breaking into the sport, thanks to the shining examples of Rachael Blackmore, Bryony Frost, Katie Walsh, Nina Carberry, and Hollie Doyle on the flat. Increasingly, women are taking key roles in the sport as clerks of the course, clerks of the scales, stipendiary stewards, judges, stud managers, and in administration, as well, of course, as trainers. "Sport," in the words of broadcaster Clare Balding, "is a powerful motivator and gives girls a much more honest reflection of the range of their strengths than they will find in a fashion magazine."

It is hard to believe that not until 1966, 212 years after the formation of the Jockey Club, were women granted a licence to train, and that success came only after the Court of Appeal out-battled The Jockey Club. It took another six years before women were allowed to ride on the flat, ten before they could ride under National Hunt rules. Charlotte Brew, in 1977, was the first female to compete in the Grand National.

Things have raced on since then. In 2021, jockey Rachael Blackmore won the Champion Hurdle on Honeysuckle, was leading rider at the Cheltenham Festival with six winners (only one short of Ruby Walsh's record seven) and went on to win the Grand National on Minella Times.

The following year, she repeated her win in the Champion Hurdle and then won the Cheltenham Gold Cup on A Plus Tard. Women now compete on a level playing field with men, a true triumph over discrimination. And they are raising the bar, as much as their male counterparts, achieving what many thought impossible. Women now outnumber men 70% to 30% in the racing industry, as they carve out their identities within the sport.

In 2011, Carlisle staged the first ever all-female-jockey flat racing day. Lead slabs were driven up from Haydock to put in the saddles, so the 'girls' could carry their stipulated weights. Twenty dressing gowns were hurriedly purchased from Marks and Spencer's for the changing areas. A crowd of over 10,000 turned up at what was proving an inspiring time for female jockeys: three weeks beforehand, Hayley Turner had become the first woman to win a Group One race on Dream Ahead in Newmarket's July Cup (she later won the Nunthorpe Stakes on Margo Did).

If anything, jump racing has changed more dramatically. In 2010-2011, only Rachael Green cracked the top 100 (58th); seven did it in the 2020-2021 season: Bryony Frost, Paige Fuller, Lilly Pinchin, Millie Wonnacott, Bridget Andrews, Charlotte Jones and Rachael Blackmore. Expectations have gone through the roof. Individual graft has been vital: "It's what you do in the shadows when no-one is watching that really matters," says Bryony. Rachael had more rides than anyone in two of the last three seasons in Ireland. But, as with the men, injury is an ever-present threat. You are going to get hurt.

Jump racing now boasts a plethora of professional female jockeys in one of the very few sports where men and women compete on truly equal terms, as is also the case in Three-Day Eventing and showjumping. In France, female jump jockeys are given a weight allowance in certain races; here in the UK, in championship races, mares are given that weight allowance, but their pilots are not. The term 'female jump jockey' is a bone of contention to some who wish to be seen – and evaluated – as simply jump jockeys, but the counterpart to this argues that highlighting gender as well as achievement can increase the profile of women in racing. Whereas there used to be viewed a significant difference between the performance of female jump jockeys and the public perception of their ability, that is no longer the case.

It was English women who led the breakthrough: Meriel Tuffnell, on her first ride, was the first female to ride a winner in Britain, on Scorched Earth at Kempton in May 1972; Gay Kelleway was the first female to win at Royal Ascot, on Sprowston Boy, in the Queen Alexandra Stakes of 1987; Alex Greaves was the first to ride in the Derby, soon followed by Hayley Turner in 2012, and then Hollie Doyle. In 2015, Michelle Payne won the Melbourne Cup on 100-1 outsider, Prince of Penzance.

'Over the sticks', sisters-in-law, Nina Carberry and Katie Walsh, together brought us more awareness of female jump jockeys. Nina was the first to win at the highest level in Britain or Ireland, when partnering Leading Run to victory in the Champion Bumper at Punchestown Festival, and she enjoyed a terrific career, having nearly 17 years in the saddle. She is the daughter of trainer, Tommy Carberry, and sister of Paul, himself a legendary jockey in both Britain and Ireland. Nina proved an inspiration over the Cross Country course at Cheltenham for Enda Bolger, who said she had no equal over the banks. In that sense, she took over the baton from JT McNamara, winning on Heads On The Ground, Garde Champêtre (twice) and Josie's Orders, as well as the Cheltenham Foxhunters (twice) on On The Fringe (2015 and 2016), and the 2011 Irish Grand National on Organisedconfusion.

Katie Walsh's pedigree is equally flawless. Daughter of trainer and TV pundit, Ted, and sister to Ruby, she, too, brought female jockeyship to a higher level, admired by Willie Mullins: "Horses jumped for her, she had confidence in her ability and in her horse, riding every one in a different way." Winner of the Guinness Kerry National, she rode her father's horse Seabass into third place in the Grand National in 2012 (the highest finishing result for a woman until Rachael Blackmore in 2021). Racing was lucky to have both these pioneering jockeys at the same time; they set the standard, and retired the same week.

In Britain, Bryony Frost, also daughter and sister to a pair of jockeys, had finished fifth in the 2018 Grand National. She captured the imagination of the racing public, when she and Frodon won the Ryanair Chase at the Cheltenham Festival in 2019, and the King George VI Chase the next year. She now holds the record for the highest number of wins for a female jockey. Describing herself as "a feral child," school was no priority for her: instead she would buy broken ponies with her pocket money, take off on her own with them and, with her jockey brother, Haddon, launch herself off hay bales so as to learn how to fall.

Haddon was badly injured in a fall at Exeter when Bryony was 14: his legs were crushed, paralysis was feared; he told his young sister, "Never race unless it is worth the risk of this," a rule that has stuck with her, although it did not deter. She had a bad fall at Newton Abbot in 2018, when, unaware she was carrying a spinal injury, her saddle slipped, she broke her sternum, lacerated her pancreas and suffered an aneurysm in the artery between those organs. Attending Oaksey House for five weeks, she built her body back up. "Broken bones are easier and predictable, but internal injuries fragile and unpredictable; you have to be 110% before you come back; you can't afford to give a horse a bad ride.

"In such an unpredictable world, when you are out there with your partner, it is like breathing, there's nothing in the world that can take you to the place where galloping your horse can take you; that is an addiction bigger than anything. It doesn't matter the way I ride, whether I am a boy or a girl, it doesn't change how much I want to be the best I can be. From an extremely early age riding was the only place where I was still – and it was uncomplicated, me and my pony were able to connect without speaking. I became addicted to that adrenalin and freedom."

She speaks of horses as her partners: "I am not racing for me, I am racing for them; what they say goes. I put in a suggestion every now and then, but they have the last say, for we are in it together. If they decide one thing and I decide another, that is when it falls apart." Every race provides information, no matter where she finishes, but "Second is always second." Like Frodon, Bryony is gutsy and never-say-die. They followed up their King George victory with success in the Ladbroke Champion Chase at Down Royal in October 2021, beating that year's Gold Cup winner, Minella Indo.

She is also philosophical, aware that jockeys are not indestructible. "All of us have our down days and up days; we are riding a wave and it can't always stay smooth; currents change against you. When that happens, you have to keep trying to paddle against them. If you do keep paddling, then, before you know it, the current will change, you will swing round again, and start to find things become easier."

That philosophy was seriously tested in 2021 by the long delay in the BHA dealing with her complaints about the way she had allegedly been treated by a jockey in the weighing room. She was sanguine, saying that she had taught herself to recognise and hold on to positivity more than negativity. The best way to keep holding on to that was to ride winners.

Lizzie Kelly was the first female jockey to win a Grade One chase, at Kempton, on Tea For Two in 2015. On the same horse she became the second female jockey to ride in the Cheltenham Gold Cup. They teamed up for a famous win in the Betway Bowl, at Aintree, seeing off the redoubtable Cue Card in a thrilling finish. Lucy Alexander, Scotland's only female jump jockey, made a name for herself riding winners, and not just in Scotland. She retired after suffering a broken back at the end of 2020, having been the first woman to be Champion Conditional, raising expectations about what could be achieved. She broke Lorna Vincent's 32-year record for wins in a season, and was Britain's most successful female jockey for several years, until passed by Bryony in the month after her final ride; she fell and was kicked by one of the other runners, which resulted in a fracture to her L3 vertebra. Metal rods were inserted into her back, and she recuperated at Jack Berry House. But, having realised that she had been side-lined through injury every three to six months for three years, on breaking her collarbone again, she decided to retire and take up a job as Andrew Balding's racing manager at his powerful Kingsclere Stables. One day, she may well take up her father, Nick's, training yard.

But it is Rachael Blackmore, the most successful female jockey at Grade One level with ten wins, who is now re-writing the record books. The daughter of a dairy farmer and a music teacher in County Tipperary, on her 12-2 pony Bubbles, "keen and strong," she revelled in Pony Club games (what Ruby Walsh has termed "lunacy on ponies") and would gallop him before hunting to take the pep out of him. She had her first win in a pony race at Cork, beating a young Paul Townend, a memory that still thrills. Paul was just 13, and promptly graduated from pony racing tyrant to track sensation. Rachael took the scenic route, but even then speed was her addiction; it had given her the taste. She thought of training as a vet, but ended up studying equine science at Limerick (she is self-deprecating about trying "every university course on the Emerald Isle," and saw that education as "a safety net until real life set in.") She rode as an amateur, competed in over 200 point-to-points, learning all the time, riding more finishes, going a whole summer without a winner, and at 25, when she thought it time to get a job, turned professional – the first female to do so since Maria Cullen in the 1980s: "Riding as an amateur was not a career." In 2017, she made history in Ireland as the first female to win the Conditional Jockeys' championship.

Since then, her rise through the ranks has been meteoric – her Grand National victory was 77 years after *National Velvet*, where Elizabeth Taylor wins the race on celluloid, and with the Champion Hurdle, and then the Gold Cup of 2022, Rachael had arrived. Nonetheless, a jockey will always be riding on the edge: falls and injuries will happen. "But, you can't think about that. If you start thinking about what could go wrong, this is not the job for you," and she is realistic, "A jockey does not just rock up for the glory of the day." After some success in 2021, she took a fall in the summer, but, to no-one's surprise, she was back in the saddle sooner than the medics had predicted.

Luke McManus has made a film, *Jump Girls*, about female jump jockeys. "You start off making this film about women in racing, but, because they don't really dwell on the fact they are women, you realise you are actually making a film about families, and the love of the sport, and the love all these people have for each other." The film, made in Ireland, has gone down well, McManus saying, "The culture in Ireland is don't be drawing too much attention to yourself, swaggering around and thinking you are great. In England, people seem to be perfectly happy doing that." Rachael Blackmore is not.

Writing a fine piece after the Cheltenham Festival in 2021, Richard Forristal paid tribute to her down-to-earth character: "She never dreamed or talked big: instead, she focused all her energy on doing and learning. That's the lesson she imparts, no concessions, no limits, just endeavour. In a race, she knows what everyone else is doing; horses run and jump for her ruthless instinct; she has her rivals where she wants them and, having ridden herself into the position she is in now, she is the full package."

Ruby Walsh agreed: "It's the grit, determination and hunger I admire most in her." In addition to her tactical nous, and a level of resilience, that sets her apart in a gruelling profession, she gives great feedback to trainers and owners after the race, and she inspires trust. Despite being box office gold, she is a pragmatist: "The more defeats you have, the more you deal with them," but choosing the wrong horse hurts, as it did in 2021 when she rejected regular partner Minella Indo for the Gold Cup in favour of stablemate A Plus Tard, only to see the former romp up the Cheltenham hill ahead of her to seize the spoils. "Choosing the wrong horse is deflating. Is there a word in the dictionary for that feeling?" Such a searching question is typical.

Shark Hanlon, perhaps the first trainer to spot her talent, said she is always a bad loser; she might never say a word, but she is tough on herself when she gets beaten, and only by choosing well has she earned the trust of high-profile trainers and owners. Alastair Down sung her praises after her Champion Hurdle victory; it was a "stirring and emotional sight to see a woman returning to the unsaddling enclosure after an undoubtedly historic triumph." To him, she is a lioness "with manners you could photograph." Despite becoming an A-lister, earning the world's (and not just the racing world's) attention on merit, she remains self-effacing. "I don't set massive goals for the future: racing is very unpredictable, so I take it week by week." Most of all, she wants just to be a jockey. Ruby Walsh has said, "Everyone has a moment; she has seized hers. Every experience in life is a lesson, and Rachael has learned many. Her ruthless instinct shows most people only see the finish, but 95% of races are won and lost long before you turn in. Rachael has a lot of her races won early." Chris Cook has commended her tactical acumen, executed in, "a wholly merciless way. She swipes every advantage she can keep for herself, thereby denying it to her opponents. There is nothing soft in her sporting soul."

Rachael acknowledges: "The achievements of Katie Walsh and Nina Carberry allowed me to go into a weighing room, into racing, once a man's world exclusively, where the stigma was gone. It is a privilege to be part of that industry, when you are given opportunities on your ability, and that is improving the whole time." She is not just in the vanguard, she *is* the vanguard for opening up the idea of professional jockey as a life aspiration for young women everywhere. In 2022, at Cheltenham, Rachael responded to pressure and huge expectation with typical dash and panache – her win on Honeysuckle for the second year running in the Champion Hurdle beat Frankel's record of fourteen consecutive wins. Henry de Bromhead said of Honeysuckle, "She is a freak, in my opinion, as regards ability and soundness, she turns up every time." The pair turned for home to a tidal roar rolling down the straight at Cheltenham, and three days later after their victory in the Gold Cup, Rachael and A Plus Tard received an even more rapturous reception. Vanquished on the horse the previous year - about which she had beaten herself up – by a horse sharing the same address as A Plus Tard - this time in that race the partnership was almost hidden for six minutes. She saved her energy and kept her powder dry until the last fence, then lit the fuse and A Plus Tard sprinted up the famous, draining hill, to win by a record margin of fifteen lengths. A little dervish in the saddle, her daring ride avenged the previous defeat with aplomb. Not panicking, having her opponents covered, waiting for a gap and pinging like an elastic band, she orchestrated a coveted win in front of a full house. The next day, she won the 4:37 at Thurles, her local track. She had grown up in Killenaule, twenty kilometres away, and had her first win there in 2011 on Stowaway Pearl, for Shark Hanlon.

With the oppressive presence of Covid and political instability across the world, Rachael's Gold Cup win gave everyone a lift. Ruby Walsh praised her technical ride, her decision to avoid the safe option and go bravely down the inside. Paul Hayward lauded her human stardust for a high-grade equine pageant, and *Racing Post* was inspired by "her racing brain, coolness and confidence, an inspiration to women, not just in racing, but in all sport, and in society." Rachael's return to the winners' enclosure was memorable, so different from 2021, during Covid sparsity, when people could hear their own claps echo. She was a ray of sunshine, which left her, the unassuming jockey, "wishing I had the English vocabulary to explain the reception I got."

Henry de Bromhead said, "She is just so tough. Races are there to be won, she wins them, she is a big race rider who can produce the goods on big days when it matters most, as she did on A Plus Tard in the Betfair Chase in 2021. She doesn't believe in fuss, and there is only one thing that matters; winning

– it doesn't matter how it is achieved. Rachael Blackmore is the poster girl, breaking boundaries for women everywhere she goes, she just wants to be the best, male or female."

Well before the Cheltenham Festival of 2023, Henry de Bromhead announced that his wondermare, Honeysuckle, and pilot Rachael Blackmore, would contest the Mares' Hurdle, not the Champion; the way in which Constitution Hill won that race with a stratospheric performance, and Honeysuckle's own bravura performance forty minutes later in the Mares' Hurdle vindicated that decision. With Honeysuckle's jockey "in her pomp," proving yet again no-truck determination and tactical acumen, the pair romped home that intoxicating afternoon to scenes of emotion perhaps never before seen at Cheltenham. Photos captured Henry punching the air. A crowd who'd just watched Constitution Hill blitz his rivals, poured into the winners' enclosure in scenes of unforgettable recognition and tribute. Racing embraced the horse and team; they had taken their final bow in a stellar career. 'Honey' secured her fairytale ending; her jockey had shone again: "She is a different ball-game," wrote one journalist, while another said, "It is a treat to share the same orbit as Rachael Blackmore." After the tragic loss of trainer Henry de Bromhead's son, Jack, killed in a race on an Irish beach six months before, this was not just a glorious victory, but a much-needed one, brave, redemptive and much more.

The 2023 Mares' Novice Hurdle was named in honour of Jack. In the race before it Henry, the bereaved father, prepared Envoi Allen to win the Ryanair Chase, again partnered by Rachael: it was a brilliant training performance. Henry had entered several for the race named after his son, and brought a troop of Jack's friends and cousins for the occasion; his Magical Zoe ran an honourable second, and the full de Bromhead team presented the prizes; it was a private tragedy made public, a huge tide of goodwill dowsing the grief. It caused Henry to say: "This is a massive day for us, a day to celebrate Jack's unfortunately very short life. We're so lucky. The support we get is ridiculous. There are so many people in our situation who don't see this support." Henry had been looking for a rainbow: "Maybe there's one starting up there just now." Sometimes, racing transcends sport for something better, something beyond just a horse race.

Enhanced by The Lionesses' success in the 2022 European Cup and 2023 World Cup, there is an increased, and still increasing, appetite in society for women's professional sport; there has been a sea-change here, and thanks to the aforementioned jockeys, a woman booting home the winner of a major race is no longer extraordinary. Ted Walsh has famously claimed, "Women are stronger than men, mentally." Regardless of gender, a jockey has to work exceptionally hard, competing in what is arguably the most life-encompassing sport, involving human, beast, nature and money. National Hunt racing is exciting and risky; it always demands maximum effort, both physical and mental, as men and women go head-to-head in the sport; women have, at last, the opportunities to compete on equal terms; the world is better for it.

CHAPTER 12: COMING SECOND - AND NOT GIVING UP

"In whose world is second enough?"

- Rachael Blackmore -

"No-one remembers who came second." Or do they? It is not easy to forget the huge Australian chaser, Crisp, weighing 700 kg, 17.2 hands tall, and strong with it, who led the Grand National field under Richard Pitman for all but the very last yard of the race in 1973, only to be collared by Red Rum, the first of his three victories in the race, which has added to Crisp's place in the pantheon, as well as 'Rummy's'. Some have argued the race would not have been so memorable if Crisp had won.

The finish of that race is played over many times on TV; its allure still captivates, and its iconic status was boosted by the fact that Red Rum was to become the noblest Aintree specialist of all time. In defeat, Crisp, a handsome horse, nicknamed in his home country the 'Black Kangaroo', gave the greatest display of jumping ever seen at Aintree. Flown to the northern hemisphere via America, where he had finished fifth in the Colonial Cup, his journey had taken its toll. When he reached Lambourn, jockey Richard Pitman described Crisp as "an enormous hairy hat-rack," the shell of a racehorse, but Fred Winter noted the depth of his chest, "He must have a big heart in there." When stable lad 'Chipper' Chape, who had come over with the horse, tried to clip him, Crisp went berserk: only a tranquiliser used on elephants and rhinos managed to calm him.

Training muscled the horse - he came to look magnificent — and won the 1971 Champion Chase at Cheltenham by 25 lengths. Come the 1973 Grand National, burdened with the top-weight of 12-stone, enough to sink a battleship, he was co-favourite with Red Rum. Crisp jumped like a stag, going at his fences as if he wanted to devour them, and sailing over open ditches with utter contempt. Richard recalls what happened next: "I found we were 25 lengths clear, the noise of my pursuers diminishing until I was quite alone. The silence was eerie."

But Crisp was a two-miler, and, although still running well, with his legs flicking out in front of him, "With two fences to go, I felt his action change slightly. Approaching the final fence, I caught the sounds of a pursuer... the flapping of nostrils as he forced each breath out of his lungs, joined by the drumming of hooves on firm ground. It was like a childhood nightmare of walking through treacle. Crisp popped over the last, but no longer had the strength to shoot away from it. Instead, his tired limbs carried his welter burden towards the winning post at only half his previous speed. The run-in between the last fence and victory is 494 yards, the most agonising I ever had to travel. My aching limbs had given their best, and every breath I snatched scalded my windpipe as if it was boiling water. The horse's light, forward action was now laboured and sideways, as if he was drunk. The tell-tale noises were close, but so was the winning post, or was it? It almost seemed as if it was moving further away with each stride. With only 15 yards to go, Crisp tightened as he felt Red Rum's presence, but it was his dying effort and only lasted for a second: he had got to the bottom of the barrel, exhausted; two strides from the post, Red Rum's head forged past my gallant partner to snatch victory from our grasp." Fred Winter was magnanimous in defeat: "Well, we nearly did it," he consoled his jockey.

The time of the race broke Golden Miller's record by no less than 19 seconds, a record that had stood for 39 years. Crisp had given Red Rum 25 pounds in weight, the equivalent of 25 lengths. With his typical understatement, Richard said that Crisp had lost nothing in defeat, and his jockey, who had gone from elation to desolation in those final two strides, only to find elation returned almost immediately, had enjoyed the best moments of his life, an experience money could not buy, which would last him to his grave. The Aussie champion never had the chance to go back to Aintree for revenge. The two horses did meet again – in a match at Doncaster – Crisp beat Red Rum by ten lengths, but broke down doing so. Crisp was perhaps the better horse; Red Rum was the legend.

Richard Pitman knew all about coming second: he was runner up again in the Grand National, in two Cheltenham Gold Cups and twice in the Jockeys' Championship. Pendil showed him how to cope with second place. The horse, though small, with legs like glass and two half-inch horns on his head, was a natural. He won 11 races in a row, clocking 42 mph at Chepstow, and he also beat crack two-miler Tingle Creek. Coming home from exercise, he would goose-step, a distinct character, who later became mean, as some great racehorses do. The best steeplechasers live on the edge – as do their riders. In 1973 Pendil was favourite for the Cheltenham Gold Cup; Richard and Fulke Walwyn had been through every scenario beforehand: Pendil jumped the last in front, but "curled up" under Richard, and lost by a short head to The Dikler. Did the crowd noise get to him as it had to Devon Loch in 1956?

In 1974 Pendil was again the Gold Cup favourite, but, unbeknownst to the public, his stable had received a threat: the horse would be shot if he hit the front. His lad, Vince 'Clogger' Brookes, told Richard to get the horse withdrawn at the start. The jockey did not. As the race approached its climax, Pendil, who had never fallen in his life, was brought down by High Ken: it looked a tripwire fall as the horse went down so fast. Vince thought the threat had been carried out, and his horse had indeed been shot.

In sport, there are heroic seconds all the time: in jump racing, perhaps because its protagonists compete for several seasons and can become household names, continually giving of their best in this hazardous occupation, runners-up are revered and remembered. Scottish-trained Wyndburgh finished runner-up in the Grand National on three occasions, most famously in 1959, when his jockey, Tim Brookshaw, whose stirrup irons broke at Becher's second time round, kicked the other foot free and ploughed on to be second behind Oxo, ridden by Michael Scudamore. Another Scottish horse, the Reg Tweedie-trained Freddie, who had come within a whisker of beating Arkle in the 1965 Hennessy Gold Cup, was second twice. In 1981, hunter-chaser Spartan Missile and his gutsy owner, breeder John Thorne, was second to Bob Champion on Aldaniti. Richie McLernon, on Sunnyhill Boy, lost out by a nose to Neptune Collonges in 2012, making him the man who has come closest of all to winning the great race. Just a few of us remember Black Apalachi's bold run behind Tony McCoy's long-awaited victory at his 15th attempt on Synchronised in 2010.

Amongst the jockeys, Richard 'Dicky' Johnson was 16 times runner up to AP McCoy in the Jockeys' Championship, always chasing the dragon, but, having been Champion Jockey four times since, he has the second greatest number of jump victories of all time. His attitude, energies, level of professionalism and ever-increasing depth of endeavour were inspirational. He would concur with the notion that champions realise defeat – and learning from it, perhaps even more than winning – is part of the path to mastery. So, second need not be a defeat: it can be a stimulation to get better, increasing a jockey's determination. Finishing second is very different to settling for second best. Endeavour is what matters most, as Michelangelo realised: "The greater danger for most of us lies not in our setting our aim too high, and falling short, but in setting our aim too low, and achieving our mark." We need to do our own reckoning in a world where so much is decided for us. For a jockey, this means never giving up, and the example of Dicky Johnson stands alone.

He left school in Hereford at 16 to work for David 'the Duke' Nicholson, "maker of horses, maker of men," a man who did not suffer fools, at Condicote, Gloucestershire. Two years later, the Herefordshire lad was Champion Conditional. The only thing he ever wanted was to be Champion Jockey – "the pinnacle," which was made a much more demanding target for him to achieve by the presence of one AP McCoy: Champion Jockey for a staggering 20 seasons. Being runner-up so often was not easy. For the first few years Dicky was disappointed and annoyed with himself. But, more than anything else, he was frustrated. As the years passed, and with a lot of work, plus family support, he changed his mindset. When Nicholson hung up his training boots, the jockey moved to Philip Hobbs, outside Minehead; he remained there. "Loyalty, trust and reliability," said his farewell tribute in the *Racing Post*, "may be unfashionable concepts in modern sport, but Dicky Johnson still proved his value, day in, day out."

For all his rivalry with AP, Dicky's resolve took on some of the perennial champion's fastidious preparation and depth of thinking, hardly surprising when for 20-plus years they had sat next to each other in the weighing room at least five days a week. With cheating and corruption prevalent in 21st century sports, their fierce rivalry was once described as having "a touching nobility" to it, for its mutual generosity of spirit. When AP retired at Sandown in April 2015, the permanent understudy, who by a lovely touch of irony won AP's last race, Dicky Johnson was choked.

But the understudy very soon assumed the lead role, having inherited AP's steadfast drive for numbers; he once confessed that he missed AP "in a weird way," but was "delighted he was not there." By dint of his ultra-reliable, relentless commitment, and, despite a broken leg, pelvis twice, cheekbone twice, thumb, foot and countless ribs, he finally became Champion Jockey the year after AP's retirement, and again for the next three seasons, only yielding to Brian Hughes in the Covid-interrupted 2020 season.

The Herefordshire man had the ability to just get on with it, and not feel frustrated by losers: "However bad my day had been, someone had had it worse." Always aware of his responsibility to racing, he carried that responsibility with distinction. He had an extraordinary work ethic, joking, "If Philip Hobbs had a runner on the moon, I would go there." The notion of giving up never entered his head: he was tireless and fearless; like one of his most famous partners, the grey, Rooster Booster, who eventually won the Champion Hurdle after a series of valiant near-misses. There is little time for celebration in a jockey's life: even on becoming champion, he was always onto the next race, admitting, "It's a treadmill I was very happy to be on, and I didn't want to get off."

Another jockey who used coming second as an inspiration rather than a defeat is Brian Hughes. In the 2020 to 2021 season, the final few weeks had seen a titanic struggle between Brian Hughes, top rider in the north, and Harry Skelton, in their bid to be crowned Champion Jockey. Harry had by far the greater horsepower – but Brian, the reigning champion, put up a Herculean effort to defend his title. The *Racing Post* said it was testament to Brian's determination and graft that his contribution to the battle will not be forgotten. For so long he led the way, but, try as he might to stop the floodgates from opening, there was no answer to the Skelton surge in the closing weeks. The tussle went to the wire, but when the season ended Brian was just beaten. Harry had so much more ammunition at his disposal: as Donald McCain said, "It became a David vs Goliath battle – in this case, Goliath won." Brian was to gain sweet revenge in 2021-22.

David Bass had loved the Grand National since the age of 6: his dad would come in for the race, draw the curtains and take the phone off the hook. Encouraged by his father, David decided to be a jockey aged 16, after a trip to Stratford with his grandfather. Having done work experience with permit-trainer Clarissa Caroe, David was taught to ride at the British Racing School. He spent time as conditional with Richard Phillips, alongside Richard Dunwoody and Sean Quinlan, and then moved on to John 'Mad' Manners, one of the sport's great eccentrics, who gave him crucial opportunities, including his first point-to-point win on Man From Highworth, and his first win under rules, on the same horse, beating AP McCoy into second. David went on to Nicky Henderson, joining Nico de Boinville, Jerry McGrath, Andrew Tinkler and Richard Killoran at Seven Barrows. With Barry Geraghty, the stable number one, it was a golden age for jockeys in that yard, and there were "loads of good horses." David partnered Sprinter Sacre when the star chaser made a winning debut over fences at Doncaster.

A spare ride for Kim Brailey was a winning one. Bailey had trained the winner of the 1990 Grand National, Mr. Frisk, who set a course record; the Gold Cup with Master Oats in 1995, and the Champion Hurdle that same year with Alderbrook. David accepted the offer to become stable jockey for Bailey, a move that, for him, felt "just the right thing."

In 2016, the pair saddled The Last Samuri, "a great little horse," for the Grand National. The jockey had said beforehand, "It's such a hard race just to get into. To have a ride in the race is good. To have a ride with a good chance is brilliant." On the day, they were sent off joint-favourite. After running courageously throughout, The Last Samuri and Vic's Canvas jumped the last fence together, David's horse battling on at the elbow, but he couldn't quite hold off the strong-finishing Rule The World, a 100-1 shot who was winning for the first time over fences, and never won again. Having finished runner-up, David went over the race countless times, berating himself for not winning. That defeat wore him down. But he now has a different view: not winning the race started to give him a different, more healthy mind-set, and thus change his life: winning it would not have done that; it would have reinforced his ego, not a good thing for him, as he explains later in this book.

There have been numerous statements about filling the second spot; some of them damning, ranging from "Second is always second," "Second is the most difficult place to finish," and "Coming second means you are the first person to lose," through to "There is no such thing as second, either you are first or you are nothing." But, perhaps there is an art in coming second. No-one can deny it is a difficult position to be in: you train to win. No-one trains to come second. It is all the more painful if victory has often been – or seemed – within reach, which renders the chasm between winning and second far wider than any other placing. But while the racing public can celebrate their horse coming second (betting each way), seeing it mark a fantastic effort in a high-profile, ultra-competitive race to outrun its odds, and outrank worthy opponents, for the professional jockey, second is never easy, in many cases never acceptable. While the British psyche is often happy to embrace second - we have had to get used to it down the years - for a jockey, there is no such thing as a glorious failure. In a sport where winning is paramount every day of the week, Mick Fitzgerald has said that winning is everything, hence coming in second is not even an option for a top jockey: "You never accept it as fatal or final... keep hustling until you come first." Long gone are the amateur days of "play up and play the game," and the Olympic ideal: "It's not the winning, it's the taking part."

To compare finishing runner-up to winning is impossible. Adrian Maguire was never Champion Jockey, but he is remembered, still recognised as a very fine jockey, who kept trying and never gave up. To be in a position to become champion means you must have had wins all along the way, wins large and small. As Tom Scudamore asserts: "We have to play the hand we get dealt." To make the best of this hand can hardly be termed a 'failure', however much a jockey might reckon they have not succeeded to the extent that, or in the way that, they would have wished. Too many people live to dictionary definitions of winning or losing: it is never that simple.

CHAPTER 13: TRAINERS

*"It is not the great trainer who can cause his horse to perform:
the great trainer can cause his horse to want to perform."*

- Monty Roberts, American Trainer and Horse Whisperer -

In the frayed and dusty tapestry of the trainer's life, days never end: they start early and roll on from one thing to the next. Trainers have to possess not just the expert eye for training each individual horse, but strong interpersonal skills to manage people, and keep ambition and morale at the highest, especially in the cold, dark days of winter. They also have to steer their jockeys in the right direction, where hopefully luck, judgement and circumstance will combine. Many trainer/jockey combinations endure throughout a career, like Philip Hobbs and Richard Johnson, the Pipes and the Scudamores, Fergal O'Brien and Paddy Brennan. What is needed above all from the trainer and the jockey is consistency: "Keep turning up for work," says Paddy, "who knows what the end result might be? Horses give you massive hope in the morning."

It is not easy to become, and remain a trainer these days. In England Paul Nicholls, Nicky Henderson and Dan Skelton have huge strings, whilst Ireland boasts Willie Mullins, Gordon Elliott and Henry De Bromhead as its powerhouse triumvirate. Facilities there are state of the art, with swimming pools, spa–solariums, indoor schools, treadmills, horse-walkers, saunas, schooling fields and all manner of gallops for all weathers. With jump racing dominated by this little group of huge yards, opportunities for the smaller stables to make an imprint at top table are about as scarce as the Sumatran rhino, but it can happen – as Coneygree proved in the 2015 Cheltenham Gold Cup – and the game is much more appealing because of it.

Coneygree was the novice, the underdog in the 2015 blue riband of chasing. His rise from cheaply produced, gangly foal to brilliant Gold Cup winner was a terrific story. The horse was bred by John Oaksey, trained by son-in-law Mark Bradstock, and owned by a syndicate led by Chicky, John's wife. The horse's dam, Plaid Maid produced 2011 Hennessy Gold Cup hero, Carruthers. Coneygree himself was fragile, prone to injuries and had spent long spells on the sidelines. But he won three chases with his powerful, front-running style, and the Bradstocks chose as their Cheltenham goal the Gold Cup rather than the Champion Novice Chase, ignoring criticism for their choice: "He was always there to race, and that was all." In the event, Coneygree set a searching gallop under novice jockey Nico de Boinville, jumped superbly, and held off every challenge to win, proving himself a chaser of the highest order. When he stopped racing he continued to be treated like royalty, as his owners had put a bit of their prize money into this retirement fund.

Many trainers are the next line in a racing dynasty, like Willie Mullins, based at Bagenalstown, County Carlow, Ireland, Champion Trainer for the last seventeen seasons. The son of Paddy Mullins, trainer of Dawn Run, the only horse – yet – to win both the Champion Hurdle and the Gold Cup, Willie, with an apparently endless conveyor belt of talent at his disposal, continues to push back the boundaries. Affable when interviewed, he knows his horses and how to prioritise their needs: "They are given all the time they need." Few trainers are so deeply in tune with their horses. Paying minute attention to detail, Mullins claims his greatest asset is his staff: "They all know what they're meant to do, and how to do it."

Before he started training in 1988, he was assistant to his father, and to Jim Bolger, the flat trainer, where he saw racing from a different angle. He learned a lot in France from Guillaume Macaire, and was an amateur jockey, winning at the Cheltenham Festival. Now training, he has won the Gold Cup, the Grand National, the Champion Chase, the Champion Hurdle and all the big races. He is regarded as the master of mares, and has the unique ability to get a horse primed to win a highly competitive race despite a lengthy absence.

His Quevega won at six successive Cheltenham Festivals, with rarely a race in between.

Above all, he enjoys training, though he admits: "The whole game has changed." He is always seeking improvement, keeping his horses enthused, healthy and focussed, tempering hard work with soft, knowing what a very fine line he must keep so as not to overwork them. "He trains off his eye," says son Patrick. "Decisions, often made at the eleventh hour, are hard to take sometimes, but he has the very annoying habit of being right." Yet being the most successful trainer in the history of the Cheltenham Festival (103 not out) has its drawbacks: "It's always in the back of your mind that we could have a blowout at Cheltenham: everyone else's expectation is going to be your failure, and that leaves a certain dread in your stomach." With Ruby Walsh, son Patrick, assistant trainer David Casey and stable jockey Paul Townend, there is much sharing of opinion ("It's mental!") and Willie listens to them all: then he will inevitably go with his gut feeling. That way, when things go wrong, the buck stops with him: "Absolutely everything is done on instinct," and that fear of failure drives him on to succeed. At the 2024 Dublin Racing Festival, Willie Mullins won all eight Grade 1s, not always with his 'first-strings': he is unafraid of his horses racing each other.

But few trainers have the backing, facilities, cash and acumen as the master of Closutton, County Carlow. The North Yorkshire-based trainer Mike Sowersby (64) revealed in October 2021 that he had suffered a breakdown earlier that year, during which he "didn't want to live" and felt "not worthy" when overwhelmed by an 847-day wait for a winner. That winner came at Hexham, followed by another at Sedgefield. Sowersby said: "I thought it was never going to happen – I was in a mess. Luckily the NTF (National Trainers Federation) got to know and they helped me. People say 'Ring me', but when you're feeling bad, that's the last thing you do, and you don't go looking for help. You feel so low."

He had his best season in 2015-2016, recording ten winners, but enjoyed only a single success in 2019-20, and a total blank from 56 runners in 2020-2021. When opening up about his dire straits, he had ten horses in his charge, many of which ran in his colours. "People expect you to provide a service and I felt I wasn't. I'd got owners, but I daren't send them bills as

I didn't feel I was giving them good enough service. I had horses to sell, but daren't sell them as I felt they weren't going well enough. I used to train horses all right. My horses now probably aren't good enough, but I love them."

After Sowersby had bravely spoken out about his mental health struggles, Rupert Arnold, then CEO of the NTF, confirmed that his organisation was working closely with Racing Welfare to introduce a more structured support system for trainers. Arnold was well aware not everyone finds themselves able to speak out, and he acknowledged that Sowersby's case was much more about a man being rescued by friends, community and other trainers asking how best to support the Yorkshireman. There was no formalised structure in place, but a project was in the pipeline to help understand the relentless nature of the racing calendar and animal husbandry, combined with the pressures of running a small business which "is a perfect storm for stress and pressure." Trainers come into regular contact with trained people in mental health, who are looking out for them, and can often help. You cannot beat talking to people directly.

Among multiple trainers in between the polar extremes of Mullins and Sowersby is Matt Sheppard, who has lived and trained on the expansive Eastnor estate near Ledbury for 28 years. His story is currently being told in his book *Slow Two-Miler*, an honest, illuminating read. He worked for such racing luminaries as Arthur Moore in County Kildare and Mercy Rimell at Kinnersley, and had a stint at Sun Valley chicken factory in Hereford, before working his way through fifteen wins in point-to-points, "that bastion of rural life," whose heyday was the eighties and nineties and now, perhaps, needs a shot in the arm. Having built his own stables, and maintaining them himself, his is the voice of a racehorse trainer who perseveres no matter what. Success to him is staying in business and keeping enough of a reputation to carry on training. Working with animals, he knows every day is "a school day" in his attempt to handle the unpredictability of his profession. Most of the horses in his care (he can have 15-25) are second-hand, though he has handled good horses like Seek the Faith, Rock on Rocky and The Bay Birch, and he still finds it satisfying to train a moderate animal "to win a race for nice owners and see them smile."

At 50, he thought he would be lucky still to be in business at 55; a new influx of horses and owners has enabled that to happen, and as one of Britain's six hundred trainers, he still relishes his job, for all its vicissitudes. But he is well aware racing is geared towards the big man, and he can be excused for feeling jaded at times, even baffled as to why, despite hard, honest toil, his career has not really taken off, and he has not attracted the big owners. The worst time he cites as foot-and-mouth and three years' bad luck, which was hard to climb out of, until he was rescued by one good owner (other owners can come from Hades). But he knows his trade, has won 200 races, enjoys training, having known nothing else, and does not shy from its perennial challenge – to keep up momentum.

His horses are invariably ridden by son Stan, though he also uses under-the-radar jockeys not attached to a big yard, accepting that the whole jockey landscape has been changed by the emergence of agents. He believes mentoring his stable staff is crucial, treating them as equals, and acknowledges that some trainers have five minutes of fame, then disappear. He takes a pride in showing the different gallops he can use at Eastnor, but is concerned that in racing, gambling has become more important than the horse, an industry, rather than a sport. It is refreshing to meet a Grimthorpe race-winning trainer so down-to-earth, who is always trying his best, accepts that in racing he'll always be questioned, sometimes blamed, and still reckons a good day in his job is second to none. His self-deprecating candour reaches its zenith when he claims he is himself "the ultimate slow two-miler…"

Martin Pipe bestrode the world of jump racing. He took much of the guesswork out of training, and was a meticulous creature of habit, many of whose horses made the running, and stayed in front to the finish. A self-taught puzzle-solver, he revolutionised the training of race horses because he knew his job and his charges. The first to exploit internal training, he weighed horses regularly, took their blood, and kept them lean during the season. He had his horses fitter than anyone else's, and put them into the right races. "It was just common sense, really; doing the simple things well." With 4,183 winners to his name, he is the most successful trainer in jump racing history, associated with several Champion Jockeys, including Peter Scudamore. It was said at the zenith of their fortunes: "None can claim to have cut such a swathe through racing's centuries-old idyll as Pipe and Scudamore, who arrived like an act of God in the closing years of the 1980s."

Richard Phillips is the youngest of five lads in a family that had not much money and no racing connections, though he had spent time around horses since the age of nine. In his teens he was headed for the priesthood, but then his father died: the man had been a civil servant, who did not enjoy his chosen profession; Richard decided to make work - training racehorses - his passion.

Bonhomme, entertainer, wit, impressionist and wonderfully dismissive of political correctness, he comes from a line of teachers: "Failed teachers become trainers," he jests, but his words are well chosen. They are disarmingly philosophical. He has always likened the role of trainer to that of Headmaster: owners the parents, jockeys the teachers, horses the pupils. Both professions demand getting the best out of all the charges in their care, preparing them for the future, whatever that may be, nurturing them through thick and thin.

On the notion of winning he asks a lot of questions: "Who determines winning? Who is a winner, and to whom? How much does it matter? How is winning measured?" He is refreshingly adamant in his view that it is not measured by what other people think. Never a man to say it other than it is, he continues the school master parallel: "The Headmaster of Eton's kids gain A-stars – they are bred to pass exams; the Headmaster of Brixton Comprehensive's charges, many of them from broken homes surrounded by problems, notch up a cluster of C-grades: who is to say which is the greater achievement? The only measure is a personal one within your own circle of life." The world in general, and the sporting world in particular, might well contest this claim. Jockeys in their championship are rated on the number of winners they partner, not on the amount of prize money won, as is the case with trainers.

Good trainers, like good jockeys, need so many facets to succeed, of which luck is perhaps paramount. Then comes determination. Richard quotes the example of Brendan Powell, who won the 1987 Grand National on Rhyme 'N' Reason: in the days before jockeys' agents, Brendan would ring every trainer he knew to try and accelerate his career – if it was running, he'd ride it – and build a platform from which to succeed, as he did particularly with Dublin Flyer.

"Everyone, trainer or jockey, has their own style, sets the parameters for themselves: is that winning?" wonders Richard. "As long as it looks like success, it will be. Winning horses make for happy owners: how happy? And what of the jockey who makes the most of his perhaps limited gifts and does O.K.? Is he a success? What about the jockey who has a thousand wins and comes out in a wheelchair? The only person who can measure it is the person themselves. Most of the general public know very little about racing. They've read a Dick Francis novel, they bet on the Grand National, they join in the office sweepstake, but have no knowledge of the sport's complexity, its intrigue, fascination, challenges and underbelly, perhaps sharing the view that the sport is a crucible of chicanery. They will only judge from racing headlines, tipsters, and increasingly, of course, online persuasion (some would say compulsion.)

"Smaller, lesser known trainers can be satisfied with small wins. They've done as well as big trainers with the best horses, but the public won't be aware of that. If a horse goes lame, is it the trainer's fault? It could be, but it may not. There is so much that cannot be known by a trainer, which stresses the importance of instinct, essential for them to be good buyers of horses in the first place."

Richard spent a year at Jackdaws Castle above the Cotswold village of Ford, home to the Plough Inn, now the training base of Jonjo O'Neill, under the patronage of JP McManus, whose green and gold silks have reaped success unimaginable across the courses of Britain and Ireland. "Having the use of these state of the art facilities was like managing Manchester United; it was a game-changer. I had a Cheltenham Festival favourite." Now he trains out of Adlestrop, the village made famous by Edward Thomas's poem of that name, written in the hot summer of 1914, a paean to the calm serenity of the English rural landscape that would never be the same again.

His horses are clearly happy, he has the ability to connect with all sorts of people, not least his owners – "very interesting folk" – several of whom he takes with him to France to look for horses to buy. He is a realist, does a lot of charity work, not least for prostate cancer, about which he is self-effacing – "I am not that nice" – and had a part-time career as an impressionist, even plying that trade at the House of Commons (though for a racing dinner, alas, not in the chamber itself).

To be a winning trainer: "You need courage, strength, determination. You might have to have a leg up, metaphorically, you have to keep going.

You don't complain. You make your own mind up about things. You have to acknowledge there is always somebody worse off than you…" He pauses to mention Sharron Murgatroyd, paralysed in a fall at Bangor in 1991 and author of four books including *Jump Jockeys Don't Cry*, which he found inspirational: "Her suffering makes our lives a success. And you have to have three things to fall back on: faith, family and friends."

Richard is ultra-competitive, not least in quizzes. He may not be the best trainer – whatever that means – but he's done O.K. He is certainly the best entertainer of owners. He believes trainers should make the most of their gifts, acknowledging they work hard for a very long time. Back in the day, comparatively few retired, but in 2024 he knows their numbers are dwindling as costs soar upwards, and bigger trainers hold the market. But horses, he claims, are always something to get up for. His parting words come from Churchill, and are on his desk: "Success is not final, failure is not fatal: it is the courage to continue that counts."

In 2019, Richard Phillips had the idea of annually celebrating the racehorse, and giving the world a chance to see first-hand the love, care and attention that goes into looking after horses. Training yards, studs and after-care centres up and down the land open their doors to showcase the fantastic animals and the lives they lead. The importance and the impact of this initiative is growing every year. National Racehorse Week shows the importance of the animals at the heart of racing. But the public needs to trust that the sport does the right thing throughout the lifetime of all horses bred to run. The 70-75,000 thoroughbreds in Britain make up 8% of all the horses in this country. Of the 30-35,000 retired, we have good data on 12,000 – but what of the others? *A Life Well Lived* is the Horse Welfare Board's strategy for a drastic improvement in this situation.

For a long time one of the top trainers in the North, Nicky Richards knows racing is a cut-throat game, particularly for jockeys sitting at home injured, watching someone else ride their horse. "Jockeys and trainers go out of fashion quickly – they're no longer flavour of the month. Owners are different now – loyalty is not what it was. Owners can demand a particular jockey and go through agents, because agents are in charge. Trainers have to be philosophical about the ups and downs; they have to have horses to compete, and they need owners who can afford good horses," says the master of Greystoke. "It's become very hard for smaller trainers to find the money to instal gallops and then maintain them, as they're living from hand to mouth. And there are huge logistical demands on them now. Racing somehow needs to attract a new generation of trainers, people with ambition and ability, but that is not easy. Today's increasing concentration of power among a decreasing number of trainers is a concern: the public will get sick of the same people victorious in all the races. There's no mystery in winning any more."

But, we are reaching a tipping point for trainers. With jump racing now largely dominated by a small group of ever-growing big yards, the pressures on a trainer, mainly financial, continue to grow. Even the bigger trainers are struggling. Having battled cancer, during which time his horses kept him "sane not bitter," Oliver Sherwood relinquished his trainer's licence in 2023. "You never forget how to do it, but you lose confidence; things aren't going well and you think you must be doing something wrong when, 9 times out of 10 the horses aren't good enough." His expertise will not be lost as he moves on to be assistant trainer to Harry Derham. But not all are throwing in the towel; peaks are still being scaled by smaller outfits, after years of hard work, showing all the graft is worth it, even when there is no tangible reward for months on end. Eric McNamara, in Ireland, and Nicky Martin, in Somerset, are two such grafters, still stealing the limelight with winners in big handicap chases. When such people in tiny, wind-blasted stables stop believing they can scale these peaks, jump racing will have lost its soul.

Recently retired trainer of the galloping grey Desert Orchid, David Elsworth, concurs here: "Racing has changed: it has created a monster we've got to feed, we breed too many horses, have more bloodstock sales, more trainers with bigger strings and more fixtures. We have so much racing you might as well be watching dogs going round Romford. There are more vets bills now." But he lauds the way vets have improved the health and welfare of horses – equine care is now on a par with human care.

That sentiment is echoed by Michael Scudamore, the youngest of the Scudamore dynasty - at the moment – to cement his place in racing. Michael, nicknamed Micky Joe by his beloved eponymous grandfather Michael senior, went to Cheltenham College like his elder brother, but for a while it was another sport that captivated him: rugby. Hartpury College, which he attended after Cheltenham, had links with the powerful Gloucestershire club: he was soon picked to play for Wales' Under 19, moving on to play for Ebbw Vale, the feeder club for Newport Gwent Dragons. The prospect of a full career in rugby appealed, but, with the ever-realistic Scudamore trait, Michael felt he'd perhaps reached stalemate with rugby. The farm his family had taken over was getting busier, as they converted it into a jumping yard. His grandfather was not as fit as he once was, so it was either take over Eccleswall Court near Ross-on-Wye, or sell it and walk away. He was thus able to have more fun days with his grandfather, building fences, putting things in place, Michael senior on the tractor, the pair of them in harmony: "People just aren't built like him any more," says his grandson.

And far from finding the Scudamore dynasty a pressure, Michael junior feels it has made him. Grandfather, Dad (Peter) and brother Tom have enjoyed great success in the sport: Michael is not going to be the one unsuccessful. He may not have hit the heights, yet, but, "The legacy left me gives me an extra kick." He worked hard taking over the yard, and developing it offered him real luxury in terms of surroundings. But the place was owned by the bank – it was "a big black hole." Luckily he didn't realise the full extent of his challenge, and along came Monbeg Dude, owned by Mike Tindall and fellow rugby stars, at just the right time. "Without 'the Dude', I'd not be here now. He was my saviour." The horse won three races at Cheltenham, got up to win the Welsh Grand National from a seemingly impossible position, then finished third in the Aintree Grand National. His trainer's reputation was out there for the first time; there were financial benefits, but, most of all, it boosted his confidence. That took another boost in the final race of the Cheltenham Festival 2015, when Next Sensation, owned by Mark Blandford, godson of Michael Senior, who had passed away the previous summer, and ridden by Tom, won the Grand Annual Chase, a hugely poignant victory for all. Though Blandford has not had great success since, he remains a loyal supporter of the yard.

Not all owners are so considerate: on the contrary, as all trainers experience, they can be unpredictable, break promises, and, arguably most of all, can be bad payers, causing a trainer to be kept awake at night. They may have their own plans for their horse, not entirely in sync with the trainer's, who is thus the middleman: he knows the horse best, but it's the owner's horse, so trainers have to live with that, to listen and be diplomatic. It is hard when a horse proves no good and the trainer has to say so: owners can take that personally, when in fact the trainer may well be doing them a favour, but it doesn't come across that way. Worst of all is having to make the phone call when the news is dire. Michael recently lost a promising four-year-old who had a heart attack on the gallops: "Such a sad event hits the whole yard. The atmosphere is one of loss, everyone is affected, so it's a hard phone call to make." For Michael, "Understanding animals is key, so after suffering such a loss, the good days mean that bit more. Horses repay our loyalty and faith."

The best owners are those with whom everything can be openly discussed. Owner and trainer may not always agree, but they are working towards the same thing: the owner may crave personal glory, the trainer just wants winners, but it's what's best for the horse that matters most. If everything is discussed, all parties know the highs and the lows so there can be no blame when things go wrong. "That is the hardest thing," says Michael, "when things go wrong: horses run badly for no apparent reason, the trainer is banging his head against a brick wall and can't work out why. "It comes down to the quality of the animals you've got."

Next hardest is injuries, which are difficult to take, and get a trainer down: "You can't just go and replace that promising four-year-old – you need to stabilise, which is easier said than done. When you expect a horse to run well and it doesn't – the drive home is the longest and the loneliest. You're tired, too, and have to get up at five next morning. A trainer has horses on his mind constantly: until you put things right, frustration doesn't leave you, and injuries can make you feel guilty. Are you doing it right? You have to justify to yourself what you are doing. But spending time with the animals gives you a lift: they are calming creatures, and being around them encourages you to start again and keep making plans."

Nicky Henderson, the five-time Champion Trainer, knows all there is to know about training horses, and is well known for the care taken with those animals in his charge, refusing to be persuaded by pressure from outside to race his horses when they are not ready. He listens to his horses, rather than telling them what they will be. 'Hendo' was destined for a desk job in London in 1978, but started with five horses and grew the equine empire that is now Seven Barrows in Lambourn. His training is all done on instinct, but, "It never works out as planned. You have to be ready for anything and everything. No matter how well a horse jumps at home, it is dangerous to be too confident until he shows it on the course." As one trainer has noted: "It's not how much pressure you put on; it is how good you are at taking it off." Hendo has a reputation for loyalty to his jockeys, as advocated by Nico de Boinville: "He has moulded me into what he needs as a rider. The fire within him burns as brightly as it ever did."

Training racehorses is a stressful occupation. With jockeys now encouraged to speak openly about the causes of depression, anxiety, and substance dependence, this has begun to erode the stigma that stifles potentially healing conversations. Encouraged by Rupert Arnold and the NTF, the Racehorse Trainers Benevolent Fund has now been set up to make it easier for trainers to share the burdens of their busy and challenging working lives. Initiatives include the recruitment of 'well-being champions' in the community to whom they can turn, and having access to trusted figures in racing, like Jennifer Pugh in Ireland.

Former top point-to-point jockey, now trainer, Evan Williams, has crystallised the trainer's lot: "You can dream all you want, but be realistic. Trainers have to put on a brave face, and always pretend all is well. You cannot push a river, but you should never be scared of having a crack at top horses. You have to enjoy the journey." For which trainers have, always, to be a force of nature.

CHAPTER 14: JOCKEYS 2 – WEAR AND TEAR

"A certifiable travelling band of madmen."

- Sue Mott -

Jockeys never stop learning. Everyone has dark days, but tells themselves, "When you doubt your abilities, keep rolling. Try to limit the effects of losing. Self-worth is not determined by what happens on the course. To hate the thing you enjoy most does not mean something is wrong; on the contrary, it's quite normal." Riding 'over the sticks' needs deep reserves of resilience.

We hear the galloping hooves, and then the crash of birch, we gasp at the tumbles, fear for the losers, see the bright colours, feel the ground shake in the carnival of high drama that is jump racing. We revere the men and women brave enough to race – hard – over obstacles. But these men and women do so at a price: they have to banish moments when butterflies in their stomach practise manoeuvres in a very small space – and then swoop. It is a cut-throat game with constant challenges, and, while they ride, jockeys have to be ambassadors for the sport, themselves, and their future careers, an aspect of race-riding which brings its own pressures to bear...

Sean Quinlan is a jockey who moved north in 2015, after years of hard graft down south. Winning the Scottish National on Takingrisks in 2019 for Nicky Richards - the horse almost fell at the first fence - was pivotal for him. After Ryan Day's retirement, Sean now rides regularly for the master of Greystoke, whose staying chasers are renowned. He is also first jockey for trainer Jenny Candlish, and northern jump jockeys' safety officer.

He was wise to move north: despite his hard work, things were not going well. Then, in February 2014, he tried to break up a pub brawl, got involved in the argument, and ended up with a six-month suspended sentence for affray. Trainer Milton Harris stuck by him, and, one day at Catterick, persuaded Harvey Smith, husband of trainer Sue, to take a chance on someone viewed by many as damaged goods. "I got up at 3, to reach Yorkshire for 7: that's how desperate I was to get back to riding winners." Sean was told by Harvey: "Work hard now – then party and do other things when you retire." The Irishman has not looked back since.

A lad from Tipperary, he didn't sit on a horse until he was 16, but got the bug at once: "I couldn't believe people actually got paid to ride horses." Having won on his first ride in Ireland for Eddie O'Grady in August 2003, he chanced his arm in England and repeated the winning feat on his first ride for Richard Phillips, for whom he was conditional jockey. He rode for Kim Bailey and started his association with Candlish. Now, only Brian Hughes is ahead of him in the northern pecking order: Sean is great mates with his fellow Irishman. "We sit beside each other in the weighing room, and share lifts to tracks. For Brian, everything revolves round racing: he works really hard and you can see what he's trying to do (become champion again). He's so far ahead of everyone up north, so the closer we can get to him, the happier we'll be." If Brian were to need an heir apparent…

Sean, (39), speaks for the more experienced jump jockeys: "I see differently from years ago. As a young jockey, you are thinking about being champion and winning the Grand National. I used to look for magpies, and all that kind of craic, wear certain socks; not now. Now I have got into reality, and see racing as a business. I can switch off as soon as I leave the course, am much more laid-back, and can't wait to get home, I like a day off."

He credits agent Richard Hale for being the making of his career, and appreciates that, on the whole, he has been fortunate with injuries, "apart from collarbones, small things, cracks, aches and pains." Lucky with his weight, he sees travelling as the hardest thing, going to work in the dark, getting home in the dark, often unrewarded for his efforts. A modest character, his Scottish Grand National win on Takingrisks was "a big surprise."

Sean always has time for people; not all jockeys are so generous.

A football fan, who had trials for Celtic, he is a Manchester United supporter, with chocolate a guilty pleasure and golf his mode of relaxation. And his answer to the question whether life as a jump jockey is all about winning, is significant: "There's no better feeling than getting on a nice horse, and coming home in front. To me, it's 90% about winning – but there's a lot of love there too: love of the horse, the thrill, the competition, the way of life… It brings unbelievable joy."

Sean's enlightened approach to life since he moved north has brought the best 5/6 years of his career. Associated with horses like Lady Buttons and Navajo Pass, he is strong, and gets a good tune out of his mounts, on whom he never gives up. This was seen in his riding of For Jim at Hexham in 2021, for which he was nominated for Jump Ride of the Year. Recently notching up his 500th winner, he is never less than passionate about his profession, and spoke up strongly about the new whip rules in early 2023. He is now riding at the top of his game. With a couple of years left, all being well, and still loving the buzz of the weighing room, he is already looking forward to retirement, seeing more of his young girls, and helping wife Lizzie prepare/train their horses in their Cumbrian village near Appleby: "There's so much to do in the lakes around here."

Ryan Mania was 23 when he won the Grand National in 2013 on 66-1 shot Aurora's Encore, his first ride in the race, for trainer Sue Smith. Ryan had known horses all his life, but admits he was not the bravest: "My tricky ponies and horses scared the life out of me." With no expectations, no pressure in the big race, he never thought he was going to win, and when he did, he was hit by disbelief, hurled into a world he knew nothing about. The next day he rode at Hexham – "I didn't need to, but I wanted normality": he fell from his mount in a hurdle race when his horse stumbled: the horse behind trod on him, fracturing vertebrae: he thought that was it… By the end of the next year, 2014, he had stopped race-riding: despite winners, he was struggling, not least with his weight, continually waking up knowing he was 11 stone and would have to lose several pounds: "Ridiculous." But he told no-one, so nobody knew, until he phoned his agent and announced he was retiring; he was eternally grumpy and didn't like who he had become. That phone call brought instant relief: the load was off his mind.

It took him two years to realise he had done the wrong thing, a feeling enhanced when he was asked to ride in a charity race – and won it. Helped by his wife, and step-father Sandy Thomson, who offered him the role of assistant trainer, he grew increasingly aware that he'd retired too soon, but knew he needed to be stabilised. A dietician's meal and exercise plan dealt with the weight problem. The Ryan Mania of 2024 couldn't be more different from that of 10 years earlier, when for him, racing was proving toxic. With a good family life, and two kids – his daughter is named Aurora – he can safely say when he gets home, racing doesn't matter. And for the future, his outlook is sunny: "Keep riding, keep turning up, keep doing the job, riding winners, keeping everyone happy."

Paddy Brennan, Irish of course, and now 43, has been a jump jockey for 24 years. He is a fine example of resilience, and remains one of the most colourful jockeys in the weighing room. He found it hard to get started when he first came to the bigger playing fields of England. But under Philip Hobbs – "proper educational" – he became Champion Conditional. Now, he has well over 1,000 winners to his name, while admitting he still gets "too excited by that winning feeling." He never thought he was any good, and doesn't yet, having always to work hard at all he does. "You never stop learning; there's always a door to open." 'Ride to win, not to lose' is imbued in his psyche, despite injuries and knockbacks over the years. In 2018, he had his teeth knocked out when headbutted by his mount in a race at Chepstow: Sam Waley Cohen's dental practice immediately helped out.

"All the falls you take need a bit of madness," he says, "and the feeling of getting beaten doesn't get better." It took him two years to recover psychologically from Cue Card's fall when going so well in the 2016 Gold Cup, for which he berated himself. Cue Card was the most popular horse in training at the time. But now he can accept that mishap, feeling it extended his career, made him more fierce, determined, driven – and braver. "After the dim, dark days, nothing can phase you. Every track is different, every race is different," says the man who had won the Gold Cup on Imperial Commander in 2010; "You have to make instant decisions, have razor-sharp reactions, learn not to press the green button too soon," something he learned in particular from Ruby Walsh, along with fractions and tactics. But a good win is worth

Sam Thomas and Denman power to victory in 2008 Cheltenham Gold Cup

Paul Townend and Laurina after winning at Cheltenham Festival 2018

Tom Scudamore as Fleance in Cheltenham College's 1996 production of *Macbeth*

Mill House leads Arkle in 1964 Cheltenham Gold Cup

Richard Dunwoody on One Man at Cheltenham

David Bass: the jockey who thinks out of the box

Rachael Blackmore wins on Honeysuckle at Cheltenham Festival 2023

Richard Davis 1969-1996

Tom Scudamore after winning World Hurdle at Cheltenham 2019 on Thistlecrack

Sam Thomas in weighing room before 2009 Cheltenham Gold Cup

Sean Flanagan jockey and pilot

Nick Oliver on Red Happy in Royal Artillery Gold Cup, Sandown, 2023

Paul Townend and Galopin Des Champs romp home to win their second Irish Gold Cup, Leopardstown, Dublin Racing Festival 2024

David Bass lands Clarence House Chase at Ascot 2021

all the toil: "You get mentally drunk for a while after it; you feel like God. But it doesn't last, of course." His is an engaging, honest story, reflecting a thoughtful man of high emotion, for whom, "Social media is the biggest disease travelling the world."

Daryl Jacob had no family racing connection, but has carved out a steady career for himself, not least in the 'double green' silks of Simon Munir and Isaac Souede. For him, key is the "focus of getting the best out of your horse and the best out of yourself." Despite his credo, "It's winning or nothing," he has an unusually altruistic approach to his riding, having shared a house and been great mates with Irish jockey Kieran Kelly, who was killed in a fall in 2003. Daryl wants to achieve things for Kieran that his departed friend can never achieve; as he did when winning the 2012 Grand National by a whisker on Neptune Collonges, dedicating the victory to his former house-mate.

"It's an obsession, an addiction, keeping your body two stone under its natural body weight. You're chasing the dream – to be successful; when you are, you want more and more. Everyone wants to be part of racing history by winning the Gold Cup or Grand National. I love my connection with horses, every one of them different for you to try and get inside their mind; you're always looking forward to tomorrow."

But he acknowledges the pressures, the sacrifices: "It's hard to plan anything as a jump jockey. There's no routine, and the shape of the day can change in an instant. And everyone wants what you want [i.e. a good horse]. There are always people snapping at your heels; you've got to keep momentum going, always looking for that next good horse. When you're lying there, injured, you count the days till your return: you have to get back soonest because other jockeys are getting your mounts. And there are lots of falls, of injuries. The joys," laughs Daryl gently. "Jockeys are meant to keep riding."

He realises the need to get away from the bubble, in his case by playing golf; the fact wives have to be strong dealing with husbands' disappointments, defeats and regrets, and how hard it is to express fully what you feel after a notable success – "Everything builds into one outcry of joy." But jockeys can never get too high; this sport will soon bring them back to earth again. As Willie Mullins has said, "You are allowed to buzz for 30 minutes."

Jump jockeys still need an arm around them; with confidence such a huge thing, they have to be told they're good jockeys more regularly than we think. One day, Daryl knows he'll have to "go and find a job, I suppose"; at the moment he cannot think of any better way to enjoy his days than riding. The fire burns on…

Still only 27, Johnny Burke has packed a lot into his young life already. Born, like so many top Irish jockeys, in County Cork, he grew up with 100 horses. His Dad, Liam, a trainer, still has a licence to race-ride, and, in March 2023, rode Teuchter's Glory to win the bumper at Limerick – aged 66. Despite two knee-replacements, he became the oldest jockey to win under Rules in Ireland. Losing his Mum aged 5, Johnny was brought up by his sister, Amy, Liam, and great neighbours, including Davy Condon, who lived next door. The lad was always going to ride…

On his first day with a licence, point-to-point day at Cork, he had two rides in Liam's colours, the second of which, Trendy Gift, stormed home at 33-1. He spent his summers with Willie Mullins, for whom he won the Land Rover bumper on Very Much So: that was his springboard to a lot of rides. He watched everyone, not least Jim Dreaper, and shared a house with Paul Townend, who has ever been his mate and source of sound advice. Taking Ted Walsh's encouragement, he turned conditional: two months later – aged 18 – he was offered the plum job of riding all the Ann and Alan Potts' horses, on several of whom, Sizing John, Sizing Europe and Sizing Granite he won, as he did the coveted Galway Plate on Shanahan's Turn. A great first year saw him crowned Champion Conditional: "I was lucky."

That luck didn't last. In a fall at Thurles in 2015 he fractured his T3 and T4 vertebrae, came back to run fifth in the Grand National on Goonyella, then broke his T6 schooling at home and needed three months' rest. He was struggling, rang his mentor, Ruby Walsh, rang Sandra and Richard Hughes – and, as ever, sought the counsel of his father. He severed the Potts bond, went freelance, and got a lot of rides quickly. But then he broke his leg – a further two months off; "I missed another Christmas." Three weeks after his return to the saddle, he crushed his shoulder, which needed a full reconstruction – a mere five months on the sidelines – and in the 2023 Grand National, he broke his arm.

It was agent Dave Roberts who texted him with the offer of coming to England as retained jockey for Charlie Longsdon: he had nothing to lose. Lodging with Will Kennedy, for four years, he won the Red Rum Chase at Aintree, rode Glen Forsa and others for Henrietta Knight and Mick Channon, settled with Oliver Sherwood until his retirement, with Tom George, where he still is, and with Harry Fry, on whose Love Envoi he won at the Cheltenham Festival in 2022. Johnny has every intention to be loyal. His progress is steady: 63 wins in 2021-2022 was his best season yet.

Is it all about winning? "Yes, but you have to see the bigger picture, especially with jump horses, who take time: next year could see them at the next level, so look after what you have." He reckons loyalty has caused him to miss winners, but has learned much, and wouldn't change where he is now, "though I'd like another go at the Potts job!" Clondaw Castle, Double Shuffle, Summerville Boy and Bun Doran have kept him in the limelight, but he is keen to find the top level again, as he did on his best ride to date in the Grade 2 Champion Chase back at Cork over the Easter weekend 2018, winning in his Dad's colours on Sumos Novios, and when he won the 2022 Paddy Power Gold Cup at Cheltenham on Ga Law.

He remains a modest man, like so many of his courageous counterparts, gaining pleasure after a win from giving a kid the odd pair of his goggles — "I was that kid" — even as he wonders, "Who am I to be signing autographs!" He firmly believes "Racing has a way of doing the right thing at the right time." Meanwhile, he loves his job, living the dream of his Dad, his feet firmly on the turf: "You're only as good as the people round you."

Social media he uses, though he'd like to be "the jockey without it." Down the line he'd like to commentate, and has already tried his hand in this at pony races and point-to-points. Richard Hoiles has helped him here. Johnny can pick out jockeys' styles as much as their colours. He has a fine valet, Simon Burroughs, who makes his racing life easy. On danger he says race-riding is such a special feeling he'd never thought of not coming back from his injuries. He secured that first Cheltenham Festival success — after three times finishing runner-up — in 2022 on Love Envoi for Harry Fry, and, on Not So Sleepy, a challenging mount, dead-heated in the 2021 Fighting Fifth Hurdle at Newcastle with fellow Cork man Aidan Coleman.

Aidan, from Ireland, like so many of our top riders, shares with Sam Thomas the distinction he's the son of two school teachers. He came over from the Emerald Isle at 18 to help school young horses at Henrietta Knight's, where he met Sam, just a few years older than he. They rode out together, Aidan finding Sam "always kind," and Henrietta and husband Terry Biddlecombe, great folk to work for. Humour was never far away; the training pair were inordinately wise, as well as genuinely encouraging, though Aidan got "some wonderful bollockings" from Terry. But the young Irishman was keen to expand his racing horizons: he had a morning's trial with champion trainer, Nicky Henderson, who told him he hadn't got enough experience. Sam came to the rescue and got his friend a job with Venetia Williams: "He did me the biggest favour."

Aidan makes – and keeps – good friends. When Sam took the job with Paul Nicholls, Aidan jumped the ladder to become first jockey at Aramstone, where he stayed for 6-7 years riding nigh-on 400 winners. He moved on, at that time taking "the best job in jump racing," with John Ferguson, then to Jonjo O'Neill and has been freelance riding for Olly Murphy, Anthony Honeyball and Emma Lavelle. At times he misses being part of a tight-knit team, aware that no jockey will get everything right. "I've trained myself not to get too up or too down. The measure of a man comes out in ordinary situations." He acknowledges how cut-throat jump racing can be; how the number of jockeys has been gradually whittled down over recent years and how fortunate he has been dining at the top table, riding the likes of Jonbon, Epatante and Paisley Park, on whom he won the 2019 Stayers Hurdle. "Spending long hours working day in day out means jockeys aren't able to strike much of a balance, let alone relax, because you're always thinking about the next day, so your mind doesn't get much rest. But, as a jockey, you mature and learnt to deal with different situations. I believe you have to try to leave everything at the races, win, lose or draw." It was hard for him to see Sam Thomas lose his confidence: "It just happens in sport – it's no-one's fault." Venetia still advises him to: "Ring Sam: see what he says," and Aidan rode a winner for Sam on Galileo Silver in February 2021 at Lingfield.

Aidan has always stood "on my own two feet, but I've always had a lot of people around me. I've never had a proper riding lesson, I just got on with things and jumped whatever came, however I could." He has climbed high in the jockeys' table, but it hadn't always been an easy ascent. "It took a while for him to handle the ups and downs of the game," said Venetia. Now he is fast becoming an elder statesman in the weighing room: "The only way to deal with the bad days is to experience them. In many ways I had it too easy: it's hard to be mentally unflappable when things go wrong if you've never had a bad experience." But he is the ultimate professional: "Every race is a big race for somebody. A moderate horse is still someone's pride and joy, and they're paying bills for it. As I see it, I'm paid to do a job I love, so should be doing it just as well on a weekday as I should be in the Grand National."

Now he brings many assets to the table; despite being almost 6 ft; his style has been lauded for being "enviably poised and forward-tilting." And his philosophical outlook is clear: "Any sportsman needs ambition. If you go home contented, you're not going to improve; you have to keep a balance, or it will drive you to an early grave." His first winner was on a little pony called Magical Dancer in a race at Buttevant, where, in 1752, Edmund Blake and Cornelius O'Callaghan had raced over ditches, stone walls and hedges, giving birth to steeple-chasing. Aidan is well aware that racing is a hard game, that there are not so many jockeys over 30 now, and he well knows just what strength of mentality is needed.

He is one of racing's deep thinkers, who learned much from Jonjo O'Neill, "a great mentor." Aidan knows that as a jump jockey, his livelihood is ever at stake: the sport is so time-consuming, "and it's not real life. You have to make your own luck, and keep re-inventing yourself," as he did when the John Ferguson job stopped, leaving Aidan in no-man's-land. But he is fiercely determined, can be stubborn, is not a selfish man, and wonders if jockeys sometimes get offended too easily, citing the essential difference between criticism and abuse. He remains a loyal rider, who doesn't expect things to fall in his favour, a man who rides, Will Kennedy has said, "like an artist would paint a picture."

Aidan (35) acknowledges the harsh truth that racing over obstacles brings with it the underlying pressure to please all and sundry. His, "When you ride horses for a living, you don't expect to come out unscathed," proved an inadequate comment on the risks faced by jump jockeys. In a freak accident on

June 15th 2023, at Worcester, his mount, the ironically named Ascension Day, tried to duck out of jumping the final hurdle and did "catastrophic damage to his right knee," shattering the top of his tibia and grinding it to sawdust. Five hours under the knife ensued, his surgeon admitting Aidan had done "the full house." Industrial quantities of antibiotics followed, and his protracted recovery called for "some kind of medieval torture device," strapping on an ungainly boot three times a day for half an hour at a time, and steadily tightening the screw, one notch every five minutes.

After 8,000 rides and more than 1,000 winners, he remained phlegmatic, determined to return to the saddle, and squeeze a few more years out of his career: "I still have a leg, and I am ready to get on with it again." In spite of the 'inhumane grind' needed to overcome his injury, he insisted he was not a slave to the game, resolved to keep striving to pass the personal milestones that pepper the career of every jump jockey.

As I stood up to go, having interviewed him in June 2020, he said, "Of course, I should have won the Grand National in 2009…" That year Venetia had two runners in the big race, one of them the much-fancied Stan, (bought by Nick Oliver in New Zealand) and Mon Mome, a rank outsider at 100-1, (although he had won a long distance chase at Cheltenham). Aidan opted for Stan; the ride on Mon Mome went to young Liam Treadwell. Stan fell at the 7th fence, Foinavon, (the smallest fence on the course). Mon Mome romped home to win. "I thought the end of the world had come at the time," said Aidan. "My head was fried. I've got over it now. The right man won the National. That's jump racing; these things happen. It was only a horse race; now it's just annoying that I picked the wrong one."

"Were you angry then?" I asked, meaning angry at himself for making the wrong decision. Aidan thought I meant angry with Liam. "Oh, no," he replied quickly, "Liam is one of my best mates. We went racing together a lot, lived next door to each other, and we often meet for a pint."

I took my leave; Aidan said to come back if I needed any more information. Next afternoon I dropped a thank you card round to him: of all the people interviewed for this book, he'd been as positive as anyone. Oddly, his car wasn't outside his house. I thought nothing of it. Only later did I discover why: Liam Treadwell had taken his own life that morning.

CHAPTER 15: SAM THOMAS: EARLY DAYS

"Racing is, at its best, an irresistible game, one of the most attractive and natural metaphors for life that sport has to offer."

- Hugh McIlvanney -

Every Boxing Day, Sam's maternal grandfather, Kenneth, would urge his family to put sixpence in the hat for the day's big race at Kempton, the King George VI Chase. In 1967 he had Foinavon (shock winner at 100-1) in the work Grand National 'sweep', and he loved point-to-point. Sam's father, Geoff, grew up on a small-holding in Wales; he revelled in its scope, and the chance of adventure. He thought Abergavenny market a wonderful place, and always came back from it with something: he once bought two ponies, Thunder and Lightning – well named, they were "as wild as hawks." Geoff competed in all the local shows on his grey pony, Topper: in time Sam would also compete on a grey pony called Topper. Sam grew up in a Monmouthshire cottage, Trevyr, with views over to the sweep of the Greig, where he rode up from Grosmont on the old road, the wood full of honking ravens, the wind howling, deer jumping across in front of a galloping horse.

On Sunday evenings he sat down with his family to watch the BBC series *Trainer*, urging horses home from the arm of the sofa. He'd always wanted to be a jockey, prompting Geoff to speak to Lord Oaksey one day at Cheltenham: the Noble Lord suggested that unless you had a racing name, or came from Ireland, the odds were probably stacked against you. Undeterred, the young Sam galloped the donkeys on the beach at Weston-Super-Mare, returning his mounts in a state of sweat: the donkey master was not amused.

Geoff took Sam to Abergavenny market when he was five: a dapple-grey pony pricked his ears, caught the eye, and was soon at Trevyr. Sam remembers seeing the pony in the pens, his dad chatting to a man against a wall, then shaking hands with him. Topper taught Sam to ride, though he was no gentle schoolmaster. "If he could drop me, he would." But the two forged a fiercely competitive bond – perhaps a hint of another, more famous partnership to come (with Denman): both Sam and Topper had "guts and balls" – and they kept winning. Often Sam had another pony in the jump-off as well, and would go round the ring "like a wall of death."

Topper was succeeded by Foxy Lady, "a bit of a madam." Sam hunted with her, and reckons that was where he learned his horsemanship. "There's no-one to look after you, and different obstacles to face. You never know what's coming up next." He was no stranger to falls, as Foxy Lady was bravery incarnate. After her came a Welsh cob named Armitage; one BSJA show was at Cheltenham racecourse: in between rounds Sam would sneak off and race Armitage up to the steeplechase fences, little knowing, but perhaps hoping that would one day be for real.

He had grown up with no-nonsense kids, all with ponies bought for a song, and no 'namby-pamby'. This down-to-earth upbringing and childhood experience gave Sam a healthy sense of perspective to complement his growing prowess in the saddle. When he was 15, acting as an outrider on the look-out for loose horses at the Monmouthshire point-to-point, a photographer told Sam he'd take a photo of him if he jumped the last obstacle after the final race, but he needed to be quick. Sam popped the fence, the photo was taken: last fences were to play quite a part in his story. Whenever he and Geoff went to a point-to-point, his father was keen Sam took his hat: "One of the jockeys could fall: you might be needed."

A local family friend, Reg Brown, good mate of Michael Scudamore, senior, lived up the road from Trevyr at Cross Ash (he was the oldest living permit-holder, until passing away in 2016). His son, Stan, let Sam ride out with his horses, a practice that began when Sam was 14, and continued for two years while the lad was still at school. Sam is eternally grateful to Stan for being the first person to put him on a racehorse. But his first time on the gallops at Caradoc Court near Ross-on-Wye was "a hell of an experience," something Sam has never forgotten. Tackling his first fence, at Hooley's, Sam jumped "like a trout": he fell, got back on, and by the year's end was flying his fences. Reg was old-school: he worked horses till they were super-fit on his Blaenllymon Farm, and this gave Sam a strong grounding. Stan, and wife Mary, remain among Sam's staunchest supporters: Stan it was who bred and named Iwilldoit, Sam's Welsh National and Warwick Classic horse, and his biggest winner as a trainer (so far), a source of great pride to Stan: "It didn't take much to realise Sam had talent, but he wasn't very big when he first came to me, so he needed a bit of weight. I bought a lead-lined saddle, previously owned by Molly Rhodes, a local eccentric and hunting doyenne, and for a while that did the trick." Sam loved riding at Blaenllymon. Stan smiles to remember the lad's own ponies "were wild: no-one else could ride them."

With both father, Geoff, and mother, Dot, now Headteachers, Sam attended King Henry VIII school in Abergavenny, where his short-term memory was not of the best: he is better with routine (and even now never quite sure as to the whereabouts of his keys and wallet). He played rugby "until I got munched," loved cricket, and took up golf. But after GCSEs he decided 'A' levels were not for him.

He asked Stan to put in a word for him with David Evans, to whom Stan was assistant trainer. Evans was turning the stud at Pandy back into a racing stable, for which Stan had to put in miles of fencing and rails. The trainer agreed, a tad reluctantly, to give the sixteen-year-old a trial, "for a month or so." It was Sam's first time away from home: he dealt with the young horses, made friends among the stable lads and took advantage of the chance to learn from those around him, not least Gandy, later a vet. The month was extended, and then Sam went to Newmarket Racing School for its nine-week Foundation Course, where he learned the need for patience with horses. He returned ready to apply for his amateur licence. Growing readily, he stayed away from the gym: "Muscle weighs more than fat." And his body was used to sweating: "Being a jockey is one of the only sports where you can be at your best dehydrated: once you're on a horse, adrenalin kicks in, and it's a different story." So he did not have problems with his weight.

With Evans, he visited every track in the land; the trainer was a tough taskmaster, and made it clear success would not come easily. Sam broke in the 2- year-olds, many of them "as wild as hawks" – as Geoff would concur - and learned much. One morning he was hurt when, during a piece of fast work, the horse dropped dead under him. At last Evans gave him the chance to race-ride; among others he partnered Master Beveled and Madam Jones, "a little fireball." He found everything happened so quickly in a race, and realises now he was not clued up enough.

His first point-to-point ride came in January 2002, at the Army meeting at Larkhill, on Ardbei, trained by Geoff. 12 stone had to be carried. Geoff had borrowed the lead-weighted saddle from Stan, but Sam weighed only 6½ stone, so his father got hold of some roofing lead, and bulked up the saddle. In May of that year, Sam had his first ride at Cheltenham, in the amateur riders meeting. He was 17.

His first point-to-point win came in January 2003 on Tirley Gale at Cottenham, but his memories of that victory are "weird. It was a photo-finish, and I thought I'd been beaten, so didn't feel an immediate buzz," (he still feels he lost out in that finish). Only later could the feeling of victory start to sink in. Photo finishes were not always accurate then, and even now he feels his premier win was not as convincing as he would have wished.

Another Stan, Turner, was estate manager for Venetia Williams, at Aramstone, her Herefordshire stables near King's Caple. Sam teamed up with him to ride Ash Green, on whom he enjoyed several wins. Stan has rich memories of those days: "Sam was always full of fun; nothing was too serious about him. He'd been kept grounded by Dot and Geoff." The man still follows Sam's career keenly. When, years later, Big Buck's, under Sam, fell at the last fence in the Hennessy Gold Cup, for which the lad received unwarranted criticism, Stan's view remains firm. "Sam made that horse. He wasn't a chaser, he was a hurdler. Things are meant to happen."

In March 2004 at Brecon point-to-point, at the downhill fence he used to stand by as a lad - "It was a combination of the entertaining and the hairy" – Sam had a bad fall. "My face was planted into the ground. I remember being stretchered away in an ambulance, put on lockdown, transported with care to hospital for fear of neck, spine and brain injuries. I can recall lifting my head up to relieve the pressure – and the relief that I could move." Years later, when he fell from Woolcombe Folly at Ditcheat, X-rays suggested the fall at

Brecon had done more damage than was first thought.

Around that time Sam spotted an advert in the *Racing Post* for a stable lad at Aramstone. Geoff took Sam along, the lad kitted out in immaculate blue riding gear. Venetia remembers a smart, youthful and raw young lad, still 17, who brought photos of his ponies and 'cups won'. Aware that Stan Brown had mentioned his potential to her, she watched him ride, offered him the job, but didn't promise any rides. "This is a racing stable, not a riding school." He accepted the job. Venetia thought him observant, able to pick things up quickly and keep his wits about him. Sam lived in a cottage on the estate, with Will Biddick and Liam Treadwell: the local pub was their university.

Venetia encouraged Sam to ride in as many point-to-points and hunter chases as possible, to gain experience. Six months after he had started at Aramstone, when he was 'setting fine' a new horse in the yard, she came round at evening stables and offered him the chance to go to Japan with her horse, Banker Count, for the Nakayama Grand Jump, the richest steeplechase in the world. He hadn't been abroad before. With David Pipe and Jeremy Young he was upgraded – not just to Business Class but to First Class. "Right place, right time," he says now, a phrase that often proved apt with his riding career (though its converse equally so). Stan Turner travelled cargo, with the horse.

Back at Aramstone, Sam learned from watching Norman Williamson, Brian Cowley and Frank Windsor-Clive. Before a race at Perth, when he had called correctly on Venetia's toss of a coin to win the ride, he was told to weigh out in "cheating boots" (paper thin and uncomfortable) but wasn't told to change back into normal boots for the race – he was mocked mercilessly. The constant humour of jockeys is still one of their eternal – and essential – features, a vital weapon in their armoury for days – which they have to endure frequently – when things go wrong.

Under Venetia's tutelage he "whizzed through." He turned conditional (equivalent of apprentice on the Flat) at 19, lost his claim (the weight concession allowed to more inexperienced riders) after a season and a half, and began to attract people's attention. Racing correspondent Marcus Armytage rarely misses a trick. For him, Sam caught the eye riding Banker Count in the Tripleprint Gold Cup at Cheltenham in 2003: the result was no fairy story – the horse was pulled up – but this was progress: for the Grand Jump,

Sam had only led the horse up. After Misty Future won a novice chase at Chepstow in November 2003, the South Wales Argus heralded "such an unassuming young man," whose "blossoming career" they would continue to cover with interest. He began to notch up victories at Cheltenham, courtesy of It's Only Me, Jasmine Guichois, Ballyconnell and Heron's Ghyll, the latter a particularly enterprising ride, and when he rode 6 winners in a fortnight one journalist in the Western Daily Press described him as the "most exciting young jockey since Adrian Maguire, a real racing find." He won several races in Stan Brown's blue and red quarters, white armbands, though he'd never been victorious in a point-to-point wearing those colours.

Venetia saw losing was hard for Sam to take, especially when he felt he'd done things right, but he usually kept frustrations to himself. Even now, he harbours "deep-down thoughts," conveyed to no-one. He didn't often lose his temper in those early days, but admits he was aggressive sometimes, earning him a conversation with the stewards. "I was, as ever, trying to emulate AP McCoy." He admired Timmy Murphy and Paul Carberry, but had to develop his own style: simply looking the part did him no good. "Venetia was fair, never harbouring grudges: she kept me level-headed." Little by little, his confidence grew. He often drove Venetia to the races, and listened to her depth of experience. There was no intention, then, to become a trainer himself, but, when he did, he resolved to put what he'd learned at Aramstone into practice, not least where planning was concerned. "Venetia wins so many races in the office."

Sam enjoyed a stellar season in 2002-2003, just losing out, by one win in the Conditional Jockeys' Championship on the last day of the season. With 46 winners that day, Sam was two behind his good friend, Jamie Moore, conditional for Martin Pipe. Jamie was not riding that day; he sat on 48 wins. Sam went to Market Rasen with high hopes of equalling, even surpassing his mate. He was down for two rides, but Alan O'Keefe 'got off' one for Sam, as did Tony Dobbin: Sam had four good rides to assist his bid. The first mount won: he was on 47. The second horse, favourite, the one he was relying on, "ran terrible" and was unplaced. The third horse finished 3rd. That left the bumper: Sam was on a horse trained by Steve Collings: he made the running and led throughout, but was chinned on the line by Tony Evans, who roared loudly on gaining his narrow victory. "Did he know I was going for the title?" Sam still wonders. It was a long drive home, but on the way he rang Jamie to congratulate him. Sam can't abide bitterness. Will Biddick has recently agreed, "Sam never burns his bridges." The tests to come on that score would be challenging…

At this time, the young Welshman was also riding out for Henrietta Knight, trainer of Best Mate and mastermind of that horse's three Cheltenham Gold Cup wins with husband Terry Biddlecombe, three-times Champion Jockey. She remembers the attention Sam paid to Terry over her breakfast table: she also remembers, "He was a bright boy, and terribly good-looking, of course, with always plenty of girlfriends." It was around this time Sam was nominated by mates for the Bachelor of the Year. A '*Racing Post*' headline read, "Is this the sexiest man in racing?" Sam was taken aback. "I nearly crashed my car when I was told it was all over page 2. It was one way to get noticed, but I didn't half get some stick. I was the cause of endless banter from the lads in the weighing room, and on balance I'd much rather make the news for riding winners." A date with a couple of handicappers down at Exeter meant Sam was unable to attend the glitzy London ceremony where the final verdict was announced. The judges opted for George Best's son, Calum, who might well have possessed what one journalist called "chiselled features and paparazzi appeal" but might not have been too keen on taking the reins for a dodgy jumper in a novice chase round Hereford.

Henrietta Knight is renowned well beyond the realms of horse racing, but the combination of her training acumen and Biddlecombe's ever-colourful personality sealed her reputation indelibly. She does not mince her words. After exercising her string, Sam would sit in her kitchen with fellow jockeys Timmy Murphy, Mattie Batchelor, Paul Moloney and Sam Stronge, listening to Terry's jokes, and stories and wise counsel, even when, towards the end of his life, the man felt far from healthy. "Terry never gave compliments for the sake of it, so when he did," Sam recalls, "it was great."

He had several big race rides for Henrietta, notably on Racing Demon, Somersby and Open Ditch, and enjoyed being on her and Terry's wavelength, a bonus that complemented what he was learning at Aramstone: "Routine is always hard grind for a jockey, so to mix it up, now and again, is healthy."

'Hen' had learned her trade from the likes of Tim Forster, and Fred Winter, and, being an ex-school teacher, was in a strong position to teach young jockeys the proper workings of a top yard. She found Sam always aware of the need to learn. Whilst riding out for Henrietta pretty frequently, Sam remained loyal to Venetia, for whom "he always worked hard to improve, and had a good eye for a stride." She appreciated his approach, responsible attitude to learning and excellent brain: "You only had to tell him once."

In January 2004, Sam rode Venetia's Limerick Boy in the Lanzarote Hurdle at Kempton: they made the running, until headed by the favourite, Perouse, ridden by Ruby Walsh. In a driving finish, with no quarter asked, no quarter given, Sam was not to be denied and battling grimly to the line, he and Limerick Boy prevailed by a nail-biting neck. It was the lad from Grosmont's first big win. His reaction was a modest one: "Riding against jockeys like Ruby makes me realise I've got to get better and better." Sam had earlier won the handicap hurdle on Cotopaxi: both races were on Channel 4, the racing broadcaster that would later become part of his story. The fact Sam had stolen the show that day by taking the notable scalp of Ruby did not go unnoticed. But Sam has always been a realist. Whilst acknowledging that, at 21, time was on his side for making his mark in top races, he was well aware that: "The big boys have nearly all the fire power, so, when a good horse comes along, you have to take your chance and make the most of it. There's only one AP McCoy, but I feel I can get stronger and more consistent to become a more solid jockey all round. My target is to break into the top ten." With AP, Mick Fitzgerald, Tony Dobbin, Carl Llewellyn, Richard Johnson and Tom Scudamore all riding with appetite and panache, the younger brigade of Sam, Jamie Moore, Paddy Brennan, Tom O'Brien and co. had no illusions about the competition they were up against. "Will I go all the way? Will I be one of the top jockeys? Let's just say that if I'm not, it won't be for lack of trying."

Limerick Boy was to prove crucial in the young Welshman's quest. In March 2005 the partnership returned to Kempton for the Pendil Novices Chase, aptly sponsored by Limerick Boy's owners, Favourites Racing. Together, they conjured up a magnificent round of jumping, comfortably accounting for the high-class pair, Lacdoudal and Duncliffe, eventually coming home clear by 12 lengths. The bay gelding produced the kind of display he had been promising since being switched to fences. He had run in the German and Italian Derbys, and finished 6th in the Supreme Novices at Cheltenham, but fences were clearly his forte, and his jockey was seizing the chance to underline his driving ambition. Sam was never selfish in this: for him the greatest joy was "getting it right on a winner, and seeing the excitement it brings to an owner."

By the end of the 2004-2005 season he had 55 winners to his name: he was going places, riding with flair – and gaining in confidence. In November 2005 he turned professional to become stable jockey at Aramstone. Soon he was racking up the winners with no mean flair. But, as he was realising, a jockey has always to "ride by the seat of his pants: it is hard to get everything right." And, as Venetia also knew, "Flair can be damaged if confidence is lost. With horses, jockeys, schoolchildren, all of us, confidence is perhaps the single most important aspect. It is a precarious balance."

CHAPTER 16:
SAM AS A TOP JOCKEY

"No-one will ever write a book about you; it's all going too swimmingly."
- Geoff Thomas -

Whilst riding as Venetia Williams' stable jockey, a position he'd held for some time, seizing the chance to partner lots of good horses like Kock de la Vesvre, on whom he won the Midlands National at Uttoxeter, Sam had also been going down to Paul Nicholls' yard in Ditcheat, Somerset, and occasionally riding for him. When Ruby Walsh, Nicholls' number one, dislocated his shoulder in the Paddy Power Cheltenham meeting in November 2007, it was the worst possible timing for him. That fall, and its complications, resulted in regular cryotherapy sessions; Ruby described the process, which he endured four times over the course of a day, as "pure torture – but you'll do anything to get back."

Before that, with Ruby based in Ireland and riding there three times a week, Nicholls had needed a permanent number two: he offered the job to Sam, giving him a golden opportunity; second jockey at Ditcheat was equal to first jockey anywhere else. It was a big decision. Sam weighed up the pros and cons; he decided to go for it. Telling Venetia was hard, but his father had wisely suggested Sam recommend a jockey to take his place at Aramstone: Sam chose Aidan Coleman, who was to remain there, and enjoy success for several more years.

Sam felt he couldn't afford to let his opportunity slip away at this stage of his career: the move could raise him to a different level. But even now, both he and Venetia recall him going in to her office to break the news "with quiet consideration." He had always ridden with great flair for the Herefordshire trainer: she was both sad and disappointed to hear his decision, having sensed this might happen. She also sensed what could happen further down the line. But she couldn't blame the lad's ambition, set, as it now was, against all the support and loyalty she'd shown him. Would he get the same support from Nicholls? The situation was compounded by the media trumpeting this news before Venetia had time to inform her owners. She knew Sam would be under pressure with Nicholls, where he'd be given tight instructions, whereas her method was to trust her jockeys: "You either trust them or you don't," a philosophy that had enabled Sam to grow in those two imposters, confidence and flair. He went to Ditcheat. Some would say Sam was not quite the same jockey after leaving the leafy lanes and cider apple trees of King's Caple.

He knew he had to continue to refine his talent to play – and stay – in the top flight, and look after the big Ditcheat horses: everything about them was so well documented; with most stables there would not be such a high degree of scrutiny. If you made mistakes there, everyone was watching: pressure was great, which is why riding winners was so rewarding. At first, restricted to Ditcheat scraps and hardly ever being in the press, Sam had burgeoning success as Ruby's deputy, which saw him regularly on the front pages, the new face of jump racing, who rode with natural composure.

Indeed, he was the rising star of the weighing room, not short of intelligence, with his pedigree, and gifted with racing acumen: "He makes the right moves at the right time in a race," said Venetia. He was helped by being physically ideal for his profession, combining instinct, nimble agility and an innate sense of balance. Instinct was key, backed up with a quiet riding style (he was chuffed to be compared with Timmy Murphy, whom he always admired) and a good eye for a fence. Getting on good horses is the real secret of success: good horses make good jockeys (as Richard Pitman's autobiography affirms). Sam was privileged to be at Ditcheat, riding for Nicholls, the champion trainer "With the horses we had to ride and with Ruby often being there as well. I learned a lot from him, an absolute genius in his race-riding. You can't teach what he did, he was very natural, but

I certainly always watched him. The way he sat on a horse over an obstacle was what I tried to take from him."

Ruby's Cheltenham fall meant Sam had to step up suddenly from the sub's bench, with the sure touch of a man at the top of his game. It is not uncommon for the understudy to take centre stage, and make a hit with the critics. Sam did just that, in a series of high-profile rides. Ruby's injuries had opened a Pandora's box for the young Welshman, who reaped a stellar harvest. The way he did so, slipping seamlessly into Ruby's shoes in what became a dream month, is a *Boys' Own* story: winning the Betfair Chase on Kauto Star, the Cheltenham Gold Cup holder, proved a pivotal moment in Sam's career, and showed a maturity beyond his years. Next day he hoovered up the Becher Chase at Aintree on Mr. Pointment, who took to the obstacles like a natural, and promptly became the new Grand National favourite.

Nicholls was impressed with 23-year old Sam. "We needed a good number 2 to Ruby: Sam's style of riding suits our horses, and he's a nice guy, which is important. I've thought for some time he could be Champion Jockey material. He's very mature for his age." Sam wasn't altogether comfortable to be the new pin-up boy of the weighing room, and found it "a bit weird being recognised in the street, but I'll take it if it's the price of success."

The dashing young Welsh pretender was an intelligent rider, who listened to his horse, and was only forceful when he needed to be. Like Ruby, he was neat and efficient, resisting the temptation to be flashy or take unnecessary risks. Tom Scudamore commented at the time, "Sam's not doing things differently, he's doing them on a bigger stage. Mentally some jockeys can't do that."

Of all Sam's race mounts, the horse he will always be associated with is Denman, a horse who pushed the boundaries of what was thought possible. The liver chestnut saw the light of day on April 17th 2000, "an enormous foal, so big we had to call for help to pull him out," said his breeder, Colman O'Flynn. The horse won a point-to-point in March 2005, and soon after, then in the care of ex-jockey Adrian Maguire, was led out of his box to be looked at by trainer Paul Nicholls and his patron, Paul Barber. Both were bowled over by the horse's presence and power: "If he'd been human, he'd have been Muhammad Ali; he looked tough, determined, would fight to the end." Despite having been hobdayed – an operation to remove soft tissue ventricles and thus alleviate breathing problems - the horse came to Ditcheat.

As often, though not always, the case with great horses, Denman could bite and kick: he was "a bit of a playboy," says his groom, Jess Allen, and, like the great Crisp, he hated being clipped. But as he grew yet more physically imposing, sages noted he was not dissimilar to Mill House, the 'Big Horse', who won the Gold Cup majestically as a 6-year old in 1963. So the horse had quite a reputation by the time he reached an English racecourse, then promptly won all his first four hurdle races, two at Wincanton under Christian Williams, one at Cheltenham on New Year's Day 2006, ridden for the first time by Ruby Walsh, who described the horse as "a big, awkward, quirky yoke, a real handful, but an aeroplane," and one at Bangor, by the length of the straight. In the top novice hurdle at the Cheltenham Festival, he was just beaten by Nicanor, a defeat for which Ruby blamed himself.

But a steeplechaser was all Denman was destined to be; hurdles only got in his way. Even though he was a brilliant jumper of the lesser obstacles for his size, and very athletic, he was clearly destined to be master over the 'big black ones'. From October 2006 to February 2009 he didn't lose a race. He won novice chases with ease, including the novice championship, the Royal and Sun Alliance Chase at Cheltenham, where he got into a wonderful rhythm, tearing the field apart and storming up the final hill as if it wasn't there, to win by ten lengths. Because he had such a long stride, it was sometimes hard for his jockey to gauge just how fast Denman was travelling.

His next race, the first out of novice company in the 2007-2008 season, was the most prodigious and competitive handicap chase before Christmas, the long-established Hennessy Gold Cup, for which he was assigned top weight of 11 st 12 lbs. Saturday December 1st 2007 was a dreich day of heavy rain and First World War trench mud. But gloom was alleviated by a young Welshman riding a strong liver chestnut in the big race. 'The Tank', as he was now christened, did not just beat his rivals, in the keen words of Alastair Down, "He demolished them, putting them to the sword with a performance that melded the magnificent with the merciless." Sam's only challenge was keeping the lid on his mount, who had jumped into the lead after a circuit and bowled along happily. His jockey was a passenger then, the horse measuring his fences well, while his pursuers started to look ragged: in the words of Marcus Armytage, "White flags were being unfurled." Sam said, "When I looked over my shoulder, turning into the straight, I couldn't believe my eyes. I hadn't even got out of first gear at that stage. He's destroyed them." Treating the opposition, the fences, and the burden of top weight with disdain, the giant gelding threw in a mighty jump at the last, and hacked up by eleven lengths, to the delight of a huge early December crowd.

The manner of his victory evoked comparisons with such previous Hennessy winners and jumping greats as Mandarin, Arkle, Burrough Hill Lad, Diamond Edge and One Man. Alastair Down's report went on to say that Denman "wolfed the last two fences with the appetite of a trencherman sitting down to a light snack as he galloped all the way to the line without the semblance of a falter, $3\frac{1}{4}$ miles of gluey Newbury turf, and a field thought bound to bother him flicked away like a crumb off a lapel. Many are the mighty deeds, but few, so very few, in this league." Jon Lees of the *Racing Post* suggested Sam request a set of wing-mirrors for Christmas that year. Denman's flawless jumping had included some spectacular leaps, highlighting, as more than one blade of the turf remarked, that this was one of those 'I was there when' days.

It was hard to comprehend how a horse could win this big race so easily. You need a bold jumper at Newbury, because the fences are coming at you fast. Denman had made use of his jumping prowess and got into an unstoppable rhythm. Hyperbole ran amok; those present had witnessed not just a clear association with superlative talent, but also a muddy marvel. Yet, racing scribes are men of experience. Alastair Down sounded a gentle cautionary note in referring back to the day in 1963 when Mill House won the same race decisively, and seemed destined to be the ultimate champion – until meeting his nemesis in Arkle. Reporting on the 2007 renewal of the race, Andrew Longmore in *The Times* wrote: "Sam should record the last few weeks for posterity; it might not get much better for him than this." Meantime, the lad was enjoying his moment in the sun.

Denman's Hennessy win under Sam, with "murderously intimidating ease" was followed the next week with an exhilarating success in the Tingle Creek Chase at Sandown, on Twist Magic. John Francome, commentating on Channel 4, said, "The jockey must have bruises on his legs from pinching himself every time he wakes up in the morning. Life gets better and better." Newspaper headlines beamed out: 'SAM'S THE MAN' and 'NO DOUBTING THOMAS': his bank account soared; his ego did not. Sam was repaying the faith shown in him, and found the month "a whirlwind… quite unbelievable," but he kept his feet on the ground. He knew Ruby would return to ride the top horses, and his own magic roundabout would slow down. He had ridden with the guile and dash of a veteran, and "discovered heaven on earth," but was still aware that jockeys can be chewed up and spat out quickly. His success had come about in a flash: "One moment Ruby was winning all before him, the next I was being hoisted aboard some of the finest jumpers in the land. Only when people spoke to me about it, did I realise it'd actually happened: all those big races, I'd never have believed it. I still can't in some ways."

Denman won his preparation race for the Gold Cup when taking the Aon Chase at Newbury – the race now named after him – galloping off into watery sunlight, his raw power reducing his rivals to distant spectators – confirming his position as a worthy challenger to Kauto Star in the Gold Cup. The mighty giant made one mistake, which allegedly "brought the ghost of a smile to Kauto's backers," but he never looked like falling: "It reminded him not to take liberties with his fences," said Sam. Not long before the blue riband of 2008, Ruby, having the choice of Kauto Star or Denman, had committed himself to Kauto: "You don't get off a Gold Cup winner." Kauto held the highest official rating for a steeplechaser since Desert Orchid. Sam, who, if he'd had the choice would have gone for Denman, was grateful to keep his association with The Tank: "The Aon gave me the chance to have an extra spin on him. They are both exceptional horses: Kauto has speed and power; Denman is an out-and-out galloper we've not seen the best of yet. We'll make the running if we have to." Before the championship race, Sam was riding like a demon: he took every race as it came, being careful with what he rode, and "cracking on as normal."

The build-up to the Gold Cup clash was enormous, racing fans pinning their colours – literally, their coloured scarves – to one or other in their pre-clash fervour. The 'freak of nature', Kauto, versus the 'force of nature',

Denman, even Beauty versus The Beast. Kauto was loved, Denman respected. Sam kept quiet, and kept the faith: "I definitely believe my fella will win." Hype was ratcheted up to the maximum. Commentator Richard Hoiles had not known a more eagerly awaited clash. It was the collision of jump racing's heavy weights, the promoter's dream show-down of two 8-year old horses, born only 29 days apart, housed in adjacent boxes at Paul Nicholls' Somerset yard: the trainer had kept them apart till now. Jonathan Powell captured the febrile atmosphere: "Kauto Star is the reigning champ, as good a chaser as we've seen for years. Precociously gifted, and sleekly athletic, he has speed to burn, and glides through his races with insolent ease, before stretching clear in the prizes that matter most in the jumping calendar. Denman is a raw-boned giant of a horse, undefeated over fences. Taller and much heavier than Kauto Star, he possesses a relentless ground-devouring stride, unlimited stamina, and a ruthless racing style that intimidates his rivals." So, the supreme stylish artist versus the big punching fighter. Nicholls wouldn't choose between them: "Kauto's the reigning champion. Denman is the challenger, still on the up, but he'll have to go to a new level if he is to emerge as the winner." Kauto Star was favourite, at odds-on, "the dancer with Beckham-esque love of the limelight against pure Mike Tyson." With those distinctive scarves peppering the whole racecourse, as in medieval jousts centuries before, the racing gods were in benevolent mood: Nick Luck's panache summed up such keen anticipation: "... and so to the uncorking of sport's most shaken bottle..."

CHAPTER 17:
DUEL IN THE COTSWOLDS

"The racecourse is a place where everyday reality is suspended, in favour of a theatrically heightened version."

- Hugh McIlvanney -

2008 was the year when high storming winds cancelled the Festival's Wednesday; Thursday and Friday cards were extended. That Friday, a local Cheltenham vicar was out for a run near his Prestbury home. Easter fell early that year, and he was composing his sermon for Palm Sunday while he ran, a small transistor pressed against his ear, as he listened to Radio Five Live. He hadn't intended to run to Prestbury Park, though he had been racing there once, and he loved the buzz around Cheltenham in Race Week.

The Gold Cup was on: he heard its growing roar on the commentary, and resolved to find out what it was like to see the great race for himself. Landing at a side entrance, he assured the gateman of his ecclesiastical credentials, and was let in. He wandered past the stands as the roar from the race, and its aftermath subsided. Without planning his route, he ended up where the horses are led to cool down after the race: there was only one horse there, with his lass, and no-one else. Something identified the mighty Denman…

Still with commentary in his ear, he later described what was unfolding in front of him as "surreal, a significant, compelling moment." He walked gently back towards the stables with the horse and his lass: minutes before, seventy thousand people had been cheering Denman's name: suddenly he was by himself; no-one knew he was here. The crowd had moved on, as they did on Palm Sunday – the vicar's sermon that year was potent.

To describe racing journalists as 'hacks' does them a huge disservice. No small number of them have fiendish writing skills, from which we all benefit. True, they apply hyperbole, but why not, when some performances by horse, rider, or both, deserve nothing less? Their ability to summon up the 'mots justes' reached an apotheosis in their dashing anticipation and evaluations of the Cheltenham Gold Cup 2008. Few could put a cigarette paper between Kauto Star and Denman...

Sam had not ridden a winner at the Festival, but he knew his mount, Denman, the tungsten-tough liver chestnut, had a brutal, almost intangible will to win. The bottom of his neck was one slab of muscle. He was building a great following because of the whole-hearted way he went about his racing: a swash-buckling hero, capable of breaking rules that apply only to mortals, a huge, rough-cut diamond polished into something close to flawless. He was the Bentley; Kauto Star, the reigning champion and favourite, the Rolls Royce.

When the race began, the top priority was not to go too hard early on; so Sam allowed Denman to settle in behind, but passing the stands to start the second circuit, he racked up the gallop to blunt his rivals' speed. Flicking over his fences with the finesse of a show jumper, he devoured them with sure-footed panache, head down, huge stride, putting the gun to his adversaries' heads. With relentless, ruinous rhythm they cranked up the pace further. His jockey had a plan, and he kept to it: with an awesome display of relentless galloping, flawless jumping and a rare and thrilling exhibition of raw power, Alastair Down saw "an air of blitzkrieg about him as he blazed away, challenging all-comers to come and lay a glove on him."

From the top of the hill, Ruby Walsh on Kauto Star could be seen sending out distress signals, as he saw the crown being wrenched from his grasp, but the pair plugged on in searingly hard and lung-shredding pursuit. Denman forged on further, drawing comparisons with Arkle, taking huge, relentless cuts at his fences, never touching a twig, putting his opponents to the sword: "The show-down was becoming a mow-down." The pair loved it in front: every time they landed after a fence they were looking for the next. They had Kauto Star in their pocket, and they kept him there. Turning for home,

Sam looked under his arm to see how his opponents were travelling: he continued to tear them apart, giving his trusty partner the freedom of Gloucestershire, and Jim McGrath wrote: "The only surprise, long before the run-in, was that white towels didn't flutter down from the packed terraces of owners' enclosures." Richard Hoiles' commentary on the race remains epic: "... relentless, remorseless, he's powered Kauto Star into submission."

Denman had put the race to bed: he had blazed into the finishing straight and kept on gamely up the run-in, although visibly tiring, to win by an emphatic seven lengths. Ruby gave Sam a congratulatory pat as the two horses pulled up, and said the best horse won on the day – though he vowed he would gain his revenge. The crowd, who know their jumpers, acclaimed both horses: two great animals running freely round a track in front of 60,000 spectators was an antidote to so much in modern sport: monumental greed, drug cheats, match fixers and corruption.

David Walsh had the sense of having watched a plan of military precision enacted before his eyes. That plan had been gone over a million times in Sam's mind: he knew he had to make the race a supreme test of stamina, and he executed that plan flawlessly. The experience is still seared into his memory – and many of ours. After a flying dismount in the winners' enclosure, where he leaped from the saddle in triumph, arms spread wide, legs akimbo, "wearing a grin the width of the River Severn," the jockey paid fitting tribute to his mount: "He wasn't doing a tap in front: he just stays and stays. He'd have gone through a brick wall for me. He's just such a good horse."

It was not the head-to-head over the final few fences many had hoped for, but some felt that in its way it was better: the monster, in the hands of a master tactician, had given a matchless exhibition, ripping the heart out of his adversaries, rising to the occasion supremely. As good as Denman's performance was, Sam's matched it: he won the race exactly the right way, sensing the weaknesses, going for them and finishing off the job. No winner, save Coneygree, ever makes so much of the running in the Gold Cup, but no-one had seen Denman so imperious before. His indomitable will to win had changed the racing landscape in the space of a few minutes, shifted single-handedly by the horse known as The Tank. Nick Luck believed that day that no horse on the planet could touch him or his giant, nimble leaps;

he was, "a cocktail mixed to perfection, floating round Cheltenham in full sail, shredding Kauto Star's cloak of invincibility borne for two seasons."

Paddy Brennan, sixth that day on Knowhere, described that Gold Cup as the best he had ever ridden in. Brough Scott quoted P.G. Wodehouse: "Being there was like being in heaven without all the bother and expense of dying." Denman's was a totemic victory that had "something shiveringly raw about it that grabbed the soul: heart first, huge frame to follow, he hurled himself at his fences like an old-fashioned war horse. Here was a dreadnought dropped in against dinghies, his precise, uncanny athleticism looking for an outlet." (Alastair Down)

The old champion had been taken to a place where he did not want to be, a tortuous world, where lungs burned, and every stride was painful. In 1964 the speed and class of Irish champion, Arkle, had proved too much for the bruising power of Mill House: this time, it was the other way round. Nicholls gave credit to Sam's "fantastic" ride. The stable's Neptune Collonges, who was destined to win the Grand National – by a whisker – in 2012, had taken bronze, thus giving trainer Nicholls a 1-2-3, which evoked memories of Michael Dickinson's yet greater achievement of saddling the first five home in the 1983 Gold Cup. It was the first time Denman had had a gun to his head in a top-class race, and many felt there was improvement still to come. Some even said that as long as Denman ran like he did, it was difficult to believe anything could live with him.

But while the eight year old was being lauded for what Peter Thomas termed "a performance of the most savage beauty that will crystallise for ever the present achievement of one of the greatest jumpers in racing" and Claude Duval enthused, "No horse has won in such majestic style; it would have taken a concrete wall or a sniper to have stopped him," one or two canny observers discerned that the horse was tiring visibly by the finishing-line, the strain was biting. He had given so much of himself. Ruby's father, Ted Walsh, echoed the lurking note of caution: "The last time there was a clash like this, Arkle broke the heart of Mill House," though not completely, for the Big Horse stormed up the Sandown Hill in 1967 to win the Whitbread Gold Cup. Walsh and Thomas know a bit about horse racing... both Denman and Sam were to pay a high price for their magnificence that March day...

Immediately after the race, before the horse was spotted by that local vicar, a vet said that he'd never known a horse to be so hot for so long afterwards – he almost overheated. When Denman came back from his summer holiday in the field, he was out of sorts for some time, and not training with his usual zest: those closest to him were shocked at the deterioration – this was not the same horse. So he was sent to Newmarket, where Celia Marr, at Rossdales, performed a full cardiological assessment on the horse, now seriously ill. She diagnosed a sustained atrial fibrillation. The horse underwent surgery and was treated with quinidine, which dampens down that extra electrical activity, and allows the heart to go back to a normal rhythm. Denman fought his illness bravely.

Despite his exertions in the Gold Cup that previous March, there was no knowing what had sparked the problem, which can happen at rest, just as it can during a race. The horse had regular checks after treatment, and no further heart problems. But he had been mighty tired up the long Cheltenham run-in: he had given so much of himself, and, with sheer guts, still tried to find more. Shrewd judges had noted he was wandering slightly in the last few yards: the roll of his forelegs showed the strain was biting. Sam was not totally surprised Denman had heart issues, because that March day the manner in which he won destroyed his opposition: "He was so competitive, he wanted to win more than anyone else. Nothing was going to come by him the day he won the Gold Cup."

So, later than planned, Denman went back into indoor training, and was gradually built up to fitness for the retention of his crown. But in the schooling ring Ruby heard barrels being clattered, bars being hit, and saw a general untidiness in the champion, so suggested schooling him over the fences to wake him up, change his mind, and spark him. Denman decided he was in the mood, reappeared at Kempton after eleven months off the track, and was well beaten – his first defeat over fences. And so, back to Cheltenham to defend his title, where, this time, despite staying on gamely under pressure, coming upsides Ruby, again on Kauto Star, and catching Ruby's eye, he had to give gallant best to Kauto, who floated over his fences and came home, the first horse to wrestle back the Cheltenham Gold Cup.

Denman ran a monster of a race, a great training performance by Team Ditcheat. "If you'd seen him last winter, you were worried would he

ever go near a racecourse again, let alone finish second in a Gold Cup," –
which he was to do three times in all. Barely a month after Cheltenham, he
ran at Aintree, but hated its tight course, as some experts had predicted, and
fell when under pressure: his season was over. Yet next autumn the warrior
was battle-ready. He had to be. Set to shoulder a crushing 11 st 12 lbs in
the Hennessy 2009 Gold Cup, this time ridden by Ruby Walsh, he silenced
any doubts with a second battering win in the race, jumping and galloping
his rivals into a state of near-exhaustion, his trainer describing the heroic
performance as "one of those experiences I'll never forget, not least
because he was so ill last year, perhaps more than we realised." Ironically,
Denman's closest pursuer at the line was Sam Thomas, aboard stable-mate,
What a Friend. Alastair Down compared the horse's 2007 Hennessy win:
"scarily magnificent" with his 2009 win: "lovably indefatigable."

But whereas in 2007 Denman was at his peak, the mighty athlete in
his pomp, carrying his 11st 12lbs as a weightlifter might carry a small
child on his shoulders, this was a different, dominant Denman who again
dazzled the Newbury crowd. Steve Dennis' fears that the horse who, up
to then in 2009 "had been made to seem mortal, a shell of his former
self laid low by his heart problems, his proud record in tatters, his crown
lost for good, his 11st 12lbs looking like a millstone around the neck of
a war-wearied veteran," were allayed in the most magnificent manner.
Denman was back...

By the time of his prep race for the 2010 Gold Cup, The Tank ran
at Newbury in the Aon Chase (now the Denman Chase). Sam had been
controversially replaced on his back by AP McCoy, The horse panicked
at the third last, stepped at its ditch, and was already in descent when he
reached the fence's apex: a carbon copy of his Aintree fall: his jockey, the
multiple champ, was "unceremoniously ditched." That day at Warwick,
jocked-off Sam won one race with what Mike Cattermole rated "the ride
of the year." 'Choc' Thornton spoke for many when he commented that
he wasn't sure if he'd have meddled with the original riding arrangements.
In the 2010 Gold Cup Denman went down all guns blazing to Imperial
Commander, ran a below-par race at Punchestown, and, reunited with
Sam, who had never lost hope he would get back on him on day, ran a

courageous third to Diamond Harry in the Hennessy, his jumping acumen and never-say-die tenacity smashing through the pain barrier – again.

The Gold Cup 2011 was his fourth appearance in the blue riband; back on board, Sam summoned up the old Denman for one last time, put his shoulders to the wheel, wore his battered heart on his sleeve, and finished runner-up, this time to Long Run, a horse five years his junior, beating Kauto Star into third. No horse had finished the silver medallist in three Gold Cups. But after an uncharacteristically tame run at Aintree, he picked up a tendon injury, and was retired in December 2011.

Sent to Charlotte Alexander, he survived a life-threatening infection, fighting for his life in a veterinary hospital for five months, before continuing his second career as a team chaser, returning for his final days in the spring of 2017 to owner Paul Barber among the Somerset lanes where he had built his legend. The following summer, after the deterioration of his stifle, equine equivalent of the human knee, the decision was made to euthanise him painlessly at home: even a big, old lump like Denman is still delicate, fragile and vulnerable to the smallest thing.

Obituaries flowed, together with a sense of regret we never got to see how good he could have been, for he was still on an upward curve when the heart injury intervened. Sam paid tribute to "The type of horse you'd want for your best friend: he'd always be there for you; you could rely on him. On his day there was no better horse in the world: he was a real power-house, who loved to attack his fences." Charlie Brooks saluted his enormous presence and ability to pummel his opponents into submission; Alastair Down wrote that Denman was "not born, he was quarried - a horse of stature, his great head lowered in battle, courage in every stride. The way he ate up his fences, giving his all, meant that the sight of Denman in full cry forged deep connections with the racing public. He was all heart and battling prowess – the perfect steeplechaser. He exhibited for many of us the sheer vicissitudes of jump racing: blistering success, severe injury and a comeback of Lazarus proportions, before being carried out on his shield."

Sam had known Denman was special because, with such a high cruising speed, he found everything easy; the jockey's main job was to get the horse to relax: he could be a jack-in-the-box, as he just wanted to get on with it.

If he hit a fence it'd take nothing out of him: he just kept putting his head out, he wanted to win. Steve Dennis saw "His name written in gold leaf for as long as leaves turn from green to gold and back again, his great achievements safe from the erasing effects of time and memory." His tribute on the day Denman would have turned 20 is gold-dust: "Death shall have no dominion. How could it when he had gained racing immortality long ago? Death takes a moment, and is gone, but a life so well lived is everlasting. Denman is gone. No more will he lift his head as pheasants rise from the hedgerows with a clatter of wings, no more will he carefully present his backside to those seeking an audience, his silent, eloquent method of deterring conversation.

"But what a treasury he left us. Death takes life, but it cannot subtract from it, cannot diminish that which came before. Denman's legacy is inviolable. What will form the main strand of a million reminiscences is the way he went about his work. At his great and glorious peak he was an elemental force like no other. He was a big horse, a throw-back to a half-forgotten age of steeplechasing, when giants strode the earth. We called him The Tank, in tribute to his size, but also to his relentlessness. He was the irresistible force, and woe betide any immovable object that lay in his way, like bulwarks of belief turned to matchwood by his might.

"To watch him barrelling down the Cheltenham hill was to witness the perfect explosion of equine power. Together with his stablemate, he helped change the aspect of his sport. Denman and Kauto Star were like United and City, Federer and Nadal, Coe and Ovett, opposing styles, opposing poles of brilliance.

"But as long as horses race, whenever the dust is blown in clouds from ancient record books, Denman will be brought bewitchingly to life. Years hence, when younger faces light up at the exploits of the next great star, (for there is always a next great star), old heads will nod, and then these words will follow: "Ah, but you never saw Denman, did you?"

CHAPTER 18: SAM POST-DENMAN

"When things hit hardest, you find something within you, an intangible force, that propels you forward... you draw immense power from this inner strength, but often you don't know you have it till you're forced to depend on it."

- Walt Whitman -

As Denman's powers declined, so Sam's star was no longer ascendant. After his Gold Cup success, racing scribe Alan Lee in *The Times* had lauded: "the new face of jumps racing: he has all the raw material – looks, youth, personable nature, and classically respectable background." This assessment was accurate: Sam only needed the breaks: as is common in this fickle arena, they come through the misfortune of others, and Ruby Walsh's horrifying fall at Cheltenham had opened the door for the young Welshman.

In the 2008 Grand National, Sam rode Mr. Pointment, a horse with solid credentials, having won the Becher Chase that season over the famous fences. Compared to Cheltenham, which Alan Lee termed "a minestrone of conflicting pressures," Sam found no real pressure in the National. "You can't really have pressure in that race, as anything can happen. So much is out of your control." His first experience of Aintree had been as a teenager in 1999, the year Bobbyjo won: he got lost in the crowd somewhere down the home straight.

Mr. Pointment was only Sam's second ride in the great race: in 2006 he had fallen at The Chair from Silver Birch – who went on to win the race a year later. That year, 2007, Sam had been knocked out in the bumper the day before, so he was left a spectator - but not entirely: a loose horse, Graphic Approach, was acting wildly with heat exhaustion. Having knocked down three stewards, the horse crashed through railings and collapsed, legs flailing. The screens went up. Sam heard the commotion, saw the horse fall, got between the kicking legs, and removed its saddle, giving the horse some relief. "I did what I could," he says. When, minutes later, the race was won by Silver Birch, it brought mixed feelings for the Good Samaritan watching on. In 2008, he and Mr. Pointment jumped for fun, and led the field bravely down the inside for much of the race, before pulling up at the final fence.

But the flip-side of good publicity is very different. In May 2008, eight weeks after his Gold Cup triumph, riding the odds on favourite, Oumeyade, in the Best Mate silks at Fakenham, where he was top jockey that season, Sam took the wrong course, riding his finish a lap too soon. It was an uncharacteristic blunder that the jockey put down to a lapse in concentration, making him only the latest in a long line of jockeys who had taken an incorrect course at Fakenham. But media knives were out: GOLD CUP SINNER; FAKENHAM FIASCO; THE MOMENT OF MADNESS; MORE WAYWARD LADS – headlines any jockey could do without. Sam was banned for seventeen days. His win in a later chase that day was virtually ignored, and Fakenham promised it would consider changes to the track. But mud sticks... Oumeyade ran again, at Stratford later that week, this time ridden by Ruby Walsh.

Twelve months on from the magic of November/December 2007, Sam experienced Dame Fortune's crueller side. At that time he was sitting eighth in the jockeys' table, with the second best strike rate after Ruby Walsh, who, riding in Ireland as well as in Britain, rode fewer, better-fancied horses over here. With Ruby now on the sidelines with his injury, Sam was on Kauto Star for the Betfair Chase; the horse was bidding for a hat-trick in the race, which in 2007 was the first leg of a £1 million bonus, if the winner went on to land the King George at Kempton and then the Gold Cup. Kauto Star's career had been punctuated by heart-stopping blunders, often at the last fence, and he was not at his athletic best that November day. After labouring in the race, he hurled himself at the third last, landed on top of it, survived, though momentum was gone. Realising he needed to jump the final fence well, Kauto, the short-priced favourite, "threw in a big, stretching leap, but slipped on landing, did the splits, slithered to the ground and, in his recovery stride, tossed Sam up round his ears, then shook him loose, like a rag-doll on to the turf." (Alistair Down). The horse was quickly on his feet, but Sam took longer, a grim expression on his face. Pain flooded in, but not to his body.

Next weekend came the Hennessy: this time Sam was again riding the favourite, Big Buck's, also trained by Nicholls. In a race before the big one, Sam had taken a fall at the final fence. Then, coming into the last in the Hennessy, the biggest handicap of the jumping year, with his race all-but won, Big Buck's still needed a good jump, but put down on Sam, veering left, as he buckled on landing. The jockey lost his balance two strides after the fence, and was ejected. (Ironically, Big Buck's never took to fences, but proved one of the best long-distance hurdlers: his last-fence fall in the Hennessy was the making of the horse, as Stan Turner had foreseen.)

At Aintree next day, Sam took a spectacular fall from Gwanako at The Chair in the Grand Sefton Chase, over the Grand National fences. His undignified exit ensured he adorned the front page of the *Racing Post* for the second day in a row. Then, on Mr. Pointment in the Becher Chase, he completed the course, an exhausted runner-up to Black Apalachi, who would finish second to Don't Push It in AP McCoy's National victory of 2010. The knives came out for the young Welshman, and were "sharpened with depressing relish on the steel of recent reverses," (Alistair Down). Sam found himself pilloried in the market-place of public criticism.

But not all the racing scribes joined in. Paul Kealy of the *Racing Post* was strong in Sam's defence: "I think people should get off his back. He hasn't become a poor jockey, he's just been incredibly unlucky. Kauto Star has a habit of clouting the last, and Big Buck's is known to be a dodgy jumper. Does one mistake make Sam a bad jockey?" Down, also, was compassionate: "Suddenly the man who powered Denman home in the Hennessy and Gold Cup is on the verge of being hung out to dry in this fusillade of frankly horrible days. If he is shuffled diplomatically aside, it will shred his confidence. If you shatter the crucial confidence or emasculate self-belief, then you render a jockey incomplete, like a fish without fins, or a bird missing its wings." The journalist asked us to reflect on what our love of the sport offers us; the opportunity to celebrate something unique. "It has something to do with the risk to life and limb, the chemistry of endeavour that makes jockeys, at the polar opposites of triumph and wrenching defeat, embrace after pulling up at

Cheltenham, and it also lies in the joy and admiration with which the public greets great feats at the end of major races that weave our history. It is about how we behave as people, the value that we place – in a world obsessed with pounds, shillings and pence – on more enduring matters, such as courage, compassion, and the sheer joy of being a part of something that marches to some mysteriously worthier drum. This was not a choice about Sam Thomas. It was a choice about who we all are."

Hailed as the second coming, the jockey had had a lot to live up to. The sight of him and Denman powering up the unforgiving Cheltenham hill had been something for which people would pay good money. But Sam was quick to point out that, during his reversal of fortunes, the depth of his fellow jockeys' camaraderie took him by surprise.

Few others seemed concerned with the jockey himself, who admitted he was mortified: "No words can describe how I feel." But in a *Racing Post* interview with Richard Forristal, Sam more than held his own, as detractors bayed for blood: "Unfortunately, the couple of races that went wrong happened to be on terrestrial TV. I knew I wasn't doing anything differently, and it's just a shame that was all the media had to write about." He was still riding plenty of winners, and people forgot about that. Forristal believed that the media had become outcome-orientated to the point of obsession when it came to Sam's rides. "… The detractors chose to ignore the realities: in the Hennessy, they didn't see a horse out on his feet put down at the last because the tank was empty, they saw his jockey lose balance and come off the favourite."

Sam tried to put the criticism to the back of his mind, and focus on each race. A trip to Yogi Breisner, the jumping guru, offered him reassurance, and peace of mind, as Breisner confirmed the jockey was doing nothing differently. But would owners sacrifice Sam Thomas on the altar of AP McCoy? A week later, Sam was jocked off Master Minded in the Tingle Creek – replaced by AP McCoy.

Sam went to Chepstow the day of the Tingle Creek. "I'll go and ride whenever I'm told to ride. I'll just keep trying to ride as many winners as I can." He dealt with the job at hand, and bounced back in the best way he could. Forristal paid tribute to his being in turn forceful, when bossing Herecomesthetruth to win at Taunton, and composed, guiding What A Friend to a bloodless win at Cheltenham: "If this was a rider suffering a crisis of confidence, as some suggested, he was doing an awfully good job of disguising it."

Forristal believed that Sam was being judged ruthlessly because of the high standards he had set the previous year. "Over a short period of time, slip-ups are inevitably magnified." And he paid tribute to Sam's determination: "As if it were ever going to be anything else, his response to adversity has been brilliantly ardent. When things went wrong, he refused to go with them." The jockey expressed humility by conceding: "I've probably learned more from what has happened this season than I did last year when everything was going so smoothly... You have to think about it more when things go wrong, and I certainly feel as though I've learned a hell of a lot more now. It just makes you stronger, I suppose."

Sam was rebuilding his reputation, but would he be given a fair go by the unforgiving racing media? He had always looked to be destined for great heights, a youngster going through the burnishing process that all big names endure as they scrap their way up one of the toughest ladders in competitive sport. But now rank misfortune was putting him – and keeping him – on the rack. Sam's decline showed racing folk and the media at their worst: knee-jerk reactions and scapegoating. The jockey remained the consummate horseman, especially adept at judging pace and getting horses into a rhythm. But just as quickly as he had registered on the public radar, he retreated into the shadows. Perhaps it was not so much that Sam had lost his confidence, rather that others had lost their confidence in him, speculated Alistair Down.

But the day after Sam's fall from Gwanako at Aintree was to prove seminal, like a portent in a Thomas Hardy novel. It was a lowly Monday at Folkestone: Sam had two rides – both fell. Watching those races, from the offices of *The Guardian*, was Chris Cook, who has since joined the *Racing Post* as senior reporter. Little of note had happened that bleak day. Cook felt sorry for Sam's continuing bad run, and decided to write a piece focusing on the jockey's ill-luck, not on any supposed lack of competence. He discussed what had happened at Folkestone over the phone with his editor, who was at an awards lunch, and whose side of the conversation was overhead by at least one other reporter. The result was more difficult headlines for Sam:

"Fall-guy Thomas' miserable run continues," on a "lamentable afternoon."…
"More falls for Doubted Thomas." The need to fill column inches and sell papers was more important than balance or integrity.

Sam answered his critics in the best way possible, when riding a copybook race on Noland, to win the Grade 1 John Durkan Chase at Punchestown in December 2008: "I went into the race with the same attitude I always do." He had the horse travelling well, and fought off the renewed challenge of long-time leader, The Listener, to win by half a length. The crowd gave him a warm reception. As Nicholls said: "That win helped get Sam's confidence back." It was much needed.

And while all around him hatchets were still being sharpened, Richard Forristal was succinct in his summary of a young jockey "catapulted into the limelight of glamour races one moment, then, not long after, enduring a torrid time where his stage appeared to be littered with landmines." Sam told Marcus Townend at the time: "When at first things didn't go right, it was devastating… you wonder what purpose there is to that. It all builds up, and the only way to get back is to start riding winners again. It's a vicious circle. I went from one end of the scale to the other, so it was a big character-building part of my life; my confidence wasn't the highest it's ever been. Confidence is everything: the more you have, the better things will run… When you've not got that confidence, it's so hard to get it back, and that state builds up and up. But when you've got it, it's the best thing ever. I like to think I've come out a better person from it all."

One day after Sam had ridden a double, "Someone in the weighing room just told me that I'm back. I hadn't gone anywhere. The whole thing was completely overblown. People went overboard about what was supposed to be happening to me." Throughout all the indignities and setbacks he endured, Sam put on a brave face. He had to confront a character examination that, wrote Julian Muscat, "would determine the long-term course of a career that had reached such a giddy trajectory when he won the Gold Cup." This relentless media scrutiny became an unseemly sideshow for the sport.

Still rebuilding his reputation, Sam was entrusted with a return to Denman's saddle for the 2009 Gold Cup, running a heroic second to

Kauto Star. Over the following months he remained philosophical. In November 2009, with Ruby Walsh back on Denman for the Hennessy, it was not easy for Sam: "Deep down, I'd love to be riding him – I don't think I'll be lucky enough to see a horse as good as him again, let alone sit on one! After all he's been through, I'd love to see the horse come back to his best." In the event, Sam was arguably in the best seat of all to watch his old ally's heart-stopping win, finishing second to an imperial Denman on What A Friend, co-owned by the loyal Alex Ferguson. And the following month Sam returned to the racing big time, winning the Lexus Chase at Leopardstown on that horse. Like so many of Ferguson's Manchester United performances, the pair scored a late winner, holding off the lunge of Money Trix on the brink of full time.

With uncertainty surrounding who was to ride Denman before the 2010 Gold Cup, and Sam's position ticklish in the extreme, Alistair Down wrote: "There would be jockeys with greater reputations, but none with better qualifications. As a jockey, or as a man." The article is set underneath a photograph of Sam in the weighing room, surrounded by all the paraphernalia of jockeys' lives: he sits alone, hands clasped, pensive...

But he was still sometimes riding out at Ditcheat, and falls do not only happen in a race...

On Thursday March 11th 2010, Sam was schooling Woolcombe Folly at Nicholls' stables in readiness to partner the horse in the Arkle Chase at the following week's Cheltenham Festival. He was jumping alongside AP McCoy. Sam's horse had been jumping boldly, when he took off too early at the final practice fence: his jockey took a heavy fall. AP heard a loud crack.

Racing Post chief photographer Edward Whitaker happened to be at Ditcheat that morning, and saw the horse crash to the ground. Sam was caked in mud and looked very pale, but never lost consciousness. By good fortune, all three pairs of horses following Sam and AP managed to avoid the stricken jockey. An air ambulance arrived in minutes. The ambulancemen had to cut off Sam's jacket; he was shaking with cold, but was able to talk, and asked Nicholls to phone his father. Whitaker was struck by Sam's bravery throughout: "I never heard him complain. He was obviously in great pain, but handled it with such dignity." When one ambulanceman, not knowing

Sam was a jump jockey, asked if he had broken any bones before, Sam replied: "Just the usual."

The jockey, airlifted to Bath's Royal United Hospital, had a hairline fracture of the T1 vertebra: the top one of twelve thoracic vertebrae in the upper back, immediately below the neck. But there was no damage to the spinal cord. Earlier reports of him being on a life-support machine turned out to be wrong. But it was still a bad injury. Paddy Brennan summed it up, saying: "You have to feel for Sam, who's had no bloody luck at all."

The final few days leading up to Cheltenham are always a precarious time; horses walk on glass for fear of a last mishap or injury; trainers pray that nothing goes wrong with them, or with their jockeys. Sam's fall left Team Ditcheat in a state of shock. In addition to Woolcombe Folly, Sam was due to partner Tricky Trickster in the Gold Cup, which may have led them to the Grand National. There was no chance of that now, so missing Cheltenham – and the rest of the season – was a huge wrench, as acknowledged by his sponsors, Markel, "after all the effort he has put in during the season." But the injury could have been so much worse, as Sam realises: "I'm quite lucky, as I'm able to move everything, and get out and about. I'll still go up to Cheltenham. It's never easy to watch a horse you were going to ride, but Cheltenham will be particularly difficult." Most jockeys choose not to go racing when injured.

Sam's injury took time: he didn't get to ride in the Grand National 2010, but instead took a holiday in South Africa. Upon his return, he found himself de trop at Ditcheat; he was not the first, history having shown several jockeys thumbing a lift from the hard shoulder of the M5. Sam soon secured the role of stable jockey to Tom George: "We've raised the profile of our team," said the trainer from Slad, the village made famous by Laurie Lee. "It's only right we had a top-class jockey to ride them, and Sam is top-class." Going to George gave Sam a new direction not dictated by the torments of the previous season, when his stock had spiralled from the giddy heights of Gold Cup glory. Sam hoped the change in status would reignite his career: he was looking forward to the challenge, the opportunity to make more contacts, greater flexibility, and getting back on the winners. Alas, George's operation was not then large enough to justify employing a retained jockey: Sam stayed there less than a year. But there is all the difference between a battered man and a broken one – and he still had moments in the sun.

In November 2010, Nacarat, a thin-skinned grey on whom every scratch showed up as a scar, trained by George, gave Sam a welcome change of luck when winning the Charlie Hall Chase at Wetherby. It was reckoned one of the best Charlie Halls of recent times; Sam and Nacarat, enjoying the decent ground, took the race by the scruff of the neck turning in, and galloped home best up the straight, despite paddling through the third last, and landing awkwardly on all fours. Sam was thrilled; Nacarat that day gave a spring-heeled display. In noting Sam had beaten Ruby and Nicholls into second place with The Tother One, Marcus Armytage wrote: "The jockey who won the Gold Cup on Denman, and was then very publicly jocked off in favour of AP, has maintained his dignity: his chances will surely flow again."

That victory for Sam was only his fifth since the season had started in April. "These have been tough times," said Sam. "I haven't been counting the number of winners I've ridden recently. To ride a winner on a horse like this means everything to a jockey like me. More than anything, it shows I can still ride." So it was more than significant, that win: Tom O'Ryan in the *Racing Post* described it as a "wonderful ride," and the horse came home to "a rousing ovation from an appreciative audience, who simply love a grey." Sam's name was back in lights in a major contest. "He has had his downs, largely through bad luck, bad injuries, or a combination of both. It is a stark reminder of how competitive racing is, and how tough it can be to make a decent living as a jump jockey, unless you have the backing of a top-notch stable, that he has had fewer than one hundred mounts this season. Everyone needs a springboard now and then: the flying grey could project Sam back to bigger and better things."

Riding was still his priority: he wanted to ride as long as he could. The *Racing Post* published a letter of support: "Defeats were not his fault, and having to deal with the resulting downturn in his career was hard; this professional and likeable rider thoroughly deserves a change of luck." For a while Sam worked for Channel 4, under Liz Amperie on *The Morning Line*, precursor to ITV's *Opening Show*. He was responsible for 'Sam's Dark Horses', a feature where he chose a racing yard, usually a lesser-known one; the trainer chose a horse, and Sam focussed on its profile. Many of the horses prospered, while Sam, a one-man band with crew, was at ease talking with the horse's connections on camera, a trait in which he shines, and which, now that he is a trainer, is essential.

But Sam knew he was not the same jockey, though still believed he might be: he had to keep the show on the road, despite being past his best. Riding a winner at Plumpton or Fakenham still gave him a real buzz, far away as these courses were from Cheltenham, where he and Denman had been in perfect harmony. In the season 2007-2008, Sam had ridden 88 winners: in 2012 he had only 122 rides, admitting: "It's a bit depressing the way my career has gone." A win on Arbeo in late December 2012 was only the jockey's sixth win of the season. As he was only too aware, the standard of jockey-ship had never been higher: there were arguably more high quality riders than ever, and even some of those were struggling to get rides. If you weren't with a top trainer, life was hard indeed.

Sam's profile since the heady days on Denman was uncomfortable and confusing. Next season brought further disillusionment, with a mortifying score of three wins: his lack of luck was encapsulated when, finally on a favourite, Niceonefrankie, in a decent race at Sandown, the pair crashed to the turf at the first fence.

Gradually he found himself winding down: he let it happen, increasingly aware that there was no inner force urging him to keep going. His winners became less and less frequent… the message was clear. Unlike jockeys who retired after a blazing winner, none more so than Ruby Walsh after winning the Punchestown Gold Cup with Kemboy on May 1st 2019, Sam cannot recall his last ride… no fanfares, no interviews… he would not weigh out again.

But what was he to do? He said he would never train, for he knew what came with that profession, and a social life certainly didn't. He missed that winning feeling that he knew would not return.

Jim White wrote a piece on Sam in the *Daily Telegraph*: "A sportsman is gifted a moment of complete ascendancy, a second or two in the arc light of history, delivering a performance so extraordinary its significance reaches far beyond the confines of his calling. Then, almost immediately, he suffers from such ill-fortune the only logical explanation is that he signed a pact with the sporting devil, and that, in return for gifting him a brief encounter with triumph, the sadistic old usurer is making him pay with crippling interest."

Alistair Down had the last word: "Racing is driven by results; it's a ruthless, cut-throat game. Sam fell from grace because he was not riding winners. But, for all the hard times the jockey had endured, the good times blazed even more brightly." For them, Sam was 'ever-grateful'. And his win in the Gold Cup, the FA Cup for jockeys, on the best day of his life remains with him...

CHAPTER 19:
SAM THOMAS TRAINER

"What lies behind us, and what lies before us,
are tiny matters compared to what lies within us."

- Ralph Waldo Emerson -

With over 500 winners to his name, since he started riding in 2001, though only three from 64 rides in his last season, Sam began to turn his sights away from riding. But, unlike many jump jockeys, he did not have to hang up his boots for medical reasons. He laughs to think he had once said he would never train, because he was well aware what deprivations came with that life: a trainer has to be completely immersed in his team. The adrenalin and exhilaration he had felt when riding a winner was special, but that would be lost now: winners, if he were to be associated with them in some way, would feel completely different: there would hopefully be exhilaration, but instead of adrenalin the feeling would probably be tamer, more a sense of satisfaction.

Nothing could compare with the buzz of your mount jumping for fun, from fence to fence, wind coursing by, then crossing the line in front. Sam knew he would miss that for a long time, one reason why he kept riding even as his star waned in the racing firmament. "The worst thing of all is to stop," Mick Fitzgerald told him. "You don't get the winning drug anywhere else." But as the months began to ebb by, whereas once they had flicked, Sam slowly found himself winding down: he let it happen, even as he sensed something was telling him not to keep going…

Looking back, he had wondered what he would do. He had no idea, all he'd ever known was riding a horse, being in the thick of it; there was no remedy for his malaise except winners, even just the occasional one. Subconsciously he had been well aware that he was no longer riding at his best, he was trying hard, but to no avail; he was not happy, but he kept up a brave face. Without any ceremony, he had ridden his last race.

Slowly, but surely, he made up his mind to start training. Though some in racing, including Henrietta Knight, who has a soft spot for him, felt he should have started off in the role of assistant trainer, as the majority of greats have done, Sam was ready for a new challenge, and keen to get cracking. He did his trainers' course at Newmarket, and immediately set to work at Winterwell Farm, 1,000 acres of arable Gloucestershire land belonging to his now father-in-law, Peter Cannon. On the road rising out of Northleach, some 15 miles from Cheltenham, Winterwell was not an existing racing stable; Sam had to work hard to secure decent facilities: his gallops were two miles away – and he had no illusions about learning to walk before he could run. He started with just three horses. And from the start he was well aware he had to play a patient game. "I'd been lucky to ride for some very good trainers, and I picked up a good understanding of their ways. I hoped to put that experience – plus what I've gained from riding some of the best horses in the land, to good use, but the horses won't be rushed." He was always going to be hands-on.

His patient manner with horses is not restricted to the public eye. At Winterwell one afternoon I was confronted by a 3-year-old galloping round the corner of his barn and heading straight at me, with only a thin privet hedge between us. Sam appeared, ice-calm, and the horse, mercifully deciding not to jump the hedge, swung away in a lather of sweat. His trainer approached the horse quietly, patted its heaving flanks and then fetched a bucket of water: danger averted. This horse, Wonga Swinger, has gone on to great heights in the show-ring with Sam's wife, Tori, and was Elite Champion in 2023, one of the most competitive awards for former racehorses.

His first runner, Miss Giselle, ran second in a mares' 'bumper' at Bangor in November 2015; Sam was pleased; he just wanted every horse to run up to its best. His first winner was the aptly named Lovely Touch at Wetherby in May 2016. He was on the way, at his 35th attempt. But soon he needed bigger premises, better facilities: when Saxon House, the famous stable in Lambourn became available on lease, Sam seized his moment.

Clare Balding has described Lambourn as an unique village, in that almost everyone who lives there is involved with the horse racing industry. At present there are some 1,500 race horses stabled in 50 yards, with several studs also punctuating the Valley of the Racehorse. Lambourn's annual Open Day on Good Friday is increasingly well-supported, and The Valley Equine Hospital, founded in 1997, is renowned far beyond the village. The place has been written about by Hilaire Belloc; G.K. Chesterton; Colin Dexter of *Morse* fame, and Sir John Betjeman, among others. Alan Lee's *Lambourn – A Village of Racing* and Robin Oakley's *Valley of the Racehorse* have also popularised the village, and it is mentioned, not surprisingly, in several of Dick Francis' crime-racing novels.

Saxon House had been made Upper Lambourn's premier address by previous occupants. Joseph Saxon was a self-made Lancastrian, who bought 100 acres on the road to Upper Lambourn and built Saxon House in 1855, where he trained a successful string of horses, including Brown Duchess, to win The Oaks in 1861. That year, Lambourn also produced the Derby winner, Kettledrum. So it was at first for flat racing that Lambourn was known. That began to change when Reg Hobbs won the Grand National with the American 'pony', Battleship, in 1938. Hobbs trained at Rhonehurst, from where Oliver Sherwood sent out Many Clouds to win the Grand National in 2015, and now the stables for Warren Greatrex. Battleship was the smallest horse in the race; his jockey was 17-year-old Bruce Hobbs, the youngest rider to win the race, and, at 6'1," probably the tallest. The emergence of serious jumping in Lambourn was soon afterwards given a huge boost when Fulke Walwyn moved to Saxon House in 1944.

On September 8th of that year, a B-24 Liberator took off with eight crew from Northamptonshire to fly supplies to the French Resistance, but soon the aircraft spouted flames, so the American pilot, 2nd Lieutenant Lawrence Berkoff, turned for home. With his plane increasingly hard to control, Berkoff ordered six of his crew to bail out, while he stayed at the controls, aiming to avoid the houses. He did so, but was killed instantly when the plane crashed by Folly Road: he had missed Lambourn by 200 yards.

Less than ten years later, the village had another lucky escape, when, on April 13th 1953, at lunch-time, a tanker carrying 3,600 gallons of jet fuel went out of control and careered into Lambourn at 60 mph, with the driver, newly married Reg Bungay, (36) desperately sounding his horn to warn residents of impending doom. He managed to slalom between parked cars in the high street, before thundering into buildings and destroying a shop front. His tanker exploded and he died, trapped behind the steering wheel. Five properties were burnt to the ground, 26 people from 11 families were made homeless, yet, miraculously, none of the locals was injured.

When Sam moved into the Grade 2 listed Saxon House stables on September 1st 2016, he was well aware of the place's potential for him, not least the gallops that would now be available: 8 miles of turf, 7 of all-weather, and 6¾ of artificial, all with the varying inclines so necessary for training racehorses in the best way. "Not a bad site for an office," said Sam.

Centred in these 500 acres of rolling green countryside, with its luscious grass and free-draining soil, were a network of horse-walks, fabulous schooling facilities, and all the machinery needed to keep the gallops operational. It is a superb location, continuously evolving, thanks to massive annual investments, from The Jockey Club, the first time that organisation had supported an area outside Newmarket. "There's no excuse not to train winners here," said Sam. "You just need good horses..." Ay, there's the rub...

Walking into Saxon House yard under Sam's care was to be confronted with a quadrangle of white-washed walls, twenty or so stable doors open to reveal inquisitive heads sniffing the air. An island of grass sat in the centre, as the eye was drawn to myriad rose bushes that had crawled up the walls for aeons, and threw their bright buds into colourful relief with the whitewash.

Tucked away inside one ancient stable was 'The Wall of Fame', a mélange of photos: great winners covering whole eras of the stable's life, tumble-down, peppering the walls: dusty, cobwebbed, weather-scarred, in faded colours, or once black and white, now gone to sepia, and all stages on that journey. Only a few hung straight. Champions abounded: Golden Miller; other National heroes, Royal Mail and Team Spirit; grey Anzio; Gold Cup winners Saffron Tartan, Mont Tremblant and The Dikler, plus several of the Queen Mother's favourite horses, though The Rip was missing. A gently drawn cartoon of Fulke Walwyn stood out among the equine warriors.

In 1936 Walwyn, an officer in the 9th Lancers, won the Grand National on Reynoldstown. He retired after fracturing his skull in a fall at Ludlow in 1939. From Saxon House he sent out a stellar array of horses including Mandarin, Mill House, Special Cargo, who had fought out a pulsating three-way finish in 1984 Whitbread Gold Cup, and Diamond Edge. He won all the big races, and was champion trainer five times, notching up 40 winners at Cheltenham, then a record, among a total of 2,000, before he died at Saxon House in 1991.

So heritage was on Sam's side when he moved his slowly growing string to Saxon House from Winterwell in October 2016: heritage, expectations, and pressure…

Like all trainers making their way up, Sam needed one good horse, and new owners. He spared no efforts in seeking both, flying to Dublin's Goff Sales one day, driving to Ascot Sales the next. Overheads at Saxon House were already pressing and winners came slowly - he needed patience. But he was learning fast, not least the need to have horses in the right races, so they were handicapped accordingly. He was constantly thinking of the future, hoping big wins would come in time, and aware of the old adage, "Keep your horses in the worst company; keep yourself in the best."

As he gradually acquired new horses, others left him for different trainers, an experience no different from being 'jocked off' in his riding days. Meantime he was buying youngsters for reasonable money and hoping… you never knew what could eventuate. Training is a never-ending wheel that has to be kept turning. Trainers can never sit back and relax, being ever conscious of the need to keep building, keep pushing.

His staff worked hard, and he mucked in (and out) with them. One good owner, Bart Beswick, was in the local pub with Sam one evening, playing the game of snagging a horse shoe on to a hook attached to the ceiling. "If you do it in three attempts, I'll buy you a £30,000 store at Land Rover sales," said Beswick. Sam did it. "If you do it again, I'll buy you another one." Sam did, having missed with every shot the evening before.

His gently-growing number of owners needed to be patient, too. But some of his horses were being better handicapped in the summer of 2017, so he was going to the races with runners that had a chance: everyone was getting something back from their toil. It is amazing what a winner can do: the good vibe spreads. But Sam was aware summer racing was not as competitive as the sport becomes in the season proper: he needed to keep the impetus going into the autumn and winter, when things became tougher.

And he was planning hard for the next season: to run a tighter ship; harness the best from his staff, which would become harder as that team grew; stick to routine; use the knowledge he was acquiring, not least on how best to use the gallops at his disposal, and look forward to some nice horses. He enjoyed his trips to the sales, like Naas, "great craic." It takes a day to look over some 350 horses, but Sam does his homework; you have to, as, on sales day, everything happens fast.

In October 2017 Sam took part in Chepstow's two-mile charity flat race in aid of the Bob Champion Cancer Trust, which focuses on trying to understand the molecular basis of the way in which prostate cancer – recently named the most prevalent of all cancers in the UK – develops. Sam badly wanted to win the race. Despite leaving it to the last minute, a trait he acknowledges, a tad ruefully, he raised over £1,500 for the Trust.

Alan O'Keeffe, a long-time mate of Sam's, now assistant trainer to Jennie Candlish, offered him the exotically named Maoi Chinn Tire, who had run the week before the Chepstow race, and spat the dummy after the second obstacle. Sam drove three hours to pick up the horse. He was looking forward to getting back on the track, but he was not at all sure what to expect. It was a weird day: going back into the weighing room made him feel he'd never been away; nothing had changed. In the event, his mount jumped off in front and found he was enjoying himself, not having to clear any fences. He remained in front until the last furlong, when he was headed by a horse trained by his old boss, Paul Nicholls; it looked as though he'd have to settle for the runner-up's spot. But Sam kept squeezing and got back up in the dying strides to win by a short head. Unlike his first point-to-point, Sam knew he'd won – and thoroughly enjoyed the experience, his first ride in public since 2015. He had not lost his riding prowess.

After the race, he said how good it was to support the charity, and how he missed his competitive life as a jockey, comments that one journalist took literally, writing that Sam was to return to race-riding on a more permanent basis, the temptation for more victories now taking precedence over his new training career. Not so. He enjoyed the day, and Chepstow had rekindled good memories: it is probably his favourite track, having booted home many winners there, so he had not needed to walk the course. But the report made him angry, off the record comments being taken as gospel, and people ringing to encourage his return. He still always thinks about riding; it's only natural after 15 years in the saddle. And understandably he had wondered about going back, but realised he'd have to be 110% committed. So he had no intention of slipping back into the old ways; his jockey days were over. He was a trainer now, and had still so much to learn. No longer one of the lads, he had buckled down and was doing his learning the hard way, ensuring he rode the tricky customers himself. Inevitably, some owners let him down, making empty promises, then disappearing; it was a worry, Sam having no big backer, no pot of cash. He was excited when picking a horse out of a field that no-one else had earmarked, like Oscar's Little Rose. But time was always at a premium, as was his patience: it's not easy to sell a horse to a new owner if it's not going to race for a while. You have to be hopeful, but you never know…

Yet his numbers were growing, albeit slowly, during the winter. Then, in January 2018, the weather was grim – horses were ready to run, owners wanted them to run, but the ground was too firm. Mornings were cold, grey and forbidding. It was a trying time, having to stay positive, despite all, and keep everyone else positive, on the same wavelength. He remained keen to engender spirit in those around him.

Nick Oliver, the former point-to-point jockey, was well aware of how daunting a challenge Sam had set himself. "You always hear of the big trainers; Sam for now is one of the others, not seen, yet always working, always striving." The Welshman has never been afraid to strive, and at Saxon House he had three good staff, Emma Hardy, Joe Knox and Frenchman, Quentin. But it was still a testing time; Sam needed that one good winner, and owners with cash. Pressure was growing. Saxon House was becoming a liability, not least where its high rent was concerned. Sam then heard the stables were coming up for sale…

Dai Walters, the former rugby player from Brecon, established Walters Plant Hire Ltd., the group of civil engineering and development companies, and had long been a supporter of National Hunt Racing, having horses with several trainers. In 2008 he set about transforming a once open-cast Welsh mine into the racecourse of Ffos Las (which means Blue Ditch), the first new racecourse in Britain for over eighty years, and was the man in charge, until he sold the course to Arena Racing Company in May 2018.

Sam had known Dai a while, and ridden for him plenty in the days just before the magnate's good horses, Oscar Whiskey and Whisper. But it was something of a surprise when Dai rang him with a view to his becoming Dai's salaried trainer, in charge of his own string of horses at The Hollies, Lisvane, east of Cardiff, just off the M4. Sam remembers the phone call well: it came at a good time. He would be able to bring his own horses from Lambourn. Dai's yard had a good gallop, with stables for 48 horses, perhaps more. It was a tempting offer. Sam had to weigh up the pros and cons: Lambourn had the best gallops in the land; he had spent time building up his career there; had lots of contacts in the area, and no great problem finding staff. But the prospect of better horses was tempting. Sam had learned from training lesser horses, which was never plain sailing; he was now ready for quality ones, maybe even a Cheltenham horse. He would start with a clean sheet. Some of the weight of responsibility would be taken off his shoulders, (not least sorting out the money side of things), which meant he would have to spend less time in the office. He would still have to ride four 'lots' (horses' exercise sessions) every day. The move would be daunting, but with the prospect of an excellent carpet gallop, outdoor school, water treadmill, equine spa, horse-walker, all-weather-schooling strip and daytime turn-out paddocks, the young trainer – still only 33 – soon realised it was a "no-brainer." He rolled the dice…

On April 30th/May 1st 2018, he, his staff and his horses moved to The Hollies. The property lies next to St. Mellon on the eastern fringes of Cardiff, an imposing set-up, with a mansion in sumptuous grounds that slope down to a lake. There are two yards for the horses, top and bottom. Sam was soon at home in his new surroundings. "It's not as picturesque as Saxon House, but it's so much better equipped." Already he was relishing the turn-out paddocks, and the chance to get his horses there after morning exercise. "It does wonders for their heads, not being cooped up inside."

Within a short time of taking over the reins he had broken in ten two-year-olds: "It gets them safe to come in as three-year-olds, and gives them something to think about over the summer; it's the making of them."

Trainers have to understand equine psychology, which can only come from experience. "Every trainer has a different understanding, of course, but it's crucial." He still had six or seven of his charges in for summer jumping, while the rest were fattening up in the paddocks. He would start bringing them back in mid-July, then get them fit for the season proper in the autumn. Dai had bought promising horses: there could in the future be 40 inmates at The Hollies, maybe more...

The yard was in good order; Sam kept it that way. The fact that his third runner from the new base, Not a Role Model, won at Kempton, under Richard Patrick, was a good portent: the realisation that he had a healthy number of horses took some of the pressure off him. At Saxon House he was always under pressure to find and buy a promising horse, with comparatively little cash. For the coming season, all the horses in the yard were capable of winning; "nice horses with which to go to war."

Dai met Sam every morning for an update. So far the trainer had kept all the details of his charges in his head, amongst the host of other issues continually on his mind (no mean feat!): he was hopeful this would still be the case with a bigger string. But he was under no illusions as to the magnitude of his challenge. Racing is all about results; always the bottom line for a trainer, and that means winners...

Dai lets his trainer get on with things, and is happy to go with Sam's decisions. Because the businessman's Plant Hire Company owns most of the horses, Sam does not have to deal with a host of different owners pressing buttons, thus being spared hours on the phone: he can concentrate on the important things. He viewed his first four years as nothing special: success does not happen overnight. He is nothing if not self-critical: "At the start I wanted things to happen all the time, was just running the horses and hoping for the best." He rarely sat down, emptied the ever-churning washing machine, answered the phone, saddled horses, brewed coffee for his staff, handed out tack, and made plans in his head, all at once. At times he felt 'down': "I wanted the best for the horses and for everyone. But in sport there are always ups and downs;

you've got to keep on a level playing field and you need good folk around you: family, mates, staff. Young horses are always going to be stronger next season: why not now?" Gradually, he came to realise you can only do your best.

The season 2020-2021 was not just his best to date, but the season in which he learned the most. There are always a million things in a trainer's head, but Sam had had time to build his experience, aware that he still attracted criticism for never having been an assistant trainer. Now he knows everything is about the preparation of his horses, about bringing them on quietly, which means things happen. He has stopped fooling himself. "They will tell you when they're ready, and if they don't run well, there is always a reason."

Getting winners gives him a buzz, albeit a different one from when he was a jockey. "It means I can wake up before dawn, and go up to the yard, with a spring in my step." He's always first in the yard, checking on each horse in turn, enjoying the lack of noise and bustle that inevitably comes with the daylight and the arrival of his staff, whom Sam is quick to praise. With a new gallop, gradually winners began to flow from The Hollies; "Moving here was the best thing ever," says Sam, "It's crazy how it worked out, even despite Covid." Walters kept all the staff on: "a real bonus."

So the 2020-2021 season was good to him. With 26 winners from 92 runners, his strike rate was a healthy 28%, putting him top of the English trainers, beaten only by Ann Hamilton in Scotland. Folk now noticed Sam Thomas' horses, referring to that season as his coming of age. He was chuffed, but had no illusions about the future: "Next season will be tougher, racing will expect things of me, but I have a lot of young horses to bring on, if anything I will have to work even harder." But winners help: "That's what winners do." Something inside drives him on: "I don't want to define it," and winners make all the wet Welsh mornings – and wet Welsh nights – worthwhile. For the moment his outside life was on hold, but that might not always be the case: "Now I let the horses run where they're ready, not just hoping for the best, as I used to, but knowing that I have left no stone unturned in the horses' preparation." He lets his jockeys use their own initiative, as he did when riding; nothing is as valuable as experience.

Sam's Head Lad for a time, Chris, was once a stunt man (veteran of *Game of Thrones*, *Transformers*, *The Crown*, *Vikings* and *Star Wars*, among others) who fell off horses for a living – correctly. He loved the challenge: "I'd do it again: you have to go with the rhythm of your horse, get the feel of it, and you're away." He was paid £500 per fall – "stupid money" – but for him it was not about cash, he did it for his love of the animal. Horses were all he knew. So he came to work for Sam with a wealth of experience, but aware that with horses you're always still learning. One day in the autumn of 2020, he was exercising a horse at the stables, when it spooked suddenly: Chris was catapulted over the beast's head, did a somersault and landed on rubble. A trip to A&E revealed he had fractured his back: Covid was running amok, which meant no visitors; he had to roll out of bed, and then use the bed to climb back up again. He faced a mental battle, went back to The Hollies for a time, though it was not easy to recapture his nerve in the saddle. "If I fell again, would I break my neck this time? I don't bounce any more!" Riding horses will always carry risks. The stuntman gave up on horses.

The 2020-2021 jump season had presented the potent challenge Sam had expected and planned for: there was pressure, horses had gone up in the ratings, and thus in the weights. But he stuck to his previous year's plan: not rush the horses along; keep options for them flexible; avoid them having unnecessary stress; maintain soundness, fitness and health wherever possible, try to ensure they were mentally strong for the rigours of the season, and trust his judgement. He endeavoured to keep them 'right' until their first run, then give them a quiet three weeks in which to gauge how they all were, and start identifying targets for them. Cheltenham was the main aim. But that was a long way off…

Next autumn he was aided by the building of a brand-new barn, containing 19 boxes, each with a window at the back, so the breeze could blow through. With 35 horses now his team was ultra-busy, riders regularly taking care of six or seven lots a day. But there was no spare muscle in his band, any accident to his staff made things even tougher. Sam had for the first time appointed an assistant, James, a graduate, who was fully hands on; a straight talker, he shared much of the planning with his boss.

At The Hollies there are horses everywhere, usually in pairs: two sedate beasts in one field, their tails flicking; beyond them two younger animals careering across a low field, bucking and rearing with exuberance, sometimes in perfect syncopation. Everywhere feels busy. The horse walker circles endlessly, its cargo usually full. The sand gallop is in constant use, and, parallel to the gallops, practice fences have been spruced up (literally), all of them different: one set of tyres; one low ditch; one brush hurdle with white poles in front (white is now the colour it is thought horses can see most clearly), thus helping them stand off from their obstacles, giving themselves plenty of daylight. There is a pool of fresh water, in which horses can cool off after exercise. On rare days of searing heat, humans can attempt the same practice – though silt dampens any sense of total abandonment to the elements.

The 2021-2022 season did not yield as many winners, but his horses won better races, notching up nearly half a million pounds in prize money, at a strike rate of 19%. Warriors such as Paddy's Motorbike, Galileo Silver, Grey Diamond, Before Midnight, Skytastic and Good Risk At All kept up his strong momentum. The highlight was winning the Welsh Grand National at Chepstow with Iwilldoit, the horse bred by Stan Brown, which gave great pleasure to all, though sadly, because of Covid, the race had to be held behind closed doors. There was no atmosphere, no crowd cheering him home; the only sound Sam heard was Stan Brown shouting. Sam had realised Iwilldoit was a promising horse and had targeted the Welsh Grand National, having won the trial for that race. His trainer was still getting to know the horse and learning about him as they went along. The Welsh Grand National was to be again the aim next season but Sam remained realistic: "You work hard for things and don't imagine them happening until they do."

The 2022 - 2023 season was quiet for Sam, in part due to the lack of rain and absence of decent going for his horses. Yet Stolen Silver, Grey Diamond, Good Risk At All, Before Midnight and London Gold Cup victor, Our Power kept things going. But then, in the early evening of November 1st 2022 Sam, with Dai Walters and three others, were injured when the helicopter in which they were returning home came down in dense woodland near Llanelidan, Ruthie, whilst combating high winds and heavy rain. Dai suffered more serious injuries than the other passengers, and was detained in hospital, where his condition deteriorated, resulting in a transfer to intensive care. Sam played down the accident: "We've just got to keep the show on the road, keep the horses in top form, and keep kicking." Four days after the helicopter crash,

Al Dancer battled to a poignant win in the Grand Sefton Chase over the big fences at Aintree.

Dai took a long time to recover. In January 2023 Iwilldoit, highest rated horse in Sam's stable, with whom the trainer had had to be patient, defied a huge weight and monster absence (383 days) to win the Classic Chase at Warwick. "You won't find another horse to try like him; it's very straight forward when they want to do it - he's the most genuine horse you could wish for." The horse was entered in the Grand National, but did not fulfil all the entry criteria, a ridiculous situation for one who had not only won the marathon Classic, but also that Welsh Grand National 2021. In February 2023, Our Power romped home in the Coral Trophy at Kempton; Sam's horses were coming back into form. But then progress was stalled by a bug in the yard, so winners were desperately hard to come by. Though Our Power ran credibly in the Grand National, Sam was again up against the fates – he battled on. The 2023-2024 season saw him with increasing fire-power; having runners at Cheltenham – with a serious chance – was no longer a pipe-dream. And with horses of real promise, like Ed Keeper, Lump Sum, and stable stalwart, Stolen Silver, there is much to look forward to in the future…

Always spotting and picking up on things, Sam is constantly seeking ways to improve, but at the same time, despite the pressures with a big winner, he knows that ultimately he relies on the horse; the key thing is to keep it simple and try to get the best out of every horse; he trains by instinct, with Walters' invaluable support.

On the question is winning everything: "Yes, for a jockey it means everything. I'm the most competitive person I know. Every time I get a horse I'm thinking how to win, I'm not going racing for a day out. For a trainer, no, winning is not everything in the same way; the trainer has to put the puzzle together, take the positive out of every situation, think about the horse and the future: jockeys don't have time for that." On the mighty challenge that helicopter crash had presented to him, Sam is sanguine, pausing, fixing his gaze and half-smiling: "What doesn't kill us makes us stronger." I know now that those are the words of Nietzsche, but, to me, they are vintage Sam Thomas…

CHAPTER 20:
TAKING THE ULTIMATE STEP

*"It's so much darker when a light goes out than it would have been
if that light had never shone."*

- John Steinbeck -

In the end, it is probably the mental health pressures on jockeys that constitute their greatest challenge.

Having left Marlborough for a primary school in Stow, James Banks came to live with the Arnold family at Nether Westcott. "From a young boy, he was always so much fun," says Jane Arnold. "He was wildly imaginative, in part due to his dyslexia, which at that time was not understood, and he had so much energy." James 'found' riding at the Arnolds, and would get on anything; one day, the lad took a saddle, so as to try and ride a cow. Years later, he rode point-to-point for Jane, got his licence, and started his professional career with Chris Broad.

Broad was James' first agent; he got the lad going as an amateur, after which James was looked after by Russ James, for the vast majority of his career. The jockey admitted he had been a hothead, but Russ saw how well he could ride. For Russ, there was more to being an agent than just booking rides; listening was part and parcel of the job. He and James spoke every day, even if there was not a great deal to say. Russ realised how much the small, insignificant things could manifest themselves in James's mind; although he was "high maintenance," the jockey was "a pleasure to deal with; he depended on good people, and needed to have that spoken contact on a regular basis." James described Russ as a calming influence, and even likened the rapport to a marriage, both of them working through difficulties, as with the injury James sustained in 2013.

One of the podcasts in *Jockey Matters* featured *A Day in the Life of a Jockey*; its subject was James Banks. It showed him arriving to ride work early: he rode out for seven trainers, a different trainer every day of the week, so was always up by 5:30 a.m. latest and there was never guarantee of a proper pay-day. The podcast stressed the physical side of the job, with its manifold risks, but asserted that: "Though the days were long, every day was different; after a low, you dust yourself off and go again." It ended with the words: "It beats working for a living…"

In February 2020, James, 36, failed to turn up to ride work at the stables in the Cotswolds where he had been Head Lad since his final race two years earlier. He was living in a cottage in Naunton owned by Jane Arnold, who went to check on him after his no show: she found his keys hanging from the lock on the outside of his front door. Once inside there was a note saying he had "done something very silly," asking the finder not to go upstairs, but to call the police. The handwriting was very neat. She called the police and waited until officers arrived. They found the jockey dead.

The note held references, his inquest heard some time later, to James's mental health difficulties, and the personal struggles with which he was dealing at the time. He had lost his home and been declared bankrupt, which led to his being disappointed with himself for not coping. He apologised to those dearest to him. His GP had diagnosed depression, but it was not clear how much James had sought help from mental illness services. He had gone to France to rebuild his life with his girlfriend, but this relationship broke down, and he returned to the UK. Despite a history of alcohol abuse, he had been dry for sometime when he died: there were no drugs or alcohol in his system.

In all, James partnered some 85 winners and, in 2015–2016, he enjoyed his most successful campaign with 24 victories from 265 rides. In early 2018, he rang Emma Bishop to whom he had remained first jockey to say he was going to retire, but wanted to go out on one of hers, which he did, on February 2nd at Chepstow: he was beaten a short head, but got a great send–off, being very popular with his fellow jockeys.

After that, he began to lose his way: he missed the discipline of riding. For a time, he was on antidepressants, but he appeared to have knocked these on the head, though sometimes he seemed unusually 'low'. Notes he had written that were found later explained how truly 'low' he had felt; when a person has always appeared to burn so bright, we may wonder if that can always be the case. James had forever been an entertaining character, the life and soul of a party, with a real talent for mimicry. "He always had time for you," says Jane, "and you couldn't be annoyed with him. He lit up a place wherever he went."

Jockey Wayne Hutchinson knew James from schooling sessions and described him as "A top guy, who always made you laugh. He was a really bubbly person to be around, someone who made others happy." Tom Scudamore saw James as a popular jockey, "One of those people you are always happy to see." The IJF and PJA praised him for his hard work and dedication to his craft. He had the support of a loving family, was close to his brother, Ryan, and was aware of the extensive support available to current and former riders, with some of which he had engaged. Robbie Dunne, jockey friend of James said, "In the end it was lack of opportunities, and getting screwed over by some trainers… that's why a lot of lads get 'down' about the job, and pack it in."

But, in the end, life had become too daunting. The vicar's address at James' funeral in St. Mary's Church, Marlborough, began with words that must so often rebound when a person, especially a young person, takes their own life: "I have no answers, and just as many questions." James had travelled to the church in a carriage pulled by two beautiful black horses; six of his mates were his pall-bearers, including brother Ryan and jockey Tom Garner, who had one hand on the coffin, and the other around the shoulder of Liam Treadwell. On either side of his coffin were pictures of his two favourite horses. James's brother's tribute said his life had "so many ups and downs, whether it was over a fence or under a sheet." There was laughter, there were tears, followed by a wake at Newbury racecourse, but nothing could alter the cold fact that James had gone to that place where darkness feels warm and comfortable, "Where you go to switch off the button."

In 2009 Liam Treadwell, second jockey to Venetia Williams, won the Grand National at 100-1 in his first attempt on Mon Mome, after first jockey

Aidan Coleman had chosen to ride the stable's first string. The victorious pair came home to an eerie silence. "Nobody had backed him," said Liam. "Everyone was as shocked as me." Clare Balding interviewed an elated Liam straight after the race, famously commenting that his share of the winnings would pay for a new set of teeth. "She did me a big favour. I can't thank her enough," said 'Tredders' later, after a dentist offered his services almost free of charge.

The jockey, an instinctive rider, rode 125 winners for Venetia Williams, including Carrickboy at Cheltenham Festival 2013. He also finished third in the 2015 Grand National on Monbeg Dude, trained by his good friend, Michael Scudamore, for whom he rode out. But Liam had been through the mill: his career and life suffered a major setback when he had a fall at Bangor in early 2016, incurring a serious head injury. Several less serious later falls created a 'cumulative concussion' with severe brain damage; he was forced to take six months off. But the pressures did not go away: for the rest of his days he was beset with headaches, short-term memory loss, problems with concentration, and depression. "I found it difficult to cope with the pressures," he admitted. "I've not felt comfy in my own skin. I've lost a lot of purpose, drive and ambition. There's no point battling on and being miserable." Retiring for the first time in February 2018, he spoke openly about his battle with mental well-being, unlike many sportsmen, and admitted he'd had no idea how dangerous untreated concussion could be: he had ploughed on, not realising the need to take time off and recover. Having lost control of his moods, he had come to the conclusion there was no point in trying to pretend any longer that he was the 'indestructible jockey.' Unable to capitalise on his early success, he was briefly reduced to doing the duties of a stable lad to make ends meet. But even then he acknowledged, "There are many in a worse place than me."

But the fall from top jockey to the anonymity of a stable lad's life is a steep one: there can seem no shard of light at the end of a long tunnel. Venetia was supportive; she'd never had an assistant trainer, but offered him the role: he lasted only a couple of months, finding it hard to cope with the responsibility. Then his marriage ended, but he spoke openly about his battles with mental wellbeing and was a great advocate for those suffering similar circumstances.

No jockey can rest on his laurels, thinking where the next ride is coming from, rather than the next winner, living in a financially holed boat…

In 2019 he returned to the saddle, but his career never took off again. The concussions had a collective effect, and he was still having falls. In this all or nothing sport, he battled on the railroad of having to be seen to be head-down and grafting, rather than taking time out. Concussion is unique among injuries; you think you are fine, and don't realise you are suffering. Over time, it slows you down: instincts and the ability to keep out of trouble in a race are dampened; it becomes a disease that rots the brain. When things settle, at least temporarily, there can be depression, so it may be a price every jockey has to pay…

Liam saw "another Liam creeping into my life whom I didn't know; I didn't realise what was going on." A proper assessment, good advice, and the right treatment were vital. He went to rehab with IJF, where he realised the full effect of his long-standing concussion, and was reassured he was going in the right direction; there was light at the end of the tunnel. But he was unable to control his moods, choosing to be a recluse and not leave the house. He baulked when advised to see a sports psychiatrist, but he went, aware he could no longer ignore his symptoms. At the time he said, "Doctors do a fantastic job; it's up to us to be more responsible and to think long term; we need to be open with trainers, and our relationship with them would be better for it. No jockey is indestructible."

He became assistant to Shropshire trainer Alistair Ralph, and was working there in June 2020 at the time of his sudden death. He was 34.

In his career, he'd partnered 308 winners over jumps, including at Fontwell on a horse called Royal Wedding the day Prince William married Kate, and 28 on the flat. Nick Gifford, for whom Liam rode for two seasons, described him as "An uncomplicated rider, beautifully balanced, especially over a fence: he wouldn't try to organise a horse too much, and tried to keep things as simple as possible. You'd never notice him in a race and he gave great feedback after one." A life-long Arsenal fan, always fit from cycling and running, Liam was seen by journalist Nick Luck as "such a gentle man, a humble man; someone who probably wasn't aware of the extent of his own gift and talent in the saddle: that gift was probably not matched by his self-confidence."

Liam was a universally popular character on the racecourse, and had sometimes spoken eloquently about his mental health struggles, both in the press and in the film, *Jockey Matters*, made by the PJA. At the inquest on his death, the coroner recorded a verdict of misadventure, pointing to the Bangor fall as a turning-point, causing the jockey anxiety and depression. Personal problems, including splitting from his wife, Emily, had built up, and Liam had found life even more challenging during lockdown. Only four months before he died, he had been a pall-bearer at the funeral of jockey friend James Banks, also in his 30s. In the end, despite strong friends, and having sought help for his mental challenges, the pressures became too much. Although he had appeared on 'top form' at social events with friends, a message to one of them the night before his death told, "I've reached out and spoken to the Crisis team this evening, I've taken a knockout cocktail tonight. It will either end it for good, or shut me down for several hours. I don't mind which."

Jumping lost a real character; his family lost a son and brother; Aidan Coleman and other jockeys lost a great mate. Liam's pals in the weighing room were devastated, bewildered, angry and more... when someone takes their own life there can never be a satisfactory explanation. Aidan spoke for many when he said, "I was so glad he won the Grand National, but so sad it wasn't enough for him." We have to face the grim fact that sometimes for a jump jockey, however hard they fight, courage is not enough. Since Liam's funeral, more than one jockey has noticed that their conversations are rather different to those they had previously.

And still the demon suicide is prowling... no small number of stable hands, the real but unsung heroes of the sport, have fallen victim recently. Trainer Warren Greatrex, who had not enjoyed the best of times in recent years – "The longer a bad time goes on, the more you want the good times back" - had to deal with the crushing blows of two members of his staff being found dead: in July 2021 Michael Pitt, and in February 2022 David Thompson, both of whom were "part of the family." "Michael was the life and soul, son of a trainer; his death was just as we'd moved to our new base at Rhonehurst: that was horrible. He was such a character and to lose him - at a similar age to my boys - knocked everyone. It wasn't easy. Michael was a happy lad and it hurt us. David was a big member of the team, his death hit me so hard.

I remember the policeman coming round, and my having to go out to the same members of staff and tell them - in the same spot - another member of their team had gone, and seeing them hit the floor - again. How do you rally the troops then? It was as hard as anything I've been through in my life." Warren tries to be not just a boss, but a father figure: "Stable hands have a tough job; they need to feel involved. Neither Michael nor David showed any sign of distress. I feel responsible for all my staff, so it is hard not to take their loss personally. At times like that, you question yourself: it's not easy to keep striving forward and believing in yourself." But, there may be some light at the end of this desperate, dark tunnel: in order to promote awareness of suicide, Richard Farquahar has set up James' Place for those who struggle, with centres in Liverpool and London: walk-in sessions are freely available, and his syndicate plans to open more places. As Warren says, "If we could help just one person, that would mean a lot."

Those who are tempted to take the ultimate step, but resist it, or who survive their attempt, have been known to feel relief: "My thinking was gone by then... imagine all I would have missed."... "I blamed everyone else; ending that blaming was the beginning of my growth. It's as simple as going from selfishness to thoughtfulness"... "Now I take life a day at a time, a great way to live... My mind is clear, not cluttered up with stuff that really isn't important... no good ever came from suffering in silence... I tell myself every morning to treat everyone I meet really well... everyone has a sign round their neck saying, 'Please make me feel important'"... "I didn't think you could have a gentler approach and be successful; I thought I had to be ruthless; I was wrong..."

CHAPTER 21: MENTAL HEALTH

*"It is during our darkest moments
that we must focus to see the light."*

- Aristotle -

The biggest killer of men aged 20-49 in the UK today is suicide – at the rate of 16 per day. When young men are more likely to die at their own hand than from cancer, heart disease or road accidents, there is something seriously wrong. The causes and consequences of this catastrophe demand much more research, study and open discussion. Simon Reeve sees mental illness, "like a virus, infecting through emotions, ego, or as a result of bereavement, loss or failure." The adventurer has warned that nobody completely understands why: "Young men, in particular, are shockingly vulnerable and every life is so frighteningly specific... the human mind is a powerful machine." He learned much from a French-speaking special forces captain on a base under attack from suicide bombers: "People don't change when others tell them they should; people change when they tell themselves they must."

Easier said than done, so how can we address this destructive malaise?

Despite the harpings-on of successive governments, mental health services today remain woefully under-funded. Tom Bradby, ITN lynchpin, who knows something of internal struggles, believes that, "Mental health understanding and treatment in England is roughly where physical understanding and treatment were 50 years ago. People say there's no stigma around mental health any more: that is not true. To get where it needs to be better understood and combatted requires a massive public programme." We men, perhaps particularly English men, are scared of discovering we're not who we pretend to be; we worry that admitting this will bring out our feminine side (whatever that is). Often, we struggle to identify, let alone voice, how we truly feel: trapped, lost, desperate. The stiff upper-lip approach to adversity remains a menace.

Only now are we realising the difference between mental health problems, which almost all of us suffer to some degree, and mental illness, which is far more complex. The former can be combatted, usually with therapy and/or medication, though recent data shows only 37% of men with mental health problems seek treatment. Three-quarters of men choose not to confide in another person about their mental struggles: this is a silent, invisible affliction, and young men in the throes of it are often expert at disguising how they feel. Often they present as positive and happy-go-lucky, making it hard for us to see the conflict raging inside their well-groomed heads. So many young men are going through this alone. In Northern Ireland the teenage suicide rate is twice that of England, and rising, so the organisation *Lighthouse* has been set up in Belfast to try and 'normalise' the problems young men face. Rather than waiting to see who will be next, the young are being helped to own their pain, fear and grief: it's a process without a silver bullet, but releasing the pressures in their thinking can only be a good thing.

Glasgow University is leading the field in suicide research, and its findings are vital in our fight to help prevent more young people taking their own lives: they feel a keen sense of entrapment; think they are a burden; have tunnel vision; and conclude that everyone will be better off if they are dead. If only victims of suicide could see what happens after they've gone: the victim has ended his or her pain, but those left behind have to carry that pain for them, for the rest of their lives.

Research is showing that suicide is preventable until the very last moment, but who can pinpoint that moment? In the tempestuous head of the victim small things can make a huge difference for the worst; it can indeed be the last straw that breaks the camel's back. They may well think that they are doing their loved ones a favour... lack of sleep, loss of appetite and energy lead to desperate frustration; hiding their stress saps mental resilience.

They are ashamed of the situation they have ended up in, fearing that no-one will understand, let alone help to cure their mental state. The very word 'mental' is fiendishly difficult to accept, which is a tangible indicator of the stigmatised nature of mental illness. And perhaps it is not so much a decision to die as, entrapped by their own mind, a desperate lunge for peace, to end their overdose of pain.

In contemporary life, mental pain is still often regarded as taboo; this needs to change. Pressures can be eased, often by medication; mood swings and social withdrawal investigated, and issues not previously verbalised – or realised – can be explored. Talking has to be key: suicidal humans feel they are in a bubble, the world is happening around that bubble, and they are helpless to act. But that bubble, like a physical blister, can be – has to be – burst. The fog will often clear with talking, for that enables sufferers to put their pain somewhere, to find a place for it. Everything revolves around asking the strugglers how they are, making that 'How are you?' question more than the equivalent of 'Hi', looking them in the eye, and following up with the vital second question: "How are you, really?," as Roman Kemp showed in his recent brave documentary on the dangers of suicide, *Our Silent Emergency*. The radio DJ has taken up this crusade, followed up that programme, and been working tirelessly to promote better mental health. His open letter to the government was penned not only to make our government aware how much care – and money – is essential, but to translate that awareness into concrete action, starting with mental health support teams in schools. Roman has had some measure of response, but will keep going until he gets there…

There's a solution to (almost) every problem, even though it may take weeks, months, or years. Being the person who asks that telling second question is the responsibility of us all. There is a risk involved, but maybe the alternative is infinitely worse: "Would one word from me have helped? Am I partly to blame for this death?" These questions open wide the floodgates to guilt. And we must be prepared for the long haul. One day in the sun will not keep sufferers safe – it takes a long time to convince potential victims that only they can change things, only they have the power to burst that pernicious bubble. They can only do that with an ongoing support network, not just of friends, but of professionals. Nottingham Mental Health Emergency Service is a forerunner in offering support here, and was particularly so during Covid; the youngest lad to respond to its offer of help was aged 11. A huge number of people using the service, especially young men, felt they were not where they should be, but have now found there is someone to whom they can run.

Even when potential victims appear to have been rescued from themselves, and to be responding positively to much-needed support, we must remain watchful. Sadly, a lot of suicides happen precisely because the victim is making good progress: that is the time when they can look back, see more clearly themselves at their worst, and do something drastic in their desperate fear of falling back into the mire.

Those of us who crave going on to the racecourse and standing by a fence, away from the cosy safety of the concourse or hospitality box, experience a sense of drama, and a thrill, that changes our perspective of the sport's brave warriors. The sound of hooves rattling on the guard rail, and fir boughs crackling like gunfire as half-ton thoroughbred horses and their pilots hurl themselves at a fence can only leave us in awe of human and beast and their Herculean endeavours. But, do we pause to imagine the amount of pressure these riders are under?

In our technological age, there is enormous pressure on sportspeople from social media: for a jockey there is virtually no protection. Increasingly, jockeys are criticised, lambasted, abused, mocked, threatened, decried, and vilified by calumnious cowards hiding behind the cloak of anonymity. As Kirkland Tellwright, until recently clerk of the course at Haydock, succinctly said: "You're either a hero or a villain these days; there are no half-measures." Congratulations are far less frequent than censure. Today's world drives us to crave more possessions: houses, cars, clothes, fancy gadgets, but research now reveals our showing-off with these possessions is fear-based. Discovering our true needs might make us more content, more determined to do something about our situation.

But that takes time and sustained effort, which is where therapy comes in. Therapy has been termed "a gym for the brain, that most important muscle in our body," as one jockey highlighted. Opening oneself to therapy is a vital step to recovery: it is not weak or self-indulgent: on the contrary, it is a sign of bravery and self-awareness, that can become empowering, even emboldening.

Good therapy teaches us to recognise our emotions - and to deal with them. It can help us develop understanding, compassion, a healthy sense of self, and give us the chance to reflect on the consequences of our actions; it is a maturing process that helps us become the best version of ourselves, rather than a second-hand version of what we think people expect us to be. By far the hardest thing is taking that first step, making that first phone call, and reaching out for help.

A wealth of recent documentaries, like *Our Silent Emergency*, are trying to combat this problem, and there has been some breakthrough, but the elephant in the room remains large, tusked − and trumpeting. Jockeys need our arm around them; sometimes there is no-one there to do that, no-one to tell them how to handle losing. "We don't need amphetamines: we need one another. No-one needs to be stuck," as psychiatrists agree. Flat jockey Richard Hughes was in a state of personal torment due to alcohol addiction; Johnny Murtagh was riding on fear, with drink his greatest motivator. To admit these problems when they came to a head was "the best thing that ever happened," as both began to discover and explore 'risky areas', learn from others who'd recovered, and realise the quicker they unravelled their addictions, the better. But before that can happen, that addiction will have had an impact. "People say you have a problem: you deny it: you think you've cracked it, and you are the last to know."

Racing is a fickle mistress. Jockeys constantly have to deal with defeat, hunger (both literal and hunger for winners) and tiredness: this can snowball fast. So they begin to doubt themselves, they try to limit the effects of the sport's downside, and move on: everyone has a dark day. When such days persist, they look for short cuts to better resilience, but there aren't any. Life becomes a relentless treadmill, with sleep, rest, recovery time and re-energising all too hard to come by. All too many jockeys remain silent, unlike Graham Lee, who realised he needed to ask for help and bravely said so.

It seems beyond cruel, and deeply ironic, that, having long conquered his mental demons, Graham should have been so seriously injured one Friday evening in November 2023, at Newcastle, when he suffered a spinal injury after being unseated from his horse as the stalls opened for a run-of-the-mill sprint. His horse seemed to lurch and duck as the gates sprang open and his rider was thrown over the horse's withers into the Tapeta surface – a mixture of silica sand, wax, and fibre. His unstable cervical fracture caused severe damage to his spinal cord. Jump jockeys wear helmets, and body protectors under their silks, but when ½ ton animal does something unexpectedly it is the equivalent of being flung from a car wearing only a pair of pyjamas. Graham's accident had a profound effect on the racing community, a measure of whose respect for the man can be gauged by a Just Giving page set up by his daughter, Amy, in the hope of raising £100: the fund has risen to just south of £200,000, and Graham, with characteristic humility, wrote to IJF, to thank everyone who had contributed: "I never really considered I'd achieved that much as a jockey, and it seems crazy so many people are thinking of us all."

Graham, born in Galway in 1975, the winner of more than 1,000 races, had enjoyed a distinguished career over jumps, which reached its zenith when he won the Grand National of 2004 on Amberleigh House for Ginger McCain; in 2014, he switched to riding on the flat after a series of serious injuries, and, in 2015, won the Ascot Gold Cup on Trip to Paris. He remains the only man to have won both these races. In the days after his terrible accident, Ruby Walsh said, "When one suffers, we all suffer: the racing community will never leave him. With a bit of luck, God can be good, and I think everyone would like him to be good right now." We could only pray that Graham's tried and tested mental strength would pull him through…

David Bass, until recently jump jockey President of the PJA, and the rider most concerned to bring about a better understanding of the mental pressures on jump jockeys, stresses the need for jockeys to switch off; think long term; control what they can; be a person as well as a jockey; believe in themselves; have the guts to express themselves, and have outside interests, so there is not just one thing in their life to focus on. If they can be kinder to, and learn to trust themselves, they will be in a better place.

In many ways jockeys must cut themselves off from emotion, which includes not getting too attached to particular horses, though most have their favourites. Their game is unpredictable, always balanced on a knife-edge between success and failure, even disaster. They can be in as much danger driving distances in wintry conditions, as they are out on the course. Weather, for a sport enduring from September to April, is another factor that can play havoc in their lives: even with today's technology, race meetings can be abandoned at a moment's notice, leaving jockeys ruing a long, wasted journey. Steve Smith-Eccles thought jump racing was at its worst on a winter Monday at Leicester.

Many jockeys spend time going over a race, or a fall, in their mind, especially if they are riding that horse again: self-criticism is vital, but in moderation: it does no good to keep re-running a race in their head, if only because the outcome cannot be changed. Unlike in cricket, where a player has the chance for redemption, often over days in the same match, jockeys do not have the same luxury: the race is over, they cannot change the result or its consequences. Redemption might come in the next race, but the memory of defeat can gnaw away for days... Jockeys always have to prove themselves to others, as well as to themselves. So comes the dilemma: should I take on this ride, or give myself a week to recover? Journeyman jockeys often have to grab every opportunity to ride, as if their lives depended on it, when in fact their livelihoods often do. Even should they decide to ride a poor horse in a poor race, there's always the risk of being 'jocked off' by other available riders. It is a precarious seesaw.

No jockey gets it right all the time. John Francome was not infallible, but what made him so good was that he made fewer mistakes. The same is now being said of Paul Townend. A good jockey can, to some extent, see accidents a split-second before they happen, but no-one is immune from danger. Fate blows in and out, in her random, whimsical way: she cannot be predicted. But jockeys feel alive mid-race, inches away from the horse in front of them, travelling at 30 mph, making those split-second decisions, challenging their gods to the utterance. They are well aware that glory is short-lived: they can be chewed up and spat out quickly: cheered by 70,000 at Cheltenham, then sitting alone in a darkening autumn room, as Sam Thomas discovered in 2008.

No comprehensive review of jockeys' mental health had been conducted until recently, when the disclosures of their non-physical difficulties demanded exploration. Jockeys present a higher level of depression/ anxiety symptoms than other elite athletes. Among crucial concerns are not just injuries but the fear of them; stress; burn-out; career dissatisfaction;

the need to prove themselves to fathers; parental split (no matter how far back) and the worry of retirement. My own research has shown that the number of jockeys actively seeking help is low. Loneliness, and their relentless work ethic add to their challenges, to say nothing of financial uncertainty: unlike footballers, paid a signing-on fee; paid when injured; paid to sit on the bench, having enjoyed a massive weekly wage, and a contract, with an agent to deal with the press, the vast majority of jockeys reap only meagre monetary rewards for their endeavours. Other key barriers to accessing professional help include lack of time; ambivalence over treatment suggestions; concerns about confidentiality, and the practical difficulty of finding good, local support.

The dark world of the male psyche thrives on fear: "If I start worrying about the meaning of life, I'll go mad. I just have to keep going," said one up and coming jockey. No small number of men feel they need to be tough, physically attractive, have sexual prowess, stick to rigid roles and use aggression to solve conflict. Some are indoctrinated to aspire, hard-wired to suppress emotion, and trained to associate success with winning, good grades and promotion with happiness throughout their education, and careers.

Research shows that many 18-year old men have never booked an appointment with their GP, and GPs are not helped by 'the tyranny of ten minutes'. Even when they secure an appointment, men often start with something small, e.g. an ingrowing toenail, so take time getting to the point, if they ever do. Testicular pain, impotency, anxieties, not coping at work constitute an 'access barrier' in young men, who either feel they don't deserve help, or are mistrustful of GPs. Discussing sexual/mental problems is hard: trust needs building up, and that takes time: while in our current health system, they may never see the same doctor again. Men have built up a powerful win/lose philosophy: "Set goals, and beat yourselves up if those goals are not achieved."

Goals could be smaller; and little things appreciated. With money, or the fear of lack of it, so often a problem, anxiety can disrupt a healthy work/life balance. Men can be left in a confusing no-man's land: emotionally still old-school, but aware, if they unbend, of huge ramifications in how they deal with problems/stresses.

Jockeys' challenges include having to choose which parts of their personality to show to the world. They often say little, or give robotic answers, so are accused of having no personality: if they speak out, everything they say is jumped on: it sometimes appears that they can't win. Paul Townend does not give pre-race interviews. Why should he? Post-race interviews are not most jockeys' idea of fun. Most such interviews contain exactly the same pleasantries. As AP McCoy said, "There's a limit to what you can say in an interview." This begs the question: can a sportsman or woman choose to be their own person? Can they have their own narrative? We need to let them pause and think before they react, but we don't do that, because we have to know everything at once. There's no mystery any more; we need to change the narrative and make it more humane...

And perhaps we're aiming for the wrong thing anyway, dictated to us by the media? Eckhard Tolle said: "Pleasure is always derived from something outside us; joy arises from within." It is joy that is so often missing. Real mates, not online 'friends', supply that. They are the folk who might see a need, encourage us to speak out, or get help, and maybe show us that therapy – of whatever sort – can help us realise, even extend, our potential.

CHAPTER 22: MENTAL HEALTH 2

"Not until we are lost do we begin to understand ourselves."
- Henry David Thoreau -

The Fall is Nathan Horrocks' short (21-minute) film on the life and trials of a jump jockey, a 'scene from a larger story', subtitled, '*The space between self and what they see*'. It had been a 'passion project' of the ex-jockey for years, after his own battle with mental health and the loss of colleagues, James Banks and Liam Treadwell. Dedicated to those two mates, the film went into production on World Suicide Day 2020, its initial idea fuelled by the support of Paul Struthers, then Head of the BHA, and recently re-appointed to that role.

Nathan, a jump jockey who had ridden more than sixty winners, tried to kill himself with alcohol and pills when the weight of his life became too much to bear. He felt unable to share his torment, feeling too embarrassed by what he was going through, and didn't want to admit it: being fragile cannot come into a jockey's narrative. He hid his black feelings, all too aware of the stigma still attached to mental health and depression, until he went online and found someone who could help him.

In recovery, he did something tangible: he made his film. *The Fall* is a psychological drama that could be about any of his former weighing room colleagues, but evokes sad memories of James and Liam in particular, both of whom suffered from the same anguish and desperation that took Nathan to the brink.

The film's main character, Tom, ("He is four or five different jockeys and only a bit of him is me," says Nathan) is undergoing the age-old traumas of a jockey's life, exacerbated by the twenty-first-century disease of abuse on social media. When Tom is alone, we can see he is breaking down, feeling a burden on everyone and with a biting urge to leave this earth, but when he's talking to others, owners and trainers in the paddock, the mask goes on and no-one notices the depth of his struggles.

James Banks was a kindred spirit, with whom Nathan had deep conversations about how they were both feeling, though neither admitted to the other quite how dark a place life was. Nathan sought counselling and therapy, the tools needed to deal with his state of mind; perhaps James chose not to. "Then we lost Liam not long after him, and Michael Curran (who worked for John Gosden) and Dean Crossman, who was my valet, and after all that I had something in my head that I needed to get out. That journey home became the film."

Nathan had his share of 'bollockings' from trainers like any jockey, but realises how demoralising these can be, especially if conducted in public, in front of other jockeys, one instance of which stayed with him for a long time. But, having quit the saddle, he enlisted the help of JETS: after time as a sales director, and an on-course rep for Betfair, he helped set up *Equine Productions*, with the aim of taking this 'extreme sport' to a new and wider audience: he also rode out regularly for Oliver Sherwood, which gave him the chance to exercise Grand National winner Many Clouds. When the 10-year old died in action at Cheltenham, Nathan's downward spiral culminated in his suicide attempt. "Clouds was my saviour," he said, "until he died. Around that time, I remember seeing James (Banks) on my couch, crying his eyes out, but I was trying to be strong, not let him into my own head. I couldn't admit what had happened to me, even when someone was having a breakdown in front of me."

Nathan made a documentary on Many Clouds, which ignited his filming journey, and in turn helped his mental state. "For me, it's been a real battle against the stigma, and I don't think I'm out the other side: even now I still get very 'down', but I've got the tools and I can make them work for me." Having done '*The Fall*', he is now constantly looking out for that hook to catch someone's imagination and help promote the sport.

His journey has been cathartic and, "Even now, it's hard to say it sometimes, but every time I talk about it, there's another person that knows, and if my experience helps somebody go and get help, it'll all be worth it." Nathan has been keen to promote pressures in the sport since he left it. But he felt keenly that he needed to do something with his own story, that the public needed to see the challenges jockeys have to combat every day of their working lives. Jockeys are always "on the front foot; they always have goals; they're the last man standing; the first to be blamed; living a different life, seen all the time." All jockeys experience the journey home after a bad day at work, expectations – real or perceived – dashed. Nathan has known huge loss and grief in his own life, but survived 'that tragic day' when it all seemed too much, and can thus dissect the extent of a jockey's pressures and demands. "AP raised the bar so high in terms of mental and physical toughness," says Nathan, confirming how jockeys need built-in hardness: they can show no chink in their armour. "It's not a team environment, except in the weighing room, where they can, to some extent, let their guard down. But that very sanctuary is full of adversaries: when you leave it, you have to take the mask off and battle the very person who could just have consoled you."

And they are constantly trying not to burn bridges. They have their agents, but, these men look after a lot of jockeys: are they doing their best for each individual? His film makes full use of the jockey cam, so viewers are themselves in the saddle. It claims that 80% of jockeys have suffered abuse online, causing Nathan to be scathing about social media: "It could be the tipping point." Having to deal with defeat endlessly, it's no surprise that over 50% of jockeys feel some sort of mental health pressure; "A lot of them are young guys. They are all, always, on a knife edge."

Nathan first sat on a horse at 16; he fell in love with the animal, and now wants to attract a new audience, get more people into racing. He is determined the sport is seen in the best light. A fervent supporter of Racing Welfare and Racing for Schools, he is keen to give the young chance to go behind the scenes – on the gallops, in racing yards – to increase their interests. Racing, he believes, can appeal to a different demographic, including ethnic minorities, so they can experience his strong feelings of empathy with horses.

His film opens the doors to show people outside the racing bubble what it's like to ride in that bubble. And it underlines the places where riders can go for help, via the IJF. "It's all about having the conversation. We just need to be kinder to jockeys, to each other and to ourselves." This ties in with what Matt Rudd has written about mental health: "Self-compassion is not something we are used to. Our powerful win/lose philosophy sets goals, and beats us up if we don't achieve those goals. We need to set smaller, realistic goals and appreciate small things. The primary cause of unhappiness is rarely a situation itself, but the thoughts about that situation; to separate the two is vital. Today's pressures demand too much."

To counter that, young men are becoming more tolerant of others; are they also becoming less tolerant of themselves? If one man in a group can break the ice, others may well recognise this and build up a more positive approach to themselves. And while stiff upper lip may no longer be rule number one for some men, we are often stuck in a confusing, mixed message state of masculinity: emotionally many of us remain in the old school, which has huge ramifications for how we deal with stress. In the 21st century there is perhaps room for a new definition of masculinity, where there is nothing to prove; we can live truthfully; express our emotions and be ourselves. We should be allowed to talk about pain, and we need the ability to cry, not to pursue a warped version of masculinity as the unforgiving world sees it.

With so much focus on women's rights, black lives, gender identity, 'sexploration' and inclusivity, some men have got lost. They have turned to ways of blotting out their pain. Not surprisingly, there is a drinking culture in racing – and a drug culture, arguably more rife with flat jockeys than their jumping counterparts. Everyone has a different challenge, many weighed down by anxiety, confusion, responsibility, circumstances and a growing fear, not just of failure, but of its consequences.

At every turn they have to be available – and answerable – to the hungry media, be upbeat as a defining figure of their sport, drive all over the country, often for just one ride, and operate at peak physical capacity, continually delving into reserves of energy. All the time, anxiety can build, triggering an amygdala hijack, when primitive parts of the brain short-circuit, bypassing more rational areas and flooding the body with stress hormones. This leads to fight, flight or freeze response, where jockeys panic and make bad decisions, or focus too much on usually automatic skills. They carry the weight of hopes – and money – of many, who can and do retaliate, squishing verbal attacks into a few words of abuse, insult or threat. Ferocious critique plays at the mind, saps confidence and belief, takes out the joy. In addition, objective scrutiny is more relentless than ever: we don't just think we know our sporting heroes, we think we own them, not realising they are vulnerable to their own demons, driven by fear. Fear can be a good motivator, but it is never satisfied.

Mark Enright was a case in point: he no longer wanted to ride; suffered from depression; had many more bad days than good, and felt he was being put daily under a microscope: all was dark. He asked himself how he could get out of riding, what excuse could he come up with next, how could he escape the gaping black hole that had become his life?

"Everything was an effort: it was hard to stay positive. The biggest problem is yourself, for you are overthinking and analysing the whole time. Sport has no level plain, and coping with the lows is harder than ever before. There are no secrets. You open yourself up to a huge audience on a daily basis: most people are able to make their mistakes in private. So you go up to your room, sit in the dark and rack your brains wondering how to get out of racing. You believe you are the only person in this cavernous black hole."

All sportspeople have issues the preying world knows nothing of: how can it? Sport is a leveller because things are not level. Mark went into a psychiatric hospital for ten days. On emerging he took a deep breath, sat down, wrote to the *Racing Post* and finally talked to people, which for him was the 'Open Sesame'. Paul Struthers understood: "Racing tests like no other sport, it is up to the individual. With up to five or six rides some days, few of them delivering a win, jockeys get beaten the most of all sportsmen." This takes its toll. Leighton Aspell knew this: "You have to take deep breaths, sit down and talk: you may not hear what you want to hear, but…"

Michael Caulfield hits the nail on the head: "The greatest strength you have as a human being is to ask for help. In the past this would be seen as a weakness, a true sign of vulnerability because you were not hard/brave enough. Not now. You need to surround yourself with the best-possible people, which may mean going further afield." Jockeys can now call the

Sporting Chance helpline (07780 008877) and book a face-to-face assessment, after which a treatment programme will be planned out: this may involve CBT (Cognitive Behavioural Therapy), counselling or full psychological help. AP McCoy knew all about the stigma, the need to remain mentally strong and show no weaknesses, because his was such a tough sport; he now adds his backing to the weight of research into the mental health, not just of jockeys but of all sportsmen and women. As Struthers has concluded: "Racing demands help more than any other sport. So seek the best advice possible: it's the most important thing you'll ever do… more important than any horse you'll ever ride."

Money remains a problem, not least because prize money for jumps racing in Britain is relatively poor. It is sobering to realise that in Australia lowly picnic races – the equivalent of our point-to-points – are worth considerably more than some of our jump races. Many jockeys commit to sponsorship – it pays the mortgage. They have to take out their own insurance policy, the annual cost of which, due to the perilous nature of their profession, is high, though they are helped by JETS. Learning new skills; getting good quality sleep; giving to others; paying attention to the present moment; mindfulness; meditation; spending time in nature; being exposed to sunlight (jockeys' helmets shut this out); staying positive; having time to open up; staying connected with family and mates; setting aside 'me'-time; seeing a sports psycho-therapist; trying not to overthink and having strong relationships with those around them; realising what they've not realised before; understanding that help comes in many different forms: all these take time to explore and make habitual. But if racing bodies, trainers, owners and pundits can acknowledge the struggles and stresses of a jump jockey, as they are starting to do, then things can only improve. There is always an alternative: it is never too late to seek help.

Everyone's challenge is different. It is no good to say pull yourself together, stop whingeing and crack on: pressures are inevitable in every sport. Brian Moore, Luke Sutton, Stan Collymore, Ben Mercer, Lee Hendrie, Emma Raducanu, Naomi Osaka and Simone Biles have all admitted to mental health struggles. Jim White of the *Daily Telegraph* wrote: "We revere sportsmen and women for their resilience, aptitude and ability to surmount challenges that make us mere mortals whimper. It is believed they can access a part of their brain that is capable of closing off any thoughts outside the game/match/race at hand, but no-one can do this all the time. The effort of this can make it hard to think of others, or make the move to help yourself when you're cocooned in a damp blanket of sadness, and all you can do is think of your own pain."

In September 2021, Ruby Walsh, and Dr Jennifer Pugh, Senior Medical Officer of the Irish Horse Racing Regulatory Board (IHRB), launched a ground-breaking mental health app., Leafyard, for professional and amateur jockeys, provides tools, activities and support to help with general mental health concerns; it was devised by the Irish Injured Jockeys Fund with the support of the IHRB. Piloted among jockeys in 2021, it soon produced significant results.

Injured Irish jockeys were 46 times more likely to meet the criteria for depression than non-injured jockeys, and reported higher levels of dissatisfaction, associated with distress and anxiety. Ruby Walsh described the app. as a tool for riders to help deal with the strictures of the profession: "I wasn't shocked when I saw the results of the survey. I've been around in the racing world long enough to see the highs and lows, but it did upset me. After consultations, the Irish IJF was happy to fund this innovative, action-driven, practical solution to support everyone in the weighing room." In its first twenty-four hours the app recorded a 24% uptake, and 88% of jockeys who registered continue to use the app.

With his *High Performance* podcasts, Jonny Wilkinson has launched a mental health campaign to help people reach out and find support, after detailing his own struggles in the sphere. His advice has been earned through suffering and sacrifice, in an honest appraisal of how he lived between the whistles. He has concluded that acceptance is the basis for good health in all its forms. Acceptance is an empowering tool, so athletes can perform without the distraction of their internal experiences and pressures. By learning to accept these experiences as 'normal' routine, part of their lives, and certainly not 'bad', they can focus their attention on what matters most in the present moment: their sport. This is no sinecure, but it helps to create a willing mind-set, adaptable to any emotion or thought that may arise in the context of a particular situation, without having to judge these experiences as positive or negative.

For all his successes, not least that winning penalty kick in the Rugby World Cup Final vs Australia in 2003, Jonny realises that it was outcomes that used to define him: had his team won, or not? "I used to meditate, but allowed the winning or losing of a game to make feeling at peace seem out of control." This led to a conflicted inner state, which he fought, but to which he then had to give in. Even the winning of the World Cup lasted only seconds; the feeling had no permanence. And always there was more and more pressure: "You are not only as good as your last game: I was living ahead of myself, always thinking of the next whistle to blow." He made himself a plug to fit the socket of rugby - and plugged in.

But self-belief was fragile; it was covering up fear: he had nowhere to turn to but inwards – and found to his horror there was nothing there. On the field he put all of himself into every moment, fully attentive, fully engaged. But he had no inner peace, no true joy, despite all his glittering successes. Something vital had to change… and his was an overnight conversion. For all his winning feeling, sense of flow, sharp intuition, undeniable grace and limitless possibilities, he was missing out on life. Painstaking self-exploration made him realise that how he performed on the pitch, how he led his life, was utterly his own choice. He needed to challenge himself differently: what could a great life lived really mean? Could he get rid of his old ideas and re-define everything?

It meant exploring the unknown, acknowledging that his potential – in its widest sense – could be fulfilled in the here and now, not by what might happen in the future. And he gradually dismantled his obsession with results: if there was a loss, and with it disappointment (more often directed at himself) he could be curious about that, not angry, seeing it as a new opportunity to explore the previously shut-off feelings, and discern a different potential in the seeking. For that he needed to be completely open – exposed, his feelings naked, and ready for what the new challenge to himself would reveal. Key to the whole process was unconditional support from those he held dearest, banishing others' judgement, or lack of it. He had to be selfish, deciding how and who he wanted to be. Whereas before he had thought leaving a rich legacy important, he now concentrates on flourishing in the widest sense – just loving life. He acknowledges that success is not concerned only with outcomes, and in response to the question as to what would render a great life lived, has concluded, "To be fully engaged and deeply invested in every moment." Jonny Wilkinson's experience – and its findings – have much to teach us...

CHAPTER 23: JOCKEYS 3 - VICISSITUDES

"Like matadors, they take their lives in their hands every time they ride. They smash collar-bones, arms, legs and vertebrae round the clock, and are back in the saddle when most of us would be taking tentative steps on a Zimmer-frame. Jump jockeys, for me, remain the bravest of all our sports people."

- Ian Wooldridge -

A recent *Racing Post* investigation into jump jockeys' earnings, where there is no fixed salary, made compulsive reading: for each ride over jumps, jockeys are paid £221.28, out of which must come their considerable deductions, including 0.6% of all prize money to their pension fund; not to mention petrol (driving 40-60,000 miles per season costs at least £8,000), their valet, agent, insurance, physios etc. Taking the average number of rides over the year means they earn less than £30,000 – but that's assuming they are race-fit throughout – and with no protracted cold spells when there can be no racing. In addition to that woeful sum, they earn 11.03% of winning prize money, depending on the race, and 3.44% of placed prize money. Racing bank Weatherbys handles their financial affairs, charging 65p for every transaction. Jockeys can supplement their earnings via sponsorship, sporting logos on their breeches, or doing a blog for the big betting firms, but they still have to pay accountants, or sweat over their own tax returns. So journeymen jump jockeys' earnings are trifling reward for a relentless job with very few breaks, high injury risks, and an enormous number of hours in the car, traipsing all over the country. Danger is not just at the racecourse: driving is a constant challenge, negotiating increasingly congested roads on our little island. In August 1988, Paul Croucher, an extremely popular jockey, with a happy-go-lucky nature, was killed in a flaming car crash on a country road near Lambourn; when he swerved to avoid a deer, his car hit a tree and burst into flames. His death robbed the new season of its innocence. Accidents and sudden road closures – not all of them legitimate – mean jockeys miss a race sometimes. With their hectic schedules, menial tasks, like getting a hair cut or seeing a dentist, are hard to come by during the season.

For aspiring jockeys trying to make it, and break into the highest echelons of the sport, it is a mighty challenge. Rob Law Eadie is one such jockey. Now 26, he grew up on a smallholding with sheep, cows and dressage horses, his Mum an agronomist, Dad a teacher. For work experience he took a job with horses, then, after 'A' levels, worked for a year in Wiltshire with Gary Witherford, an expert in breaking 2-year-olds, teaching horses how to enter and leave a starting stall, and correcting the problems of the worst behaved of these: Rob was thrown in at the deep end, and not paid much. The job was tough, and got tougher. He remembers a 4-year-old colt, Radar, who continually 'napped' (whipped round with him), and then bolted, until Witherford cured the horse. Witherford was a hard task master; Rob was never good enough, despite a vibrant work ethic: "I was up at 02:00; in Newmarket, at the stables for 08:00." When he crashed the work car, the writing was on the wall: he gave in his notice; it was not well received.

From there the teenager went to work for Ed Giles, near Ledbury, where he found himself working 80 hours a week during the winter, along with other 'stable rats', but he was in a 'proper racing world', finding the sport an escape from life's other challenges. Then he met Michael Dickinson, "a great man" to the lad and went to work for him in Maryland, US. "With Gary, I learned how to stay on; with Michael I learned how to ride, race plan and meet big owners." Rob found himself as much the trainer as Dickinson, who had a yen for teaching. The boy was desperate to race- ride: "When you're ready, I'll tell you," said the ex-Yorkshire jumps training supremo. "It takes twenty rides to realise you're in a race." Rob got match fit: in his first race he finished fourth, having dropped his stick, and as Dickinson had predicted, felt like a rabbit caught in headlights. His second ride was a grey, Inittowinit, in the Athenia Idol on Maryland Hunt Cup day; he won by eight lengths – "a great experience."

Then he came home – why, he now wonders? But he couldn't settle, so went to work for James and Jane Evans. He rode out, along with Liam Treadwell and Ben Poste, and obtained an amateur licence, but his job was not full-time. He went to Jonjo O'Neill's for a while: nothing happened. He rode two days a week for Adrian Wintle, had six months with Dr. Richard Newland, riding five lots between 7 – 9.30 a.m. and every Sunday: "Flat out, but I enjoyed it," and in his afternoons worked with remedial children. "I have to keep busy." But again, nothing positive was happening: he needed a change of scenery. With Wintle's help he rang Jamie Snowden; he finished 4th in a point-to-point, but was called into the stewards for not driving his mount hard to the finish, when his horse was clearly struggling. He persevered, overdoing the work - but he was getting sour.

Rob is well aware of the price jockeys pay, a price also paid by no small number of stable lads and lasses struggling with workload, their weight, and the ever-present threat of criticism, even abuse: "It's a fickle sport," says Rob. "I can see why stable hands take coke." The fates of these vital members of the industry are rarely in the papers. He laments that, "Racing is all about how things look; first appearances, first impressions may only last 30 seconds, but they can take a lifetime to change."

Jockeys need an outlet; like many of his counterparts Rob plays golf, but there is no denying they must sell their soul to jump racing. He is still striving to establish himself in racing's world. But he has a wisdom beyond his years in thinking where he might be in three years' time. "You've got to dream. I'd love to be with top horses, but you've also got to be realistic: so few make it to the top. So, you have to find a balance, find what makes the job bearable. You've got to find something for a bad day, find something you're pleased with, keep going, keep something private to go home to, keep trying to find the key. There's never an easy day." And on success that wisdom obtains: "Everyone wants to be brilliant at something, to succeed, but you have to define that for yourself, it's completely individual; you have to find what makes you. It's easy to say what makes you happy, but not so easy to carry that out."

Josh Moore, youngest son of trainer Gary, younger brother of jump jockey, Jamie, flat champion Ryan and sister Hayley, and one of the weighing room's most popular jockeys, had been an aspiring top jockey for some time, knowing all there was to know about injuries. He suffered more than his fair share of setbacks in his 14-year career: "I got smashed up a lot." He was a keen runner and didn't ride till he was 10. But when Hayley started riding and show jumping, he joined her: "And then racing took over." After his best season in 2020-2021, when he booted home 40 winners, and had completed the London Marathon, he incurred his worst injury thus far in a fall at Plumpton in October 2021, fracturing his T4 and T5 vertebrae, and breaking several ribs. He had an eight day wait for his surgery in hospital in Brighton, his spinal operation delayed six times due to ongoing emergencies, and Covid. Throughout that time he had to remain flat on his back, with nil by mouth, not allowed to move. But he was philosophical: "There were people in a far worse state than me."

When it was finally his turn in theatre after, "a bit of a wait" he acknowledges, his T3 to T6 vertebrae were fused and two titanium rods inserted into his spine. The fixation was done internally, so all the metal was inside him. "It was quite an invasive procedure. They cut a lot of muscle to get to the operation site… you feel like you've had your back cut open." He was adamant he would return to the saddle: "When you've got horses like we have, it gives you a reason to return."

His positive outlook was tested when his father's horses, usually ridden by brother Jamie in his absence, hit a rich vein of form straight after his injury, but shared success is what matters to Josh: "I love having my own successes, but it's important to me that Dad and Jamie are doing well." Meantime, he made a daily pilgrimage to Peter O'Sullevan House, the IJF's rehab and fitness centre in Newmarket. As soon as he could, he was back in the saddle, riding out at home, and stepping up his exercises: he typified jump jockeys' level of resilience: they keep getting back; their bodies still function; there is more to achieve. Josh had come to know hospitals all too well over the years, and lauded the excellence of nurses in trauma wards. He made no fuss, just handled the situation as best he could.

One of his first winners after returning to the saddle was in Fontwell's National Spirit Hurdle on Botox Has, the horse who had buried him in a novice chase four months before, and out of whose owner's silks he had been cut. His family, who had won universal popularity with Champion Chaser,

Sire de Grugy, gave sterling encouragement, and have remained his greatest strength and support. Josh never had any illusions about the sport, and its mammoth risks: "Being a jockey is a bad way of being educated." Taking over Gary's licence one day had been on his mind, "Hopefully down the line. Jamie and I might be able to keep going what Gary's built…"

Then, in April 2022, he was again in the wars: a heavy fall at Haydock from the stable's reliable jumper, Gleno, resulted in a broken leg, broken ribs, punctured lung, and more damage to his lower back. But a rare reaction while under sedation for yet another operation led to a serious chest infection, which required him to remain sedated, on a ventilator, and delayed treatment of his injuries. When about to be anaesthetised for surgery on his leg, Josh was confused and unable to answer simple questions. He was placed in an induced coma at Aintree hospital, immobilised, and transferred to the critical care wing, the situation then made worse by pneumonia. "There were wires and tubes everywhere. They completely took over Josh's body with machines doing all the work for him," said his partner, Phoebe Cruse. The jockey's life hung in the balance. The phone rang at two o'clock one morning telling Phoebe and Josh's mother, Jayne, to go to the hospital at once: there was little more they could do: the worst was feared… "All we can do is pray," said father Gary, "he hasn't turned the corner. We are nothing without him."

Jayne had read up on fat embolism syndrome, first mentioned to her by one of the Aintree surgeons, and she became convinced this was the principal cause of her son's desperate predicament. Josh's eyes were open, but he wasn't responding to anything: "I was there, but nobody was home," says the jockey now. On completion of his spinal surgery, his treatment was altered accordingly… After several weeks in hospital in Liverpool, he was moved closer to home, and then, on the advice of BHA chief medical advisor Dr. Jerry Hill, to London's Wellington Hospital for brain rehabilitation work. There he improved rapidly. After months of anxiety he was finally in recovery. Daryl Jacob spoke for the whole weighing room: "Josh was never going to give up without a fight; he's done that all his life. He's hugely popular, a brilliant horseman, but an even better character." David Bass echoed these sentiments: "We were all so relieved to hear the positive news. Josh is used to being mentally very strong as he's had a lot of injuries, so his toughness is obviously coming through again. He's from such a well-respected family," the head of whom, Gary, commented: "If he turned up in a taxi tomorrow morning it wouldn't surprise me." Not for the first time Josh had baffled the doctors with his grit and determination.

He would not race ride again, but his recovery meant he still had a future in the sport, once he had accepted the harsh reality of retirement. "A lot of the lads get lucky with their falls and some have never even broken a bone. The thing is I enjoy riding horses. I enjoy racing them even more. It's hard to let it go. I've learnt that the human body is incredible. And I feel very lucky – a lot of jockeys haven't been so fortunate. There's no good being angry or bitter. It's a funny old game." He is now assistant trainer to his father, and back to fitness, having run in the 2023 London Marathon.

Will Kennedy may not be the winning-most jockey of all time, but he is certainly top notch when it comes to being honest. His response to the question, "Is jump racing only about winning?" was refreshingly measured: "I'm obsessed, not with winning, but with finishing in the best possible position. If, on any given day, another horse is better, you can't do anything about it." His chief concern had always been "doing it right, and getting it right."

Now 41, he had been a jockey almost half his life. When he was six, his brother, Vivian, was killed in a fall at Huntingdon: "That's why I wanted to be a jockey." His parents were not the keenest for him to don silks, but from the age of ten he had decided he only wanted to ride horses in races. He carried brother Vivian with him, in the form of an angel tattooed on his back: "He was going really well and got robbed of a chance, so I was doing it for him as well." Will had great help from Michael Caulfield, was Champion Conditional with Noel Chance in 2005-2006, and had no mean success afterwards, winning the Lanzarote Hurdle twice, the Imperial Cup and the Summer Hurdle. He always ran the track before racing. His best horse, Time for Rupert, won at Aintree and Cheltenham (twice), finished second in the World Hurdle, and took his jockey to places he'd always hoped he'd reach. In 2016-2017 Will rode 63 winners, mainly for Donald McCain.

But although he'd ridden for a lot of trainers, he had never been a stable jockey, more than once finding himself on the end of the dreaded phone call from a trainer saying he was being replaced – "on the owner's instructions."

This strikes a shrill chord with Will: "Jockeys are always concerned about upsetting trainers, trainers of upsetting owners, so only rarely do we hear the truth in interviews. Always we hear the same, "Have saddle, will travel." We need to tell the truth as it is, not how we want it to be. A lot of it is dog eat dog." The truth does not always go down well in racing; he has always spoken honestly though not in a "chippy" (i.e. bitter) way. "We jockeys need to show our emotional sides; racing needs raw emotion to link with the public more."

And he had always been level-headed, striving to improve. "I didn't achieve nearly close to what I'd have liked to," and, as a journeyman jockey, picking up spare rides wherever possible, felt he continually had to prove to people he was still there. Meanwhile, the risk-level rose on bad horses, day in, day out. His honesty sears when he wonders if he'd missed something in his career – the X factor – though what it might have been he doesn't know. But he lived his dream – "and there are few people in this world who can say that. I know how lucky I've been to have that opportunity." He has been pretty fortunate with injuries, keeps naturally fit "and away from the fridge," dealt bravely with setbacks – "so many highs and lows" – and has a savvy businesswoman, Rachel, as his rock. He regularly consults the man in the mirror.

That man is his friend, despite all. And perhaps his therapist: "If race-riding was easy, everyone'd do it." Not getting as many rides as he was, he was aware it was not so easy to "get back in and get back going." But he was still trying and started training to be a jockey coach. Olly Murphy offered him the chance of some rides. Will did not want to walk away, he wanted to go out on his own terms, even if he was only kicking that day down the road: "The day was close." He took up Murphy's offer, remembering how his Dad always told him to "keep a little bit up your sleeve," knowing full well "a jockey's lifestyle looks fantastic from the outside, it always does," but he still had a good sponsor, Rob Edwards, good mates, like Aidan Coleman, Kielan Woods and Johnny Burke, a DNA redolent of honesty, and, that man in the mirror... In April 2023, he finally retired. "The time is right now, I have had a good innings and not many jockeys go to 41." Murphy paid tribute to Will: "He was a grafter, someone all these lads starting out should look up to, because his work ethic was second to none."

After 25 years in the saddle, Brian Harding knows all about the vicissitudes of a jump jockey's life. In 1998, with regular pilot Tony Dobbin injured, Brian, who had himself been on the injured list for 12 months with a fractured skull, torn kidneys, two broken ribs, and a fractured TS vertebra, all discovered when his sample contained nothing but blood, was called up by Gordon Richards to ride the immensely popular grey, One Man, winner of the Hennessy Gold Cup and two King Georges, in the Champion Chase at Cheltenham. No small number of jockeys were keen to replace Tony, but Richards stayed loyal to his stable number two. The horse had been beaten on his three previous appearances at the Festival, his stamina ebbing away on the punishing Cheltenham hill, but his trainer elected to drop him back to two miles for the first time since his novice hurdle days – and the outcome was extraordinary.

In a real throat-cutter, One Man, who never ducked a challenge, set a searching pace that proved too much for his opponents as the race boiled up coming down the hill. With his rivals gasping for air, One Man simply did not stop in an exhilarating display that brought him striding up that Cheltenham hill victorious, to euphoria from the packed grandstands. He had laid his Festival ghost, and been vindicated, finally acclaiming championship glory. But, after reaching that career high, and with Brian again on board, 16 days later the gallant grey went from triumph to tragedy at Aintree on his next start, and was killed.

Richards, the taskmaster, who had been too ill to go to Cheltenham, but had gone to Aintree with the horse he always rode out himself, was "brilliant" with his dejected jockey the night of One Man's fatal fall, despite being so ill. In soft ground, the horse, normally a fabulous jumper, had dived to the right as he jumped a fence. "It was not nice, not nice for anyone," said Richards, with typical understatement: "Son," he said to Brian, that evening, "we'll just have to go and get another." The trainer died of cancer only months later.

The third of eight children, Brian was born in Castletownroche, County Cork, the same village as Jonjo O'Neill. His father rode as an amateur, farmed, and always had horses – he it was who broke in Dawn Run. At 19, Brian was sent to Gordon Richards, and he stayed there a quarter of a century. He describes Gordon as "the hardest man I ever worked for, the most loyal, and the fairest."

Brian rode renowned chasers and hurdlers, though perhaps not with quite the same following as One Man: Feels Like Gold, The Grey Monk, The French Furze, Harmony Brig, Twin Oaks, Addington Boy, Grey Abbey and McGregor III, on whom he won three of the newly introduced cross-country chases at Cheltenham, brain child of former CEO, Edward Gillespie.

Gordon's son Nicky has taken over at Greystoke, Cumbria (its castle still visited by *Tarzan* fans) where Brian boasts, "The gallops are as good as any in the country, though it can be a cold place in winter: that makes it a great place for horses," as Monet's Garden, Noble Alan, Eduard, Gold Futures, Duke of Navan and Simply Ned have more recently proved. The jockey's last serious injury came in January 2016 at Musselburgh, when Shot of Wine crashed out of his race. Brian was on 45 wins for the season, and heading for his best year yet. His recovery took a long time, demanding great patience, but he'd already decided to stop after one more year. He'd had a long innings, was determined to go out in 'one piece', and underplays the respect he'd earned from other jockeys: "That was only because I was around for so long! But I was lucky, I'd had more good days than bad."

Following in the steps of Peter Niven and Chris Grant, who had also hung up their saddles on the peg closest to the door, denoting their seniority, Brian retired at Perth in the shadow of Scone Palace, where Scottish monarchs were traditionally crowned, in April 2017: "It had to happen. I wanted to stop on my own terms and work towards the future while things were still going pretty well, while I still enjoyed riding very much." While some of the jockeys he rode with had long since swapped riding boots for slippers, Brian had kept going, though he had been planning his retirement for some time. But walking away was still hard, and he left a big hole in the weighing room. Soon after that last day at Perth he went racing at Cartmel: people were pleased to see him, but he felt alien, a stranger, not having his place in the weighing room, and left after the third race. He has been back since.

Only a few months after retiring, "evergreen Brian" beat a stellar collection of veteran flat riders in the September Leger Legends Charity Race at Doncaster; the popular race raises money for the IJF's Jack Berry House and the Northern Racing College. He had shown the promising young jockeys he now coaches exactly how it should be done. After his win, Brian was honest in evaluating that experience; "Race-riding was my life for so long, then suddenly it was all over. Giving it up was a wrench, and my immediate thought at Doncaster was that I was half tempted to come back." But the Cork man was prepared for a challenging readjustment, well aware that no small number of jockeys get lost after retiring: "Someone needs to keep an eye on them." He quotes Jason Maguire, one of the many who had to retire through injury: "On one of his first day's racing after being told he'd be unwise to continue, Jason had to ask the location of the gents."

Brian is a plain talker: "Speak as you find, but be as nice as you can saying it." He had been a jockey coach long before he retired – now in that role, he is still up at 5 a.m., in the yard by 5.30, pulling out at 6 – and now he has to muck out like everyone else. But he enjoys the chance to be a touchstone of experience for his young charges, with more of them waiting on the books. He is kept fit and busy, able to use Greystoke's facilities just a few miles from his home. "You've got to be proactive." He has an ever-growing passion for the chance to pass on his own experience in every nuance of race-riding to jockeys such as Danny McMenamin and Callum Bewley, already making names for themselves at Greystoke, and is particularly concerned to teach his charges about mental strength, as well as to encourage them on equicizers and through videos. Brian works with sports psychologists as part of their training: Mick Fitzgerald, himself a coach, advocates the importance of a strong arm to cry on: "It's not just about riding a winner, but needing to ring your coach on the way home and have a whinge. Then, when issues crop up, young jockeys won't panic because they are already latched on to a support system."

In addition, Brian breaks horses in – "the most important thing in a horse's life" – with wife Kelly, he pre-trains horses, building them up slowly on the Cumbrian Fells and nearby beaches. Being a northern jockey was important to him: having ridden in the halcyon days for jump racing in the north, he is well aware of the current north/south divide, with many of the best horses, jockeys and trainers now in the south of England, though Sandy Thomson, Lucinda Russell, Tim Easterby, Ruth Jefferson, Micky Hammond, Jedd O'Keeffe and Nick Alexander, as well as McCain and Richards, are working hard to redress the balance. They all face the same pressures and demands in 21st century jump racing, for which there are probably more aspiring youngsters, for fewer full-time jobs, and fewer rides.

With many of these lads and lasses working in more than one yard, everything is more spread out. As a consequence, trainers, who are busier than they were back in the day, are not solely responsible for their jockeys – all the more reason for retired riders to become coaches. "It's all about giving them confidence," says Brian, "something to bounce off, especially when things – or trainers – get tough." Brian, who had no coach, but was much encouraged by Neale Doughty and Graham Lee – that man again - makes sure his pupils see the bigger picture. A man of gentle surprises, he is always good 'craic'. As I left his yard one time, the place was buzzing with lads changing into riding kit. One of them looked up with a ready smile: on being asked how he fitted into the Harding team, he paused a second: "I'm his… his project!"

Having always said he would never train, Brian has 'got a kick' out of saddling a few runners, like Senor Lombardy, "a gorgeous-looking horse who had lost his way." The man who rode 496 winners out of 5,490 starts in Britain – and an important one in Ireland, Granit d'Estruval in the Irish Grand National – and finished third in the 2005 Aintree National, has always had an exemplary work ethic: now he passes it on. Admired by Michael Caulfield, for being "straight as a gun barrel," Brian remains anchored in the harsh reality of his sport, his way of life evoking Shakespeare's: "To thine own self be true." He has always been his own man; it is somehow right that his crowning moment as a jockey came at Cheltenham in the Champion Chase on the daredevil grey, One Man.

CHAPTER 24: DEATHS

"I saw the danger, yet I walked along the enchanted way."
- Patrick Kavanagh -

Pressure on jockeys is immense, and though some, perhaps most of all AP McCoy, thrived on it, and Barry Geraghty said, "Pressure's for tyres," many others down the years have yielded to its cruel insistence.

Fred Archer was born in Cheltenham in 1857, the son of jump jockey, William, who won the following year's Grand National on Little Charley. Young Fred was surrounded by equine companions, which helped him develop a sense of how they thought and reacted: he had soon acquired an uncanny judgement of pace, together with an obsessive will to win that saw him 13 consecutive times Champion Jockey on the flat, with 21 classics to his name. Not surprisingly, the phrase 'Archer's up' encouraged gamblers everywhere. But Fred could be merciless and harsh, with both other jockeys and the horses he rode so hard to win. There was even a story that he once wept, miserable that he couldn't have ridden both winners in a dead-heat.

Fred was very tall for a jockey, particularly in the Victorian era: throughout his career he had to battle with the scales. In order to help him lose weight, a Newmarket doctor prepared him a special concoction that became known as 'Archer's Mixture'. To say it was a fierce laxative is an understatement, but Fred drank the potion by the sherry-glass full – to complement his diet of castor oil, one biscuit and a small glass of champagne at midday.

But in 1886 it is thought the long-term impact of wasting (to lose weight) on his physical health and psychological well-being, allied to the grief he experienced after the death of his wife in childbirth two years earlier – just a year after their marriage – caused him to become seriously ill. While suffering from a fever, he put a shotgun to his head and took his own life. He was just 29. Such was his standing with the public that his death released a huge outpouring of sorrow: it was said that London buses stopped every few yards so the passengers could buy a paper. The Prince of Wales sent a wreath to "the darkest of funerals as Archer was buried next to his wife and his son, William, who had also died prematurely." (John Carter)

The effects of trauma are borne for many years. On Derby Day, 1913, Emily Davison was fatally injured when she ran out under the King's horse, Anmer, at the top of Epsom's Tattenham Corner. The royal jockey, Herbert Jones, had won the Derby twice before on Diamond Jubilee in 1900, and on Minoru for the King in 1909, the only time that a horse owned by a reigning monarch has won the classic. His collision with Davison resulted in concussion. 15 years later he laid a wreath at the funeral of Emmeline Pankhurst, leader of the Suffragette Movement, in honour of her and Emily Davison. He retired from the saddle in 1923, claiming that he was "haunted by that poor woman's face." In 1951 he was discovered to have committed suicide when his son found him in a gas-filled kitchen.

Serious injury, even death, is not a longshot when it comes to jump racing. For all that safety measures, jockeys' kit and tighter stipulations on protocol have undoubtedly helped prevent more fatal accidents, no small number of jockeys racing over the sticks have paid the ultimate price. Death is always "proud, august and raw."

While records of jump racing tragedies may not always have survived until today, there can be no gainsaying that many riders – and, of course, their gallant mounts – died whilst doing their job in a race. Joseph Wynne is the only known jockey who died in the Grand National, when he fell from his mount, O'Connell, at The Chair in 1862. Michael Scudamore remembered the deaths of two contemporaries, Ivor Beckinsale (24) on Boxing Day at Wolverhampton in 1951, and Micky Lynn (23) at Sandown in 1955. In 1973 Doug Barrott (26) was killed in a fall at Newcastle, while 1986 was a desperate year, with three jockeys dying in rapid succession: Jim Lombard (22), at the Punchestown Festival, Michael Blackmore (30), who had never ridden a winner, at Market Rasen, in April, and Jayne Thompson (22), the first lady rider to perish, at Catterick in May. Three years later, Vivian Kennedy, aged just 21, but already one of the most popular riders in the weighing-room, fell two flights from home at Huntingdon: he broke his neck, incurred serious head injuries and never regained consciousness. In August 1988 Philip Barnard (24) was killed at Wincanton. Tom Halliday (20) died after a fall at Market Rasen in July 2005. The following month, Kieran Kelly (25) who, in March of that year had ridden Hardy Eustace to victory in the Sun Alliance Hurdle at the Cheltenham Festival, and who had ridden his last winner just 90 minutes beforehand, took a fall at Kilbeggan, in County Westmeath, which left him so badly injured that he died four days later in hospital. Statistics appear to show jockeys in Ireland fall less often, and sustain fewer injuries than their counterparts in Britain, but the incidence of fatalities and serious injury in both countries is strikingly high compared to other sports.

And these statistics do not include death in yards, or on the gallops, that rarely make the pages of newspapers, nor indeed in point-to-points. John Thorne, who had ridden the gallant hunter-chaser, Spartan Missile, a horse he had bred himself, into second place behind Bob Champion and Aldaniti in the 1981 Grand National, finishing like a wet sail, was a great sportsman. After partnering this gallant runner-up, he had enjoyed a drink with Bob in the pub the evening of that race. Himself a champion amateur, with countless victories to his name, he was killed aged 55, in a point-to-point at Mollington in March 1982. He had ridden Spartan Missile to victory in the Aintree Foxhunters twice, the Cheltenham Foxhunters, and the Champion Hunters Chase at Stratford, as well as finishing second in the 1978 Whitbread Gold Cup, behind Tommy Stack on Strombolus. The horse is still considered by many the greatest hunter chaser to have graced British point-to-point fields.

Richard Davis came of honest racing stock. His mother, Ann, had ridden in point-to-points, and his father, John, had drawn up the plans and built the first block of stables for 16 horses at Aramstone when Venetia Williams was starting out in Herefordshire. After a stint in Ireland, and time with John Edwards, at Ross-on-Wye, son Richard moved to Aramstone in 1994, and helped Venetia for 18 months before Norman Williamson arrived. Richard was ambitious, dedicated, lean; his workroom pals ribbed him for being as fit as Bruce Lee. A proper athlete, he never drank milk, and when haymaking on the family farm, he wore a PVC suit to lose extra weight.

Friday July 19th 1996 was not a big race day. Journeyman jockey Richard had one ride in the bottom-drawer novice chase at Southwell on a complete outsider, Mr Sox. Together with his mate, and fellow journeyman jockey, Guy Lewis, he had been working on a book to describe the ups and downs, exhilarations and depressions in the life of an ordinary jump jockey: he had kept a diary of his own experiences for that enterprise.

Richard, and many like him, might never have been a multiple champion jockey like John Francome, Peter Scudamore, AP McCoy or Richard Johnson, but these men exist on hope: that one day, perhaps, should all the fates be smiling at once, a chance ride on a good horse might do what Sean Magee describes in his book, co-written with Guy Lewis, *To Win Just Once*, as "pluck him out of the ranks, and place him, at last, on that upward escalator" so vital to becoming known – in other words, a "winner."

Together with Guy Lewis and two other jockeys, Richard had recently visited Pardubice in the Czech Republic, where few British jockeys had at that time competed. The course is famous in jump-racing circles for its gruelling race, the Velka Pardubicka, with its extraordinarily convoluted cross country course, and daunting obstacles like the Taxis, a fence that from the take-off side seems inoffensive enough, but has a huge drop on the landing side, with an enormous ditch and a long lip sloping out of it. Horses do not realise this until clearing the hedge, so they need strong momentum in order to land clear of this ditch: the fence demands great respect, and cannot fail to evoke the element of fear. Even the notorious Becher's Brook on the Grand National course at Aintree pales into insignificance by comparison with the Taxis. Peter Gehm, the now-paralysed German jockey, won the Pardubicka four times. Those who ride in this gruelling race are beyond brave.

Although not riding in that year's big race, Richard had prepared for his ride over the cross-country obstacles: he walked the course for hours, only to discover, just before race time, that his mount had been withdrawn. He still rode in the Czech Gold Cup, run over the more orthodox steeplechase fences.

The weather was diabolical, causing the start to be delayed; when the race finally took place in still bucketing rain, the kickback from the mud made visibility almost impossible, but Richard had clung on to finish fourth. Despite atrocious weather, there was the usual vibrant atmosphere at Pardubice, with a huge crowd, and abundant goodwill. Czech hospitality had been an unexpected surprise to Richard and the other English jockeys, who had not anticipated such a warm welcome from the former Communist country.

Richard Davis was well aware of the challenges he faced every day he rode in a race: up at the crack of dawn to drive, bleary-eyed, through the dark to ride out for a trainer who had agreed to put him up on one of their horses. Richard's father, John, had, for two years in the 1950s, worked at Fairlawne for the Queen Mother's trainer, Peter Cazalet. Landing there, he had half a crown in his pocket, was paid £2.00 per week and given his keep. He had ridden gallops on such famous horses as M'as-tu-vu, Lochroe and Devon Loch. John was well aware that his son travelled up to 50,000 miles a year, dashing round the country clocking up mileage, piling up petrol receipts, sharing journeys with other jockeys to spread the load. Not for these men the heights of Cheltenham, Aintree or Punchestown: they had to eke out a living at the gaff tracks (smaller, less well-known courses), often in bad weather, for just one ride – on an outsider, of course…

… which is just what Richard was doing that July day in 1996. Mr Sox, trained by permit-holder, Laura Shally, had no chance whatsoever in the Fiskerton Novices Handicap Chase at Southwell, Nottinghamshire. A five-year old gelding (castrated male), Mr Sox had been switched to jumping after a career on the flat that was utterly undistinguished: his rating that fateful day was a mere 60, which put him in the bottom 2% of racehorses – indeed only 13 animals then in training in the country were on a lower mark.

Guy Lewis noticed in the paper that morning that his mate was going to Southwell, for just one ride, flogging halfway across the country to ride a useless horse with no possibility of winning. Why was he doing it? Guy made a mental note to ring Richard and ask him to jot down his thoughts on this, which they could then use in their book.

Mr Sox's recent form had been dire: in three of his four previous races he had started at 100-1, and finished a race only once. Not surprisingly, he started as the rank outsider in that Southwell race. Sean Magee described what happened: "Having made the short run from the start to the first fence, Mr Sox failed to judge his take-off correctly. Although he just managed to get his front legs over the fence, his hind quarters did not give him enough power to clear it properly, and his underside slammed into the birch. The impact of hitting the fence so comprehensively at a speed of around 30 mph. flipped the horse's rear end into the air, and his head sharply downwards: as he descended steeply Richard was shot over the horse's head. Half a second after his jockey hit the ground, the full ½ ton of Mr Sox, pivoting on his nose, somersaulted down squarely on top of him. The horse quickly regained his feet and made off after the other runners." His jockey did not rise…

Richard, in the gruesome jargon of jump jockeys, was 'buried' by his horse and knocked out by the impact of the fall: he lay on the ground as the paramedics rushed to his aid. Lying on his side, he was unconscious, blue in the face and showing signs of respiratory distress. His eyes were open, but he could not respond: his skin colour turned from blue to pale, and he was very sweaty.

Placed on a spine board to be stretchered off the course, he began to regain consciousness, and kept repeating, "I came on my own and have already had my spleen removed." He was taken to the racecourse medical centre, where it may well have been that the racecourse doctor assessed him wrongly, though attending paramedics did not. Crucially, there was a lengthy delay as Richard had to wait for a county ambulance to take him to hospital. (Jockey Club regulations then stated that two ambulances must be in attendance when a race is run, so critically, the fear of holding up the next race was placed before the stricken jockey's needs – a situation which has now changed).

During the wait Richard was conscious enough to ask for analgesia for his back pain, and to fret about what would happen to his beloved dog, Henry, given him by the trainer, Henry Oliver, for whom he had ridden out. Nick Oliver had canine Henry's brother. Richard's valet took his clothes and wallet to the ambulance, and fellow jockey Warren Marston made arrangements about his car: jump jockeys don't always get home at night. Richard was loaded into the county ambulance, but the racecourse doctor, assuming the jockey had back injuries, instructed the ambulance to drive slowly to the nearest large hospital, the Queen's Medical Centre in Nottingham, some dozen miles from the course. By another cruel twist of fate, that hospital having been given a wrong diagnosis, the consultant cardiologist was, at first, not available. Only after a delay did Richard undergo surgery, where the extent of damage to his crushed internal organs became apparent: his inferior vena cava – the main vein leading to the heart – had been torn three-quarters of the way across, flooding his abdomen with blood, and his liver had been split. Remarkably, not a single bone in his body had been broken. He had lost masses of blood: the severe haemorrhaging and shock due to this blood loss caused his heart to arrest: he was pronounced dead at 5.40 p.m., three hours and twenty minutes after Mr Sox had tried to jump that first fence. The official cause of death was given as a lacerated liver, combined with severe, uncontrollable internal bleeding. His estate would receive his fee for riding Mr Sox: £80.

His death quickly reverberated through the world of racing: next day, racegoers at the day's six meetings stood for a minute's silence. Richard Dunwoody, in sweltering heat, led his fellow jockeys in an act of remembrance, placing flowers under the number 1 marker board in the unsaddling enclosure. The racecard that day had Richard Davis down to ride a horse called Magic Bloom in the 3.40: the horse had been declared to run the previous morning, as Richard drove to Southwell.

According to Dr Michael Turner, there was nothing that could have prevented Richard's injuries, other than not riding. The immediate shock gave way to questions – about the horse, his trainer, the racecourse itself (racing in 2020 was suspended at Southwell for a while after the BHA took a safety-first approach), the medical facilities, the racecourse doctor, all of which needed probing, but nothing could alleviate the deep and tangible grief of his loss…

His funeral took place in the thirteenth century village church of St Nicholas, in Earl's Croome, Worcestershire, on a warm, sunny Friday July 26th, just a week after his death. The famous and the lowly of the racing world gathered to mourn one of their number killed in action. Long before the service began, the church was full, as were the grassy banks flanking the path to the church door: so many had come to express the collective grief of the weighing room, which boasts the tightest bond. Richard Dunwoody, three times Champion Jockey, spoke the words of The Saw Doctors, Richard's favourite group, in their song, *To Win Just Once Would Be Enough*; there was an address from Michael Caulfield; a recording of Don McLean's *American Pie* – Richard's favourite track; the hymn *Fight the Good Fight*, and, as his coffin was borne back down the aisle came a haunting call from the hunting horn, *Gone Away*. On the headstone which now marks his grave, the letters RIP are enclosed in a horseshoe.

Luke Harvey was the last person to speak to Richard as they left the weighing room that July afternoon. He remembered that, a few days before the race, his friend had gone to Mr Sox's stables, but there was nowhere to school the horse over fences, so Richard had given him a gallop instead. Luke recalls that in the race the horse seemed dumbstruck as it approached the first fence: "In that situation, you're just a passenger." AP McCoy won the race, and had seen what happened. "It was the most apparently run-of-the-mill fall in the most apparently mundane, run-of-the-mill race. Alas, not so..." Richard's death had an effect on all jockeys, and all associated with jockeys. His family was brilliant, not at all bitter, never trying to blame anyone. Richard had died doing what he loved, that was their way of dealing with the tragedy. AP heard the fateful news whilst stuck at traffic lights on the way home; when the lights turned green, he was unable to move. He still has a picture of Richard on his wall at home.

Richard had made the most of the opportunity for foreign travel, and had forged a deep impression on his Czech hosts that day in 1996, when he had ridden in their Gold Cup, so much so that ten weeks after his death the course staged the Richard Davis Memorial Chase, just prior to the Pardubicka. Guy Lewis rode the horse his great friend had partnered in the Czech race, and finished fourth. Richard's younger brother, Stephen, presented the prize; the following year, Stephen's twin brother, Andrew, did the honours. Both men, like their courageous parents, blaze, still, with the memory of Richard.

And jockeys do not only die on the course, or on the gallops. In 2012, the Grade 1 three-mile Novices Hurdle at the Cheltenham Festival was won by Brindisi Breeze, ridden by the irrepressible young Scot, Campbell Gillies. By midsummer, both horse and jockey had died. The horse was trained by Lucinda Russell and her partner, Peter Scudamore. For no known reason, one night in the summer of that year, Brindisi Breeze jumped his way across two fields to get to the road. He evidently hurt himself, because a trail of blood was found leading into the driveway of Arlary Stables. Sadly, the horse had been hit and killed by a tanker.

One month later, Campbell (21) and some friends went on a hastily arranged holiday to Kavos while the racing season was quiet. They arrived in the early hours, went out, and came back to go straight into the pool. Campbell suggested seeing who could swim the fastest two lengths underwater. He went first, did a length, turned, got halfway back, then just went to the bottom. Thinking he was joking, as usual, the mates ignored him – until too late. His mother, Lesley, now believes he was a victim of shallow-water blackout, a phenomenon that particularly affects the physically fit. Peter Scudamore, Lucinda, and Campbell's family were left to deal with the death of this brave young lion: "It was a James Dean thing," says Peter of the young jockey with a spaniel-like charm, a questing quirkiness, grim self-belief and unfailing joie de vivre.

John Thomas McNamara, always known as 'JT', from Croom, County Limerick, was a glittering Irish amateur rider, with over 600 victories to his name, the vast majority of them for trainer Enda Bolger in the green and gold hoops of owner JP McManus. JT shone at Punchestown, not least 'over the banks' in races like the coveted La Touche Cup, which he won five times. He had sixteen victories at Cheltenham, including four at the Festival: among his celebrated partners were Risk of Thunder, On The Fringe, Spotthedifference, Garde Champêtre and 2012 National Hunt Chase winner, Tea for Three, ten years after his most celebrated ride on Rith Dubh, whom he 'kissed over the line'.

He had told friends he intended to retire from the saddle in the summer of 2013, but at the Cheltenham Festival in March of that year he fell from Galaxy Rock in the Fulke Walwyn Kim Muir Chase, fracturing vertebrae C3 and C4. He was left paralysed, but returned to Ireland after 15 months in hospital in the North West Spinal Injuries Centre in Liverpool, having earned the admiration of many for his positive determination. But in July 2016 he suffered complications, and died at the age of 41. Poignantly, the Galway Festival was taking place at the time.

Among the many tributes paid to this 'prince of racing', who they called God in Ireland, God of the point-to-point circuit, Aidan Coleman said JT: "transcended all sport because he was all heart." Greg Wood in *The Guardian* wrote: "JT blurred the distinction between amateur and professional," and reminded us that "these things don't just happen to the less well-known jockeys, they happen to the best as well." A plaque in the weighing room at Cheltenham sits above where he changed, and honours the King of the Banks' sixteen wins there, the skill of a "proper horseman, proper old-school." His injuries brought a lot of people in the racing world together, and a part of his legacy is that through his injuries – and reaction to them – there will be more understanding of how best to help jockeys in the future. Ruby Walsh, with his typical acumen for 'calling it as it is', praised not only his friend's wicked sense of humour, but his mental and physical strength, his fine judgement of horses – and people – the fact that no matter who you were you got the truth from him: "We come and go as jockeys, but he was just a wonderful, wonderful man."

On April 8th 2021 Lorna Brooke, riding her mother's horse, Orchestrated, fell at the third fence in a handicap chase at Taunton. She was airlifted to Southmead Hospital, Bristol, for observation and tests on a suspected spinal injury, but, after complications, was placed in an induced coma eight days later. Her condition deteriorated over that weekend, her brain tissue having suffered serious swelling from the injury. Despite doctors fighting tirelessly to save her, she died on the evening of Sunday April 18th. She was 37.

The racing community united in its grief; silence was held at the following day's race meetings, jockeys wore black armbands, though David Jennings argued strongly that was not enough: he firmly believed racing should have been cancelled that day. Lorna had ridden as an amateur, notching up forty point-to-point victories, the last of them at Sandown just five days before her fall. David Maxwell spoke for all such jockeys who receive no remuneration for their brave endeavours: "Amateurs do it for love, the love of the game, and, more important, the love of the horse. There's such passion in the sport. At amateur level, nobody has to do it. Lorna was at the forefront of the Corinthians."

On the racecourse, Lorna had ridden seventeen winners, the most celebrated being the inaugural running of the Ladies' Handicap Chase in 2015, where, riding Moonlone Lane, at Fairyhouse, she came home in front, beating Katie Walsh, Nina Carberry, Lizzie Kelly and Rachael Blackmore. In her own way she was one of those who set he standards for females to compete on level terms in the jockey world, and her thirst for racing was 'unquenchable'. Her death "puts everything into perspective," said Harry Bannister, a feeling endorsed by Paul Struthers: "Racing is not about big prizes at big meetings. It's about the Lornas of this world, and what's happened is a devastating reminder of the dangers our brave men and women face. We have lost one of our own, and she will be sorely missed." Brian Hughes was equally moved: "When jockeys get a fall like this, competitive edge goes out of the window. The whole racing family is affected; that is the harsh reality of our sport."

We are all reminded how close jockeys are to the limit, how we should never underestimate the risks they take day after day, only millimetres from their doom. Matt Chapman, who for all his bantering bravado is unafraid to show open emotion, paid tribute to Lorna's family, not least her mother, the trainer Lady Susan, for whom Lorna rode: "Their family spirit is at the heart of our sport. Racing is full of fractions and factions, but, when required, racing steps up… this is beyond sad." Lorna's death as an immediate result of a fall on the racecourse was the first since 2005, and only the second woman ever. In a poignant postscript to her death, the last horse she'd ridden to victory, Garde Ville, won a race at Ludlow three days after Lorna died, the knot she'd tied in his reins still there.

On February 4, 2024, West Country jockey, Keagan Kirkby, (25), died after a fall in a point-to-point race at Charing, Kent, when the horse he was riding ran out through the wing of a fence. An affable and immensely popular young man, Keagan, who had ridden six winners, had made it through to the final of the 2024 Thoroughbred Industry Employee Awards.

But, most tragic of all was the death in early September 2022 of pony racer Jack de Bromhead, thirteen-year-old son of revered trainer, Henry. His was the first death on an Irish course since another Jack, Jack Tyner, fell in a point-to-point at Dungarvan in 2011. Jack de Bromhead fell from his pony when, under a bad weather day, it slipped in the water while turning on Rossbeigh beach, during part of the Glenbeigh Festival in Co. Kerry.

Just the week before, he had won a race at Cahersiveen on a pony ironically called The Highest Level, which the young lad may well have reached in time.

Stephen Ferhane wrote: "Chance has rarely looked more cruel. No analysis is worthy of coherent understanding; only heartbreak and dismay seem to make sense. To say he died doing what he loved sounds empty and hollow. But it's true. Horses reinforced Jack's precocious identity." The lad, who was making quite a name for himself as a young jockey, wanted to learn all the time, and was often seen at Henry's side; he could not have had a better master tactician than his dad, who courageously delivered his son's eulogy at the funeral. The words:

"And He will raise you up on eagles' wings,
bear you on the breath of dawn,
make you to shine like the sun,
and hold you in the palm of his hand"

struck home then, and still do now. The parish priest said Jack was "an incalculable loss, a young man who captured the hearts of not just a parish, but of a nation, and far beyond. His was a life jam-packed with love and laughter."

The previous week, after riding his last winner, he had said to Henry how much he loved pony racing; he got such a buzz out of it: "Henboy, [the nickname he used to call his father] if you can't take the falls, you shouldn't be doing it." His grandfather's tribute told how "in a fateful riding accident on the late afternoon of September 3rd, in the dark, murky Atlantic waters washing on to Rossbeigh beach, his horse came down. Jack was thrown, and, in an instant, the horse delivered a fatal blow to Jack's head."

"Frozen in time, with a beautiful soul, he had packed a vast amount of life into his 13 years, living so many more years than that stark number. And he made a mighty impression," (David Jennings) as well as leaving a legacy for all pony riders to come… But, alas, that won't bring him back.

CHAPTER 25: THE EMERALD ISLE

*"The Irish inject into the unique spirit of jump racing an
uplifting liveliness, love of the horse, and contagious humour;
theirs is the most glittering thread."*

- Hugh McIlvanney -

At the moment, Irish jump racing is going through a golden age: long gone
are the days when a solitary Irish winner graced the Cheltenham
Festival. The Prestbury Cup, between Britain and Ireland, has recently been
dominated by our near neighbour, with Willie Mullins' stable alone notching
up more victories in 2021 than the whole of UK forces combined. But is
there something more than just the quality of the horses and the expertise of
their training? To what extent have the Irish jockeys themselves contributed
to this domination? Has there been something discernible in their characters
and horsemanship that has also played its part in this modern Irish golden
age? Will the tide turn inevitably in the fullness of time, or is there something
more in the domination than that old chestnut, 'the luck of the Irish'?

Ireland is the acknowledged home of the horse. Perhaps it's all that lush
green grass of the Emerald Isle that has led to this pre-eminence. The country
has always enjoyed a more temperate climate (and more plentiful rain) than
Britain, a feature that has been increasing during our recent severe climate
change. Whatever the cause, Ireland currently breeds the best horses; and, if
the English go to Ireland to buy horses, they understandably only come away
with second best.

Former trainer Henrietta Knight, when interviewed on the Nick Luck
show, offered interesting insights into this Irish domination. She feels their

animals are given a better chance of being top class because of the way in which they are brought up: broken in, and taught to jump, having had their muscles strengthened earlier in pre-training yards. The Irish equine education and point-to-point system is top class. Taken to racecourses, like Tipperary, for training days, horses become practised in big fields and competition, thus gaining good experience, adapting and adjusting on a steady learning curve. For the Irish, horses are in the blood, understood, and given a feeling of confidence. In the UK, by contrast, trainers operate under considerable disadvantages. Many British yards are more isolated, training days are not allowed on racecourses, there are too many races of a similar calibre, and too few horses by comparison with Ireland, where trainers are more patient, and play for time. There, each horse is treated differently, and attention to detail is first-rate. The UK does not pursue the same avenues.

Ireland has a terrific legacy of great jockeys. Michael Moloney won three Grand Nationals and the 1951 Gold Cup on Silver Fame; he was Irish Champion Jockey six times. Tommy Carmody won the Gold Cup on L'Escargot (The Snail) in 1971; four years later he rode the same horse to win the Grand National, lowering the colours of the race's mightiest hero, Red Rum, who was going for his third consecutive victory. Tommy was also associated with the battling grey Flying Wild. Conor O'Dwyer had just four wins at the Cheltenham Festival, but all in blue riband events, two Champion Hurdles with Hardy Eustace, and two Gold Cups: Imperial Call and War Of Attrition.

The modern golden age could be said to have begun with Adrian Maguire, who started his career at nine; Charlie Swan, a master tactician, was a top rider in the 1990s, most famously associated with Istabraq, who won three Champion Hurdles (only foot and mouth disease foiled his 2001 attempt to become the only horse to win four); Barry Geraghty was twice Irish Champion Jockey, the second most successful of all time at Cheltenham (43 wins) thanks to such warriors as Moscow Flyer, Kicking King, Simonsig, Bobs Worth, and Sprinter Sacre. In his 23 year career he dealt well with pressure, and claimed: "A good jockey doesn't need instructions." When he drove to the races with Paul Carberry, David Condon and Robbie Power, they were known as 'The Wolf Pack'.

Another Cork man, Davy Russell, as a young amateur had to combine his riding with working in a fish factory. In 2002 he came to England to ride as a professional for Ferdy Murphy – "the biggest culture shock ever"; after two years he returned to Ireland and became stable jockey to Gigginstown, where he stayed for seven years until, after a win at Punchestown on New Year's Eve 2013, he was sacked by Michael O'Leary over an infamous cup of tea. In 2014 Davy won the Gold Cup for Jim Cullotty on Lord Windemere, and was associated with other good horses like Sir Des Champs, Forpadydeplasterer and Presenting Percy. He was Champion Jockey in Ireland three times, and also won the Grand Steeplechase de Paris. Having loved every minute of being a jockey, he still believes "There's a certain art to walking into a field with a bridle in your hand and jumping on a horse's back." With Jim Bolger he organises an annual club hurling match in aid of the Irish Cancer Society, and has raised over €1,000,000. Davy had so many injuries, his teacher wife used to mark these on a skeleton for her class. In the Munster National 2020, he suffered a bad fall, fracturing and dislocating vertebrae: bolts were drilled into his head, and weights added to the back of his skull in order to address the dislocation in his back and spine: he had 341 days off. The rehab was "torturous," but he came through, against the odds, and considered himself fortunate just to be able to walk again.

He retired for the first time on a quiet Thursday at Thurles, "the stars just seemed to align," going out on his own terms, with 1,579 wins after a stellar career. You knew you could trust this man, and he was a great help to young riders. At 5'11," with gaunt, intense facial features belying ice-cool composure, he had a constant struggle with his weight that sometimes impacted his mood, but never impeded his single-minded desire to make the most of his talents in the saddle. Despite a plethora of injuries through the years, he looked adversity in the eye, and never wavered. Two Grand National victories on the smallest horse in the race, Tiger Roll, especially the second in 2020 with Davy the oldest rider in the race, revealed his ability to "distil a task of colossal magnitude down to that of a clerical chore." (Richard Forristal). His trademark celebration: to look at the skies, arms aloft, hands dipped, was dedicated to a friend he lost at an early age. At his greatest moments, he thought of those at their lowest ebb: Pat Smullen and Cork footballer, Kieran O'Connor. Davy returned to the saddle in 2023, aged 43, to ride for Gordon Elliott, while Jack Kennedy was injured. He remained a genius in the saddle, even as he realised he was emptying the tank. His second retirement marked for no small number of racing devotees a final conclusive disbandment of the old guard.

Jack Kennedy leads the advance of the up-coming brigade of Irish jump jockeys. Born in Dingle, Co. Kerry, he has won multiple big races already: he rode his first Cheltenham victor aged 17, and in 2021 became the youngest jockey – at 21 – to win the Cheltenham Gold Cup, on Minella Indo. Already he has ten Festival successes, mainly as stable jockey for Gordon Elliott. But he has been beset by injuries, and missed well over six hundred racing days, having broken both legs, countless ribs, shoulder and collar bone. In January 2023 at Naas he broke his leg for the fifth time: he was leading the Irish Jump Jockeys' Championship at the time. Next morning he was back at Naas to watch schooling. Ruby Walsh was not alone in believing the young man from Co. Kerry, with youth on his side, could come back stronger than he was, though it would be a huge test of Jack's mentality and his confidence. But he is level-headed and phlegmatic: "You could say I've been lucky, too. They're just broken bones, and they heal."

Kevin Sexton's story is proof Irish fields of dreams are not guaranteed fairy tales. He was Champion Conditional Jockey in Ireland in 2014, but then things began to slip away from his grasp. In November 2016 he was suspended for two years, after testing positive for cocaine: the final eighteen months of that were deferred, as all tests returned negative. He returned to the saddle, rode a couple of winners, then everything went quiet again – "driving round the country not riding winners – exactly what I didn't want to do. You're going to Sligo for one ride at 100-1. I had injuries, then I began to let people down: instead of working harder I got a bit sour over it. I got into the wrong mindset. I never thought of doing anything else outside racing, because I didn't really know how long I was going to be around. Every day for over a year or more, I thought about doing away with myself. I'd sleep all day, and be awake at night, because I didn't want to be with people. I felt there was no fixing what was going on. So for me to get the help I needed was massive. I hadn't dealt with things." He spent three weeks in St Pat's (mental health service): "I didn't know what was happening. I was so used to dealing with everything myself." When he came out of St Pat's he was helped hugely by Jennifer Pugh, who sent him to RACE (Racing Academy Centre of Education). He had decided to go to America, and try his luck out there, when a text to Peter Fahey, asking if he could ride out for him, changed everything, though it was no silver bullet. When his mount Belfast Banter was beaten, at odds-on, at Killarney, the jockey had seventeen notes of abuse by the time he got back to the weighing room, some of them containing death threats, suggesting he had 'stopped' the horse on purpose.

But then in 2021, again on Belfast Banter, he won the County Hurdle at the Cheltenham Festival, and followed up at Aintree in a Grade 1 race. Belfast Banter put trainer and jockey back on the map, so Kevin can now say: "Life is good again." But he sounds a note of caution on the menace, cocaine: "It's scary, and the situation isn't getting any better. I don't know how they're going to go about dealing with it."

This is one huge challenge for racing…

In Ireland there is arguably more room for the amateur to thrive, every meeting ending with an Irish National Hunt flat race for non-professionals. Jamie Codd, Derek O'Connor (with record point-to-point wins in excess of 1,200), and Jody Townend, sister of Paul, reap regular rewards here. But Patrick Mullins, son of maestro Willie, is the most successful amateur jockey in the history of jump racing, having booted home over 800 winners, and aiming for 1,000. He studied equine business for three years, then went back to Co. Carlow to his family steeped in racing, where: "there's never a moment's let-up." But at 6'2", he is not light enough to turn professional: "My height would support any sporting ambition except my chosen one." And he rides more winners as an amateur, where he is not competing against Paul Townend and co. "The great thing in this job is that you always have the chance to get the next race right."

It might, perhaps, come as no surprise that, as a fan of the taboo-busting Red Hot Chili Peppers, he can sometimes be refreshingly controversial about the realities of his life. "Riding allows you not to grow up!" he says with a smile. "You don't have to grow up while you're a sportsperson!"

But a serious reflection follows: "I do think there's a part of me that has a fear of being born, growing up, living and dying in one small part of rural Ireland." Not that his winning exploits are confined to Eire; he has enjoyed success at the Cheltenham Festival, though admits that this sporting mecca has seen for him: "far more disappointments than the realisation of dreams." He has unfinished business there, and ambitions left. Like his father, to whom he is assistant trainer, he has a thoughtful and broad-minded approach to the sport, and may well take over from Willie one day. In the meantime this man, 'amateur' only by name, is exploiting another serious talent in his writing for the *Racing Post*, where his deep knowledge of his sport is telling: a recent piece on jockey Paul Carberry saw Patrick describe that great jockey, at one time dubbed 'The Head Waiter' because of the way he delayed his challenge to the very last minute, as: "an untouched snowman in a forest fire." And the obituary he penned for his grandmother, Maureen, in February 2024, was pure gold.

Senior Irish jockey Denis O'Regan, yet another Cork man, was no one-trick pony. He always monitored his riding: "I was very black and white like that," and had a distinctive style in the saddle: relaxed, patient, kind, "his back flat enough not to spill a drop of champagne out of a glass." He spent several years in England, riding good horses like Inglis Drever and Tidal Bay, then endured a lean patch, but came out of that, and returned to Ireland. Being one of the senior jockeys there gave him a "different confidence." He remained fiercely competitive: "That'll never change. Don't ask anyone else what they're doing; I already know: that stems from riding with the lads early on: Ruby, Barry and co. Ruby always tried to beat you with his mind: he'd try and unnerve you, beat you that way, but in a fair way. I miss that."

A superstitious man, who always put his left boot on first, he won a lot of races in the last two strides: "In the end, you win with your brain." He put his stamp on horses, well aware of the pressure on jockeys from trainers: "When the chips are down they demand the best of you and you have to deliver." He credits Rachael Blackmore for the role she plays in making the weighing room a better place: "It used to be a very hot environment with big personalities." Uniquely among jockeys, he won at every one of the 85 currently active tracks in Ireland and England, and having achieved that distinction with a success at Hereford in November 2023, he retired a few days later: "It's been phenomenal and I've loved it." He was ready not to be a jockey any more. Denis is a warm figure, who gives you his time. He recalls his escapades with Black Apalachi, "a great horse," in whom he took real pride. Now settled into his retirement, he is happy in his skin, and hits the nail on the head when he says, of leaving the saddle," I'm busy, but not mentally busy."

Sean Flanagan from Co. Wexford has ridden for fifteen years, having begun as an amateur, and had his first win at Down Royal in 2006. Then he gave up on racing. After two and half seasons in America, he returned to Ireland with a different outlook on life, and in 2016, replaced Paul Carberry as first jockey for Noel Meade. Associated with good horses like Snow Falcon, Road To Respect, Disko, and Voler La Vedette, he also won the Aintree Stayers Hurdle on Identity Thief, the Thyestes Chase on Whinstone Boy, and in 2021 romped home in the Fred Winter Hurdle at Cheltenham on 80-1 shot Jeff Kidder, the longest price winner at the Festival since Norton Cain's 100-1 Gold Cup in 1990.

What made that win more special was that he had flown himself over to Cheltenham, as he vowed he would, having earned his private pilot's licence. Flying started out as an adrenalin buzz, but then he came to really like it. He knows how important it is to get your head away from racing sometimes: "You get completely engrossed in racing, and it can be testing on the mind." With a smile in his eye, he likens landing a plane to jumping a fence: "You're going down to it, and it's either going to work or it's not." He calls flying a "nice, safe hobby," and wants to be a full-time pilot after hanging up his stirrups, though even that will not "tick the boxes of winging down to a fence on something really good." For now he is realistic about the challenge of race-riding: "You can't tell someone not to be afraid," and, in the hurly-burly of "a very self-centred game," he keeps the balance between sharp focus and being a good family man.

With a personal trainer, a liking for the word 'albeit', and the admission that seeing his horses ridden by others is worse than any physical pain, Sean is proof, if ever proof were needed, that jockeys are wired differently to mere humans. Having been lucky for a time with injuries, more recently he has been in the wars with a fractured skull, shattered jaw, cracked tibia, and splintered sternum, and in November 2021 he broke his back schooling for Noel Meade – from which he made a miraculous recovery: "I needed to get back." Small wonder he is now on the Irish Injured Jockeys Fund board.

But he is well aware how precarious is the jockey's position: in May 2022, after seven years as a stable jockey, he was sacked by Meade "in favour of using the best available," but said he was still grateful to the trainer for getting his career back on track, and propelling him into the big time. "That's racing," he said – how often does that phrase come out, more often than not in disappointing rather than heroic circumstances? "It was a bit of a shock, but you have to take these things on the chin. I had some unbelievable days, including School Boy Hours winning the Paddy Power over Christmas 2021, and five Grade 1s. Now I'm freelance, my appetite for winners has never been bigger. I'm going to put my head down, work hard, and see where that gets me. The new challenge will be tougher, without the security of riding Noel's horses, but I'm looking forward to the next few months." He realised that opportunity can be found lurking in the midst of difficulty.

Sean recognised that some avenues had been closed off to him, but there were new ones ripe for exploring. Aware that he had become a luxury at Meade's stables, losing the job left him with "that lack of sureness about where you stand." For a jockey the perils are not confined to racing: being a stable jockey does not come with a contract – you are a sole trader reliant on staying in your employer's good books. "So many riders are struggling, many are getting on grand, but only a handful are really going well." Since leaving Meade, he has been surprised by the "phenomenal reaction" from other trainers wanting his talent. Like many of his cohorts, he acknowledges the support afforded to Irish jockeys by Jennifer Pugh. But he still doesn't believe jockeys' voices are heard as much as they should be: too often they are told they are 'whingeing'. "Racing needs a good shake-up: things need to happen faster."

On injuries he is sanguine: "That's just the joy of it." He is aware of his responsibility to pass knowledge on, the need to take his opportunities, and that riding in a golden era of jockeys meant progress was often slow. He is realistic: "Things will start happening when confidence is high." Seasons are long, there are no guaranteed outcomes. A horse can tear the sand off the gallop at home, but not show it on the course. "You need to be mentally tough."

When things weren't going well he describes his state as "not depressed but numb," – knowing full well "a lot of jockeys end up on the scrap heap. Ours is the best sport to bring you from hero to zero." He has a good agent, and a strong partner: "It takes a very special person to be with a jockey: they have to go with the ups and downs: all they can do is sit and wait."

In October 2022, Sean was again badly injured in a fall, 'doing' three vertebrae in his back, and two ribs; he was in a body cast for weeks, and off for three months. His catalogue of injuries was growing even greater, but so was his determination to get back. Being a glass half-full type of lad, he has kept forging alliances with different stables (he had ridden for 66 different trainers between his last two injuries), seeing his situation not just as a new chapter, but "a whole new bonus level being unlocked in a computer game." By the end of 2022 he needed to be back in the saddle more than ever: "You take it and you go again." His first win back in January 2023, where he forced his mount for a dead-heat, showed the strength – and the hunger – are still there. "It is still Gameball: time to keep kicking," as he showed when runner-up in the 2023 Grand National on Vanillier. He is going strong…

With a firm handshake, and that ready twinkle in his eye, Sean hopes to keep riding for as long as he can, "hopefully five or six years." Road to Respect was his best horse, and he still aspires to get back on one like him. In the meantime, he and his wife have taken over as valets with a view to that unpredictable future, and are now working with half the jockeys in Ireland. His stamina and sharp perspective are contagious, and prove it a privilege to be allowed below the working surface of a jump jockey.

Paul Townend's story illustrates many of the clinching points in Ireland's current domination, but he had to wait for his star to rise. He grew up on a farm in Cork, where his father, Timothy, trained a few point-to-pointers; racing was in the family's blood – Paul's cousin Davy Condon was a fine jockey for Willie Mullins – and the lad grew up riding horses, competing in pony races, where he won the Dingle Derby in his last year at that level, already living out his dream.

Davy Condon had a huge influence on his cousin, who aspired to be like him. Davy it was who introduced young Paul to Willie Mullins; at Thurles races Paul went up with his Dad and asked Willie for an apprenticeship at his Co. Carlow stables. The request was granted. He spent summer holidays there, watching the massive operation when Hedgehunter, winner of the Grand National under Ruby, was probably the stand-out. Already the young teenager sensed he was privileged to see such a prosperous stable from grass roots level: he also sensed that Willie and his team were always seeking improvement. So he had no illusions about starting from the bottom and working his way up. "I kept my head down, my mouth shut, mucked out, rode lots: there were plenty of lads to keep my feet on the ground."

When he was 15, Paul took a transition year out of school to do work experience at Willie's yard. Come the following September, he was nowhere to be seen at school! But things were hard; he lost his mother to cancer when he was 16, so being away from home was double-edged; his mother is still only a thought away, especially when he lands a big race – after every big race triumph he gently raises his eyes heavenward. But he was putting a few pounds in his pocket: "I wouldn't have had that at school," and was learning all the time, though well aware that he was trying to live in an adult world, and that so few young race riders make it into the big time. He rode on the flat at first, where it took him eighteen months to ride a winner for Willie, which frustrated him. He was also putting all his eggs into one basket, and that was a real risk. He had thought racing was simple, but had a rude awakening when turning professional, as a jump jockey.

At first he lived with cousin Davy, content to be bottom of a very long list at the Mullins yard. Then Davy went to Cumbria, to work for Nicky Richards; Paul remained at Closutton, gradually working his way up. He spent time with Rebecca Curtis in England, in order to familiarise himself with the country, the jockeys, the tracks – and the English way of racing, which is different to that on the Emerald Isle. "You need to get to know the traits of other jockeys; then you can second guess what they're going to do. Well, sometimes you can..." Paul has never made any secret of the fact that he does his homework thoroughly: "The more you study the race beforehand, the better." He still never goes to the races without making a plan for every race: "If I make the wrong decision, there's no-one to blame but myself."

He was lucky to be on the cusp of the glorious generation of National Hunt jockeys, and learned heaps from watching them: Paul Carberry he idolised for that man's style; AP McCoy ("of course") – and he gives Ruby huge credit. But as time went by, back in Ireland, he began to find himself called upon, and thus in a position to ride winners if Ruby was injured, or riding in England for Paul Nicholls. He made the most of Ruby's absence. With the backing of Team Mullins – especially Willie, who promised Paul he'd do all he could to make him Champion Jockey in Ireland, he achieved that goal in the 2010-2011 season. Ruby had first choice of mounts – as Paul does now – and for all his brilliant expertise on a racehorse, inevitably Ruby was not correct in every choice he made, so Paul picked up winners in this way sometimes. All the time, he was determined to learn from getting beaten. Willie's constant backing of the young Cork man made a huge difference: "When Willie has confidence in you, you can only grow in confidence yourself." And grow he did, though even now – after his sixth Jockeys Championship – he still seeks to improve. "No two races are the same: you have to factor everything in to each race; even winners can help you improve. Every year I try to build on the season before; there's always improvements to make, even after winning."

At Punchestown in April 2018, he was riding Al Boum Photo (from whom Ruby had fallen and broken his leg in the Royal Sun Alliance Chase at Cheltenham). He came to the last fence with a narrow lead, but just then Paul thought he heard a voice telling him not to jump the fence: he pulled his mount sharply to the right, taking out an English horse in the process – and was at once besieged by angry shouts, questions and oaths. Keeping his counsel, as pundits, punters and racing correspondents questioned the reason for his 'brain-fade', he turned off his phone, went home to his girlfriend, Anna, and hunkered down, wishing to speak only to his family, though he did take a long call from Ruby.

Next morning, when he arrived at the stables, Willie having requested he come in an hour early, he was ribbed mercilessly by the whole team, for two hours – until Willie stopped that, saying there'd be no further mention of the mishap. Paul went back to Punchestown that afternoon, was greeted affectionately by racing folk, and rode a treble. That treble helped clinch the trainer's title for Mullins; it also showed the calibre of his jockey. Messages of abuse had come winging in, and were ignored: "There's so much negativity:

I don't need that in my life. I'm a professional, with a job to do: the world was not going to stop. When I make a mistake, I just try and avoid the same mistake in future."

Al Boum Photo and Paul won their first Gold Cup in 2019, and the first for Willie Mullins after having come so close six times. During that 2018-2019 season Ruby had stepped back somewhat, to aid Paul's chances of again becoming Champion Jockey, which Paul duly achieved after a great battle with Rachael Blackmore. Then Ruby caught the racing world by surprise when he won the Punchestown Gold Cup on Kemboy, beating Al Boum Photo into second, and announced his retirement immediately after dismounting. Paul was suddenly the number one jockey to Willie Mullins. But he was grateful he'd had time to prepare for this; he wasn't being thrown in at the deep-end – far from it. With Ruby out with injuries far too often, Paul had become first jockey in all but name. What he did on officially assuming the mantle, quietly, as is his wont, during the summer of 2019, was win the French Champion Hurdle at Auteuil on Bénie Des Dieux, a race he'd always wanted to win: he'd got one monkey off his back.

He realised that now he had the chance to fulfil his potential, that he could, "Please God," ascend gradually and, now that he had waited so long, and had a taste for it, could again aim to be Champion Jockey: he was in a position to set his eye on that title – a feat he managed again in 2020, despite the season being curtailed by the pandemic, and in 2021 after a battle royal with the ever-advancing wonder girl of racing, Rachael Blackmore, who dominated Cheltenham, and then won the Grand National on Minella Times. To make matters tougher, Paul injured his foot in a fall at Easter, so could only watch as Rachael ate into his lead. With both Harry Skelton in Britain and Rachael in the ascendancy, and Paul referred to as Rachael's 'nemesis' in her bid to make yet more history, it almost seemed as if he and Brian Hughes became the villains, out to spoil a new pretender's bid for glory – one of the many occasions when jockeys are faced with labels people put on them: the majority do not succumb. Paul kept quiet, had a special boot built for his injured foot, returned to the saddle at Fairyhouse, and ran out Champion again, as he did in 2022 and 2023. But Rachael was not going away.

Paul is well aware that to be 100% fit, which every jockey needs to be, nothing can beat match practice. When unable to ride, as he was in the summer of 2020 (due to Coronavirus), or injured as in the summer of 2021, and the autumn of 2022, he will always seek to heal his body's bruises, recharge his batteries, and prepare for his next race: "You have to sacrifice a lot, but on the horse you're in charge. There's a huge team behind you: grooms, outriders, the trainer, your agent, your valet, without whom you wouldn't have a job." There's always pressure, but if there wasn't, race-riding wouldn't be the job it is. Willie Mullins has gone on record as saying: "Paul is probably best with pressure. If someone is leaning on his neck, he excels. He just gets out and gets that job done: poetry in motion."

For that first Cheltenham Gold Cup, on Al Boum Photo, owners Joe and Marie Donnelly had remained faithful to their jockey. Paul said that he and the horse had unfinished business after Punchestown, which had now been dealt with. Yet whereas that year Al Boum Photo had perhaps crept in under the radar, in 2020, as the defending champion, the pressure was on. But his jockey had coped with Cheltenham pressure before – he just takes every race as it comes. In the event he rode a superb tactical race in his defence of steeplechasing's crown, he and Al Boum Photo hanging on by a neck from fast-finishing Santini, and the young fighter Lost In Translation. Interviewed after the race, Paul, when asked to compare his second victory to his first, said he'd love to be able to remember more of his first win, but, as he was experiencing again, everything was a huge blur. They were two very different races, but when things had been going badly, he admitted to playing the tape of the Gold Cup 2019 "to bring up the spirits." Whereas the previous year he had said that he owed the horse everything, after Punchestown, this year he heaped praise on the animal. And, as he was coming to know increasingly often, "When things happen for you at Cheltenham, they really happen."

Ruby Walsh, Willie's "ace in the pack" as Paul refers to him, had presented a trophy for the Top Jockey at Cheltenham 2020; he it was whose boots Paul, in many people's minds, had to fill – but his successor never saw it like that. It was more than fitting that his winning ride on Al Boum Photo took him to the top of the Jockeys' Festival table – which saw him back on the podium, being presented with that trophy by his mentor, brother-in-arms, and mate.

Having known extreme disappointment, as that day as Punchestown, his "steely resilience" always strives to stay level – "worse things happen in life." And the bad days he can "leave outside the back door." Ruby Walsh had not left many things undone at Closutton, though there was one: he had never won Willie a Gold Cup. Here, no longer his understudy, Paul had won two. But none of us few watching the gentle display of camaraderie and gratitude between Ruby and Paul that March afternoon had any idea we would not go racing again for many, many days...

Patrick Mullins has known Paul since the Cork lad walked into his father's yard: "He's a fella always quick with a laugh and a joke. In the last few years he's got a good bit more serious and mature, perhaps. He's still never far off a laugh, and it doesn't seem to weigh heavy on him, the whole thing. He had a bit of a wild streak in him when he came up from Cork: he's a bit different now. But he's not afraid to laugh at himself – he learned that off Ruby."

Paul is no crossover star: the big time had held him at arm's length for quite some time. He well appreciates what can go wrong: "There are plenty of morning glories... every race is different, it's a privilege to ride such class horses." And injury gets to him, of course: "Coming back takes time, courage and mental strength; it does your head in watching others on your horses, so you need to get back quickly. At least with Willie I know I have a job to go back to." On his first afternoon back after three months out with a damaged shoulder in 2021, he returned with a treble on the day at Fairyhouse. With agent Ciaran O'Toole, he evaluates risk vs reward, always having to think ahead.

His thoughts on winning were recently recorded in an interview:

"I was always told when I started riding: mistakes happen. You're the one out there, so if it goes wrong, you're the one to blame, but there's a huge team behind getting the horse there. You're also the one who gets the applause if you win, not the people who've got you there. Thousands of things go through your mind pre-race; then at the end there could be thousands of people in the stands, and you're only a couple of feet away from them. You can't hear a thing till you go through the line, then the place erupts.

"I grew up on a farm outside Midleton, Co. Cork: we always had horses. As long as I can remember I was always able to ride ponies. The obvious thing for me was to become a jockey, with all my family in racing. The Dingle Derby was a big deal, the Gold Cup of pony-racing. That gave me a taste of the pressure when riding, and when I was lucky enough to win that, I got a taste for the winning as well." At first he thought racing was simple: he had a rude awakening when becoming a professional: "Your world changes in many ways. I did well early on, so was never striking out, but it was hard when I saw my peers going out on a Friday night and having fun, when I was heading up to Dundalk in the freezing cold. But that's what I'd chosen to do. I loved it.

"Dealing with winning was made easier by the people ahead of me at Willie's: they kept me grounded. Ruby was there – he was brilliant for advice, but able to tell you when you were doing things wrong as well. Obviously Willie has a way with words. He wouldn't say a whole lot to you, but he'd keep your feet on the ground. At the time I was probably too naive to understand any of it. I didn't look beyond that. I just knew I was going to be surrounded by horses, and that's all I wanted.

"My family and mates probably get to enjoy all my wins a bit more than me: we've a quick turnaround. When you ride a winner, brilliant, you can celebrate for a few minutes, but then your mind has to switch and focus on the next race straight away. They can head to the bar, and we head to the start again. You need to be around friends and family who are going to calm you down and keep things as normal as possible. You're mulling over something in your head the whole time. You'd be sitting down to watch TV, and your mind just wanders. You do it unknown to yourself most of the time. The hardest part is before you get up on a horse: once you get down to the start, happy days. You're in charge of the situation then.

"I keep myself as private as I can. I'm there to perform, do a job: the media side just comes with it. It's important, of course, to promote the sport as best you can, but sometimes it's nice to be just left to it. I don't do social media: it's trolls sending private messages. That's ridiculous; a nuisance to me.

"Ruby's misfortunes in missing bits of seasons meant I had a taste at the top. The safety net of him coming back was always there. You just have to make the best of your time: you're there to be shot at, which brings added pressure and stress, but that gives me adrenalin. I'd rather have that than someone else have the job. Everyone loves the glamour and limelight of Cheltenham,

Punchestown, Aintree, but I still enjoy the smaller wins: sometimes you get an extra special kick out of your smaller wins.

"I have no idea regarding the future – I haven't looked beyond riding: all I know is horses and racing. That's been my life all along. I can't imagine I'd ever be able to walk away from the sport, but what role I'd fill, I'm not sure. Who knows?" In his sights now are 'a kick' at the Grand National, and the Grand Steeplechase de Paris, but he retains a sense of perspective. Emulating his predecessor, he can put the memory of a lost race/disappointment behind him, and move on.

Paul was again leading rider in the scorching cauldron of competition at the Cheltenham Festival of 2023, with five wins, all in grade 1 races. He and Energumene retained their Champion Chase crown, with the horse's magnificent rolling stride, again lifting the spirits, giving hope for the future. In the Gold Cup on St Patrick's Day, Paul was on the hot favourite, Galopin Des Champs, the most precocious apprentice seen for some time who, as a novice, danced in front of his fences. Riding the favourite brought pressure on the jockey, but as Leighton Aspell commented: "You might not have noticed it." A ragged start, and some less than perfect jumps saw the pair towards the back of the field, about which Paul was "not happy;" they dodged the mêlée when Ahoy Senor fell, bringing down Sounds Russian, and clouted the third last fence. But Paul was keeping a lid on Galopin (French for rascal), picking off his rivals one by one, and they turned for home ready to deliver the killer blow at the perfect time. Neck and neck with Bravemansgame, best of the English, Paul had a double handful coming to the last fence, where everything had gone wrong twelve months before: not this time: Galopin put in a mighty leap, landed running, and stormed into unknown territory stamina-wise, pulling right away from his field up the hill for a magnificent victory. The further he went, the stronger he looked.

The jockey had executed his plan perfectly, as Sam Thomas had done fifteen years earlier with Denman. AP McCoy was full of praise, calling the win: "As brilliant a ride as I have ever seen in a horse race: talk about riding with 'bottle': talk about pressure and the privilege of pressure. Paul coped with it better than anyone I have ever seen." The jockey deflected the praise to his mount, as he always does. "I had full faith in my horse. He dug me out of a hole; good and brave, he has to be the full package to win where we came from ; he seemed to have got himself into trouble with the sole intention of getting himself out of it. When things go wrong, he gets better, he just fights back. He is a proper, proper horse." Reacting to the plaudit later, Paul admitted: "You have to take the praise the same way as you do the criticism, but it's nice to hear it." Since his win, Galopin has been termed the Lionel Messi of racing.

The indomitable Paul and Willie Mullins had combined to win their third Gold Cup in five years. Having navigated landmines, Paul was hailed for his defiant capacity to deliver when the chips are down, but that is the measure of the man: he takes everything in his stride, has a level head, and is made for the big occasion. "It's a tough job," Willie Mullins has said, "and Paul handles it very well. He has mental strength; when things don't go according to plan, he dusts himself down, and acts as if nothing has happened. Dealing with despair is what separates the best from the rest. He pulls races out of the fire, races he shouldn't win." The last word on the 2023 Gold Cup was the jockey's: "This race is just different. It brings winning to another level. There's a different spice about it."

Two weeks after his victorious Gold Cup ride on Galopin Des Champs, Paul landed the Irish Grand National on I Am Maximus, earning more plaudits for his cool big-race nous: he brought his mount from a seemingly hopeless position to pounce late and plunder his first Irish National after a gruelling race. Old-fashioned horsemanship, perseverance and ingenuity won the day. Willie Mullins praised his jockey for ignoring instructions: "Paul takes it into his own hands when things aren't working out"; the jockey said simply, "We got lucky," but David Jennings called it "the greatest ride I have ever seen."

At the Cheltenham Festival 2024, Paul added the Champion Hurdle to his c.v., with his win on State Man, and, having won a second Irish Gold Cup at Leopardstown that February, after a 'demolition job' in the Savill chase the previous Christmas, Galopin Des Champs defended his Cheltenham Gold Cup crown in the 100th anniversary race under a superb ride from Paul – "the man has ice in his veins" – thus boosting the horse's claim to be the most exciting steeplechaser on the planet at the moment.

With Paul, first jockey for Willie Mullins' stable, perhaps the best job in jump racing, but also the one carrying most pressure, there are some 10 other riders, but no official number two. Danny Mullins, 28, nephew to Willie, is happy to be among that squad. He is a great mate for Paul, with whom there is mutual respect, but, "Friendship is left in the weighing room and picked up on the way back." Paul is sharp at picking the right mounts, but, inevitably, like Ruby, not always right, so Danny finds it great to "catch Paul out occasionally and win on another of Willie's."

In the summer, when Willie doesn't have many runners, Danny rides for the smaller trainers: he is grateful that Willie has bought him to "the next level," and put him in a position to be picked up by other yards – an able deputy at the highest level. He thus has chance to establish new connections, and he works hard at these. Once allied to a new horse, or new owners, he endeavours to remain connected with them – and, all the time, he has to keep performing in the saddle.

Danny's best moment so far came in such circumstances: Flooring Porter's regular jockey, Jonathan Moore, was injured before Cheltenham 2020, and trainer, Gavin Cromwell, called up Danny for the Stayers Hurdle at the eleventh hour: Danny had a nice few mounts for Willie, but this was a plum ride in a championship race. "Everyone remembers their first festival win," says Danny, "and that was mine." The following year, nothing had gone right with Flooring Porter's preparation, but, undaunted, Danny rode as if defeat was out of the question, "This is going to happen – and it did." What gave connections particular joy was that "Everyone from the west of Ireland who could be there, got a ticket – and was there." The result was good for the sport, and jocund photos of Danny carried shoulder-high by the colourful winning syndicate underlined this – twice.

Danny, who has well over 500 victories to his name, is well aware that so much can go wrong – always, but "Once you taste the rewards, you crave them more: you push the risk element to new limits. You still get broken and beaten, so need even more strength and courage to bounce back. Only by working harder can you aim for the next level: you cannot relax: you have to reach for, and explore, the unknown, which costs…"

The hardest thing, says Danny, is, "Accepting defeat and failure so often. But you urge yourself on; there is always much homework to do if you are still to perform at your best." Convivial, modest, honest and driven, with a keen sense of perspective, he reckons Ireland is "on the whole, nicer than Britain when it comes to social media," which perhaps helps Irish jockeys in their quest to squeeze out every last drop of endeavour.

In Ireland, a leading jump jockey is something to be: unique in the sporting world, it is a country of one-name jockeys: Ruby, Barry, Nina, Katie and Rachael. There are no small number, such as Michael O'Sullivan, coming through to the top echelons, keen to build on the legacy of their predecessors, keen to see every opportunity, keen to win... perhaps there is more to that depth of yearning to fulfil their destiny, for the flash of quicksilver in a lightning bolt, than just "the luck of the Irish."

Ireland does not have the same system of jockey coaches as in the UK, but the country has a tradition of horses and horsemanship that runs deep. There are plentiful heroes of Irish folklore for young riders/potential jockeys to look up to − and emulate. Horses are part of a daily fabric over there: historically, their importance has left an enduring legacy. Pony racing is bigger in Ireland, so young jockeys can cut their teeth on its competitive circuit, thus experiencing close riding, tactics and pace, aspects that cannot be taught. Ireland has less of an urban society and culture. A higher proportion of children grow up in rural areas, and have more to do with horses from an early age. Jump racing there attracts more spectators.

To experience Irish jumping, not least at the Dublin Racing Festival, a real highlight in the calendar, growing in popularity every year, is tremendous craic. The welcome is warm; the degree of friendliness striking, and the provision for racegoers outstanding. British courses would do well to emulate this.

Perhaps, in the last analysis, jump racing is just in their Irish blood.

CHAPTER 26: RETIREMENT

- When the phone stops ringing... -

It has been said that sportspeople die twice...
Retirement is a challenge for many, but most of us have at least some time in which to prepare for that day. Current jump jockeys' average retirement age is 31: statistics show they sustain an injury one ride in every eighty-three; that 18% of falls result in some kind of injury; that they average 215 rides per year; and, in so far as can be ascertained, their average annual salary is around £28,500. It is not all about winning, trophies and adulation. Although jockeys are riding for longer now, they cannot keep doing it forever; age is like a petrol tank: when you're young it goes on forever, but when you get to the second half of the tank, it just drops away. For us, there is always a stab of regret when we learn that a jockey who has provided us with excitement and enjoyment has left the arena for the last time, but a fresh generation is already emerging, for whom no small number of former jockeys will be just names from the past.

Whether it comes early, and is not predicted, or later, retirement is hard to handle for many whose identity is intimately entwined with their career as a rider, and whose social networks are closely linked to the racing fraternity. There can be a real sense of loss, of uncertainty, of bereavement. Having to stop through injury inevitably means jockeys can no longer be the same person: they are ex-jockeys in an instant, and there is, suddenly, a huge void to fill, a whole new future to ponder. Jockeys are more liable to face this prospect than most of us; they handle it with varying degrees of success. Richard Pitman, whose life has revolved around horses, did not accept the finality of retirement until he woke on the last morning of his career. "The road to Stratford seemed longer than ever, but I knew when I arrived it was the beginning of the end. To give up when the fences seem bigger, and open ditches wider, would be easy, but when your heart is still in the game, to stop is both hard and sad." His last ride finished a distant sixth. But he was starting a new adventure, going on to spend 37 years with the BBC. He said of his retirement, "The last line of my jockey's medical book read: 'Fit to ride', and above that statement of fact was written in red the evidence of my falls, breaks, cracks, dislocations, at least twenty periods of concussion." He counted himself a lucky man to finish after riding 7,400 miles on the racecourse, over some 85,000 jumps. His memories are still strong: "In the weighing room the buzz of chatter is louder than at any W.I., jokes are banded around, heroes being congratulated, others recalling their bad luck, a few injured jockeys eager to start afresh." On his last day, he felt quite numb because he was about to leave this room and its inmates, never to be allowed in there again – a mighty wrench.

Adam Kondrat, the French jockey who rode The Fellow to victory in the Cheltenham Gold Cup of 1994, after hitting the bar three times, retired on his 44th birthday in 2010, and found he needed to take a different path in life; there are very few advantages conferred on an ex-jockey in France. It was difficult to turn his back on racing, especially with nothing else lined up. For him, as for so many, riding racehorses at speed over obstacles was a passion that endured, despite the difficulties and dangers it presented. After some months rudderless, Adam opted for a complete change of pace and lifestyle, relocating to south west France, setting up a fruit and veg business, and spending more time with his family. That time was not to be long: he died at 53. The majority of jump jockeys live longer, though, with our ageing population, the full effects of a life punctuated by falls, injuries, recovery and, perhaps especially, concussion are only just becoming recognised.

Many jockeys find satisfaction in a new career, of which there is a wide range: soccer coach; chef; landscape designer; saddler; equine dentist;

starter; fitness coach; jockeys' agent; clerk of the course; accountant; farrier; commentator; stewards' secretary; photographer; bloodstock agent and more... Noel Fehily typifies no small number who break horses in, take an interest in the breeding side, and still ride out: "That's where I can pretend I'm still a jockey." Some find they miss the buzz, and the weighing room, like Leighton Aspell, who quit, looked elsewhere, plucked up the courage to try again – and promptly won two successive Grand Nationals, on Pineau De Re (2014) and Many Clouds (2015), before finally hanging up his boots early in 2020. He had been, for a time, the only jockey with an official fan club – for which he received huge amounts of stick. When Wayne Hutchinson retired, David Bass knew it would be hard for him, so formed a syndicate with Jerry McGrath, Wayne, Ciaran Gethings, 'Bagsy' Painter and another valet: they bought a greyhound, Hello Gabby, to run at Swindon every couple of weeks, something to look forward to.

In an ideal world, jockeys could dovetail a gentle retirement with a Plan B for the future, their new career – but their world is far from ideal. Riders are cocooned in a jockey bubble: they have to be. But recently they are being more encouraged to prepare for that second career, to look forward, broaden their horizons and plans, so the culture of adapting to new job opportunities is growing fast. Whereas before, using JETS could be seen as a sign of giving up, now the scariness of life without racing, of hitting a big low on quitting the saddle, is tempered by the realisation that riders can have a jockey profile – and another profile.

They won't always find something they enjoy immediately, so are being encouraged to try different things before they stop riding, to show themselves rounded individuals, whom people will respect. This process can be triggered when they are injured: JETS and Friends of JETS have lots of contacts, who can give direction and help with funding, job applications and interview techniques. A sporting CV will always stand out, as jockeys have so many assets: focus, resilience, commitment and established networks with a wide range of different people. Luke Harvey has helped publicise the many courses that can be fitted around injury or riding commitments: there is even the opportunity for 1-1 tutors. In response to the assertion that jockeys are busy all the time, he argues that they do have time, can make time, to meet different people and establish contacts; the key thing is to prepare their mind...

Ryan Day's story bears this out; he loved horses, but not being a jockey. How he became one was, "an accident — it just happened. I had ponies as a kid, went to school in Cockermouth, rode in the sixth form for something to do, went to racing college, got my licence, went to Brian Harding (being one of that man's first graduates) and then Nicky Richards offered me a job at Greystoke Stables."

Ryan incurred many injuries during his short career: he broke ribs and punctured a lung at Wetherby; just months later, he broke ribs again when Baywing suffered a fatal fall going for a repeat Eider Chase triumph at Newcastle: the jockey also ruptured his spleen and lacerated his kidney. With the help of the Injured Jockeys Fund he battled back to health, riding in 120 plus races the next two seasons. He quit the saddle in May 2021, only months after hitting the one hundred winner milestone, calling time on a career that had seen no mean success since his first win on Solway Sam in 2014. His biggest win came on Guitar Pete in the Caspar Caviar Gold Cup at Cheltenham in 2017, only his second ride at the course, two days after the death of his grandad. Looking back, he now admits some of the smaller successes on a rainy day in winter meant just as much as the big days.

Interestingly, it was not his injuries that forced his decision: on the contrary, he is now thankful the injuries slowed him down: it meant he could breathe easier. When he checked in with Jerry Hill, Ryan told him, "Don't sign me off just yet," although he is aware that may have cost him the winning ride on Takingrisks in the Scottish Grand National 2019, a ride taken by Sean Quinlan. "Making the decision to stop was not difficult: taking the action to do it was. It had taken so much thought... I knew it was coming, it had to be, but I tried not to put a date on it. You put a lot of pressure on yourself; it shows you're human. I knew I was struggling mentally; I'd threatened to give up a couple of times, but this time I had to do something about it. I'd spoken to my psychotherapist, and realised it was right." He went to Stratford to ride the admirable veteran, Duke Of Navan, having resolved "to do it that day, but the words didn't come out." He told his boss a couple of days later.

A few months on, he could admit calling it a day was the most liberating thing he'd ever done; he'd not stopped smiling since. "It took a global pandemic to make me focus on my situation: racing stopped – I went out to try other work; for the first time in my adult life I felt I was in the real world. There were so many things I was missing out on." Sporting Chance helped him, especially Tony Evans and Phil Kinsela, and the PJA paid for six sessions of counselling. "When I met the psychotherapist, I asked him if I had an issue with mental health. "No, but you will have," came the reply." It was time to take action. Ryan had never thought about his own identity: who he was, what he wanted from life. He was just floating along. The psychotherapist let him talk, then seized the initiative and offered help. "It took a while; no single switch clicked. Covid helped; I'd been injured and I was missing out, then suddenly everyone was missing out. Racing consumes your whole life. I wasn't going to be dictated to, and the process takes time. I am still in the middle of it, but now into the world of self-development, I'm excited as to what will happen." He resolved to stay on at Greystoke until the end of the season, then see the world and sort himself out. "Stopping race-riding meant I could see clearly."

Ryan was not an open book: like so many young men he didn't talk about his feelings, so the pressure built up and up. "Every eighteen months/two years I could feel it coming again; this time when I felt a bit wobbly I made up my mind to make leaving the saddle a prevention against further mental strife. I'd been living with the choke out, holding in my feelings for so long; I needed to step back and take a look at myself, to try and be honest, and admit I was burned out."

About mental health he is adamant: "There is still a massive stigma; you have to act." With his reasoned arguments he now sounds wise. "Yes," he says, "that's exactly the problem. I think too much." But he knows his core value is freedom. "Depression and anxiety are terms thrown around too much. I needed to look after number one; for so long I was always overthinking everything. Now, though stopping is still raw, I've got the tools to stop that thinking. But I've met a lot of great people; the car journeys home were good, all those laughs." When journalists asked him his best moments, he found it hard to answer on the spot – now he can answer: "It wasn't the winning, it was everything else that came with it. Like the night I'd won that race at Cheltenham on Guitar Pete: it wasn't passing the post, it was the music and karaoke that night at Greystoke. That was the best part of winning for me." Looking back, he is proud he made friends for life in racing, and thankful for the opportunities the sport gave him. What he terms his 'analysis paralysis' is over, and his overwhelming feeling is relief.

Dick Francis, the jockey on Devon Loch in that sudden collapse just before the finish of the 1956 Grand National, turned to writing novels in his forties "to pay for a new carpet," – and after *Dead Cert* he wrote one every year from 1964 to 1996. His son, Felix, now continues the line. Francis' novels appeal to almost everyone. The Queen Mother loved them, and Philip Larkin rated him his joint favourite novelist – with Thomas Hardy! The thrillers are all set against a background of horse racing, usually with a first person narrator, who turns amateur sleuth and makes very dangerous enemies. These protagonists are often loners who "at least manage to start the journey to realising their self-worth." One ex-jockey said that "Dick Francis proves reinvention is possible for us all, as it is for his heroes." Reinvention is not always easy, though; the riders have to face hanging up their boots and silks, which is never an easy thing, even if the decision is made instinctively, with the jockey still in one piece, as with John Francome, Peter Scudamore, Brian Harding and AP McCoy.

At the age of 19, and in his first ride in the race, David Mullins won the Grand National on 33-1 shot Rule The World, the first maiden to win the great race since 1958. The year before, he had inflicted a first defeat on Faugheen at Punchestown, delivering a masterclass from the front on Nichols Canyon to win his first Grade 1. Three years later he teamed up with Faugheen to win the Champion Stayers Hurdle at Punchestown; he also won the 2018 Ryanair Gold Cup at Fairyhouse on subsequent dual Gold Cup hero Al Boum Photo. In all, he won forty Graded races, an impressive 19% of his total winners in Ireland.

In January 2021, he surprised the racing world by announcing his retirement from the saddle; he was just 24. Neither injury nor advancing years were the reasons he was stopping. He told the *Racing Post* that he had known for more than a year that race-riding was not the right career path for him. "When you're in the racing bubble and riding horses, it's very difficult to think outside the bubble; I needed to get out of it… it's relentless. There is no break. You're always on call." He was planning to quit the saddle at the end of the season, but said it would have been unfair to owners and trainers if he continued to ride when his heart wasn't in it. The vicissitudes of a jump jockey's life were highlighted by the fact that his next ride after winning the National was the following Friday at 8:30 p.m. in Ballinrobe on a 25-1 shot in a low-grade handicap chase: he pulled up. He had ridden forty-four winners in his best-season 2016-2017, and hung up his boots with a total of 211 victories in Ireland. But "the bad times outweighed the good. There were times when I rode a winner, but would come home depressed because the other three didn't win. Every jockey out there is fully entitled to every penny they earn, because it is not easy. But at the end of the day there is not much job or financial security. I didn't want to end up at 35 having to start up something from the bottom. I'd rather be doing that at 24."

In October 2019 he had been airlifted to hospital after a horror fall at Thurles, when he fractured his clavicle and his T12 thoracic vertebrae, but he said that injuries were not the main motive behind his decision. With regard to his future, he is carving out a niche in the bloodstock world. "I really love going to Goffs or Tatts, buying and selling horses. I like judging, and trying to figure out what I might make." While some in the racing world lamented his decision, his uncle Willie Mullins, while hailing the "natural instinct" his nephew possessed in the saddle, and feeling David's last Grade 1 win on Kemboy in the 2018 Savills Chase was his best, backed him whole-heartedly: "It was a great decision by David to retire; he has the pedigree to be successful on both sides of his family." David had the final word: "I didn't have the hunger for it, and there were a lot more jockeys lined up behind who would lose a limb just to try and get into the position I was in. I'm very grateful. This sport owes me nothing. I've had some amazing days out of it. I still love racing. I'm going to be a part of it for the rest of my life. I'm just not going to be getting the leg up in the parade ring any more."

Brian Cooper recently retired at 30. He rated his best horse, Our Connor, killed in the 2014 Champion Hurdle: Dessie Hughes, the horse's trainer, said: "He was too brave." Brian had "a very natural talent and super hands."

Success came quickly to him as a young jockey, including the Gold Cup on Don Cossack in 2016, but he was unfortunate with injuries, at one time suffering "the worst lower limb fracture" Dr Adrian McGoldrick had ever seen. Brian said his life had become "like doing repeated squats in the gym with a heavy weight on my shoulders": his decision to retire took that weight off: it was a huge relief.

Page Fuller suffered a mono-stroke in a race at Fontwell in October 2022, losing her vision in one eye, and having spasms in her arm. She managed to negotiate the first fence before pulling up. Dual champion amateur, she fought her way back into the saddle, and was happy she did so. But a fall at Plumpton in March 2023 knocked her out for three minutes: she came round, and realised she was ready for something new. She had been catapulted around on the "ridiculous roller-coaster" that is jump racing, aware that resilience is key. She had that resilience, but, still only 27, wanted to move forward, so retired: "I was fed up of sitting in a gazebo." With 108 winners, she made her mark on the sport; she had also done a lot behind the scenes to improve female jockeys' facilities.

Dicky Johnson announced his shock retirement after finishing third on the Philip Hobbs-trained Brother Tedd, in a chase at Newton Abbot on 3rd April 2021. Having faced the starter in more jump races than anyone in history, he had ridden 3,819 winners, a figure only surpassed by AP. Visibly emotional, Dicky said: "After nearly thirty years in the saddle, the time has come for me to retire. I have been so extraordinarily lucky to have ridden so many wonderful horses for so many incredible trainers and owners. It was particularly important for me to finish on a Hobbs' horse. The Hobbs, like Henry Daly, have supported me for twenty years. I will never be able to articulate what their loyalty has meant to me."

AP, Dicky's nemesis and great friend – how often do those two words go together? – paid a glowing tribute to his erstwhile rival's career: "Sometimes those who challenge us the most, teach us the most. You did both for me over twenty years. I will be forever grateful to you. Thanks, buddy. When you go home tonight, look in the mirror. You will see what a champion looks like." He later added: "He has a great work ethic and is the fairest jockey you could ever ride against, so has deserved all of his success. But however good a jockey you think he is, he's an even better person." For Dicky, his highlight was the day at Sandown in 2016, when he was finally crowned Champion Jockey. He rode twenty-three winners at the Cheltenham Festival, the last being Native River's memorable Gold Cup victory for Colin Tizzard in 2018, a supreme triumph for horse and man, for courage and endeavour; poetry in motion that day, as on so many days. Philip Hobbs praised his jockey's ability to be a terrific role model, to be honest with owners, "particularly when one has run badly, which is the important time." Henry Daly said, "He has ridden for me for twenty-three years and never missed a Tuesday morning. People have so little understanding of what he has done, what jockeys do; it is his decision to retire and it is the right time when you decide." With typical humility, Johnson himself said, "Thank you for every cheer, every shout of encouragement. It's given me enormous strength over the years." From then on, his family, not his punishing schedule, was to be the most important thing.

When Peter Scudamore, eight times Champion Jockey, retired in 1993, he was fortunate enough to provide for his future as newspaper man (for the *Daily Mail*), broadcaster with the BBC (at that time the only terrestrial channel for racing) and part-time training with old pal from pony-racing Nigel Twiston-Davies. Colin Cameron wrote in the *Independent*: "Scu invested the spoils of the saddle wisely, and nurtured outlets for that wisdom." He painted a strong picture of Scu in his retirement from racing: "Even in civvies he stands with legs apart, arms folded or behind his back, invisible whip in hand. You half expect him to touch an imaginary jockey's cap. His hands betray a yearning for the reins; asked questions, he wrestles with the bridle in his head." He also commented how the Old Brigade of Terry Biddlecombe and co. would have thought it laughable for a jockey of their era to plan so thoroughly for his retirement.

But many jockeys are not able to make the retirement decision themselves: Richard Dunwoody was forced to retire on medical grounds: "I always knew I could not go on forever, but I had hoped to go on for a few more years at least. Though I had ridden my luck over the last years, no one fall had kept me out for too long, but the effects had begun to damage the nerves in my neck. I make no excuses; I found retirement from the saddle frustrating, like many before me, and many, no doubt, who will retire in the future. I still miss the camaraderie of the weighing room, and daily adrenalin rush of race-riding, and was still contemplating a return to the saddle, but specialists put an end to those ideas."

Having to turn your back on the chance of that winning feeling happening again is tough. Mick Fitzgerald, who was forced to retire through injury after suffering neck injuries in a terrible fall from L'Ami at Aintree in 2008, found stopping was the hardest thing: "You don't get that buzz anywhere else. Sportspeople often compare the feeling to a drug: that comparison falls short." 'Fitz' is by no means the only jockey forced to retire through injury: Willie Twiston-Davies and Jason Maguire are among this number. Lucy Barry has spoken candidly about depression and eating disorders. She battled the scales for a long time to make her name, and achieved much at an early age, but then her struggles with weight got the better of her. That, and the pressure she put on herself, set her on a slippery slope, and she ended up in hospital. She fought her way back into the saddle, yet her career failed to take off; she retired following a winning ride on Hawthorn Cottage at Warwick in May 2021. But she has no regrets: "All that happened made me who I am today, and taught me success is not a number of achievements, it's being content with life."

Amateur jockey Sam Waley-Cohen was not forced to retire through injury. He won the Cheltenham Gold Cup in 2011 on six-year-old Long Run, the youngest champion since Mill House in 1963. His horse outran two great champions in Denman and Kauto Star, both of whom showed grandeur in defeat. Sam said afterwards that ultimately it was "about doing it for fun. Not making your living out of it. It doesn't mean being amateur in the sense of amateurism: there isn't any space for that in sport anymore. So you have to take a professional approach, even if you're doing it for fun." The jockey worked hard at the gym, schooled horses at dawn, studied the tapes – and then went to work, as head of Portman Healthcare, a firm he set up to revolutionise dentistry. A confirmed thrill-seeker, who escaped life's stresses by climbing mountains or piloting helicopters, Sam was cool under pressure, as he again proved in the 2022 Grand National on Noble Yeats.

His win on the 50-1 shot, in what two days earlier he had vowed would be his final ride before retirement, was a surprise to many people, but not all.

He was only the eleventh amateur to win the great race in the past hundred years, but his record round the unique Aintree fences, not the conventional 'park' obstacles, was second to none, having, on Katarino, won the Liverpool Foxhunters twice, and, on Liberthine, the Topham. "Life comes together in mysterious ways," he said after his success, recalling the years he'd watched the Grand National as a youngster: "The big thing for me was the spectacle, and the incredibly positive energy, even more so back then with the size of the fences. The sheer madness of it excited me, and the fact outsiders won it, anything was possible..." Along with the challenges of his riding commitments, he had juggled his city career, but never contemplated changing his amateur status. "I think you have to be insane to be a professional jump jockey. It's the most nuts way to make a living you could ever imagine." He knows the Grand National is particularly prone to jeopardy: "Every year someone will go to hospital, often badly hurt. And someone has won. It's quite an extreme environment. That is life condensed into a millisecond; there is something poetic about that – and mad. For those jockeys who can break a leg and lose a living, is it worth taking that chance?"

He knows about tragedy, having lost his brother, Thomas, to cancer in 2004, aged only 20. "When you are racing, you can feel beaten up when it doesn't go well. But then you think about Covid, or the war in Ukraine, or Thomas. He gives me the sense not to be overwhelmed by it all. It's a horse race. It matters now, but how will you feel in ten minutes, ten weeks, ten years? I can see why sport can be so overwhelming." But he still sees racing as poetry: "It has jealousy, ego, greed, compassion, loyalty and glory, encapsulating life and death, from victory to defeat."

Winning the National, he had no recollection of the crowd at all, no sense of the noise: "You are so focused and committed... at the end there is this huge release." His £150,000 prize went to the Amateur Jockeys' Association to encourage those in the future who have the discipline to weigh, and stay, 10 st 8 lbs, and be on just an egg a day for a week. "It can really take its toll. It's bad for your temper, your well-being: I wouldn't do it day after day." But he had taken his passion to the ultimate level.

Robert 'Choc' Thornton, who had enjoyed a string of big race wins with Alan King, fractured a vertebra in a fall at Chepstow in April 2014, and was forced to retire. One of the leading riders on the northern National Hunt circuit, Danny Cook, needed sixty stitches in the face after a heavy fall at Market Rasen in October 2021; he returned to action that November, but in the Rehearsal Chase at Newcastle suffered a fall from one of his favourite horses, Definitly Red, on whom he won nine times. With fears of sight loss mounting, he has not ridden since: "I've had to face reality, and base my decision on going forward. Things were going well, and my best years were probably still to come, so it's a shame the injury came when it did. Ideally, you'd want to retire on your own terms, but sometimes these things are forced on you."

Eddy Greatrex, son of trainer Warren, had to retire at 23 after a litany of injuries, including a split bowel. He decided, "The grind was not worth it, just to end up with a 100-1 shot up north. I felt I was pushing water uphill in the end." Conditional jockey Finian O'Toole, who rode for Micky Hammond, was forced to leave the saddle in 2019, after being unable to recover fully from a horror fall at Kelso. Paul Carberry, Champion Irish Jockey twice, and Grand National winning rider on Bobbyjo, trained by his father Tommy, called time on his illustrious career at 42, due to ongoing issues caused by a leg injury. He was regarded by many as 'the ultimate horseman', not least for his audaciously shrewd Welsh Grand National win on Monbeg Dude. Padge Whelan, who was for ten years a jockey before serious injuries forced his retirement, said: "The shelf life of a jump jockey is so short, you are only briefly passing through in the scheme of a working life. You have to have mental strength, even in retirement, with the strength to accept you had that life and now it's gone: that's perhaps why all the young lads and girls give it that bit extra, so they have no regrets at the end of it." As a recent bonus, from 2021, the RCA (Racecourse Association) now offers the Jockey Recognition Badge, and complimentary access to every racecourse, an acknowledgement of the dedication and service given to the sport by all riders who have ridden seventy-five winners. In 1984, the PJA had set up a pension scheme for jockeys funded by a deduction of 0.6% from all prize money.

In February 2024, Jamie Moore was "gutted" to be forced to retire from race-riding on medical grounds, after sustaining serious injuries in a fall at Lingfield in November 2023, the last in a litany of damages he had incurred, leaving him with a scattering of brain bleeds. But, at 39, he considered himself "lucky that I can walk away" from the sport, after being counselled by neurological and spinal experts that to pursue a comeback would be too big a risk to take. Jamie had won seven Grade 1s; his greatest moment came in his first Tingle Creek win on Sire de Grugy. The pair also won the Champion Chase in 2014. Brian Hughes recalled "The way the weighing room turned out in force after that Champion Chase success, such was the desire to hail Jamie's achievement. He is an absolute gent in every way, shape and form; a great rider and as tough as teak." Dale Gibson paid tribute to "Jamie's remarkable fortitude and appetite for race-riding, which shone like a beacon throughout his career. He was universally popular; his down-to-earth, no nonsense approach, alongside his genuine love of the horse is wholeheartedly applauded."

But, despite all the advice, training, vocation courses and psychological support, when the scoreboard stops clicking the transition to ordinary life can be immeasurably hard. Statistically, our two most dangerous years are the years we are born, and the year we retire: depression, lethargy, loss and lack of status often lie in wait to ambush us. Jockeys have sacrificed so much over the years, not least in a continuous battle with the scales, so part of them dies when they stop riding. For some, who have sustained a career, and exhibited a remarkable array of skills, calling time, or having to call time on a career, is far and away the greatest challenge they have faced.

CHAPTER 27:
EMPERORS OF THEIR CRAFT

"Great athletes are mentally as well as physically exceptional, capable of concentration beyond the reach of ordinary mortals."

- David Papineau -

Jump jockeys in countries other than England do not have the benefits of the Injured Jockeys Fund, or, indeed, as many opportunities to ride. While Australia has almost ceased racing over the sticks, some nations cling to its heritage and traditions, none more so than the Czech Republic, with its Velka Pardubicka. The race, held 100 km east of Prague, in the place where Semtex was invented in 1964, was first run in 1874. It is the oldest, and most challenging, race in Continental Europe. As well as the Taxis, arguably the hardest fence to negotiate in jump racing, of which Marcus Armytage has said, "If you can imagine the lovechild of Becher's Brook and The Chair on steroids, this is it," other forbidding fences include the Irish Bank, the Popkovice Turn, the Big Water Jump, and the Snake Pit, and part of the race is run through ploughed fields: small wonder the contest is nicknamed 'The Devil's Race'. Only two English horses have prevailed in its history, Chris Collins with Stephen's Society, and Charlie Mann's It's A Snip.

When, on 10th October 2004, German jockey Peter Gehm won the race for the fourth consecutive year, riding the Czech-trained mare Registana (also victorious in 2003), he broke the then track record. A headline in Czech read, "*Registana celebrates Bohemian Rhapsody,*" and *The Times* praised her jockey: "The German with sculpted features, a haughty bearing and a craftsman's touch on this singular course." Only a couple of weeks after their second success, Peter Gehm and Registana came to Cheltenham for the cross country chase over its unconventional obstacles in the centre of the course. Registana had won her last nine races, and turned for home with a commanding lead. But when Peter had walked the course, the final fence, a simple brush hurdle had not been in place. Up the draining hill to the finish, the jockey knew he had one more obstacle to negotiate. Ahead of him stood a large black steeplechase fence: he jumped it. His pursuers veered over to the other side of the course, picked their tired way over the brush hurdle and on to the winning post. Registana was disqualified, as Peter knew the moment he jumped the big fence. Some of the crowd jeered, but, as Peter walked the horse back to scale, the jeers softened, and then went silent as sympathy took over. There was something about Peter Gehm that repelled vilification, and in the racing papers the next day the same was true; he had made a mistake, and that was acknowledged.

In mid-December of that year, Peter was riding out for trainer, Christian von der Recke at Forstwald, his Weilerswist stables, in south west Germany. It was a Monday morning; he was only cantering, but his young horse slipped, hurling the jockey into a practice fence. Peter sustained multiple injuries, including a punctured lung, which put him into an induced coma - and he was paralysed.

Peter is the youngest of seven children: nine times Champion Amateur in Germany, and four times Champion Jockey, he lives in Bergheim, near Cologne. As part of the genesis for this book, I had the good fortune to meet him, twice, in Germany, where he was adapting – not without some frustration – to life in a wheelchair. A trip with him to Mannheim races, one of the most beautiful courses in Germany, was enlightening: everyone seemed to know Peter and came up to greet him, albeit briefly. He managed his wheelchair with some aplomb, but needed pushing up any incline, curling himself up to make the pushing easier. There is no bitterness in him. He told me of the horse responsible for his accident. It was a nervous, young animal. When it threw its jockey that morning at Forstwald, the horse fell, too. Throughout his time in hospital, then in rehab, Peter had thought of the horse, and on his first time back at the stables he had been determined to see it; he was understandably angry. The moment he saw the horse, a moment to which he had not looked forward, Peter's anger left him; he realised it, too, had been angry; it, too, had fallen. He could not berate the beast.

He has a specially adapted BMW, and, like many jockeys, is not averse to speed when driving it; that is something his paralysis has not stopped. But there have been challenging moments adapting to losing control of both legs, condemned for life to what PC Philip Olds, paralysed many years ago when attacked attending an off-licence robbery, called his "pram." Peter is determined, aware, and optimistic. In the mobile bar at Mannheim race course, the shirt-sleeve crowd milling about us, I passed him a sparkling wine. He clinked glasses, lifting his a little higher. I thought he said something unusual. Two words. Only on reflection do I realise I might have misheard his Germanic inflection. Reason now suggests he could have said, "Good health." But I'm sure what I heard was, "God heals."

Peter had made many friends among his English contemporaries from his visits to ride in the UK: including AP McCoy; these fellow jockeys raised considerable funds for Peter with a golf day held for several years after his accident. But Peter badly needed something to do on which to focus his energies. He has several wheelchairs, one permanently in the car boot, one by the gate to his house, and another couple, hi-tech and gleaming dark in his gym. He has a bicycle with power-charged wheels, which he rides when things are good. The house has been adapted for him. His mobile is his lifeline, and he remains a popular man, though on one of my visits a call caused his face to darken. I heard the words: "hospital... not good... no signs." A good friend of his, Paul Johnson, was in a coma after a fall. Peter shrugged: "Always accidents... we have always accidents." There is no denying that.

He had a go at training, taking pride in a fine stamp of a horse, Sorrow Negro, almost black, as his name suggests, and with liquid black eyes – black horses are rare in racing. I witnessed his first race, at Düsseldorf, and the pride Peter took in his horse's performance. Again, I was struck by the friends he met that day: not many did more than greet; few asked how he really was; paralysis will not improve – at least, not immediately – its sufferers need to be cherished.

Having now taken up wheelchair table tennis, and become proficient, Peter is still fired up by the world of racing, and his part in it. He has a clothes-basket brimful of photographs – and can remember every course, horse, every result, even. One cluster of these photos catches the eye: horses racing through water and over jumps; the streamlined reflections make each picture doubly effective.

He still requires hospitalisation sometimes, but he presses on. The courage needed as a jump jockey makes even more demands on a paraplegic: dark days still ensue. His photographs sustain him, two in particular: one holds just Peter and his mount: green banks of the racecourse, black water, sharp scarlet silks; the other, taken in Murano, shows him clearing a fence in purple silks against the dramatic backdrop of snow-capped hills. "The horse is Great Day," says Peter, eschewing irony: he is in the moment, and he fights on…

Although he didn't do pony racing, Nico de Boinville, proud of his French heritage, but aware that many of his ancestors were sent to the guillotine during the Revolution, grew up in a competitive equine environment, with show ponies, in Hampshire. He went to Bradfield College, "bunking off to watch Best Mate," and tried university in Newcastle, which wasn't for him – "no structure" – though he took advantage of the chance to ride for Howard Johnson, trainer of Inglis Drever and Tidal Bay. Spending 7 months in Chantilly with English-born trainer, Richard Gibson, he became fascinated to observe training methods, and took out his amateur licence. He then went to Nicky Henderson's stable at Seven Barrows, Lambourn, aged 19. Now 33, he has been there ever since: "It's all I know." He started as a stable lad, and third amateur; his mate, David Bass, was the conditional.

Nico was keen to make it as a jockey, but saw that in such a highly competitive environment, he hadn't a hope. Up to ten, even twelve lads were competing for rides, single lions in the bush. He struggled. But Seven Barrows was a home from home; 'Hendo' looked after him, and it was a great place to learn, with AP McCoy and Barry Geraghty riding there regularly. The trainer was very supportive, and gave Nico chances: he rode good horses at home, but things weren't clicking for him on the track.

David Bass' growing success spurred Nico on: the two shared a house and had a lot of fun. Having given himself time (he set the target to succeed by the age of 25), he was a "steady burn," but needed a few things slotting into place. Gradually, things started to turn around; still a 7lb claimer, he owed much to the efforts of Petit Robin, then won a race on Carruthers for John Oaksey's daughter, Sarah Bradstock, and her husband, Mark, on Tingle Creek day at Sandown. That partnership clicked: the Bradstocks embraced Nico, and he loved their set-up. He and Carruthers won the 2013 West Wales National at Ffos Las.

Then came Coneygree, a fragile racehorse, "a dream born of two grand," but graced with long hind legs that powered him through mud. Nico was still a conditional jockey – just; the horse was still a novice, but the Bradstocks stayed loyal to him for the Gold Cup. He was the underdog, taking on the big guns. On the Wednesday of the Festival, Nico had a bad fall in the Coral Cup, and cracked a collarbone; his valet looked after him. The Gold Cup is always attritional, but Coneygree had his ground that March day in 2015; his trainers had even put a downhill fence into his preparation ("How many trainers would do that!" says Nico) and the pair set a searching gallop, jumping superbly from start to finish. At the top of the hill in the previous race, Dicky Johnson had said to Nico, "There's a long way still to go in this ground," but, in the blue riband, the pair stuck it out, fought off every challenge and stayed on for a famous win. It was a romantic story of epic proportions, though many people had worked like Trojans to achieve the victory.

Propelled into the big time, everything changed for Nico: "Things kicked on." With Barry riding for JP McManus, Nico had more chances and made steady progress, though it was still a hard struggle: "You have to fake it to make it." And he saw relationships change. But 'Hendo's' way of training got everyone together, the whole stable was behind its runners, and the yard was a strong environment in which to be.

"The work/life balance is the difficult thing," says Nico, now married and father of two young children. "In your twenties you are often single-minded, and obsessive, then other people become more important than you, which leads to conflicts. It's all to do with ego: ego plays a big part: how to take criticism: how comfy you are in your own skin: how you work with people." He is not a man for social media. He shares with David Bass the full understanding, for jockeys, of consciousness: a higher level of awareness of who they are and what they are doing. Both are determined to enjoy the journey, its freedom, its exhilaration, the way they can express themselves through it: "Don't think: feel."

Grade 1s are reserved for the most prestigious races, contested by the top horses, with the biggest prize money up for grabs. With over 30 Grade 1 wins to his name already, the most of any current rider, Nico is happy to continue as he is, riding good horses like Shishkin and Constitution Hill – and working on his house, with his family, that vital balance. But there is always pressure: "Jockeys are constantly risk-assessing: does the reward make the risk worthwhile?" Success to him is happy owners, happy trainers, and helping horses achieve their maximum potential, as when Brain Power won the American Grand National for Michael Buckley: "It was a massive party, a hunt meet with 40,000 in their pick-ups, just like a point-to-point."

Nico lives for the big days; his winning rides at the great festivals, Cheltenham, Punchestown and Aintree, have often been copybook: he has an acute sense of timing and is unfazed by external factors, cool and unflustered under pressure. This he proved constantly on Sprinter Sacre and Altior. Having been in the game for so long, he is able to compartmentalise the many things going on his head, but remains a harsh critic of himself – and a realist, unafraid to ponder the deepest questions of his chosen career. "The closer you are to death, the more you appreciate what you have: that's the one thing we all have in common." His experience keeps him cheerful in the face of adversity; he establishes great trust with his horses and gives them confidence.

Structure is essential to Nico; already he knows it will disappear "when that day comes" to retire. But, this thoughtful, honest man, still in some ways a mystery figure, brings maturity to the table. "The calmest bloke I've ever come across and the man you'd want in your battalion," says Tom Scudamore. Nico remains aware that "To do what we do, you can't be a perfectly balanced individual: there have to be a few kinks there."

In conversation, Nico affords a deep analysis of himself and his sport. He freely admits it is a running joke in the weighing room that he is "the posh t...." "There's a very fine line between success and failure in all we do. But I wouldn't do what I do if I wasn't competitive and ambitious." Having 'grown up' at Seven Barrows, he feels tied to the place; Nicky Henderson, the ultimate diplomat in Nico's eyes, has been "incredibly loyal" and moulded Nico into what he needs as a rider, being sure to get the best out of him at all times. Nico is in an enviable position: "I get my kicks from top class horses being able to do incredible things." Sprinter Sacre and Altior were superstars: now he has the mount on Constitution Hill, a very relaxed horse with a phenomenal engine and mighty potential – when winning the Champion Hurdle in 2023 he took off acres before the final flight, a breath-taking sight, like Colin Jackson in his pomp. "I don't think the horse understands how good he is." For Nico, "Working with horses is a wonderful thing," but he is only too well aware that: "You cannot control the uncontrollable."

He still thinks, often, of the two jockeys for whom it all became too much: "James and Liam died far too young, and before their time. Racing is very transient, but their deaths were major moments for the weighing room, and racing. They won't be forgotten. They are a big part of the reason we are now focused on mental health challenges. The more we talk about suicide, the more we hope those situations don't arise in the future. By talking about it, we might also be better able to step in and offer help."

And there are always up-and-coming aspirants keen to scale the heights, or just to take part in the sport. Point-to-point jockey, Dan Cherriman, 37, and "completely amateur," is Master and Huntsman of the South Shropshire hunt from September to February; he races point-to-point from March to June. From a farming background, not racing, but with lots of 'pointing interest', he grew up with ponies; worked for Alan Hill; went for a charity race at Newmarket; won it; loved the experience, and built from there. Veteran of 120 rides – he started at 29 – he has booted home 14 princely winners. "There's nothing like the first," at Umberleigh 7 years ago, on a big black horse, bought unseen. His ambition was always to ride in the Aintree Foxhunters: despite lockdown, a broken pelvis, and being brought down at the first fence on initial attempts, he has now completed the course, twice. Even at his level, the 'emotional rollercoaster' is his hardest challenge as a jockey: "You can't switch off: you anticipate; wait anxiously for the race; ride it, to thrill or disappointment; can't sleep the night after, as you are still 'high' on adrenalin; play the race on replay in your head many times; then, a day or two after, experience an emotional flat. Initially, I thought every mount of mine had a chance; now I am more realistic, and don't flower it up. I still hope a lot, but expect less, trying to cope with the adrenalin-spike. Like every jump jockey, my brain is always on repeat…"

The opposite bookend to Paul Townend is Walter Barnett, who has ridden just 1 winner – so far. Like many, a graduate from pony racing, he is now working for Lawney Hill in Oxfordshire. Walter relishes his days racing at different tracks, whether leading up a horse or riding it in a point-to-point; the atmosphere grips him. That win, on only his sixth ride, in his first season, took time to sink in: "I was waiting for someone to pass me in the home straight, but they didn't. When my horse and I passed the line in front, I stood up in my stirrups and laughed to myself in disbelief." Before a race, he gets nervous, but feels no fear: "I can't wait to get going." He knows the dangers, the flip-sides of jump racing, finding nothing worse than losing a horse you spend nearly all day, every day with at home, and he already understands he will need resilience in spades to be able to keep riding. For him, the game isn't just about winning: "Sometimes horses run amazing races in defeat, and just because they didn't win doesn't mean they didn't bring thrills and excitement to the race – watching a horse jump and travel is a spectacle in itself."

Few jockeys can know more about the vicissitudes in jump racing than Ruby Walsh, the man from Kill, Co. Kildare, 12 times Irish Champion Jockey with over 2,500 wins and the record (59) number of victories in the unrelenting maelstrom of the Cheltenham Festival. He was champion amateur while still at school and rode three winners during the week when taking his last exams. Race-riding never felt like work; it was always an adventure, from the first day after those exams, when he went to Willie Mullins. Richard Dunwoody was his hero, along with Charlie Swan: "Those senior jockeys were brilliant teachers: there was no bullying." Ruby was always working to get better, "to chase the dream." He took one day at a time, and the dream never became reality: there were always more targets to aim for, though he never set out with these in mind. He admits he had lucky breaks, being in the right place at the right time, but he also had unlucky breaks, a full litany of injuries ever since turning professional in 1998-99. When he became – and remained – Champion Jockey, he was still in fantasy land. But work had been instilled in him from an early age: he remained grounded in that ethic.

Alistair Down always saw Ruby, "perched over his horse like some cross between a question mark and a half-cocked pistol, reigning supreme. Riding with vice-like legs, he proved the seemingly endless multiplicity of methods by which a horse could be ridden, not least when dropped in for a spot of masterly late smuggling. He illuminated racing, roaming another plain like some apex predator who could always ambush, crunch and chew the other creatures fighting to survive a brutal life."

Winning the Grand National of 2000 in his first ride in the race, aged 20 on Papillon, trained by his father Ted, was the turning point: "You often hear jockeys saying a big win passed them by, or they didn't appreciate the actual event until they did it again. Not me. Riding in the Grand National was a dream come true; to finish was an achievement; winning it never crossed my mind. For me it was getting over the first fence, then the next..."

Following up in that year's Irish Grand National on Commanche Court cemented his propulsion into a different league – and that came with pressure, which he handled with aplomb throughout his career. He was always driven. Many of his best victories were on horses that shared his durability: Hurricane Fly, Kauto Star, Faugheen, Annie Power, Quevega, Djakadam and Kemboy. He regards himself as fortunate to have been among a generation of brilliant jockeys. As for his injuries, he lived by the motto, 'If you can get up, get up', though that was tested when he ruptured his spleen in a fall at Cheltenham: after having the spleen removed, he was back riding in 27 days. Small wonder the racing world admires the mentality of jockeys, but Ruby demurs: "Don't think poor me; think how soon can I get back? Don't try and blame people or circumstances, just get on with how can I fix it?" He always rode to win and kept the pressure on himself. He lit up countless afternoons, en route to his record number of wins, and his genius, for all its diverse range of skills, was rooted in simplicity.

There was no stronger mind than Ruby's: after injury his psychological resilience brought him back time after time. He could take pressure, having craved it from an early age, and though he couldn't claim to get inside a horse's mind, he could always get it to co-operate, guide it – even con his mount into thinking it was going better than it was, in the hope he'd got it right. His temperament and attitude were the gifts he'd been born with. But his success in the saddle was often dearly bought, by that extensive catalogue of serious injuries during his career, breaking 67 bones in his leg, arm, hip and wrist, not to mention dislocations of the shoulder, and a ruptured spleen. Yet, he did not let these rattle his conviction: it was testament to his hunger and dedication that he rode for so long.

"The affection he built up naturally with the racing public as an instinctive horseman was endearing to witness: he was the 'go-to' man down all his years, but remained his own person, a beacon of honesty and knowledge at the top of a hugely demanding sport. The winning-most rider of all time in Ireland, his timing, his guile, and his tact were unsurpassed – made evident with a technique reassuringly old school – and a racing brain perhaps sharper than any. And he was not shy with his views: sharp, pertinent, uncompromising – and unfailingly accurate. "What he thought was what we got: he had no time for the delicate sensibilities of our era. He was refreshingly his own person, who found a means of remaining human at the top of a hugely demanding sport, content to offer opinions, prepared to make mistakes, never afraid to stand up and be counted. Though physically fragile, in terms of broken bones, his psychological resilience was remarkable, like his unflinching composure. His Christian name was all that was required." (*Racing Post*)

His sudden retirement from the saddle left an enormous gap, but he went out on his own terms. He put himself – and us – through the relentless process of recovery so often, but, "My journey was a dream: I was never going to end it on a nightmare. I wanted to finish it my way"… and he did. And he didn't retire: he changed careers: riding out, recording podcasts, writing for the '*Irish Examiner*', hosting radio programmes, and commentating for Racing TV, RTE and ITV. He was an immediate hit as an analyst on TV, where he is quite comfortable, and never short of an expert's view. Many feel he has the sharpest mind in jump racing. When he speaks, we listen. Factors which won him multiple races – his timing, subtlety and depth of thinking – are now brought to bear in his race evaluations, together with an understated but keen wit. And he still has a huge role to play at Willie Mullins' Closutton stables.

David Jennings has called Ruby "racing's shiny new pundit, fuelled by fact, not fiction"; his transition from pilot to philosopher was seamless. Ruby wants to get people thinking for themselves when watching racing: he's keen to explain tactics so that what's happening in a race can be understood. His acumen wants to talk about how a horse might win, not which one is going to win. He admired the difference made by John Francome: "He said it as it was, and more often than not he was right." The only thing Ruby has missed since retirement is walking back in front of the stands after winning.

He remains as fine an ambassador for the sport as he was in the saddle, strongly believing racing can be tightened up, better co-ordinated, and showcased more smoothly. There is no longer so much pressure and expectation; now he is less guarded, more relaxed. He is in as good a position as anyone to bring about – and quickly – the changes in jump racing that he believes are essential.

CHAPTER 28: TOM SCU

"Nobody's anything without the team behind them."

- Peter Scudamore -

Tom Scudamore always dreamed of being a jockey, and fortunately didn't grow too much. Born into the dynasty, he was bound to be steeped in the sport, and, as a kid, was already a little walking encyclopaedia of racing. Brought up to be level-headed, he saw early in his life that the sport has many avenues to explore but, through his grandfather and father's catalogue of injuries, was also made aware that, for all the glory and glamour, there was always the flipside. Having originally fancied going to Millfield, the young lad stood at the window of Cheltenham hospital, when visiting Peter after one of his frequent injuries, looked at the school opposite, and decided that was where he would like to go. This school was Cheltenham College. He won a scholarship, and duly became a Cheltonian.

Academically bright and sportingly gifted – he was a speedy 1st XV wing – he originally planned to leave education at 16, but his mother, Maz, and a handful of masters, with whom he got on well – "the right people at the right time" – persuaded him otherwise. He had reaped a healthy set of GCSEs so entered the sixth form, where his housemaster, Martin Stovold, himself a 'fine blade of the turf', and I, Tom's tutor, were able to plan for the lad an unusual timetable, that allowed him to study for two 'A' Levels – English and Economics – and also to ride out regularly, a programme that worked well for all. Having witnessed his first win at Cheltenham on the

Friday of the October meeting – "quite a day" for him – I walked into my classroom later that afternoon to teach a lesson on *Hamlet*, and, to my eternal surprise, found Tom sitting on his desk, regaling his mates with the details of his victory. My "What are you doing here, Tom?" was met by "I've got English, that's the deal." He was always keen to keep his bargain, and the lesson was spent viewing a video of his race.

About that time, Peter asked me whether his son could take up drama as an extra academic subject: "Then, if he's lucky enough to win a race or two, he'll be able to handle the media." Tom had played Fléance in the school production of *Macbeth*, and had enjoyed 'treading the boards'. So, off-timetable, I taught Tom the theory of drama. But with him being the only Cheltenham College scholar studying the subject, he had to join the silken ranks of Cheltenham Ladies' College for the practical side, worth far more marks than the theory. History does not relate whether he or the green-clad demoiselles of that prestigious establishment enjoyed the experience more. But he notched up A+, and has never had any problems expressing his ideas.

The Monday after his last exam, as Tom's mates were preparing for their gap years, he went down to the Pond House stables of the Pipe family in Somerset – and never left, until the day he hung up his boots, early in 2023. He spent one year as an amateur, then turned professional. That move to Martin Pipe was the defining moment of his life: he was to learn much. His father had been looked after by Pipe; Martin's son, David continued the link with Tom: both men are proud of its longevity. "There were no easy days when I started, but I trusted the Pond House set-up implicitly, because it demanded the best of me." There, he was entrusted with some fine horses, including Lough Derg, whom he rated highly for putting him on the map, and giving him his first Grade 1 win, at Ascot. "I owe him a lot," Tom says, of the horse who had "resolution and stamina in spades." Mischievous at home, Lough Derg was tough on the track, especially round Ascot. Stable name Douglas, he wore his heart on his sleeve, and gave his all in races: "You knew you were going to sleep well the night after riding him," says Tom. "Every jockey needs an ace in their pack: Lough Derg was that for me."

Greys Dynaste and Grands Crus did well under him, The Giant Bolster so nearly gave him a Gold Cup in 2012 (one race Tom would like to go back and ride again), but caused him heartache instead. The stars were aligned for Next Sensation's win at Cheltenham in 2015, which gave him his most treasured moment emotionally, but the best horse he rode was the Colin Tizzard trained Thistlecrack, emphatic winner of the World Hurdle 2016 at Cheltenham, devouring the hill to win by twelve lengths. He was a big horse, but light on his feet, and became the first horse to win the King George Chase at Kempton as a novice: "I was very sure what to do on him, and it worked out. That day he was the best jumps horse in Europe with his dynamism, lethal acceleration and display of sheer power. His exuberant jumping, often taking off outside the wings of a fence, was an exhilarating joy to behold, let alone be sharing in the victory." That was to be Thistlecrack's last win; the horse had physical issues which prevented further heights, "yet he gave me some great thrills. I got a thrill from any winner. But most especially with Thistlecrack. The privilege was all mine. He was a hell of a horse, the best I've ridden by quite some way. We had so many good days; even the bad days in defeat were good, because he'd come back off injury and run his race."

Tom was "pretty lucky" with his weight, but was also well-disciplined. From a lad he had always been clear about what to do, and how to do it, at the same time keen to improve every day. Any weaknesses he needed to iron out were confronted and flattened: he knew the need for jump jockeys to adapt and change. He learnt how to deal with disappointment, like sometimes choosing the wrong horse: "Be tough, man up, grow a pair of balls and move on," though at times he just wanted to be in a dark corner. There he parked his negative thoughts (he also parked the big wins), and resolved not to allow it to happen again; the next race was the most important. He quotes Mick Channon junior, "Today and tomorrow are all that matters, not yesterday."

He found all the travelling hardest: days of getting up at 4.30 a.m. and returning home at 11 p.m. were commonplace, which inevitably had an impact on his family. "You have to be prepared to put yourself and those around you through the mill." But he was 'very driven' in the psychological sense. Riding never felt hard work to him, and he came to enjoy no mean success: "Success gets to you: you want to continue enjoying it, you become obsessed; you get greedy." But he endeavoured to keep a strong sense of perspective. "Ride the race, not the occasion," his father had instilled into him, and he remembered that when riding the favourite, Cloth Cap, in the 2021 Grand National. The horse was going really well, until suffering a wind problem, which had never happened before, and never struck afterwards. Lady Luck deserted the partnership.

In his attitude to the big races, Tom owed much to the example of rugby player Neil Jenkins, "the most reliable goal kicker." When the Welshman was lining himself up for important conversions, he tried to block everything out, imagining he was back practising at Pontypridd, as a kid. Tom did the same: when turning for home with a chance of ultimate glory in that Cheltenham Gold Cup of 2012; thoughts of that situation and opportunity which he had nurtured as a boy flew into his brain.

He remained, throughout his career, sensitive to his responsibility to owners, trainers and stable staff. "Their livelihood depends on your performance, and that keeps your feet on the ground." Rachael Blackmore has his admiration here: "She lets her deeds do the talking; deeds are what counts. What she stands for is an inspiration." The two have a lot in common, much of it instinctive: "You practise instinct constantly," says Tom.

Among the things that have changed during his career – and he hopes there will be more – Tom lauds the use of jockey coaches, and the way jockeys now look after themselves, which runs deeper than before. He finds UK horse welfare second to none, but feels there are perhaps too many factions in racing. People with weighty experience are not asked for their opinions. Tom sees no clear strategy for the sport from BHA Board. The same problems keep cropping up. Racing management probably needs refreshing: "There is always so much ground to cover, but it needs to happen now." More concern at grass roots level, and a wider understanding of the full context of jump racing would help hugely. As a senior jockey, he was embroiled in the Frost vs Dunne case, and felt simmering anger for the way things were reported about the weighing room, not least where leaks were concerned. He was more angry about the way the case was handled than the case itself, and was made to feel uncomfortable. "It was a very emotive issue; people have views and it's hard to stay neutral, but we need to stay balanced.

The case needed closure. But it was a wake-up call: much needed changing, especially ladies' facilities, which are very poor and have often been the same for twenty years: there are many more girls riding now." But lots of questions about the culture of the weighing room were not answered by the case, and Tom asserted: "Everybody has to get better; there'll be a place for everybody, but we want to move on."

The Scudamores are a golden thread through racing; they are sturdy supports to each other, Tom reckoning brother Michael's Welsh Grand National victory with Monbeg Dude gave him as much pleasure as many of his own big wins. Riding any winner trained by his brother gave Tom great satisfaction. Tom shares the record with Willie Robinson for Hennessy Gold Cup – now the Coral Gold Cup – wins; after Madison du Berlais and Sizing Tennessee came the aforementioned Cloth Cap, his first victory for Jonjo O'Neill, a horse on whom he rolled along in glorious rhythm throughout the race, clearing the birch with athletic accuracy, affording his pilot a depth of euphoria only jump jockeys know. Willie Robinson, partner of Mill House, was "a natural rider, a beautiful horseman, with great hands, a man you felt better for being with": it has been said of Tom too, that after talking with him, you feel better. Tom also won the 2021 Scottish Grand National with a fine ride on Mighty Thunder for Lucinda Russell, making the most of his partner's stamina and sound jumping to overhaul Dingo Dollar in the shadow of the post. A Scottish winner was welcome, even though the stands were bereft of Scots (and racegoers of any nationality, due to Covid).

"On days like that, adrenalin mixes with the euphoria to pulse through a jockey's veins. You want to win the big races, and it's hard to let it sink in really," said Tom after that success. "You get pleasure when you look back at things. It's a great honour when you see the list of winners." But he was quick to recognise Mighty Thunder was usually Blair Campbell's ride – and he would be getting it back. Tom had no success in the English National, his best being sixth on Vieux Lion Rouge, but he won a Becher Chase over the big Aintree fences, and also a Grand Sefton. He had clear thoughts about his aims as a jockey. "Winning – and the thought of it – gets you up in the morning, though you can't get too tense or try too hard in that quest, as you always chase the impossible dream. Take it day by day. Break it down into manageable bits, as advocated by Steve Redgrave in his book *Chasing Goals*. You have to keep improving, keep changing your mindset. You have to want to win badly, all the time realising you will never be satisfied." But, Tom's perspective on success is unusual: "Even though winning is the only thing that matters, I think jockeys can win in a lot of ways: their memories; a really good horse; fulfilling their or their mount's potential; subduing their (own) demons; and defeating the odds in the widest sense of that expression." Tom is grateful for his shining pedigree, but he never felt pressure to live up to that. "I wasn't competing against Dad and Grandad."

But the advice and experience of Michael senior and Peter was never lost on Tom, who jokes that when he started he didn't need to buy new gear, because he could use theirs. Whereas Peter admitted to having felt a responsibility to live up to his father, Michael, Tom saw the dynastic side as something to honour. His sense of family is strong. Scu senior, Peter, godson of Arkle's jockey, Pat Taaffe, was eight times Champion Jockey, with 1692 winners to his name, two Champion Hurdles, four Welsh Grand Nationals and two Scottish Nationals, the first jockey to ride 200 winners in a season. Peter's trailblazing partnership with the Pipes being continued with his son as stable jockey for sixteen years, David Pipe regarded Tom as "the ultimate professional, both in and out of the saddle." Teamwork was everything for so long with the successful Pipe/Scudamore liaison. Peter takes fierce pride in both Tom and younger son, Michael, of whom he has said: "The way he trained himself as a professional sportsman, when younger, has helped in the way he trains his horses now." Like Gary Moore and his sons, the Scudamores are a huge part of jump racing's story.

Gifted with a strong sense of perspective, even as a schoolboy, Tom always chose not to look back, but forward. "I've got to be realistic. I might look like Peter Pan, but the dreaded day will come: few jockeys get to choose exactly when they retire." Training wouldn't necessarily be the go for him. He was looking forward to much, not least Ahoy Señor, trained by Lucinda Russell and his father, a horse whose frame and attitude to racing reminds him of Thistlecrack.

For Tom, that day of reckoning landed on 12th February 2023; it came as a surprise, after a fall at Leicester, only days after time out for concussion.

He sat on the ground thinking, "That's not happening again. Normally you sit there thinking what went wrong, how are you going to put it right and prove everyone wrong. Not this time." When he took the cap off, his helmet had a big crack down the side of it. A fall two weeks earlier at Chepstow, which left him concussed, may have been the catalyst. "I didn't leave the house that morning for Leicester thinking this will be it. But it was a bizarre feeling, a lightbulb went off and that was it." Tom, who had won at every racecourse except Catterick, was still operating close to the peak of his riding powers. He is proud of his body of work over the last quarter of a century, and the knowledge that he conducted himself with the same professionalism both his father Peter and grandfather Michael brought to the weighing room before him, which gives him peace of mind. "What I can look back on with pride is that I have no excuses and didn't leave anything behind; I can take solace in that. Other than getting into a time machine, I can't do anything about it, and I've got an opportunity now to have a crack at something else.

"I got a right kicking that day at Leicester and thought – I've had my warning now. I'm going to be 41 in May, and the body doesn't bounce like it used to: that is the key. I would have been riding on borrowed time; we are all of us on borrowed time. I've given all I can give and don't want to let anyone down. I knew I was on the back nine of my career: my grandfather had his career taken away from him, through no decision of his own, after a bad fall. I didn't want to be in that position." When asked how he would feel if any of his three daughters, Myrtle, Margot and Ava-Grace, wanted to continue the Scudamore thread of race-riding, Tom bellowed, "Furious!" before his face relaxed and he showed the strong sense of humour with which he has been gifted. "No, they need options; it's not something to play at. I feel very grateful and privileged for the life I have had in racing and I feel it's your duty – big word 'duty' – to follow your passion: so if that's what they want, that'll be fine." Margot had her first ride, on the flat, at Redcar in October 2023.

Tributes from his weighing room colleagues were fulsome: Tom had earned "huge respect within the industry;" "his mindset made him stand out;" he "never let the atmosphere faze him;" "he was funny and witty, and tactically the best around;" "he always had a good story to tell;" "many people looked up to him, and he'll be missed." With ten Cheltenham victories to his name, his best score in a season was 150 in 2014-2015: he notched up 50+ wins for 17 consecutive years. Amateur champion in 2002, he was always proud of his working relationship with Martin and David Pipe. Nicky Henderson said: "If one of my jockeys got hurt, I'd go to the weighing room to see who was available – if Scu was, I'd nab him. He was a lovely rider." Tom may not have won many of the really big races, but went about his trade relentlessly and genuinely, punters loved his busy style, his 'stickability', and his will to stay on a horse. He blended purpose with enthusiasm for a drive that never deserted him, always endeavouring to minimise anxiety and stress which he thinks can affect a sportsman's performance by up to 20%. His balance was laudable. Always giving 100%, he was a fine role model, always having time for younger jockeys, who looked up to him; he gave great feedback after a race, and his distinctive laugh was going to be missed. Sean Bowen said, "He was one hell of a jockey, and an even better man." Since his first win, on Nordic Breeze at Warwick in 1998, Tom had ridden 1,511 winners in his 25-year career, and he remains fiercely appreciative of all who have helped him along the way.

When Peter retired at 34, with a similar shock announcement, he said he was "immensely fortunate to get out of the sport, and still earn a living and have my good health, which is more important than anything." Having voted Sabin Du Loir his favourite horse: "You get attached to the honesty and bravery of horses like that," he was asked what was his finest hour. He replied that he hoped it was yet to come... His partnership with Lucinda Russell is now bearing rich fruit: the pair trained One For Arthur to win the Grand National of 2017, and repeated the feat in 2023 with Corach Rambler, a horse of vast potential...

Peter and Lucinda had lost One For Arthur in March 2023: he was their springboard to lofty heights. Corach Rambler proved a worthy successor and inherited Arthur's mantle. For all his special bond with Peter, the horse is not always the most docile: "He is not quirky, he just enjoys life," says the ex-Champion Jockey. "He's so brave and tough: he just loves racing. For him, it is a game, dodging between horses. It's resilience. The way he fights and goes through gaps is what I see in his character every day."

In the summer of 2023, it was announced that Michael Scudamore was to join forces with Lucinda Russell and Scu senior up in Scotland, while Tom would take over Eccleswall Court near Ross-on-Wye as a pre-training and additional yard. This, it was hoped, would make campaigning their northern horses in the south so much easier, and open up more opportunities.

Tom's retirement called time on a glittering career that saw him the tenth most successful jump jockey of all time. And he made it clear: "It's not a retirement, it's a change of jobs. I was given a deck of cards, and feel I've played them the best possible way I could. I'm proud of what I achieved, and feel content." He has already proved a source of expert knowledge and welcome good humour as a guest presenter on *ITV Racing*. Having been involved in consultations about the new rules concerning the whip, he is keen for everyone to work together, where no-one has their own agenda. It's been suggested that if anyone is to unite the weighing room and the rulers, given the fact he is universally respected, it could be Tom. "I've come to the end of Act I, now there'll be a short interval, and on to Act II," he says, his sense of drama still potent. Always fond of the deck of cards analogy, he now waits to turn over the next card in his hand...

CHAPTER 29: THE JOCKEY WHO THINKS OUT OF THE BOX

"Never a dull moment."

- David Bass -

David is an atypical jump jockey, who plays the drums, is often ribbed for being vegan, does not come from a racing dynasty/tradition, and is a canny, unconventional man of thought. Long-time stable jockey to Kim Bailey, only a few miles out of Cheltenham, he is not afraid to say things as he sees them, and was described by Lewis Porteous in the *Racing Post* as "a deep thinker, who's interested in understanding his own mind."

Much of David's success springs from the positive way he attacks his fences in a race – and his challenges in life - but his answer to the question of what drives him on is different from a few years ago. Then, he was motivated by – indeed committed to – winning, success, maybe ending up Champion Jockey. Not now. These days, at the age of 35, he enjoys his races, he appreciates the chance to ride at the top level, acknowledging that he may not always be as fixated on winning as many of his weighing room colleagues – "so often it depends on the horse" – but he has to enjoy race-riding. Realistic to a fault, he is well aware that he may not – in some races he won't – win, but he will still be 'in the moment', doing something he loves. Even in 2020-2021 with a strike rate around 20%, and in the top 10 of jump jockeys, he made it simple: "A 20% strike rate means 80% losers, so most of the time I'm not winning."

He is interesting about fear. "Jockeys are always said to be fearless, but that's "not helpful" [one of his favourite phrases]. Sometimes it's good to have a bit of fear, especially on a tricky jumper, which is scary. But the key thing is how you deal with – and overcome it. When I am on a good jumper, that is something extra. I'm 'in flow', living on instinct, completely engaged with my horse and my challenge: there's no room for fear." Anyone who has seen him hurl First Flow at the Ascot fences can only stand back and admire.

But he has no truck with cosy statements about heroics on horseback. A jockey's career is ultimately a short one, even though jockeys today go on riding longer than they used to. They have to be hungry, to have that edge. But they also have to make many sacrifices: they cannot plan and make assumptions for the future. And they have to suffer deprivation in all manner of ways: "It's not a good idea to tell young jockeys that. They have to experience it for themselves." David goes further: "We think we're building a legacy, but…" To him that is a misconception. Jockeys have to have talent, but, of course, they also need a lot of luck; really good horses are hard to come by. And there is always more to learn: the saying 'Jockeys are only as good as their last ride' is not helpful. They have to work on their skills, and, even more importantly, on their mindset. There is, always, the fear of not being good enough, which David feels has to be questioned. What drives that fear? The answer is pressures from owners, trainers, punters and the jockeys themselves. Paradoxically, he acknowledges, "The better you do, the more pressure there is." In response to the notion that jockeys feel they did their best, and it wasn't good enough, David believes, "Their best has to be good enough: there needn't be a battle in riders' minds, a craving to reproach themselves and the fear of failing."

He is proud his mindset has changed, and pinpoints the catalyst for this as the Grand National 2016, when he finished second on Kim Bailey-trained, The Last Samuri – "a great little horse" – to 33-1 shot Rule The World. He had said beforehand, "It's such a hard race just to get into. To have a ride in the race is good. To have a ride with a good chance is brilliant." Even though his horse put up a remarkable performance on ground that didn't suit him, and ran his heart out, David went over the race countless times, berating himself for the defeat. Being banned for 'overuse of the stick' (whip) added to his depth of dismay: he became fixated on the result, obsessed with his performance, so much so that his memory of what happened in the race is still blurred: "It shouldn't be." The jockey was forced to realise his dissatisfaction with his acumen in the saddle had been building up for years, but this was the crux… instead of brooding on it, kidding himself the feeling would pass, not telling a soul; this had to change: he sought help.

If he'd won the Grand National it wouldn't have changed David's life: coming second did. "I'd say for years leading up to that Grand National I was mentally fragile, but that was the end of a long struggle. We talk about how winning a race like the Grand National leaves a legacy, how, when you're beaten, you spiral into blaming yourself and believing that you've let everyone down. For me, there was a lot of self-loathing after that… I wasn't happy with the way I was riding. I went down a dark, self-sabotaging road. Sometimes it's after your biggest defeat when you learn a lot more about yourself, and I definitely learned that after finishing second in the National. I was depressed, there's no other way of looking at it. The pressure to succeed was sucking the joy out of winning." Something drastic needed to be done.

With the help of JETS and the PJA, he was put in touch with a sports psychotherapist, whom he still sees. He is unafraid to admit that his first session of therapy was the hardest thing he ever had to do: he was utterly vulnerable. "But, when things aren't right, you sort them out." The jockey remains passionate about seeking help: "A lot of folk need help in the racing world: a lot don't. But seeking help needs to be normalised, not headline-making." When he first sought help it had to be something kept in confidence, but he feels things have changed since then. In cricket; Marcus Trescothick and Freddie Flintoff have spoken openly about their mental health struggles; in soccer, research is now being conducted on injurious effects of heading the ball innumerable times, while in rugby, Jonny Wilkinson has opened the door to honesty about admitting mental health challenges, in his *High Performance* podcasts. "Racing is behind in this," says David.

When he was struggling post-Grand National, he was where Jonny Wilkinson had been, and had a sense of doom about life and mortality: "You can cope with that by being excessively competitive – for a while…" David found the great English scrum-half's experience crucial: "Connect performance with life and well-being; it doesn't have to be a story of stress. Swap stress and the need for control with the thought of possibilities: see how things turn out.

Have/put different thoughts in your head. It's always struggle and sacrifice, but there is room to let sporting life be a surprise, so don't try and work it all out beforehand. Holding on to defeat is negative. Let go of self-importance, in favour of courage and humility." Jonny now advocates a 'live more, feel better' approach to life's endless challenges, urging us to be fully engaged in the moment, to be more 'conscious', i.e. adopt a deeper, more probing awareness of who we are. David has taken this thinking onboard and feels the better for it – in every respect it has liberated him.

He still sees his psychotherapist regularly: "Talking about issues has to be an accepted practice, and an ongoing one, because we have to work on our mindset all the time." He reveals that even when he thinks he has little to say, the 50-minute sessions are still brimful of import.

"When they are together in a group, jockeys won't talk about mental health, because they are always in such a fiercely competitive environment; with just one other person, they certainly could speak freely. But it doesn't just happen. Everyone is different: everyone has their own challenges, even demons: there is nothing to be ashamed of in bringing these out into the open, and then dealing with them." Knowing how reserved young Englishmen/ sportsmen/jockeys can be about appearing vulnerable – and well aware that by far the hardest step of all is that first reaching out for help, thus admitting 'weakness' in the world's eyes, David encourages a gentle, but determined, approach with his peers, suggesting that if they 'see someone' it will improve their performance. That could put jockeys off, he rationalises. "But with riders who spend their lives risking life and limb several times every day, in the scale of things it is no risk at all. Looking inside ourselves is scary, of course, but it has to be done."

The thought of jockeys suffering in silence is unsettling. "I still think there's a stigma there," says David. "As much as I don't want attention from it, it's an issue I think needs to be discussed in the right way. We feel as if we need to suffer to justify any sort of success, or at least that's how I felt. I felt I needed to drive all over the place to ride out, ride with broken bones, do all the lightweights possible, punish myself when I didn't win on a horse, and suffer, to be successful. I've come to realise it's not healthy to keep going with that mindset. Of course, it's a tough job, and you have to have a level of resilience to do it, but for me, I needed to look after myself mentally. Ten years ago I thought it ridiculous talking to someone about mental health: you're a jump jockey, you suffer, you don't talk about it, and that's that. Now, I firmly believe people need help and encouragement. Racing is a job that has for too long been seen as a long road of suffering that leads to success, which isn't helpful. A lot of people have changed their mentality, but there's a long way to go. I feel I'm in a much better place now, but it's something you need to work on, just like your physical health - if you want your fitness to improve you have to work on it and it's the same with our mental health. 'Mental fitness' is arguably a better term than 'mental health'; use of it could help take some of the sting out of the stigma."

Not winning the Grand National gave him a more healthy mindset, made him more 'conscious', and thus changed everything; winning it would have cemented his legacy and reinforced his ego; it would not have changed his life, or his in-depth thinking: the latter he now considers infinitely more important.

But he remains as self-critical as ever: "Jockeys are taught to aim for perfection, driven, always, by 'the numbers thing'. When I lost my claim, I realised I had to do something differently: ride 'shorter' (i.e. higher up in the stirrups); have more individuality; work on my own style, be even more positive." Now he tempers that aim with realism... and always there looms the possibility of injury: one bad Ascot fall resulted in his face being trodden into the turf, which for a time meant his confidence was shot. He got it back, remained utterly committed, without pushing himself quite so hard.

From 2021 to June 2023 David was the jockeys' representative, and thus their president on the advisory panel of PJA. As a senior rider with high standards and an unusually strong sense of perspective, he experienced racing's old school being reluctant to change. Being president was, for him, a full-time job in itself, not easy for a full-time jockey with responsibilities to many: the role consumed a lot of his energies. He learned much, and was helped considerably by Simon Cox, but the experience cost him: one fellow jockey commented: " David stuck his head over the parapet, and got the bolt from a crossbow for his pains." He resigned the post. But he remains grateful for having been in a position to help improve things; fellow jockeys still consult him because they know that he is approachable and will fight their corner.

Much has been written in recent months about ways in which racing can move forward. One of the many changes David believes vital, is giving jockeys a decent break between seasons. These days, the jumps season ends with the Sandown Bet 365 – aka the Whitbread Gold Cup meeting; in 2023, it resumed two days later at Uttoxeter, though it takes a complete break for 12 days in August. David is urging a longer break in the summer, so jockeys could get out of the racing bubble. Small fields and low-quality racing during July and August are hardly encouragement for the sport, as Alan Lee observed several years ago: "Summer racing limps apologetically onto the sporting calendar like an unwanted stranger using the back entrance." The whole premise of summer racing needs an overhaul; there is a paucity of jumps meetings between May and September, when the best horses are recovering from exertion. Jockeys are expected to be on-call, yet are often left twiddling their thumbs. One of them has said: "Summer is sitting with yourself; no-one wants you if your main yard is less active. You risk not riding at all, never mind not riding winners, which is what your whole existence is about. So, you are filled with doubt in the quiet periods: "What is the racing world thinking?"

Other sportspeople cannot understand why there is no off-season for jump jockeys. Whilst it might be impossible not to stage National Hunt racing from late April until gentle Devon holiday meetings in August at Newton Abbot and Exeter, as of yore, a decent recuperation time is surely vital for riders. And with no Sundays off, jockeys cannot plan ahead, even just enjoy a Saturday night out, let alone guarantee to attend family celebrations, or a funeral; they would have the chance to do something different if there were more of a gap in the fixture list. David advocates two Sundays off in a month, "to clear the mind - it's the mind that needs clearing, not just the head."

He feels strongly that while jockeys are part of something bigger than themselves, and have to fit into that role, they are not easily replaceable items. Scratching around, riding for a lot of different trainers is hard; being more closely involved, and part of an established team would help jockeys. "It is such an individual sport; we jockeys need to band together more. We need encouragement to stay tough, for that resilience is what separates 'making it' from not. The sport could be more concerned with people, loyalty and honesty in its dealings if the racing community were more 'conscious', more aware in the wider sense. "So many people in the sport don't 'get' it."

Whereas in the past, if he had not managed a winner – particularly at the Festival with all its raw emotion – (the altar of Cheltenham is understandably the be-all and end-all for so many: you have to ride a winner), he would leave Prestbury Park beating himself up seriously; now he exhibits more sang-forid. "Winning is not what defines you as a human being" has become something of a mantra for this man, whose realism is refreshing: "Of course you want to win, you need to want that win – but not too much." That said, he adores that indescribable winning feeling – even if, as when he won that Grade 1 at Ascot on First Flow, he has to put up with the post-race interview, which is hard: "You're still in the zone, but you have to say the right thing – and cope with the day after a notable win, when, inevitably, you feel so flat after such a high."

The aged cliché of winning being a drug that tempts you on to more and ever greater success, leads to the question whether winning is enough. "But what is enough?" asks David. "Will anything ever be enough? You will always want more." Such is life, but a level-headed approach – with no small tincture of the philosophical – makes for a happier man, perhaps a better jockey. And it keeps you out of the dark places. He has no time for the Bill Shankly evaluation of winning, (that, of course, was in reference to football): "It's not a matter of life and death, it's much more important than that." For David, "What defines a true sportsman is not success, but failure: the best learn from defeat, use it to improve, and move on."

As their profession becomes evermore rigid and controlling, sportspeople need to hang on to both their sense of fun and their passion: Jonny Wilkinson calls this "connecting with the unknown." In order to do this, they need "the beauty of multiple perspectives on the many unanswered whats, whys, whos and whens, floating like snowflakes through racing's spectacular deception." [Declan Murphy]. "Those snowflakes can become an avalanche," says David. "To win, we have, still, to numb ourselves, which can give birth to a lack of self-worth: you can't be seen as soft. To snap out of this numb state straight after racing is not easy."

David's philosophy, in and out of the saddle, has been tested recently. After a successful 2020-2021 season, things since have been quieter, though he won the Peterborough Chase at Huntingdon on First Flow in 2022 and the valuable Fleur de Lys Chase at Lingfield on Two for Gold, about whom Lewis Porteous wrote: "He loves a battle and knows how to win." David appreciates his long associations with good horses, not least these two sterling warriors. Having steered First Flow to 12 wins, David, not surprisingly, rates that horse as his favourite warrior. The jockey rode his 500th winner on 7th February 2022, and is always up for the next challenge: "Challenges teach us something about ourselves: we are always learning, exploring who we are."

With no rain, and his stable's horses not firing on all cylinders, by the end of February 2023, he was way down on previous years' rides, and the concomitant loss of earnings that brought about. It's not always easy to be philosophical: pressure can suck the enjoyment out of race-riding. But, even as his new mindset was being tested, he tried to appreciate not just the race, but the whole process, the full spectrum of preparation for winning, rather than the winning per se.

He believes racing is, "all about the next generation." Today's jockeys are living through the legacy of previous cohorts of jockeys: one-third of them ride out for no money; one-third - perhaps the same third - take home less than £10,000 a year; 89% have no contract or retainer; 47% make less than £40,000 per year. As the second most watched sport in the UK, racing needs to evolve with the climate in many different ways. The next generation of jockeys has the chance – and the challenge – to improve things. With that in mind, David, together with Nico de Boinville, is seeking to earn jockeys more respect, and thus heighten their quality of life.

Racing folk can be black and white. People need the truth. Jockeys have a role to play here, but it is not an easy one. They can exist in a prison of fear: they always need to win more, and are obsessed by numbers. That can leave them in a hole, their confidence goes downhill, and they are prone to overthinking... They have plenty of time to dwell on things: jockeys spend endless hours driving endless miles earning very little. David's drive to Kelso for one ride, only to fall at the first fence, is not uncommon. A bank holiday weekend can see riders at Cartmel on the Saturday, Fontwell in Sussex on the Sunday, and back to Cartmel for the Monday's card. When they go long periods without a winner, doubt creeps in, and they become desperate to win again. Trying to be a somebody takes its toll. Then fear raises its head: they have to fall back on their store of courage. Mark Twain wrote: "Courage is a resistance to the mastery of fear, not its absence."

David is not a fan of social media, its polar compass showing only fame or ignominy, with no half-measures. Like every jockey, he and trainer Kim Bailey suffer abuse online with venom: "I hope I don't find out where you and that scumbag jockey David Bass live: I'll smash a baseball bat over your heads." Bailey's response was strong: "There is no-one quicker than the keyboard warrior: people say they'll break a jockey's legs, break horses' legs, burn stables down, all because some odds-on shot gets beaten. Young jockeys ride one bad race, or are unlucky in it, and are given the impression they've ruined someone's life." This is what gambling does to people. The racing world has to be responsible. But, is it?

Jockeys are vulnerable: that feature is often admirable in others, but not in ourselves. David got to the stage where he couldn't help being vulnerable: he is now aware of who he is, rather than thinking he had to live up to being someone that wasn't him. It is about having self-worth, as opposed to needing self-esteem. As a young jockey, he admired Richard Dunwoody, who was obsessed: "You've got to be – as a young jockey, but that can kill the passion – you are never going to reach that level. David sees the racing game as "such a bubble: it's hard to have an identity away from being a jockey, to take yourself out of racing. Long before it's all over, you have to prepare yourself for that, you have to work on it." That is not easy.

Having spoken out about the mental health side of racing for years, David is aware of the extent to which racecourses and bookies are in control of the sport. Too many low-grade horses run in low-grade races for poor prize money, and with courses paid £1,000 per runner, and up to £12,000 per race, low-level races are encouraged. Yet there is money around, mainly at the other end of the scale, rather than at grass roots level. "A lot of people need to make a noise about the sport's paltry financial rewards," says David, though he acknowledges the PJA are trying to change things here.

His trip to Ireland for the Punchestown Festival of 2021 cheered him.

"I loved it: the fences, the track, the ground, everything is so well presented, so much more inviting than is often the case in Britain. We could learn a lot from the Irish" – perhaps it is no wonder they wipe the floor with us at Cheltenham and Aintree. He applauded the Irish Horseracing Board's recent decision to give top, senior jockeys in Ireland 24 days off. During that time racing continued, with conditional/younger jockeys having the chance to ride more frequently – "They listen over there more," says David, "journeymen jockeys need to eat."

David has enjoyed four wins at the Cheltenham Festival – so far: Darna, Willoughby Court, Imperial Aura and Chianti Classico in 2024. He is still aiming high. Among ambitions still left to the Swindon man remains the desire to ride at Auteuil, outside Paris, the top French racecourse. But, now, he can ignore the voice of his ego. He would like jump racing to be more about its participants, not its controllers; he would like the small man in the sport to have more of a chance; he is well aware that suffering and self-sacrifice are part of a jockey's DNA. He believes a jump jockey's life is built on punishment, and he acknowledges that successful jockeys need to possess 'something different' to make it to the top. Whilst he cannot single-handedly push back the steamroller of our nanny state, he is more at home in his own skin than ever before. He wants, still, to make a difference to jump racing.

He still talks of the 'poison of fear': the fact jockeys are not free, in that they always need more, they crave the drug of winning. He himself had his best season in 2020-2021 – but not because he rode his most winners. Why, then? Long pause! "Because I enjoyed riding, doing the thing I'm passionate about: the winning was a bonus."

Such words are heartening, but they come at a cost; they have taken a lot of working towards, finding a balance between being hungry enough, but not too hungry, between wanting/hoping to ride a (notable) winner, and needing to: "When it's need, you're trapped. That's when you're not enjoying it." And when winning comes before everything, as it has with sportsmen in and outside racing, that can cause huge pressures: "You have to ask yourself if you are enjoying it. How can you prosper if not?"

A Spurs fan, who likes spontaneity, his love of alternative music leads him to Glastonbury, and other festivals, often abroad, and decided on in a flash. He is well-educated on nutrition, and follows a plant-based diet, to the amusement of his fellow jockeys. His underlying humour- keen, dry and quick- complemented by a canny vocabulary, makes him lively and colourful company: time with him is always rewardingly spent. "All jockeys are different," says Chris Broad, "but David especially so. He has a huge heart, can take being ribbed as a 'leftie', stands up for other jockeys, and, for all his ready humour, is a serious, terrific ambassador for the game."

He remains a man who loves people. His career has enabled him to meet a huge and colourful variety of folk, and he firmly believes, "Without people, we are nothing. And we need to cling on to the passion; it can all too easily get lost." Having been driven by the urge to leave a legacy, obsessed with numbers, and needing success, now it is all different for David, it's about the preparation for winning, being appreciative of what you have got and enjoying that, not always comparing yourself to others. The fire still burns deep within him, as he showed in March 2024, when landing his second Grimthorpe at Doncaster on the ever-frisky, Does He Know, and in the Ultima Chase at Cheltenham, with an audacious ride on Chianti Classico. Somehow, David's wins make people happy. "I want to be as good as I can be, and keep trying to improve. I feel I'm enjoying race-riding more than ever now, that's the most important thing to me. What I really want is the passion I have for my job at the moment, to stay this strong for a few more years."

CHAPTER 30:
WHERE TO FROM HERE?

"There is something mysterious about the depth of pleasure
millions of us take from jump racing."
- Hugh McIlvanney -

W hy would any sane person choose to wear parachute–thin trousers, six feet off the ground, atop half a ton of rippling muscle, at the risk of becoming completely out of control, relying on split-second thinking, risking everything from concussion to paralysis, even death? Jump jockeys are the only sportsmen and women who, every day of their lives, are followed around at work by not one, but two ambulances.

John Carter puts it: "What possesses someone to earn a living by placing him/ herself in mortal danger every day, often several times a day? Who would want to starve the body of food and hydration 24/7, while attempting to maintain an elite athlete's level of fitness? Why would anyone want to get up at – or before – the crack of dawn 7 days a week to wrack up hundreds of miles on motorways for an annual income professional footballers earn in a week, or even a day?"

Jump racing is perhaps the most demanding sport of all. It is a cruel leveller for racing's multi–coloured gypsies. With its constant, voracious demand for power, speed, tradition, and the winning post, the sport for these riders is a way of life, not a job. They are all too well aware of the dark side of jump racing: death is an ever-present threat, and 37 of them have been permanently disabled in UK jumps since 1950.

A jump jockey's lifestyle is crazy: a diet restricted to meal after meal of steamed fish, and spinach, or steamed chicken, and lettuce for variety;

the ever-present dehydration; the risk of injury; carrying an injury – or hiding it; long days of travel; uncertainty, about finance and their future; going from high adrenalin moments in front of a crowd to long, solo drives home; forensic public scrutiny, and endless criticism. Every jockey I have met answers that this is the life they have chosen: "It's what I do."

They ride in mud and cold, the awful, white cold that stiffens their fingers, lightens their head, and sears like a poker down through the lungs as they ride. Their mouths are often dry. They are addicted to winning; they have to be. The more they win, the more they want – and need – to win: it hurts not to win. They talk to themselves, question themselves, ponder the 'what ifs', always aware of, and trying to play down, the enduring physical strains and mental pressures that demand instant decisions. They have to learn early, and go on leaning, how to live not just with losing, but with losing painfully, sometimes in ICU. It all boils down to opportunity – and luck. There is something different about the jump jockeys' band; their being so unified, yet ultra-competitive, in a sport where danger presents itself constantly, where everyone, sometime will face the impact of a horse's iron shoe, and smell the antiseptic of a hospital ward.

Racing can be cruel to its jockeys: few other sports can give a competitor so much pleasure and reward, only to snatch it back almost immediately, and inflict an equal – or greater - dose of pain. Jockeys have to keep training hard, honing their fitness skills, and can only get truly fit by race-riding; muscles used in a race rarely come into play in any other sport, or form of exercise. Holding their legs in position until the lactic acid build-up gives way, they can reach a state where the fitter they are the more painful it gets. Theirs is a brutal regime, harder even than training as a boxer. They measure distances in time: jockeys' cars are their offices. Their lives are an ever-shifting cocktail of dedication, courage, skill, sweat, blood, tears, passion, pain, trust, mutual respect, responsibility for each other – and instinct, which cannot be taught.

So much is concerned with the future – the next year's plans for the Cheltenham Festival swamp the press as soon as one year's races have been run. Jockeys have an ever-new yearning for what is to come. With instant information, people know the result of races immediately, know what has taken place, so want to know what will happen next. This puts pressure on journalists to come up with something not immediately obvious. And pressure on jockeys grows all the time. They have to cross the pain threshold many times over, step out of themselves, and take their mind to a different place… they have to laugh at despair, have to battle the demons, have to lie to themselves, and believe their own lies… they have to become someone else.

As things stand at the moment, jump jockeys face, a long, hard road. Their relationships with trainers often lack respect. Racing, in the view of this invested advocate, needs to regulate more, challenge some of its draconian conventions, and make the sport more professional. The industry needs to look inwards, give its staff – from grooms to jockey – more security, especially on race days. At its heart, jump racing reflects the best of us: optimistic, heartfelt and pure. It remains- just- more of a sport than a business, and more than a numbers game. With its pageants, colour, noise, excitement, danger and unpredictability, it is still wonderful theatre. What most drives jockeys is riding winners. It's the force which compels them to be competitive day after day. They have to steer their mounts; galvanise them at every jump; put them right if they blunder; position, and reposition them, so as to maximise their chances, and then urge, or cajole them to pass a white piece of wood, topped by a red circle, with their head in front.

Racing perhaps needs more jockeys from non-racing backgrounds to usher in a change of outlook. It can appear to be a closed shop, but John Francome rode donkeys on the beach, Rachael Blackmore is the daughter of a teacher and a farmer, and David Bass has a vicar and music teacher for parents, so at least there is a modicum of diversity. But many riders, like Izzy and Eleanor Williams, daughters of Evan, follow in their families' footsteps, especially in the rural world, where jumping so firmly has its roots. It is clearly a big advantage to have blood in the game, as racing's dynasties continue to prove.

In football, rugby, tennis, cricket, swimming, athletics, even snooker, we can admire the great practitioners: we can play their game and marvel at how much better they are than us. In jump racing, we can watch the sport all our life and not know what jockeys are doing. We can only imagine how it feels to guide a horse over fences at speed in the heat of fierce competition at the highest level; perhaps that is part of the mystique that every good rider conjures up. But it is not something that can be plucked from the ether; only months and years of relentless repetition can bring about the artistry of all qualified jockeys with the courage to step into the arena.

Contentiously, an article in *Racing Post's Weekender* claimed that: "Very good jump jockeys make more difference to the result than their counterparts on the flat, primarily because the partnership between them and the horse under them is much closer to being one of equals. Good jump jockeys, just by the way they present a horse at an obstacle, can persuade that horse he's enjoying himself, and bring about a performance you wouldn't expect. Great jump jockeys can persuade an exhausted horse that he would rather win than displease the creature on his back. Flat jockeys can do this, but don't have the same amount of time in which to exert their influence. Great jockeys, like great horses, have always got the ability to surprise."

Covid allowed our sport to pause, and ask itself whether racing had lost something of its identity, and if it needed change from grass roots level. Joe Rendall, of the Jockey Club, wondered if British racing had become too complex in the way it operates, with too many factions competing for control. The sport's governing body had been criticised by one ex-jockey for "one cock-up after another; the whole big industry being run like a gymkhana." Field sizes are often too small, and prize money low, though some courses have improved here. Racing is still in danger of becoming anodyne; the names of most races are stultifying dull, too often characterised by internet-speak. Numbering 350, the BHA has so many members as to become unwieldy; racecourses are often doing the sport a disservice, with initiatives blocked, and precedents feared. There are too many races for 'bad' horses. Races need better planning, and new ideas to replace fossilised procedures. Change is vital.

The BHA was under pressure to be seen to act for "the good of racing" and improvements have recently been made to improve matters, not least with the fixture list for jump racing. Racing's governing body tries to get jurisdiction passed through quickly. This was seen with new whip rules, introduced on 13th February 2023, just a month before the Cheltenham Festival, with only a short bedding-in period, which could have been better timed: for example, in the previous summer, while things were quiet, not in the lead-up to the most important week of the season. But despite controversy and a small number of infringements, jockeys adapted well to the new demands, showcasing the sport in a positive light and proving that with proper consultation jump racing can go forward. Racing still has "a raggedy image," but it also has a committed workforce, brimming with energy, character and resolve with a strong support system to match; that cooperation has to keep growing as the pressures and demands on the industry – and on jockeys - continues to burgeon. The sport needs to be made more elite, more professional, especially with regard to horse welfare, where improvements have been noted, but there need to be more: fewer fatalities are essential. Racing is at last starting to respond to the need for more regulation to reconfigure its hitherto backward stance.

We live in a safety-first world, as if, somehow, an ever-increasing list of dull, restricting government regulations can eliminate life's central risk of cars, bikes, horses, diseases – and mortality. Perhaps we need to embrace that risk, as jump jockeys do, not run from it. Winston Churchill said: "Don't give your sons money, give them horses. The worst that can happen is that they break their neck, and that, taken at the gallop, is a very good death to die." An extreme opinion, but in a restless, demanding world, men and women riding in a jumps race have the chance to pull down their goggles as the starter calls them to the track, and pursue an urge they believe truly worth living for: all their endeavour is brought to a thundering climax that always holds the opportunity for dreams to come true.

Michael Caulfield has extensive experience of sports and their challenges; he 'gets' jockeys' madness. "The racing community is demanding, relentless and judgmental. So much is out of its control: you do everything right and still get beaten; small wonder jockeys use the Sporting Chance helpline more than other sportspeople. But racing looks out for its own, which is vital, and has much in its favour: working in nature is good and so much work is done outdoors; being with animals is therapeutic. Yet life is getting faster: time is everyone's enemy nowadays… we used to have more. We need to use time and make the most of it. Despite online benefits and contacts, informal conversations are best: it's not good to retreat into our own bunkers. We have to keep going and sort things out with talking. The stigma of mental health will always be there: break it down centimetre by centimetre; build trust;

connect face-to-face. "Have you got ten minutes?" will lead to an hour, after which we will feel better. We have to look out for each other."

The jockeys' lot needs understanding; their considered, informed suggestions and ideas demand to be taken more seriously in order to fully comprehend what it is like to be in a jump jockey's shoes, who is fighting their corner, who would spend a day with them to see the constant demands put on them, who really cares?

Jockeys cannot fully explain why they do their hazardous job... It's the depth of connection to their horse, a mindset that becomes the sport, and vice versa; it takes them out of their usual head space; gives them the illusion of control; represents the most extreme freedom; pushes their boundaries, and more... When the tapes go up, and their mounts spring forward from bunched haunches towards the first fence, jockeys are never more present, never more in flow. Fear evaporates; the horse beneath them is a sentient being that trusts the person on its back, and communicates with that person for their journey. Most of the time, horse and jockey will emerge unscathed, which affords them a safety blanket. They love their profession – they have to, precisely because it is so brutal: everything is a measure of how tough they are. Adrenalin and euphoria throb through their veins: they live for moments of epic victory, somehow shaking off the grim moments. And they can never rest on their laurels; they have to keep working. A Cheltenham victory brings short-lived euphoria, but they know the next race brings them back to square one. There is no code to crack; they don't solve the puzzle and keep the solution locked away for next time. And the trapdoor of anguish, always, is waiting and hungry...

Few of us can understand the depth of focus and emotion jump jockeys have to possess, the compromises they have to make – and make daily – the cost of what it has taken to get where they are, the amount of energy, physical, mental and spiritual, to capture this out of body experience in their aim to reach what, for each of them, would be their pinnacle. Or how much preparation they put in before the race, how much reflection afterwards, what they have to do to get under the skin of their pulsing emotions, what to aim for next. They may only be one cog in a massive wheel, but nothing can happen without that cog.

Brough Scott, former president of the IJF, who was himself a jockey, understands the plight, the thrill and the compulsion of race riders: "Facing up to risks enhances our hold on existence. For jockeys, knowing the rules are there gives every ride, every race, that extra feeling of fulfilment. For all the hard hours, bad weather, painful bumps, hungry days and ugly-mouthed, as well as sweet-tempered horses, there are the jockeys' silks, the paddock pantomime, the goggles pulled down, the tapes flying up: you and your rivals are the only beings alive in the spinning, galloping, jumping, crashing, strained world that is the race."

Jockeys have to keep asking themselves if they are enjoying the sport: it is not always an easy question to answer. It is a hazardous balance to keep. Their careers pass so quickly: if they find a purpose, they have light at the end of the tunnel. Confidence in themselves, and in their horses, is perhaps the single most important aspect: keeping that confidence intact is a precarious balance. Self-worth remains essential.

Horses and winning and supportive environments give jockeys confidence; that confidence can be eroded by the tide of vicious comments hurled at them, often anonymously. They know when they have got it wrong; they don't need trolls on *anti*-social media, to whom they are all too accessible, to berate them: that makes a loss worse. Sardonic comments like, "9.9 marks for artistic merit," on a jockey being unseated undermine that jockey's confidence severely. One reason why they are so sensitive to criticism is because they are so demanding of themselves. Jockeys have no shield: in football a bad result is blamed on the manager; in racing it is usually jockeys who are held responsible and thus abused. They have to deal with this. Or do they? It's easy to say jockeys should ignore the onslaught from the faceless critics. After all, what have these people achieved from their couches as they scream abuse into the online vacuum? It's a contract to take on when you're in the public eye, isn't it? But jockeys now have grown up at a time when our worth is judged through 'likes', comments and clicks, and where virtual life is almost indistinguishable from the real. It's as hard for them to ignore the criticism flung online as it would be for one of my generation to be unscathed by the vituperation of a spouse, community-member, or revered colleague. Whether we like it or not, the online environment magnifies everything, from minor miracles to major mishaps. The stakes are worse than they should be.

Jockeys ride on air, minds floating, always seeking the next big thing, always wondering if or how they could have done things differently. Peas on a drum as they sometimes appear, they must make the most of every ride – every opportunity - on the training gallops. As jockey John Valazquez has written: "We are there to guide the horse. We have to know the trainers. We have to learn how to ride against the other jockeys, the competition. We have to learn how the horse would like to be ridden, and it's about trying to read all those things at the same time. It happens so quickly, and sometimes all the homework you do, all the experience you have, doesn't prepare you for the race. But sometimes you get a really great connection with the horse, and that's what it takes." The jockey is at one with his horse, in a different world, timeless, never so absolutely present and flowing; it is as if he himself has dissolved, an experience as never before. It has been said that there is no secret so close as that between a rider and his horse.

And when a jockey is not winning, not capturing that "lightning in a bottle," they ask themselves whether there can be any joy, and, where that joy comes from. Can life be the same winnerless; can I still celebrate my sport; is winning the same as refusing to lose; can I cling on to my identity, day after losing day? It is no easy journey. They need to work hard on mind and body, constantly stretching that work ethic, ever-ready to listen, learn and grind on…

In 1996, Dr Michael Turner undertook an analysis of the dangers in racing: in terms of fatalities, jump racing is four times as hazardous as motor-racing, less dangerous only than climbing, air sports, and riding in point-to-points. Protective equipment can only go so far. Sean Magee pinpoints the dangers – and the deep lure of race-riding – when he describes National Hunt racing as "a visceral sport: its cocktail of strength, speed, noise, colour, muscle, drama, danger and leather unlocks deep emotions." In considering the palpable thrill for spectators "standing at the wing of a fence as the thunder in the depths of the earth rolls ever louder, with runners flashing into view, launching themselves over the fence, landing in a swirl of legs and flying birch, and galloping off as the thunder subsides," he warns against romanticising this experience, quoting Will H. Ogilvie's poem:

Taking what the Fates provide them,
Danger calling, Death beside them -
'Tis a game beyond gainsaying,
Made by gods for brave men's playing.

The obstacles jump jockeys have to negotiate have become less formidable in recent years. Hurdles are soft, sloping away, gorse-packed obstacles, ideally brushed and even flattened by a passing horse. Fences are solid, upright, birch-built: you need a horse brave enough to go for the obstacle, and smart enough to respect it. Hurdles falls are often worse for a jockey, with bigger fields, less time in the air, and greater speed with which to contend. But fences are easier to negotiate than they were: then, they were stiffer and straighter, so you had to be more of a horseman, and make horses jump properly, or you'd end up on the deck. Then, in Michael Scudamore's words, "We lived for today: bugger tomorrow, that'll take care of itself." Now, jockeys are more concerned about their future.

Improvements made to the Grand National in 2013, and again in 2023, testified to progress being made to improve the safety of the sport. Aintree used to be a chamber of horrors: Dudley Doust viscerally likened Becher's Brook to a shotgun suicide: "The face looked fine, but the back of the head had been blown off." In 1839 the *Liverpool Mercury* had been scathing about the course: "The Grand National is no doubt a very exciting spectacle, but we can be no more reconciled to it on that account than we are to cock-fighting, bull-baiting, or any other pastime which is attended with the affliction of wanton torture to any living being." The race today is a good example of change so vital to jump racing; it is safer now, as it had to be, now with 34 runners, still a mighty spectacle, and the quality of the contest is better. The famous obstacles used to be constructed from natural thorn hedges, over a hard wooden framework, but are now created from Norwegian spruce, brought from the Lake District and woven into plastic structure, which provides flexibility should a horse make a mistake at the jump. Over the past fifteen years a greater understanding of the race has caused its fences to be made less dangerous: Becher's Brook has had its landing slope eradicated and its ditch all-but filled in: one inch of water now trickles through the famous stream.

It has been said that sport doesn't build character, so much as reveal it. We care not only for winners and losers, but for how they go about it, each in their different ways, with courage, resolve, humility and grace. We wonder what jump jockeys are really like and how they are different from us. They are often private people, consumed in and by their own worlds, and wary of the media, where 'spin' on a tiny detail can suddenly become a landscape problem. Footballer, Gareth Bale, formerly of Real Madrid and Tottenham Hotspur, has spoken out about the social media enemy: "At a time where people are taking their own lives because of the callousness and relentlessness of the media, I want to know who is holding these journalists and the news outlets that allow them to write critical articles, accountable. These articles cause damage and upset, personally and professionally, to those at the receiving end of these malicious stories. The media expects superhuman performances from professional athletes, and is the first to celebrate with them when they deliver, yet instead of commiserating with them when they show an ounce of human error, they are torn to shreds instead. Everyday pressure on sportsmen and women is immense. Negative media attention can easily push an already stressed athlete over the edge. I want to encourage change in the way we publicly talk about and criticise people simply for not meeting the often unrealistic expectations projected onto them. We all know who the parasite is."

Over the last few decades, the nature of dealings between sports figures and the media has changed hugely. Broadcasters gain access to sportsmen and women because they pay for it: this is the business of modern sport. Now we have more media, press conferences, words and chatter, but that is not necessarily better than hitherto. It has taken much of the mystery out of sport, leaving many wanting to hear still more. True mavericks are harder to find now, but we want, more than ever, to hear their stories and discover what makes them tick. Agents, marketeers, newspapers and the media are in control, so honesty is harder to find. The England team manager, Gareth Southgate, has encouraged footballers to talk about their backgrounds and the obstacles they've overcome, to help deconstruct the idea that a footballer's life is a feckless and carefree existence of wealth, women and fast cars. Hopefully, thanks to the candour of David Bass and co., racing can begin to do the same.

At present, in the UK there are 290 professional jockeys, many of them in the shadows. All are under immense pressure to perform, i.e. to win. Every jockey craves a flagship, a 'Saturday horse'. All know that many people want to speak with them, not least bookies, who are always seeking contacts and privileged information, for obvious reasons. Jockeys are consistently wrestling with the complexities and contradictions of their participation in this professional sport. As England Under 21 hockey goalkeeper, Tom Pinnegar, has said: "You are running the race of ambition, only to be pulled back by the weight of anxiety and doubt. Each time you get stronger, and feel your weight lift, your race pulls further into the distance, your expectations grow and your legs feel heavier." Perspectives shift all the time.

Towards the fore of today's upcoming jockeys is Freddie Gingell, nephew of Joe Tizzard. He had his first win at the age of 16, after which he paid an emotional tribute to his mum, Kim, Joe's sister, who died of cancer in 2020, aged 43. The lad was "chucked in at the deep end a bit," said Joe, rider of Cue Card, and forever associated with Thistlecrack, "but he's responding all right." Freddie had his first Grade 1 win at Cheltenham in January 2024, when guiding Elixir de Nutz to produce a huge upset in winning the Clarence House Chase, just beating hot favourite, Jonbon. The pair returned to a great welcome in the winners' enclosure at buzzing jump racing headquarters. This breakthrough victory for Freddie came at an earlier stage than some of the weighing rooms greats; at 18 he represents a fantastic advert for racing.

A jockey's greatest gift is perhaps a good pair of hands, the ability to have just the right contact with a horse's mouth through the reins. And the art of diplomacy is increasingly essential: for jockeys of a beaten horse, after dismounting from their steaming partner, reporting back to a disappointed owner requires skills just as nifty as, and very different from, presenting their mount at a fence at 30 mph.

A jump jockey's vocation is part of their fabric as, with their horse, they aim to achieve that smooth co-ordination of muscle and mass that is nature's gift to the lucky few, in whom grace of movement equals speed. Their minds constantly flow, courage and intent their lodestars. They ride standing on stirrups, or sitting not on the saddle, but on air, until sometimes they fall, like an arrow that suddenly loses its flight. They need the strongest work ethic, having to pre-plan where their horse, in itself a powder keg of risk, puts its every step, aware that, however carefully they and the trainer plan how things are going to work out, racing doesn't let that happen. Young jockeys are capable of going all the way to the top, but such are the vagaries of racing that the wrong break (physically, say with a leg, or metaphorically with a job not working out) takes them back to square one. Rachael Blackmore embodies the modern mindset: "You go out there, you concentrate, you do not muck around, you play to win, you do all your talking at the track. And, always, confidence is paramount." In front of crowds with stretched ears and curious eyes, they start every race with hope, urging their horse to jump off smartly as they pursue that win, or the next big thing.

If it were easy, everyone would do it.

Michael Scudamore's line, "A jump jockey has to throw his heart over the fence,… and then go over and catch it" shows the stark necessity of courage, which jump jockeys have in abundance. They keep going. When things hit them hardest, they have to find something within themselves, an intangible force that propels them forward. They draw power from this inner strength, but often don't know they have it until forced to depend upon it.

They are always looking to the future, to the crop of promising horses they might one day get to ride in an epic race. Such an event took place at Ascot in January 2022 in the Clarence House Chase. Shishkin, champion chaser of England, ridden by Nico de Boinville, took on Energumene, upcoming horse of Ireland, under Paul Townend. The race did not disappoint. Both horses put an unbeaten record on the line, and brilliantly lit up a winter's afternoon with their slick jumping and breakneck pace. It looked for all money as if Energumene would prevail, with his unfaltering gallop, but Shishkin fought back relentlessly, unstoppably, to lead in the shadow of the post and land the spoils. Paul held out his hand to grasp Nico's, as the crowd's spirits soared with excitement – and fervent hope for the future. David Bass, third on First Flow, described the contest as the best race he'd ridden in – or ever would, a sentiment quietly echoed by the winning jockey.

Supreme spectacles are rare; racing on a Monday at Southwell or Ffos Las would not inspire the same depth of emotion – but could still see that depth of endeavour from beast and rider. And lesser races can engender great endeavour, even for 'unknown' jockeys. Luke Harvey has long advocated a change in thinking for the sport, whereby it would, for example, provide races for those jockeys who have not ridden twenty winners over jumps. The people who had the greatest influence on him, ITV's 'fall-guy', but a knowledgeable presenter, were at the bottom of racing's ladder, folk who couldn't possibly have been earning a living as a jockey. The racing community is strong; people can become involved in it in so many ways: it can restore the most tattered faith in humanity. The many and wide-ranging characters who make up the racing industry are brilliantly diverse; the sport employs huge numbers, and lives can be enriched by the opportunity to meet people from all over the world. Racing folk always have a good story to tell…

The IJF is always coming up with new initiatives, including Jockey Profiling Days to gain deeper insight into each rider's strengths and limitations, and find bespoke programmes to work on these key areas: these days usually end with a social event. April 2022 saw the first IJF conference, where consultant clinical psychologist Dr. Duncan Law, whilst finding the new cohort of jockeys were more open to discussing mental well-being, still felt there were "certain pockets where the stigma is still high and strong." Concerns having been raised over the inflexibility of current body protectors, manufacturers Racesafe are now working on an updated model. Energies are being focused on jockeys' spinal injuries, with the aim of discovering the 'spinal loading threshold', and how spinal fractures occur.

Jockeys cannot always be winners. Knowing they've done their best sometimes has to be enough. The experience of learning goes deep. But in order to keep learning, grow, take feedback, and criticism they need time – something jockeys do not have. They have to learn acceptance or, perhaps, contentedness: it can shed a different light on their achievements; give them different insights. Acceptance does not happen overnight; it can be seen as negative, or passive, alien words in a jockey's vocabulary. But once attained it can increase their insights, improve their lot in racing, and in life.

To the casual racegoers, a day at the jumps can be memorable, with all the finery of a medieval pageant, jockeys in their colours like figures from a pack of Tarot cards, and the crash of flying birch in the spectators' ears.

But racegoers will go back to their lives, unaware of the sunrises and sunsets that bookend the daily life of a jockey, the unseen margins in their endlessly fascinating and alluring world of racing. Jockeys are essentially optimists: one day the big win *will* come. They will partner an equine great. Every era has its superstars, as we now have with such marvels as Constitution Hill and Galopin des Champs. There is always a coming champion. Belief may one day be shattered, but, whilst it lasts, we hang on to its crystal spirit. Jump jockeys will always strive, their blood ice-hot, to feel themselves carried into the race's fire-fuelled realm of existence.

In the end, that jump jockey's world - colourful, unpredictable, perilous, fast, ever-changing, privileged – is essentially private. There remains something inexplicable, something ethereal about their chosen profession. Longfellow's lines are apt here:

> "Wouldst thou," so the helmsman answered,
> "Learn the secret of the sea?
> Only those who brave its dangers.
> Comprehend its mystery."

It is one hell of a journey for all of them, from the one who ends up top of the championship, down to the journeyman jockeys who slip under the radar, but still keep trying to let their riding do the talking. They keep going because they have to, continuously driven on their crazed merry-go-round: they come back from injury to battle on against the fates; they are unique among sportspeople. They have to make themselves numb; remain tougher than steel, whatever befalls; constantly venture beyond resilient, and never show vulnerability. They remain, always, desperate to win. They dare, and keep on daring…

Perhaps ultimately for jump jockeys, the aim is to stay alive, to leave the weighing room for a race in a positive frame of mind, to do their very best and to walk back after that race in 'one piece'.

This book started off – on nephew Alfie's 12th birthday, in April 2015 – as a biography of Gold Cup - winning jockey, turned trainer, Sam Thomas. It was edifying to watch his response to challenges, and witness his expanding skills with his horses. Somewhere along the line, and by mutual agreement, we decided to widen the book's scope to include a detailed study of the perils, challenges, ordeals, deprivations, and occasional rewards that constitute a jump jockey's life.

Writing this book has been a great experience; I have learned much, not all of it within these pages, for some jockeys were searingly honest: what they told me essentially personal. But I am grateful to everyone who has helped in this venture. The book's gestation period has been elephantine – Alfie celebrated his 21st birthday at the time of its publication. But I have appreciated the chance to show the intrepid daring of those men and women who choose to be jump jockeys. I salute them all.

Many people have given their support, encouragement, and guidance on this book, all of which has been hugely appreciated. Particular thanks are due:

... *to jockeys:*

> Sam Thomas, David Bass, Tom Scudamore,
> Nick Oliver, Aidan Coleman, Johnny Burke,
> Brian Hughes, Brian and Kelly Harding,
> Will Kennedy, Nico de Boinville, Sean Quinlan,
> Charlie Deutsch, Jerry McGrath, Ryan Day,
> Luke Harvey, Nick Schofield, John Francome,
> Richard Pitman, Rob Law-Eadie, Peter Gehm,
> Dan Cherriman, Walter Barnett, Denis O'Regan,
> Sean Flanagan, Ruby Walsh and Paul Townend.

... to trainers:

Peter Scudamore and Lucinda Russell,
Venetia Williams, Nicky Richards, Matt Sheppard,
Henrietta Knight, Warren Greatrex,
Michael Scudamore and Richard Phillips.

... to copyreaders:

James Freemantle, Nick Clements,
Warren and Louisa Richards, Mark Thompson,
Tony and Heather Meredith, Philippa Atkinson,
Simon Brazier, Lorraine Dodd, Ros and Brian Art,
John Sevior and Rebecca Gorman.

... at Oaksey House:

Debbie Grey, Clare Hazell, Clare Hill,
Jayne Matthews and Chicky Oaksey.

... on the 'techno' side:

Karen Langridge, Katie Newcombe, Mel Shaw,
Richard Suckling and Mark Mulley,
all of whose help has been invaluable.

... in the wider racing sphere:

Dot and Geoff Thomas, Stan and Mary Brown,
the family of Richard Davis:
parents Ann and John, twin brothers Stephen and Andrew,
Joe Rendall, Richard Hoiles, Edward Gillespie,
Emma Richards, Russ James, Chris Broad,
Jane Arnold, Milly Kirtley, Matt Chapman,
Mick Fitzgerald and Bernard Parkin.

... racing journalists:

Alastair Down, John Carter, Jon Lees,
Peter Thomas, Alan Sweetman, Tom O'Ryan, Steve Dennis,
Lee Mottershead, Richard Forristal, Lewis Porteous,
David Carr, David Jennings, Tom Jenkins, Maddy Playle,
Michael O'Hehir, Jonathan Powell, John Randall,
John Karter, Julian Muscat, Paul Haward, Stuart Riley,
Scott Burton, Charlie Huggins and, most of all, Chris Cook.

... other journalists:

Matt Rudd and Jim White.

... loyal mates:

Mike and Lucy Muller, Judy Grill, Nick Sketchley,
John McBroom, Will Nelson, Will Grill, Tim Grew,
Tom Pinnegar, Briony Smith, Simon Cruickshank,
Liz and Neil Suckling, Richard Allen, Tina and Nick Jefferies,
Doug Grubert, Jill Shaw, Tim Turton, Ben Smith,
Simon Hornby, Charles Montgomery, Andrew Hobbs,
Jamie Leich, John and Ann Sutcliffe, and the Harper team.

And, last, but never least,
... the family:

Gillian, Steve and Alfie;
Vicki, Myles, Bryce, Lloyd,
and brother, Noj,
whose sustained depth of counsel has been remarkable.

BIBLIOGRAPHY

McIlvanney on Horseracing	-	Hugh McIlvanney
Good Horses Make Good Jockeys	-	Richard Pitman
To Win Just Once	-	Sean Magee & Guy Lewis
Warriors on Horseback	-	John Carter
Born Lucky	-	John Francome
A Share of Success	-	Peter Scudamore & Alan Lee
221: Peter Scudamore's Record Season	-	Dudley Doust
The Scudamores: Three of a Kind	-	Michael, Peter and Tom Scudamore & Chris Cook
Turf Account	-	Steve Smith-Eccles
Ruby: The Autobiography	-	Ruby Walsh
Centaur	-	Declan Murphy & Ami Rao
Bred to be Champion	-	Richard Dunwoody
Rough Magic	-	Lara Prior-Palmer
The Horses of my Life	-	Richard Dunwoody
Riding This Life	-	Sam Morshead

RACING WELFARE...

... is the sport's most comprehensive support package. This charity champions the full workforce of British horse racing, offering professional guidance and practical help to stud, stable and racecourse staff, whose dedication is vital for the well-being of racing. It helps people, from recruitment to retirement, to thrive in day-to-day life, and through the full range of life's challenges. With headquarters in Newmarket, its mission is to enhance the all-round good health of all involved in the racing industry by providing enabling and proactive support throughout, and after their working life. Its ethos urges people to remember what is strong, not what is wrong, offering two types of mental health courses, including mental health first aid, as well as assistance for those suffering from domestic violence, pain, loss, addiction, trauma or need.

Sundry racecourses like York, Ascot, Beverley and Aintree regularly raise money for the charity, and every year it secures places at some of the world's most iconic events, from the London Marathon to epic hikes. Its 24-hour helpline and befriending service is readily available to bolster the whole workforce's well-being, with particular focus on the young and the retired.

Racing Welfare Helpline: 0800 6300 443

"The essential joy of being with horses is that it brings us into contact with the rare elements of grace, beauty, spirit, and fire."

- Sharon Ralls -